This book offers four perspectives on the p[illegible] conversations among the authors of those p[illegible] both the riches and the ambiguities of Marka[illegible]ology. The book would make an excellent contribution to a course on Mark or on early Christologies.

Adela Yarbro Collins, Buckingham Professor Emerita of New Testament Criticism and Interpretation, Yale Divinity School

"Who is Jesus of Nazareth?" The best readings of the Gospel of Mark puzzle together with the narrative's own characters in answering this question. Is he an extraordinary human or the very presence of Yahweh? The Isaianic Servant or the Davidic Messiah? The Son of God or the Son of David? Perhaps John the Baptist raised from the dead? Can Jesus be categorized under one title, or does he transcend them all? Mark's Gospel invites its readers to puzzle over these questions from the beginning to the end of the narrative. This book offers a rich smorgasbord for its readers to engage the question of Jesus's identity in the Gospel of Mark. Readers can listen in on the back-and-forth conversation between four expert scholars on Mark and early Christology and can, in the process, become learned readers of the Gospel themselves—readers who will undoubtedly grow in their ability to give a response to the question: "Who is Jesus of Nazareth?"

Joshua W. Jipp, associate professor of New Testament, Trinity Evangelical Divinity School

Not many books offer a constructive conversation in which the expert contributors are given "equal time" and voice. This is, however, precisely what happens in *Christology in Mark's Gospel: Four Views*, and the result is compelling. By granting integrity to the Gospel of Mark, the contributions and interactive discussions throughout this volume will leave readers in no doubt about this Gospel's declarative yet mysterious take on the human and divine in the person of Jesus of Nazareth. The conversation demonstrates why distinct features of Mark's narrative, embedded in Jewish traditions that took shape in the Levant, would have challenged ancient audiences no less than it inspires those who listen and read it today.

Loren T. Stuckenbruck, Ludwig-Maximilians-Universität München, Faculty of Protestant Theology, Munich, Germany

Christology *in* Mark's Gospel

4 VIEWS

Christology *in* Mark's Gospel

4 VIEWS

Sandra Huebenthal
Larry W. Hurtado with Chris Keith
J. R. Daniel Kirk
Adam Winn

Anthony Le Donne, *general editor*

CRITICALPOINTS

ZONDERVAN ACADEMIC

Christology in Mark's Gospel: Four Views

Requests for information should be addressed to:
Zondervan, *3900 Sparks Dr. SE, Grand Rapids, Michigan 49546*

Zondervan titles may be purchased in bulk for educational, business, fundraising, or sales promotional use. For information, please email SpecialMarkets@Zondervan.com.

ISBN 978-0-310-53870-7 (softcover)

ISBN 978-0-310-13905-8 (audio)

ISBN 978-0-310-53872-1 (ebook)

Unless otherwise explicitly noted, biblical translations are the authors' own.

Cover design: Tammy Johnson
Cover image: © FotograFFF / Shutterstock
Interior design: Kait Lamphere

Printed in the United States of America

21 22 23 24 25 26 27 28 29 30 31 /LSC/ 15 14 13 12 11 10 9 8 7 6 5 4 3 2 1

In Memoriam L. W. H.

Contents

Abbreviations

ABD	*Anchor Bible Dictionary*. Edited by David Noel Freedman. 6 vols. New York: Doubleday, 1992
ABRL	Anchor Bible Reference Library
AJEC	Ancient Judaism and Early Christianity
AnBib	Analecta Biblica
Ant.	*Jewish Antiquities* (Josephus)
BBR	*Bulletin for Biblical Research*
BECNT	Baker Exegetical Commentary on the New Testament
BibInt	Biblical Interpretation Series
BNTC	Black's New Testament Commentaries
BTS	Biblical Tools and Studies
BZNW	Beihefte zur Zeitschrift für die neutestamentliche Wissenschaft
CBQ	*Catholic Biblical Quarterly*
ConBNT	Coniectanea Biblica: New Testament Series
CurBR	*Currents in Biblical Research*
DJG[1]	*Dictionary of Jesus and the Gospels*. 1st ed. Edited by Joel B. Green, Scot McKnight, and I. Howard Marshall. Downers Grove, IL: InterVarsity Press, 1992
DPL[1]	*Dictionary of Paul and His Letters*. 1st ed. Edited by Gerald F. Hawthorne and Ralph P. Martin. Downers Grove, IL: InterVarsity Press, 1993
ECL	Early Christianity and Its Literature
EJL	Early Judaism and Its Literature
EKKNT	Evangelisch-katholischer Kommentar zum Neuen Testament
ExpTim	*Expository Times*

FRLANT	Forschungen zur Religion und Literatur des Alten und Neuen Testaments
HBT	*Horizons in Biblical Theology*
HThKNT	Herders Theologischer Kommentar zum Neuen Testament
HTR	*Harvard Theological Review*
JAJ	*Journal of Ancient Judaism*
JBL	*Journal of Biblical Literature*
JCTCRS	Jewish and Christian Texts in Contexts and Related Studies
JJMJS	*Journal of the Jesus Movement in Its Jewish Setting*
JSHJ	*Journal for the Study of the Historical Jesus*
JSNT	*Journal for the Study of the New Testament*
JSNTSup	Journal for the Study of the New Testament Supplement Series
JSP	*Journal for the Study of the Pseudepigrapha*
JTS	*Journal of Theological Studies*
J.W.	*Jewish War* (Josephus)
LSTS	The Library of Second Temple Studies
NICNT	New International Commentary on the New Testament
NIGTC	New International Greek Testament Commentary
NovT	*Novum Testamentum*
NovTSup	Supplements to Novum Testamentum
NTL	New Testament Library
NTOA	Novum Testamentum et Orbis Antiquus
NTS	*New Testament Studies*
PRSt	*Perspectives in Religious Studies*
RB	*Revue biblique*
SBB	Stuttgarter biblische Beiträge
SBLDS	Society of Biblical Literature Dissertation Series
SBLMS	Society of Biblical Literature Monograph Series
SBS	Stuttgarter Bibelstudien
SJLA	Studies in Judaism in Late Antiquity
SNTSMS	Society for New Testament Studies Monograph Series
SNTSU	Studien zum Neuen Testament und seiner Umwelt
SP	Sacra Pagina
STDJ	Studies on the Texts of the Desert of Judah
SUNT	Studien zur Umwelt des Neuen Testaments
SVTP	Studia in Veteris Testamenti Pseudepigraphica

TdT	Themen der Theologie
TU	Texte und Untersuchungen
WMANT	Wissenschaftliche Monographien zum Alten und Neuen Testament
WUNT	Wissenschaftliche Untersuchungen zum Neuen Testament
ZNW	*Zeitschrift für die neutestamentliche Wissenschaft und die Kunde der älteren Kirche*

Introduction

I was a seminarian once upon a time. It was an exciting time in my life because my mind was nurtured, rather than hindered. Asking hard questions about the Bible was encouraged. None of my professors were worried that a probing, questioning reading of the Bible might damage my theological assumptions. In fact, pursuing the curiosities of my sacred text enhanced my appreciation of it. Seemingly insignificant puzzles opened doors to incalculable mysteries. I was drawn into this sacred, textual world by passages that defied the neat, easy answers of doctrine. This is probably why I was drawn into Mark's world.[1] The Gospel of Mark remains a curiosity for several reasons, but there was one question that has continued to fascinate me.

After class one day I put this question to a professor. I asked, "In John, Jesus says 'I and the Father are one.' But what about Mark? Where is Mark's evidence for Jesus's divinity?"

"Whoa, slow down!" he cautioned, "Start with the right question! You're on safer ground with Jesus's status as a messiah. That's a question Mark is prepared to answer."

I was scandalized. Because behind my question was a worry. I knew that Mark's story came first (in those days we used the form-critical phrase "most primitive"). And I assumed that Jesus's status as God was still under construction in the Christian imagination. I was worried, then, that the earliest story about Jesus's life might not portray Jesus as divine. If so, it would confirm my suspicion: Jesus's divinity was invented by Christians at a later date (e.g., the author of the Gospel of John). My professor was trying to be helpful, but I only heard what was implicit in his answer: *if I*

1. By "Mark" I mean the sixteen-chapter document, not the supposed author.

kept looking for doctrinal support for my trinitarian agenda, I was going to be disappointed by Mark.

Decades later, I'm still asking questions about Mark's portrayal of Jesus. But I no longer harbor the worry that once drove my inquiry. Rather, I'm drawn to Mark because the story is alluringly strange and because the main character of this story is delightfully mysterious. Even so, my professor's warning remains. It is best to allow Mark to speak for Mark. This means allowing the story to create and develop its own categories.

Allowing Mark to Speak for Mark

Jesus's identity as revealed in Mark continues to puzzle me. *As we meet Jesus in this story, who is he? What does this story convey about Jesus's status? How is Jesus's identity revealed?*

Following my professor's advice, I try not to import my doctrinal assumptions (as best I can) into Mark when I'm reading it. But the unsolved puzzle of Jesus's identity in Mark continues to intrigue me. I think about Mark's unique portrait when I'm reading John, Matthew, Paul, etc. I'll be reading the ancient hymn of Philippians 2, for example, and my mind will wander back to Mark.

> Christ Jesus who, although He existed in the form of God, did not regard equality with God a thing to be grasped . . . (Phil 2:5–6 NASB)

I wonder, *would Mark agree with Paul on this point? Would these authors interpret this hymn in the same way and for the same reasons?*

Sometimes in my Presbyterian worship service we recite the Apostles' Creed. While reciting, a quiet dialogue will play out in my head. After each line of the creed, I'll wonder if Mark's story would lead to such a statement. Does Mark's Gospel give me enough orthodoxy to affirm each statement of the creed? Simply put, did the author of Mark believe what most Christians now believe about Jesus?

Here is my attempt at transcribing my ongoing internal dialogue. The words in bold are from my church bulletin. The words in italics are my own guesswork, keeping Mark's unique story in mind.

The Apostles' Creed

I believe in God the Father Almighty,
Maker of heaven and earth.

Yes, the author of Mark probably assumes this.

I believe in Jesus Christ, his only Son, our Lord,

Mark's author would probably have no problem with this title. But would he consider Jesus the "only Son"? Mark would probably say "beloved Son."

who was conceived by the Holy Spirit,
and born of the virgin Mary.

These plot points are not mentioned in Mark. If we were going to construct a creed based on Mark, we'd mention Jesus's baptism instead.

He suffered under Pontius Pilate,

Yes. In fact, without Mark's impact, Pilate would not be nearly as prominent in Christian thought.

was crucified, died, and was buried;

Yes. This point is key to Mark's story.

He descended into hell.

No. Mark tells us nothing about this. Would the author even agree with this?

The third day he rose again from the dead.

Yes. Although Mark's ending is ambiguous, the empty tomb points to the resurrection. The duration between Friday night and Sunday morning isn't exactly three days, however. Is "third day" meant to be symbolic?

He ascended into heaven
and is seated at the right hand of God the Father Almighty.

There is no mention of Jesus ascending in Mark. But Jesus does say, "'You will see the Son of Man seated at the right hand of the Power' and 'coming with the clouds of heaven'" (Mark 14:62 NRSV).

From there he will come to judge the living and the dead.

While Jesus-as-judge is at home in Matthew, this idea doesn't feature prominently in Mark. But perhaps this is implied if the title "Son of Man" is taken from Daniel 7?

I believe in the Holy Spirit,

Yes, Mark mentions the Holy Spirit. But would the author capitalize the "H" and "S"?

the holy catholic church,

I'm not sure that Mark would know what this phrase means. The word in Greek for church is ἐκκλησία, which is the same word used for synagogue. Would Mark's author know the difference?

the communion of saints,

Would the author know what this means? Do I even know what this means?

the forgiveness of sins,

Yes, forgiveness is an important theme in Mark.

the resurrection of the body,

Yes, bodily resurrection is probably implied by the empty tomb.

and the life everlasting. Amen.

This sounds more like John's Gospel. If we were going to construct a creed based on Mark, we'd probably want to mention the "kingdom of God" instead.

This last point about the "kingdom of God" illustrates the problem with expecting Mark to fit neatly into any sort of orthodoxy that came after. Mark's Jesus is a kingdom preacher. In fact, the kingdom of God seems to be Jesus's primary message. Any creed that intends to be faithful to Mark would have to spotlight this concept.

Inevitably, this thought experiment is frustrating because the Apostles' Creed and Mark do not fit together hand in glove. They don't even fit together hand in shoe. So trying to read Mark as a building block for orthodoxy may be a fool's errand.

As you've probably already concluded, my internal dialogue is misguided for a number of reasons. As one colleague told me, *no single biblical document is exhaustive for the purpose of theology*. What if, for example, we were to try this creedal experiment with the prophet Isaiah? I imagine that we'd find that a few lines of the Apostles' Creed cohere with Isaiah's poetry, but using Isaiah in this way is wrongheaded. Even more so with documents like Jonah or Philemon. Simply put, these documents were never intended to serve as the foundation of a creedal statement. So too with Mark. Isn't this the same lesson that my seminary professor was trying to teach me?

Another reason why my internal dialogue is misguided is that the Apostles' Creed itself is not exhaustive. It may be sufficient for its own liturgical purpose, but it will never be able to explain the importance of Peter's confession (Mark 8) or the significance of the transfiguration (Mark 9). These are climactic moments in Mark that reveal aspects of Jesus's identity, but the Apostles' Creed wasn't composed to showcase any particular Gospel's story. There is a reason why the church has celebrated four Gospels rather than one. Each is unique and should be allowed to speak for itself.

Admittedly, my Apostles' Creed thought experiment is foolish. But it is how the book before you got started. In service to my continued preoccupation, I wanted to gather a handful of scholars to discuss Mark's portrait of Jesus. I knew that I wanted scholars who were focused on Mark's literary context rather than the doctrinal interests of subsequent generations.

The authors of this project take seriously the unique portrait of Jesus found in Mark. These scholars are committed to reading Mark in its first-century, Greek, Roman, and Jewish contexts. Each author has tried to understand Mark's unique portrait without the baggage of the later creedal beliefs about Jesus. In other words, they aim to read Mark without forcing the Gospel to make claims that it doesn't make. For example, this volume doesn't debate the virgin birth because this plot point isn't important for Mark. But this volume does debate the meaning of the phrase "son of man" because this phrase is indeed important for Mark.

Narrowing further, I have asked each author to address the question of Christology in Mark. This, for many of the reasons already discussed, is not an easy task.

What Do We Mean by Christology?

Any simple internet search will tell you that Christology is the study of Christ. But there is a difference in connotation between Christology as a field of study and Christology as a doctrine. This book is about the former, not the latter. The authors gathered here have been asked to *study* Jesus as a character within Mark's story. They have not been asked to debate this character's doctrinal significance.

As a doctrine, Christology presupposes the idea of the Trinity. Most Christians of subsequent generations have understood Christ (both man and God) within a Trinitarian framework. But Mark's Gospel does not provide readers with a clearly Trinitarian framework. Mark doesn't speak directly to the coequality and/or distinction of Father, Son, and Holy Spirit. No doubt, these concepts are at play in Mark. But the term "Trinity" is not. Moreover, Trinitarian questions are neither asked nor answered by the story. And yet many Christians over the centuries—those for whom the Trinity was paramount—continued to hold Mark's Gospel as sacred, inspired, and authoritative. Put another way, Jesus's unique portrayal in Mark continues to be important whether or not it affirms a particular doctrine.

The authors of this book aim to meet Mark's story on its own terms and remain open to the theological categories it presents. In their reading, they will examine questions of Jesus's person, his relationship to Israel's God, his authority, his words and deeds, and the titles applied to him. These are topics that may inform doctrine, but they are not primarily guided by doctrine. So by Christology, we mean the study of Christ rather than the doctrine of Christ.

Questions of "High" and "Low" Christologies

The phrase "high Christology" is sometimes used of orthodox, Trinitarian doctrine. Because Mark is not a story framed by this doctrine, we might be tempted to say that Mark has an implicitly "low Christology." But if we allow this anachronism to place its thumb on the scale, we risk devaluing the discussion before it begins.

It is, however, not unreasonable to wonder how the authors of this book come down on the question of Jesus's status relative to divinity and humanity. For the sake of offering a spectrum, we could say that two of our authors read Mark's portrait of Jesus with transcendent status, while the other two do not. All agree that Mark's Jesus is decidedly human. The question, then, is about the sort of human we meet in Mark. What does divine sonship mean for Mark? Why does Jesus prefer the phrase "Son of Man" (alternatively translated "human one")? What do we do with Jesus's amazing feats, like when he walks on water?

Scholars answer these questions in different ways and for different reasons. The book before you offers only a handful of views, but it reflects well a wider spectrum of approaches. These contributors are ordered alphabetically.

Sandra Huebenthal provides a close reading of the world that Mark's Gospel creates, rather than the world behind or around the author. Within the narrated world, she argues, we meet Jesus as a human messenger (or prophet) of Israel's God. Using eschatological categories borrowed from Isaiah, Mark's narrator portrays Jesus as a man with an extraordinary life and extraordinary abilities. Moreover, Mark preserves the varying perspectives of the narrator, the characters around Jesus, and Jesus himself. Each perspective reveals Jesus in a different light. The textual world of Mark leaves little room for interpreting Jesus in divine or even semi-divine categories. Huebenthal observes, however, that Mark's story opens rather than closes at its end, allowing readers to encounter Jesus as divine even if the preceding text does not encourage this view.

Larry Hurtado argues that Mark's Jesus, while genuinely human, has a unique relationship with God that cannot be likened to other figures. While there is no Trinitarian theology in Mark's framing, Jesus breaks all previous molds of Jewish holy men, so much so that he holds transcendent status and significance, and he acts with divine agency. Mark's story puts forth a Jesus that is worthy of veneration as God's unique Son. But even more importantly, Mark is a story intended to teach worshipers of Jesus how to be faithful followers, especially in the context of opposition. As such, Jesus who is venerated provides a pattern for the Christian life—that of suffering and death followed by ultimate (even if still unseen) vindication.

Daniel Kirk argues that Mark's Jesus is presented within the bounds of his earthly life. Kirk explains that Jesus's character develops in dramatic ways over the course of the story. The Jesus we meet before Peter's confession (Mark 8:27–38) and the Jesus we meet after stand in stark contrast. Mark 1–8 establishes Jesus as a human messiah with the authority to govern matters that otherwise would have been governed by God through Jewish law and tradition. Even so, God and Jesus are distinctly different characters. Jesus is so distinct, in fact, that in the end he is abandoned by God (Mark 15). After a holistic reading of Mark's entire story, we see Jesus as the Spirit-empowered messiah who must suffer and die to enter his glory.

Adam Winn argues that (1) Jewish theology in the Second Temple period was flexible enough to include "two powers in heaven," in which both powers were rightly identified as YHWH, and (2) some Jews associated a heavenly "Son of Man" figure with one of these two powers. In short, in Mark's context the notion of monotheism is flexible, allowing for plurality within the conception of the one God of Israel. Mark's portrait of Jesus seems to fit quite well within this framework. This reading can be inferred from Jesus's ability to forgive sins (Mark 2), Jesus's status as "Lord of the Sabbath" (Mark 2), Jesus walking on water (Mark 6), and the charge of blasphemy against Jesus (Mark 14). If so, both God and Jesus can be rightly identified as YHWH in Mark's Gospel.

If it's necessary to draw a dividing line, we could say that Winn and Hurtado read the Markan Jesus as both human and transcendent. Conversely, Huebenthal and Kirk read the Markan Jesus as not transcendent. But this delineation doesn't tell the whole story. First, Winn and Hurtado arrive at their views for very different reasons. Second, it seems that Hurtado and Kirk have much more in common than their opening paragraphs would suggest. Third, Huebenthal explains that Mark's ending is open for interpretation, leaving space for readers to draw their own conclusions. These are just a few examples of the robust conversations in what follows.

Rather than seeing these scholars along a christological spectrum of "low" to "high," it might be better to think of them as a book club. Each voice presents a compelling argument. But, as with any good book club, it's not important that a single argument triumphs in the end. What is crucial is that the book—in this case, the Gospel of Mark—is better appreciated because of the debate. My hope is that you savor the delicious mystery that Mark provides.

A Shorter and Longer Ending

Finally, it's my somber duty to note that Larry Hurtado passed away before this book was finished. Toward the end, Larry wrote to me saying,

> These may well be my final, formal, written contributions to the field. I'm still feeling comparatively good . . . we can't be sure how long it may last. I think now I'll turn to recovering some of my guitar playing!!

Larry was determined to keep his commitment to this project and submitted his chapters earlier than the due date. Sadly, Larry passed about a month after this email and before he could complete his final rejoinder. So like Mark's Gospel, Larry's final work was completed with an editorial epilogue.

Chris Keith—Larry's former student, colleague, and friend—agreed to pen a final rejoinder. While Professor Keith cannot write with Hurtado's voice, there is perhaps no scholar better suited to step into the gap.

CHAPTER 1

Suspended Christology

SANDRA HUEBENTHAL

Introduction: A Gaze through the Keyholes of History

"Christology" is a theological latecomer. Reformed theologian Balthasar Meissner coined the technical term for the question about Jesus only in the seventeenth century in his book *Christologia sacra*, published in Wittenberg in 1624.[1] This is a long time not only after the New Testament was written but also a long time after the councils of the fourth and fifth century had defined the orthodox perspective on Jesus, that is, had determined who he would be for the Christian community, regardless as to whether they call themselves Anglican, Evangelical, Lutheran, Orthodox, Pentecostal, Reformed, or Roman Catholic today. Our common foundations are the New Testament texts *and* the ecumenical councils, and thus our notion of Christology comes with a long history, which only began after the New Testament was put to page. We must keep this in mind when we apply the concept to the New Testament and ask for a New Testament text's "Christology."

German New Testament scholar Reinhard von Bendemann is aware of this gap and proceeds with caution. Bendemann suggests that when it comes to the New Testament, the term "Christology" should only be used in quotation marks.[2] Elizabeth Struthers Malbon, a well-known scholar of Mark,

1. Gerhard Ludwig Müller, "Christologie," in *Lexikon der Katholischen Dogmatik*, ed. Wolfgang Beinert (Freiburg: Herder, 1997), 59.

2. Reinhard von Bendemann, "Die Fülle der Gnade—Neutestamentliche Christologie," in *Jesus Christus*, ed. Jens Schröter, TdT 9 (Tübingen: Mohr Siebeck, 2014), 71.

does in fact do so in some of her publications, providing the same rationale.[3] The awareness is that we are dealing with a late theological category applied to earlier texts that might even be at odds at times with the texts themselves. This is an important insight for any discussion of Markan Christology. What was defined by the council fathers and later dogmatized in the particular confessions is the result of a longer process of theological reflection and need not automatically be present in every biblical text. Or, put differently, there is not necessarily a direct line from Mark to the Nicene Creed, and the current debate about early, high Christology in Mark's Gospel might say more about current than ancient theological issues.[4] "To ask whether the Markan Jesus is 'divine' or not," Markan scholar M. Eugene Boring warns, "is to impose an alien schema on Markan thought."[5]

In his book *Gospel Writing*, Francis Watson makes what is at first glance a somewhat disturbing claim. He argues that had the early Christian discourses run just slightly different, we would not be reading Matthew, Mark, Luke, and John as canonical Gospels today but possibly the Gospel according to Thomas or even the Gospel according to Peter instead.[6] "The distinction between the canonical and the noncanonical," Watson argues, "arises not from the differences between the texts but from their circulation and currency in wider or narrower spheres of the early Christian world."[7] In other words, canonical discussions are not unavoidable and remain contingent to a certain extent. Watson's observations allow a glimpse into the processes that took place both on the way to biblical canon and christological dogma:

> If Gaius of Rome had won the anti-Johannine argument, and if Serapion and others had aggressively promoted the cause of the *Gospel of Peter*, then that Gospel might have prevailed over both the Gospel of John and the only indirectly Petrine Gospel of Mark. John and Mark would then

3. Elizabeth Struthers Malbon, "'Reflected Christology': An Aspect of Narrative 'Christology' in the Gospel of Mark," *PRSt* 26 (1999): 127–145; cf. idem, *Mark's Jesus: Characterization as Narrative Christology* (Waco, TX: Baylor University Press, 2009), 1–19.

4. Michael Kok, "Marking a Difference: The Gospel of Mark and the 'Early High Christology' Paradigm," *JJMJS* 3 (2016): 102–24.

5. M. Eugene Boring, "Markan Christology: God-language for Jesus?," *NTS* 45.4 (1999): 456.

6. Francis Watson, *Gospel Writing: A Canonical Perspective* (Grand Rapids: Eerdmans, 2013), 307, 612–13.

7. Watson, *Gospel Writing*, 612.

> have disappeared from sight, their memory preserved only in disparaging remarks by Eusebius. At a later date, post-Enlightenment biblical scholarship would have initiated an intense debate over the genuineness of the canonical *Gospel of Peter*, conservative scholarship would have fiercely resisted critical arguments for its pseudonymity. If, later still, fragments of a noncanonical "Johannine" gospel emerged from the sands of Egypt, they would have been consigned without hesitation to the category of the apocryphal. Appeal would be made to gnosticizing tendencies in its opening and dependence on the canonical Peter in its conclusion; and such arguments would no doubt have carried the day, disputed only by a minority of willfully provocative critics.[8]

What seems to have the character of a "what if" game is at a second glance a depiction of typical patterns in social processes. Issues come up and are discussed, majorities are organized, and decisions are taken. There is no reason to believe that social negotiation in early Christianity was any different from what we experience today. German patristics scholar Christoph Markschies claims (for good reason) that the church, especially in the second century, seemed like a huge laboratory for trying different forms of theology, hierarchy, and ethics.[9] In hindsight and with the distance of only a few decades, decision-making often looks much more harmonious than it actually was—a lesson that can also be learned from a comparison of Acts 15 and Galatians 2. In Paul's letter to the Galatians, his dispute with Cephas (Peter) is paramount. But the issue that was burning for Paul had cooled down by the time Acts was written. As the author of Acts, Luke presents a cordial and united Christian community in a mostly gentile-Roman environment. Luke does not, therefore, revisit the problems of an earlier generation. It is not by accident that he does not mention the incident at Antioch but describes the Jerusalem meeting as a unanimous decision taken under the guidance of the Spirit. His question was no longer how Jewish and gentile Jesus-followers could live, eat, and worship together but how Christian communities could make their living within Roman urban society without being considered a threat to social stability.

---

8. Watson, *Gospel Writing*, 613.

9. Christoph Markschies, *Das antike Christentum. Frömmigkeit, Lebensformen, Institutionen* (München: Beck, 2006), 42.

Similar negotiations can be observed in the ecumenical councils some hundred years later. They, too, are examples of social discourse and were influenced by their respective historical contexts. It is intriguing to consider for a moment the possibility Watson explores and apply it to the councils: What would our Creed look like if groups of Jesus-followers like the Adoptionists or Ebionites had prevailed in the discussion? The thought is particularly stimulating for reflections about Markan Christology because those groups based some of their arguments on Mark's baptism scene (1:9–11).[10]

The crucial question discussed in Nicaea was what "Son of God" (ὑιὸς θεοῦ) means. Is Jesus the Son of God as Mark 1:11 implies? If so, how many gods exist? The idea of two gods, YHWH and Jesus, is not reconcilable with Jewish monotheism. Adoptionists solved the problem by assuming that God adopted Jesus as his son during or after the baptism. Ebionites, going down a slightly different route, defended the position that Jesus was God's messenger. What Adoptionists, Ebionites, Cerinthus, Marcion, Paul of Samosata, Photinus, and others share is the denial of the divine nature and preexistence of Christ. For them, Jesus was just a human being, even though a special one, and Mark's Gospel was their key witness. The Nicene Council, focusing more on John's Gospel, which, as we have just seen was highly disputed in the third century, gave a different answer: *Jesus Christ is begotten, not made, one being with the Father* (γεννηθέντα οὐ ποιηθέντα, ὁμοούσιον τῷ Πατρί).

This brief glance at history also shows that in the beginning there was not only one idea about Jesus but a variety of different impressions, ideas, and concepts that were mediated and reconciled over time. As the ecumenical councils show, this was not always an easy process and very often included definitions and drawing boundaries between what was considered orthodox and what was not. Over time, the different ideas about who Jesus is and how he is best understood were narrowed down to a few concepts that were defined and dogmatized. The textualization of particular perspectives on Jesus as we find it in the canonical Gospels is an important step on the way from the first impressions of early Jesus-followers to the formulas of the

10. Cf. Michael Goulder, "Jesus without Q," in *Handbook for the Study of the Historical Jesus*, ed. Tom Holmén and Stanley E. Porter, 4 vols. (Leiden: Brill, 2010), 2:1296–97; Bart D. Ehrman, *The Orthodox Corruption of Scripture* (New York: Oxford University Press, 1996), 48–57.

ecumenical councils. These texts did not aim at recording the history or the events themselves but at recording a particular theological perspective on them, which they contributed to the early Christian discourse.[11]

This chapter will discuss Mark's contribution to this discourse. Our journey through the Gospel will introduce us to a fascinating narrative that discusses different ideas about Jesus. In its conclusion it will suggest one particular perspective that the Gospel of Mark visibly treasures. As we will see, Mark's Gospel does not visualize Jesus as a divine or preexistent being but rather depicts him in Isaianic categories as a human messenger of God with an extraordinary experience and, as a result, extraordinary abilities.

Reading Mark's Gospel as a Story about Jesus and the Beginning of the Gospel

Before setting out on this journey, let us get our gear together and consult some travel guides. As we are embarking on a trip into a biblical text, our travel guides come from biblical scholars. Those books resemble the old Baedeker guides more than Lonely Planet, and thus they tend to be somewhat theoretical and difficult to read. To make things as convenient as possible, I will give a brief survey of exegetical insight that I found particularly helpful for this journey. They consist of a global insight in the mode of traveling (reading Mark as a narrative text), a hint how to look at the different places in order see the fascinating sights (worlds and perspectives in the text), and a brief glance at the topography of the entire country (structure of the text).

There is a growing consensus among Markan scholars that we are dealing with a narrative text that is much more than just the sum of its parts. It is clear that the text has a narrative character, and it is equally obvious that it is not just any narrative. Mark's Gospel is neither a novel nor a work of history. Its truth lies neither in a spotless preservation of the past nor a pious imagination of what Jesus might have been like. Regardless of whether we term it an ancient biography (a *bios*), it is a text that treasures experiences

11. Cf. Tom Thatcher, "Why John Wrote a Gospel: Memory and History in an Early Christian Community," in *Memory, Tradition, and Text: Uses of the Past in Early Christianity*, ed. Alan Kirk and Tom Thatcher, Semeia 52 (Atlanta: Society of Biblical Literature, 2005), 79–97.

people have had with Jesus and his message. These experiences have been verbalized in the form of episodes and integrated into an overall story about Jesus and his proclamation.[12] While historical-critical research for a long time was predominantly interested in how the particular episodes and units came about—and what they might have to say about the historical Jesus and the passing on of Jesus traditions—Markan scholarship of the past few decades has shifted attention to the entire text as a holistic composition. Even though the approaches might differ, Mark's Gospel is now commonly read and interpreted as a story.[13]

Approaching a text like Mark from a literary-studies perspective gives a different outlook (as compared to approaches that look for editorial layers with the text) and thus leads to different results. The underlying assumption is that the Gospel's text as we know it today is a final product that carries meaning in itself. Moreover, it can be meaningfully understood and interpreted without knowing its prior stages of composition. This does not say that a text like Mark's Gospel does not form part of a larger communication process. The narrative can nevertheless be understood independently of its original historical situation. Being a *text-oriented* approach, the task of a narratological analysis is not to describe the world from which the text has originated or which it seems to refer to but to depict the world of the text itself. The point is not to shed light on the historical author and the real world but on the narrator and the narrated world that comes alive while reading the text.[14]

This approach also changes the type of questions posed to the text. As regards Christology, the question is no longer what *Christos* (χριστός) means

12. Cf. Cilliers Breytenbach, "Das Markusevangelium als episodische Erzählung. Mit Überlegungen zum 'Aufbau' des zweiten Evangeliums," in *Der Erzähler des Evangeliums. Methodische Neuansätze in der Markusforschung*, ed. Ferdinand Hahn, SBS 118/119 (Stuttgart: Katholisches Bibelwerk, 1985), 139–69. See also Sandra Huebenthal, *Reading Mark's Gospel as a Text from Collective Memory* (Grand Rapids: Eerdmans, 2020), a translation of *Das Markusevangelium als kollektives Gedächtnis*, 2nd ed., FRLANT 253 (Göttingen: Vandenhoeck & Ruprecht, 2018], 179–84, 214–26.

13. Elizabeth Struthers Malbon, "New Literary Criticism and Jesus Research," in Holmén and Porter, *Handbook for the Study of the Historical Jesus*, 1:777–807.

14. Cf. Willem S. Vorster, "Markus—Sammler, Redaktor, Autor oder Erzähler?," in Hahn, *Der Erzähler des Evangeliums*, 30; Pheme Perkins, "The Synoptic Gospels and Acts of the Apostles Telling the Christian Story," in *The Cambridge Companion to Biblical Interpretation*, ed. John Barton (Cambridge: Cambridge University Press, 1998), 244; David S. Du Toit, *Der abwesende Herr. Strategien im Markusevangelium zur Bewältigung der Abwesenheit des Auferstandenen*, WMANT 111 (Neukirchen-Vluyn: Neunkirchner, 2006), 9.

in general but rather what it means in the narrative world of Mark's Gospel. Researchers need to put their twenty-first century christological spectacles aside and read Mark's Gospel asking what it has to say about Jesus.[15] Who is he and what is he doing? What does he say about himself and what do the narrator and characters say about him?

Reading *Mark as Story*[16] means being occupied with what happens in the text. The basic question is: How does Mark work as a narrative? One basic observation is that Mark—like any other narrative—operates on different levels. On the one hand, there is the narrated world, namely, the universe that the characters inhabit. It is the world in which they live, love, quarrel, and reconcile with one another, where they eat, sleep, and die. On the other hand, there is the world of the narrator in which the narrator lives, thinks, and develops the story. Both worlds are features of the text and can clearly be distinguished from the real world of the author and, admittedly with a bit more of an effort, from each other.[17]

In addition, stories do not only consist of different *levels* or *worlds* but also of different perspectives. They contain both the *characters' perspectives* and the *narrator's perspective*. The *narrator's perspective* is the narrator's idea or construct of reality.[18] The concept of the *narrator's perspective* introduces another helpful, new agent, for it allows us to clearly distinguish different perspectives and voices within a given story, for example, when you realize that Jesus and the narrator both use the word "gospel" (εὐαγγέλιον) but do so in different ways. While the narrator proclaims the "gospel of Jesus" (1:1), the character Jesus is said to be proclaiming the "gospel of God" (1:14), though in fact Jesus uses the term "gospel" without additional qualifiers (8:35; 10:29; 13:10; 14:9). Jesus's proclamation concerns the "kingdom of God" (βασιλεία τοῦ θεοῦ), which he proclaims to be at hand (1:15)—an expression the narrator avoids as long as Jesus is alive.[19] Or, even more striking, while the narrator seems anxious not to pick up Jesus's use of the formula "Son

15. Von Bendemann, "Die Fülle der Gnade," 72.

16. David Rhoads and Donald Mitchie, *Mark as Story: An Introduction to the Narrative of a Gospel* (Philadelphia: Fortress, 1982).

17. Cf. Huebenthal, *Reading Mark's Gospel*; see also Malbon, *Mark's Jesus*.

18. Carola Surkamp, *Die Perspektivenstruktur narrativer Texte: Zu ihrer Theorie und Geschichte im englischen Roman zwischen Viktorianismus und Moderne* (Trier: Wissenschaftlicher Verlag Trier, 2003), 43.

19. Cf. Malbon, *Mark's Jesus*, 173.

of Man," the character Jesus never vocally accepts the title "Son of God." Even when he is asked by the high priest whether he is the "Son of the Blessed One," he sticks to the formula "Son of Man," equipping it with an eschatological twist (14:61–62).[20] In the case of Mark's Gospel, observations of this type are particularly helpful, for they aid in solving a quite difficult problem, which goes to the core of the christological question: Who is Jesus?

In Mark's Gospel, the question about Jesus's identity is explicitly asked several times, and it remains an ongoing theme in the background. The quest for the right understanding of Jesus is a dynamic plot of the overall narrative. Reading the whole story, the following structure unfolds. The narrator opens the narrative universe with the words "beginning of the gospel of Jesus Christ, Son of God"[21] (1:1, all translations from the Greek text of the Gospel are mine). Taking seriously this first line, it also introduces the matter of the narrative: Mark's Gospel is more about *the beginning of the gospel* than about the character Jesus, even though Jesus is intrinsically tied to it. The story of the gospel, nonetheless, extends far beyond the life of the character Jesus.[22] This can easily be illustrated by a brief glance at the text's structure: the *inner story* (1:16–15:39) narrates the *story of experiences with Jesus and his proclamation*, and the outer parts (1:1–13 and 15:42–16:8) insinuate the further story of the gospel. Two narrative bridges (1:14–15 and 15:40–41) connect the inner story and the outer parts, forming an overall outer story. The outer story has an open end and bridges into the lives of the recipients (see the table below).

20. Cf. Malbon, *Mark's Jesus*, 238.

21. The text-critical question about the originality of υἱοῦ θεοῦ in 1:1 is still subject to scholarly debates. On the basis of the manuscripts, a clear decision cannot be made. C. C. Black, "Mark as Historian of God's Kingdom," *CBQ* 71 (2009): 65, notes laconically that "adjudicating the text-critical problem in Mark 1:1, the jury remains out. When it will return with a generally acceptable verdict is anyone's guess." In the latest contribution to the problem, T. Wasserman, "The 'Son of God' was in the Beginning (Mark 1:1)," *JTS* 62 (2011): 20–50, lists once more the arguments for both sides and opts on the basis of the manuscripts ("earliest and strongest support," 50), the inner logic, and the likelihood of omitting the title in the copying process for the longer reading. In the same way, D. B. Deppe, "Markan Christology and the Omission of υἱοῦ θεοῦ in Mark 1:1," *Filologia Neotestamentica* 21 (2008): 45–64, challenges the "new consensus . . . in textual-critical circles that favors the omission" and concludes after an evaluation of the arguments that "both external evidence and Markan Christology argue in favor of the inclusion of 'Son of God' in the first sentence of Mark's Gospel" (64). In the present article, I follow this argumentation.

22. Huebenthal, *Reading Mark's Gospel*, 189–94; David S. Du Toit, "'Es ist nichts Geheimes, das nicht ans Licht kommen soll': Verhüllung und Enthüllung als Erzählmotiv und als narrative Strategie im Markusevangelium," in *Christ of the Sacred Stories*, ed. Predrag Dragutinovic and Tobias Nicklas, WUNT 2/453 (Tübingen: Mohr Siebeck, 2017), 27–56, esp. 51–52.

Outer Story (1:1–16:18)
Beginning of the Gospel of Jesus Christ, Son of God

Opening (1:1–13)	**Narrative Bridge** (1:14–15)	**Inner story** (1:16–15:39)	**Narrative Bridge** (15:40–41)	**Open End** (15:42–16:8)
	Focus on Jesus who proclaims the gospel of God	*Experiences with Jesus and his proclamation*	Focus on those who should be the ones who proclaim the gospel of Jesus Christ, Son of God	Bridge into the lives of the recipients

This visualization shows that the beginning of the gospel is inseparably linked to the fate of the character Jesus. In 1:14–15 Jesus is presented as the one who proclaims and explains the gospel of God. This has implications for the structure of the narrative: the sequence of events told in Mark's Gospel is oriented toward the protagonist, Jesus. The story unfolds along the other characters' experiences with Jesus, his actions as well as his message, and it is these experiences that lead to the characters asking who this Jesus is and how he is best understood. As regards evaluation within the inner story, Jesus's message is dependent on how he is evaluated by others. Approval or refusal of the person implies approval or refusal of the content, and thus the story of experiences with Jesus becomes the beginning of the story of his gospel and the founding story of the Markan group.

As Mark's Gospel is a sandwich composition narrating two stories into each other with both stories operating on different levels, the question is not only how the characters evaluate their experiences with Jesus in their world but even more how the narrator evaluates their different perspectives in *his* world, that is, on the level of the narration. This evaluation is the perspective that Mark's Gospel contributes to the early Christian discussion about Jesus.

Mark's Gospel: Different Perspectives on Jesus and Their Evaluation

Now we are ready to begin our journey. Let us start by turning our attention to the different worlds and perspectives in Mark's stories. First, we will begin with the presentation of Jesus in the narrated world and see how characters and readers perceive him. Second, we will move to the perspective of the narrator and see that a correct understanding of Jesus is not possible without reading him through the lens of the prophet Isaiah. Third, we will turn to the question of Jesus's own experience and how he sees himself in comparison to the other characters and the narrator. The fourth step will focus on the question as to how the different ideas and views are brought together and how the narrator ensures that characters and readers arrive at the right conclusion. Finally, it will turn out that when it comes to christological questions, Jesus's death on the cross is the elephant in the room with which the Gospel has to deal.

1. Jesus as Presented and Received in the Narrated World

How does Mark's Gospel present Jesus? In the inner story, the reader and the other characters meet Jesus for the first time as he walks along the Sea of Galilee and calls his first disciples Simon and Andrew, James and John, two pairs of brothers, all of them fishermen. In the following scenes, it becomes gradually clearer that, apart from calling the disciples, Jesus does not directly approach individual people but rather preaches to groups. It is, on the contrary, individual people who approach him. The word spreads quickly, and people seek out Jesus with the result that he rarely finds peace and space, let alone time to eat. Jesus's reaction is to withdraw and try to hide from the crowds. He is unlikely to take part in a public meal or symposium hosted by Pharisees or others. Although food, eating, and commensality are important issues, only a few meals are reported: the meal with sinners and tax collectors (2:15), the meal at Simon the leper's house (14:3), and the meal Jesus shares with his disciples on the night before his death (14:17–25). This adds to the overall picture; although he is teaching crowds, Jesus is rather a private person and frequently seeks solitude. At times even his disciples do not know where he is.

Jesus's attempt to keep a certain distance is a constant and reoccurring theme in the Gospel and achieves the opposite of the desired effect. The more Jesus withdraws, the more he attracts people and the more they search for him. When the disciples find him on the morning after the Sabbath, they tell him "everyone is looking for you" (1:37). This pattern of hide-and-seek is repeated several times. Whether he is in Capernaum or the region near Tyre and Sidon, in the first main part of the inner story (1:16–8:26), Jesus cannot hide for long. People seeking for help seek Jesus. In reaction, he withdraws and tries to continue proclaiming in a different location that the kingdom of God has arrived (1:45; 2:2; 3:7–12). Again, he does not achieve the desired effect. People do not look for Jesus or follow him because they want to hear what he has to say, but rather they turn to him because they have heard he has healing abilities (3:8). Jesus is a rather unwilling healer and public person, as his answer to Peter indicates: "Let us go somewhere else to the towns nearby that I may proclaim there also; for that is what I came out for" (1:38). Sometimes Jesus is lucky and can teach for a while (2:1, 13; 4:1), but soon enough the next healing candidate shows. They appear unpredictably and everywhere. On one occasion one of them is even let down through the roof. In the end, Jesus gives up going into cities and stays in unpopulated areas.

There is no end to people seeking him for physical health rather than eternal salvation, which renders Jesus increasingly unhappy. His outburst, "O unbelieving generation, how long shall I be with you? How long shall I put up with you?" (9:19) might reflect Jesus's frustration with people who approach him on the superficial *health* level instead of turning to him on the deeper *salvation* level. No matter where he turns or how well he tries to hide, the sick and possessed are already there or seek and find him (5:1–2; 7:24–25, 32; 8:22; 9:14–15). It is only in the second main part of the Gospel (8:27–10:52) that he finds some peace and quiet to teach his disciples. After leaving Galilee, Jesus generally ceases to speak in public until he turns back to teaching in the temple, where he is no longer approached by the sick and obsessed.

Taking a closer look, Jesus appears to be struggling with the fact that people he teaches make so little progress. He seems frustrated when he finds especially the inner circle of the disciples to be rather slow on the uptake. As we will see later in more detail, for Jesus himself it is clear after his baptism and his time in the desert that a direct relationship with God is possible not only for him but for everyone.

Apart from that, the content of Jesus's teaching remains rather unimpressive. One might even wonder how well versed in his own Jewish traditions he really is. The conversations in the temple could as well be seen as shrewdness; Jesus does not let his opponents trap him. When questioned about his authority he asks a counter question (11:27–33), when questioned about paying taxes he first wants to see the coin (12:13–17), and when questioned about divorce—the reader might still remember from 6:17–29 that critical statements about marriage and divorce can be highly dangerous—he wants to know how they receive the Mosaic command (10:2–9). When asked about resurrection by the Sadducees (12:18–27), Jesus's argument is more narrative in character than one based on the teachings of the Torah; and in his word about whether or not the Anointed One (χριστός) is the son of David (12:35–37), there barely seems to be an argument at all. His discussions with scribes, Pharisees, and Sadducees refer to the common cultural frame, and it seems that Jesus knows the Prophets and Psalms better than the Torah. When he teaches the crowds, there are no references to the Torah. The teaching in 7:14–23 is similarly based on common sense, as are the words about the scribes in 12:28–40, and the observations about the poor widow in 12:41–44.

Jesus's conversations with the Pharisees in Galilee, too, have already been rather colloquial. The words about fasting (2:18–20) draw from everyday images. The dispute about picking grain on the Sabbath (vv. 23–28) is slightly strange. Markan scholars often assume that the narrator got the story in 1 Samuel 21:1–7 wrong.[23] It might, however, make more sense to assume that the narrator deliberately depicts Jesus as slightly insecure when it comes to factual knowledge, in order to present him as an ordinary Galilean who has a quick brain and is at home in his own religious tradition but is nevertheless not a learned person. Jesus appears to be someone perfectly ordinary who has had an extraordinary and life-changing experience with God and is now trying to convince others that they can have the same experience, too.

While his teaching remains rather unimpressive and mostly relies on seemingly easy-to-access parables, Jesus's deeds are more attractive to others. The advent of *God's kingdom* that Jesus proclaims begins to take shape and become visible in their world. The ability to work these signs impresses people much more than Jesus's words. Apart from that, Jesus seems to be a quite normal and everyday person, as can be guessed from the reaction of his family and the surprise on part of the people in his hometown (6:1–4). Jesus lining up with his Galilean fellows at the banks of the Jordan (1:9) speaks as much of an ordinary Jew from Galilee as his behavior when he first enters

23. This would not be the first instance of the narrator getting it wrong. He also falsely ascribes the initial quotation in 1:2–3—in fact a conflation of Isa 40:3, Exod 23:3, and Mal 3:1—exclusively to Isaiah.

the temple in Jerusalem. He "looked round about upon all things" (11:11), as the King James Version nicely puts it. Jesus does not stay in the city that night but goes back to Bethany, and the reader must wait until the next day for the story to be resumed. It seems, after all, that Jesus is not too impressed.

One can be sympathetic with this Jesus who sees the small and is not too impressed by the large. This is a Jesus who speaks in plain and simple language that ordinary people can relate to and yet is ambiguous enough to provoke those who have a say. What is most striking about Jesus is the amount of time he needs to digest all this, the time he needs in silence, in communion with God and in prayer. The Markan Jesus gradually learns both to understand how the encounter with God changed him and to deal with the crowds, but he does not seem to be a born charismatic. Mark 5:30–33 even presents a Jesus who is *surprised by God*. Compared to the later canonical Gospels, the Markan Jesus is far more rural in his travels. He avoids cities. He does not seek publicity. He is ineloquent almost to the point of terseness and is perceived to be a gifted healer rather than a teacher. In general, publicity seems to be an obstacle to a healthy relationship both with God and fellow human beings. Jesus takes people aside and addresses them away from the crowds. Those who have just undergone an intensive experience especially need time and quiet and are urged not to seek publicity. At the end of the narrative (16:1–8), the pattern of extraordinary experience and withdrawal into silence is repeated for one last time. The reader leaves the world of characters at the point when the women, those who should continue the proclamation, are in the initial phase of digesting their experience and—for the moment—remain silent.

The reason why Jesus is able to heal and perform exorcisms is directly addressed twice. In 3:22–30 his opponents assume his capability to perform exorcisms to be the result of possession by Beelzebul. In 11:27–33 he is finally asked directly from where his authority originates. This question is also posed in 2:1–12 and is implied in 6:2–3. The key term to consider is authority. What or who allows Jesus to do all these things? Jesus and the narrator both have the same answer: Jesus's healing ability is a result of his unique closeness to God. This explains why Jesus is occasionally accompanied by theophanic motifs (i.e., motifs that habitually occur when God appears in the Bible; see 4:35–41; 6:45–52; 9:2–8) and why he, in the same way as God in the Old Testament (cf. Ps 103:7 LXX), can *rebuke* (ἐπιτιμάω) demons (1:25; 9:25) and natural forces (4:39). One could of course, like Jesus's opponents, assume that possession, that is, direct contact with Beelzebul, the highest of the demons, gives Jesus command over the subordinate ones (3:22). At a second thought, however, this explanation does not make sense. Why would the head of the demons weaken his own reign? It is only too obvious that the reason for Jesus's extraordinary abilities must be found elsewhere. Jesus special relation to God grants him a share of the divine power to heal, perform exorcisms, forgive sins, and clarify the purpose of the Sabbath.[24]

In general, the content of Jesus's proclamation is less discussed by the other characters than the question about who Jesus is and how he is best understood. The question "Who then is this?" (4:41) opens the floor to a general discussion. Everyone involved in the Gospel participates in the quest for the correct answer. Opponents come up with the idea that Jesus is possessed because they have no other explanation for his healing abilities and regard him as a heretical phenomenon. Ordinary people take him to be Elijah or another prophet of old. Herod Antipas—due to his encounter with John the Baptist and his feelings of guilt for having killed him—thinks that Jesus is the returned Baptist. Family and people from Jesus's hometown do not quite know what to make of him, and some assume he has lost his senses. The disciples, after several attempts to understand, have Peter say that Jesus is the Christ (χριστός), the Anointed One. Even the narrator participates in the general discussion; the initial statement in 1:1 that Jesus is the anointed Son of God sets the scene for the further discussion.

In Mark's Gospel, different characters have different ideas about Jesus and struggle to understand who he is or could be. With a distance of two thousand years and as people who read the story without being involved in it, we would say that they are discussing the christological question. A first set of observations and answers, briefly sketched in this section, does not point to Jesus being a divine or preexistent being but rather depicts him as a human being with an extraordinary experience and extraordinary abilities. Both experience and abilities remain in the realm of what the narrated world deems possible. The question debated among the characters is less

---

24. C. Drew Smith, "'This Is My Beloved Son; Listen to Him': Theology and Christology in the Gospel of Mark," *HBT* 24 (2002): 63–64.

about how Jesus's deeds are possible than where he got the potential and authority to work them. Opinions on that point differ greatly. The most remote explanation from the other characters is provided by the narrator, who introduces Jesus as God's anointed Son or, translated slightly differently, "the Messiah and Son of God."

2. The Narrator's Perspective: God's Anointed Son according to Isaiah the Prophet

When it comes to explaining who Jesus is, the narrator loses no time, opening with "beginning of the gospel of Jesus Christ, Son of God" (1:1). When we stick to the assumption that Mark's Gospel tells two stories at the same time and we are here concerned with *christological questions*, we can for the moment leave aside the expression "gospel" (εὐαγγέλιον) and focus on the narrator's perception of Jesus that is enunciated in the expressions "anointed [one]" (χριστός) and "son of God" (υἱὸς θεοῦ). Remembering Malbon's research question, the point is what these two expressions mean in the world of the narrator, not what they mean in general. As the scope of possible meanings of both expressions in Second Temple Judaism is rather broad and becomes even broader when possible gentile contexts are also considered, some hints as to how to understand those in the world of the Gospel are most welcome.

The narrator indeed provides such a hint in the following verses 2–3 beginning with "as it is written in Isaiah the prophet." Regardless what potential for understanding the three expressions "gospel" (εὐαγγέλιον), "anointed" (χριστός), and "son of God" (υἱὸς θεοῦ) might have outside Mark's Gospel, the way the beginning of the text is phrased indicates that in this narrative they are determined by a fourth: "Isaiah the prophet." It is obviously not enough to read only the first line. For Mark's Gospel, making sense of Jesus and the experience with him and his proclamation must take place within the broader cultural framework of Israel's Holy Scriptures and especially the prophet Isaiah.

Let us take a closer look. The word χριστός ("anointed [one]") occurs seven times in Mark's Gospel. A side glance to the Pauline letters clarifies that Mark is drawing from ideas that already existed. It seems that some people who had heard about Jesus already knew that he was called "the Anointed One." Biblical scholars would say that Mark

> is drawing from existent tradition. The use of the motif in the text is, however, interesting: the narrator and the other characters apply it to the earthly Jesus (1:1; 8:29 [Peter]; 14:61 [high priest]; 15:32 [mocking bystanders]) while the character Jesus uses it either in eschatological contexts (9:41; 13:21–22) or with reference to the concept of royal Davidic messianism (12:35; 13:21), which he clearly does not support.[25]

Messianism and messianic concepts have a long history, and it would be misleading to assume that there was one homogenous idea in Jesus's time. As Paolo Sacchi illustrates in his brief history of messianism, Jewish messianism has its origins in royal Davidic messianism, based on Isaiah 11 alongside a number of other texts, traditions, and expectations.[26] In later times, Davidic messianism is only one variation of messianism, and this particular version ties the advent of the golden age to a figure of Davidic origin. The title *Son of David*, which is also applied to Jesus in Mark's Gospel, makes use of this motif. The idea of a royal messiah reoccurs also, for example, in Zechariah 9:9–10, which is alluded to in the story of Jesus's entry into Jerusalem. The Septuagint version of Zechariah illustrates the messianic reading of the passage by the use of the expression "saving" (σῴζων) to substitute the original "victorious." "In the second century BCE, the book was certainly read within messianic categories."[27] When Bartimaeus calls Jesus "Son of David" (10:47–48) and the crowd that accompanies Jesus riding on a donkey into Jerusalem cry, "Blessed is the coming kingdom of our father David" (11:10), it is difficult not to note Davidic-messianic overtones. Messianic expectations, however, do not necessarily have to be connected to a royal figure. Other variations might be expecting the messiah to be a priestly figure, or expecting two messiahs—one of royal, one of priestly origin.[28] Messianic features might also be ascribed or transferred to superhuman figures like the returning Elijah (Mal 4:5–6), Enoch (1 En. 72–82), Melchizedek (2 En. 71.29; 11QMelch), and the Son of Man (cf. Dan 7:13–14) or transferred to

---

25. Mattias Konradt, "Das MtEv als judenchristlicher Entwurf zum MkEv," in *Studien zum Matthäusevangelium*, ed. Matthias Konradt, WUNT 358 (Tübingen: Mohr Siebeck, 2016), 59–60.

26. Paolo Sacchi, "Messianism and Apocalyptic," in *Jewish Apocalyptic and Its History*," trans. William J. Short, LSTS (Sheffield: Sheffield Academic, 1996), 149–67.

27. Sacchi, "Jewish Apocalyptic," 155.

28. Cf. Zech 4:14; 6:11–15 as well as texts from the Dead Sea Scrolls collection: 1QS 9.11; 1QSa 2.11–22; and CD 7.19b–21; 12.23–13.1; 14.19; 19.10–11; 20.1.

the people as a whole, as in Isaiah's Servant Songs. These traditions were all to a greater or lesser extent current in the first century. The question is thus what *christos* (χριστός) means in Mark's world.

As the expression occurs already in the first verse and is connected to Isaiah, it makes sense to assume that it is be best understood as denoting an eschatological messenger according to Isaiah 42:1; 52:7; and 61:1. David du Toit has made a convincing case for this interpretation. He writes:

> The references to Isa 42:1 and 52:7 in Mark 1:9–15 similarly contain an implicit yet clear allusion to Isa 61:1—the references give reason for the biblically informed reader to regard Isa 61:1 at this point as a most relevant intertext. If the reader recognizes the allusion and follows its trail, he/she recognizes that Jesus is presented in Mark 1:9–15 as the prophesied eschatological messenger of Isa 61:1 who (in the LXX version) is the bearer of God's spirit because God anointed him—as narrated in Mark 1:9–11—in order to proclaim the good news to the poor—as narrated in Mark 1:14–15! The implication should be apparent: The episodic deployment of the summary of Jesus's ministry as proclamation of the gospel (1:14–15) described in the previous section should be seen as narrative deployment of Isa 61:1a–c.[29]

Read this way, Mark 1:9–15 makes a strong case for identifying Jesus with the eschatological messenger, anointed with God's spirit, and thus the Son of God according to the prophecy of Isaiah. This implies two things: (1) after listening to or reading the prologue of Mark's Gospel, the recipients already have all the information they need to understand Jesus and his fate, and (2) it will be difficult to arrive at the right conclusion without a thorough knowledge of Isaiah and his prophecy.

When *christos* (χριστός) is not read as "Christ" but as "Anointed One," it is easy to see how non-Jewish audiences, who were neither familiar with the Jewish concepts nor subscribed to them, are able to connect to the idea. *Christos* was not an expression reserved to a Jewish encyclopaedia; non-Jews would have understood the expression in the context of antique rites of

29. David S. Du Toit, "Treasuring Memory: Narrative Christology in and beyond Mark's Gospel: Miracle-Traditions as Test Case," *EC* 6 (2015): 334–53 (340); see also idem, "Es ist nichts Geheimes," 28–33.

anointment that were fairly common in the Mediterranean region. The language used in different sources indicates that whatever was anointed was regarded as sacred, consigned to the deity or at least near to the deity. Used for Jesus, the title *christos* would thus have been understood both by Jews and non-Jews as denoting a unique closeness to the God of Israel.[30]

The same holds true for "Son of God" (υἱὸς θεοῦ), the other expression used in 1:1. In Jewish use, the word "son" expresses general affiliation that is not necessarily based on physical procreation. "Son" could denote both bodily lineage and affiliation with a particular group, profession, or people. Even an affiliation with God could be expressed by the word. For example, the expression "sons of God" is used for the angels as members of the heavenly royal household (Gen 6:2–4; Job 1:6; 2:1; 38:7; cf. Ps 89:7). God calls Israel his "firstborn son" (Exod 4:22; see also Hos 11:1), and the king or the (suffering and just) sage, too, could be called "son of God" (2 Sam 7:12–14; Ps 2:7; Wis 2:13–18; Sir 4:10; Jos. Asen. 6.2–6; 13.10). In some of the Qumran texts, the royal messiah could be referred to as "son of God" (4Q174 1.10–13; 4Q246). In Mark's Gospel, the expression "Son of God" might simply reflect the tradition of understanding Jesus as closely affiliated with the Father and the idea that he plays a special role mediating salvation between God and humanity.

The motif of Jesus as God's Son appears seven times in the text, four times directly (1:1; 3:11; 5:7; 15:39), and three times in variations: the voice from heaven speaks twice of "my beloved Son" (1:11; 9:7), and the high priest asks about the "son of the Blessed One" (14:61). Calling Jesus "Son of God" is also not a Markan innovation but derives from previous tradition. The motif already occurs in the Pauline letters, which were written prior to Mark' Gospel, for example, in Romans 1:3–4, where Davidic lineage and the Son-of-God motif are connected, and with a slightly different connotation in Galatians 4:4 and Romans 8:3–4. Galatians is particularly interesting, for the following verses indicate that sonship of God is not reserved to Jesus but open to everyone (Gal 4:5–7; cf. Rom 8:15). Here, too, the motif expresses closeness and affiliation with God, and the concept is connected with being gifted by the Spirit.

---

30. Cf. Udo Schnelle, "Paulinische und markinische Christologie im Vergleich," in *Paul and Mark: Comparative Essays. Part 1: Two Authors at the Beginnings of Christianity*, ed. Oda Wischmeyer and David C. Sim, BZNW 198 (Berlin: de Gruyter, 2014), 283–311 (296).

Once more, Isaiah is the key to unlock the idea. In Mark 1:9–15, the idea of Jesus as the one who is gifted with God's Spirit and who is called "Son" by God are brought together in the moment of Jesus's baptism.[31] Read with Isaiah 61:1, Jesus becomes the *anointed son of God* who is the eschatological messenger of God's kingdom and thus able to heal the sick and cast out demons. The second time that both ideas appear together is the question of the high priest in 14:61: "Are you the Anointed One, the son of the Blessed One?" Coming from an Isaianic background, the question would be whether Jesus is *God's eschatological messenger*.[32] Read this way, Jesus's reference to the Son of Man as an eschatological category makes as much sense as the high priest's reaction to someone who—in his perception—falsely assumes a prophetic role.[33]

Both expressions, "Anointed One" and "Son of God," have in common that they can be accessed both from a Jewish and a non-Jewish background. Non-Jewish Roman readers might have also connected sonship to *divi filius*. This was a concept initially used for Julius Caesar and Augustus, which understands the emperor to be the son of a deified emperor.[34] The Romans had a clear distinction between deified (*divus*) and divine (*deus*), which cannot be expressed in Greek. Already the Greek version of the *Res gestae divi Augusti* uses "divine Augustus" (Σεβαστοῦ θεοῦ) for the Latin "deified Augustus" (*divi Augusti*). It is thus no surprise that the imperial cult had a quite different face in the Greek-speaking eastern part of the Roman Empire, where the idea of a *sacred kingship* was known since the time of Alexander, and subjects had a long history of deified rulers who carried names like *Theos* ("god," cf. Antiochus II Theos, 261–246 BCE) or *Soter* ("savior," cf. Antiochus I Soter 281–261 BCE; Demetrius I Soter, 162–150 BCE). Understanding kings as sons of gods had greater currency in the eastern part of the empire, where kings introduced themselves as divine incarnations or

---

31. Cf. Michael Theobald, "Gottessohn und Menschensohn: Zur polaren Struktur der Christologie im Markusevangelium," SNTSU A/13 (Linz, 1988): 37–79 (57).

32. David S. Du Toit, "'Gesalbter Gottessohn'—Jesus als letzter Bote Gottes: Zur Christologie des Markusevangeliums," in *". . . was ihr auf dem Weg verhandelt habt": Beiträge zur Exegese und Theologie des Neuen Testaments. Festschrift für Ferdinand Hahn zum 75. Geburtstag*, ed. Peter Müller and Christine Gerber (Neukirchen-Vluyn: Neunkirchner, 2001), 49.

33. Theobald, "Gottessohn und Menschensohn," 47–49.

34. Babett Edelmann-Singer, *Das Römische Reich von Tiberius bis Nero* (Darmstadt: Wissenschaftliche Buchgesellschaft, 2017), 16–19, 159–162; Lukas Bormann, *Theologie des Neuen Testaments* (Göttingen: UTB, 2017), 2235–36.

of divine origin and thus as guarantors of the gods' attention or mediators between the divine and human sphere.[35] When the title "Son of God" is applied to Jesus by a Roman centurion (15:39), non-Jewish readers might find it easier to tune in than when it is used by the narrator (1:1), by characters from the numinous sphere (3:11; 5:7) or by God himself (1:11; 9:7).

Non-Jewish audiences might indeed have picked up the notion of the *good news of the emperor* and understood "son of God" (υἱὸς θεοῦ) to be referring to the emperor as the "son of a deified emperor" (*divi filius*) and the idea of an "anointed one" close to a deity. It is, however, much more convincing that the "good news" (εὐαγγέλιον) is alluding to the good tidings proclaimed in Isaiah 40–55.[36] Given the use of Isaiah in the whole of Mark's Gospel, and particularly the reading instruction in 1:2, it is more likely that the expression is derived from the Greek version of Isaiah 40:9; 52:7; and 61:1, which uses a verb form of the same root.[37] The reference in 40:9–11 is particularly interesting, as it follows the passage that is quoted in Mark 1:3.[38] It expresses that there will be a time when the announcements of Isaiah 35:5–6 are fulfilled, provided that people change their ways. The call to return to God is another feature that Mark and Isaiah 40–55 share, and it will be the content of Jesus's first words in Mark 1:14–15.

The narrator presents Jesus to be the *anointed Son of God*, God's eschatological messenger. This is the one who proclaims the arrival of God's reign as it was already prophesied in Isaiah and accompanied by circumstances anticipated there—the eyes of the blind are opened, the ears of the deaf are first stopped, then unstopped, the lame walk, and there is shouting for joy,

---

35. Thomas Witulski, *Kaiserkult in Kleinasien: Die Entwicklung der kultisch-religiösen Kaiserverehrung in der römischen Provinz Asia von Augustus bis Antoninus Pius*, 2nd ed., NTOA/SUNT 63 (Göttingen: Vandenhoeck & Ruprecht, 2011), 32–36.

36. Cf. Morna D. Hooker, "Isaiah in Mark's Gospel," in *Isaiah in the New Testament*, ed. Stephen Moyise and Marten J. J. Menken (New York: Bloomsbury, 2005), 36–37. Not every recipient will have instantly understood the term εὐαγγέλιον this way. As the noun is not used in the Septuagint, there have been speculations that the term could rather be derived from the imperial cult where it denotes "good news" about the emperor. Especially non-Jewish audiences in the Roman Empire are likely to have made this connection, and even Jewish audiences might have heard an echo of this use. The connection to Isaiah is, however, too strong to be excluded completely; cf. Sandra Huebenthal, "Anti-Gospel Revisited," in *Reading the "Political" in Jewish and Christian Texts*, ed. Julia Synder and Korinna Zamfir, BTS 38 (Leuven: Peeters, 2020), 137–58.

37. The Septuagint uses a participle of the Greek verb "proclaiming the good news" (εὐαγγελίζω) in Isa 40:9; 52:7, while an infinitive of it is used in 61:1. The "good news" (εὐαγγέλιον) of Mark 1:1 is thus readily understood as a noun related to this verb.

38. Heike Omerzu, "Geschichte durch Geschichten: Zur Bedeutung jüdischer Traditionen für die Jesusdarstellung des Markusevangeliums," *EC* 2 (2011): 77–99 (91).

because the tongue of the mute is loosened. "Anointed [One]" (χριστός) and "Son of God" (υἱὸς θεοῦ) might be the two ideas about Jesus that offer the most connectivity for non-Jewish audiences; the narrator leaves no doubt, however, that they must be read in the light of and through the prophecy of Isaiah. Mark's proclamation of Jesus is framed in categories of Isaiah.[39]

This way of reading Mark, of course, requires an audience familiar with Isaiah or willing to make themselves familiar when they realize the significance of the prophet and the book assigned to him.[40] If the initial quote is the indicator that the whole story should be understood in the light of Isaiah's prophecy, it explains why such an emphasis is put on Isaiah in Mark 1:1–3, and it is no surprise that this is the only authorial quote in the whole text. This does not exclude the possibility of a *different* perception of Jesus, for example, as a returned Moses or Elijah. It is indeed possible to understand Jesus as a prophet, Son of David, or royal aspirant, but the narrator clearly promotes a different perception. At this time, in this place, and in this text Jesus is understood to be *the anointed Son of God according to Isaiah's prophecy.*

3. Jesus's Perspective: The Eschatological Prophet of God's Kingdom

The opening of Mark's Gospel (1:1–13) is not only the key to understanding the narrator's perspective but also the perspective of the protagonist, Jesus. This becomes clear from the first narrative bridge (1:14–15) when Jesus begins the proclamation of the gospel of God: "The time [καιρός] has been fulfilled and the kingdom of God has arrived. Change your ways and believe this gospel." Whatever was necessary for Jesus to arrive at this insight must have happened prior to these verses, which means that if it is narrated, we will find it in 1:9–13.

In 1:9 Jesus appears without further introduction as one of the Galileans who line up at the banks of the Jordan to be baptized by John. Nothing seems special about him, and John proceeds with his work. The baptism scene turns out to be the key moment for understanding Jesus's perspective.

---

39. Sandra Huebenthal, "Framing Jesus and Understanding Ourselves: Isaiah in Mark's Gospel and Beyond," in *Creative Fidelity, Faithful Creativity: The Reception of Jewish Scripture in Early Judaism & Christianity*, ed. Michael A. Daise and Dorota Hartmann, JSJSup (Leiden: Brill, forthcoming).

40. Cf. Omerzu, "Geschichte durch Geschichten," 79–81.

What happens in this and the following scene is essential for the further course of events. It is thus necessary to take a closer look at what happens and how it is narrated.

The moment Jesus ascends out of the water, he sees the heavens torn apart and the spirit like a dove descending upon him (1:10), and he hears a voice from heaven saying, "You are my beloved son, in you I am well pleased" (v. 11). Several features make this scene remarkable. The most intriguing point is that for two verses, the narrative changes perspective. It is no longer the narrator who gives an overall view; rather, the reader is allowed to share Jesus's point of view. This is especially striking as only Jesus and the reader share this moment. All the other characters, including John the Baptist, neither see the heavens torn apart nor the spirit descending nor hear the voice from heaven.

The reader is granted the opportunity to share the intimate moment of Jesus's extraordinary experience, which constitutes or at least makes obvious the special bond connecting Jesus with God. The words from heaven assure Jesus of a unique relationship with God that is expressed in terms of sonship, recalling Psalm 2:7. The "spirit" Jesus sees descending upon him like a dove recalls Isaiah 61:1, "The spirit of God is upon me because God has anointed me." As we have just seen, the reader could gather from this scene that Jesus's special relationship with God is that Jesus is *God's anointed son*, while Jesus will use the idea of sonship differently.[41]

In 1:12, the narrative situation returns to being properly authorial, and the Spirit puts Jesus instantly in motion. He throws him into the wilderness or desert, an abandoned place (ἔρημος). The forty days Jesus spends there brings to mind the motif of the people of Israel in the desert and their being put to the test. Again, this is an additional piece of information for the reader to make sense of the event. The character's own experience is that in the desert Jesus comes to realize how close and special his relationship to God is. Put to the test, Jesus experiences being drawn into the cosmic battle between God and Satan. Being with the wild animals and with the angels serving him, he realizes that God is on his side and Satan cannot harm him. Jesus's conclusion can only be that Satan has already lost the

41. Cf. Du Toit, "Es ist nichts Geheimes," 35–36; idem, "Treasuring Memory," 339–43; idem, "'Gesalbter Gottessohn,'" 39–40.

cosmic battle and will thus lose the battles on earth as well.[42] All is possible, because God reigns.

When we consider the first part of Isaiah 61:1, "the spirit of God is upon me because God has anointed me," as forming the interpretative background for Jesus's experience and assume that he might have seen it similarly, it is necessary to add the second part of the verse to the scheme: "He has sent me to bring good news to the oppressed, to bind up the brokenhearted, to proclaim liberty to the captives, and release to the prisoners." The entire verse, used as an interpretative lens, would provide Jesus not only with an explanation for what has happened but also with a clear idea what follows from it. He could see his assignment as the eschatological messenger of God's kingdom who is supposed to proclaim people the good news that will change their lives and heal and liberate them. Jesus's experiences in the river and in the desert provide him with a particular insight and equip him with a deep trust (πίστις) in God who is capable of all things (Mark 9:23; 10:27; 11:22–25). This is how Jesus realizes that he can do things others cannot. The anointment with God's Spirit changes him, and in the course of the narrative it also changes the way he is perceived by others. This helps to understand why he is perceived as an authoritative preacher and healer.

One last point that requires attention in the context is the point in time when Jesus starts to proclaim his message about the kingdom of God. It is not directly after he has returned from the forty days in the desert where he has been part of the cosmic battle between God and Satan—and experienced that God has won. Intriguingly enough, it is only after John the Baptist, who has opened the way to his special experience, is handed over and arrested (1:14) that Jesus begins to proclaim the gospel of God. The catalyst for the beginning of his public proclamation is not the overwhelming experience of God's closeness and its confirmation during the forty days in the desert but the traumatic experience of John's imprisonment. What might seem strange at this point will eventually become comprehensible at a later point in the reading process.

In the narrative bridge in 1:15, Jesus's voice is finally heard for the first time: "The time [καιρός] has been fulfilled and the kingdom of God has

42. Cf. Malbon, "Reflected Christology."

arrived. Change your ways and believe this gospel." Jesus has, it seems, coined his own formula for this experience of God's closeness and his victory over Satan: *the kingdom of God has arrived.* Once more, we note peculiarities. The first is that as long as Jesus is alive, he is the only one to use the expression "kingdom of God." The second is that Jesus never goes beyond this expression or explains it in greater detail. The readers learn several times that the audiences are astonished (ἐκπλήσσω, 1:22; 6:2; 7:37; 11:18), amazed (θαμβέω/ἐκθαμβέω, 1:27; 9:15), and astounded (ἐξίστημι, 2:12; 3:21; 5:42; 6:51) by Jesus's teaching or marvel at it (θαυμάζω, 5:20), but they do not learn what Jesus actually said. The pattern is repeated several times when Jesus is depicted to be teaching without the narrator giving away what he says (1:21, 27, 39; 2:2, 13; 6:2, 6, 34; 10:1; 11:18).

Taken together, the experience Jesus had and that he passes on through the expression "kingdom of God" is that the special relationship to God he has been introduced to and that he happily embraced is open to everyone.[43] The only thing people have to do is to be open to it and be willing to put away every obstacle that might get between themselves and God—regardless of whether it is an obsession, sickness, ritual or cultic regulations, misguided ideas about God and his commandments, or simply money. Jesus is willing to offer every help necessary in this process, and his own example shows that for those who live in this new reality of the kingdom of God, it is not disease or impurity that is infectious but purity and health. The message is very simple: put first things first. Or, phrased differently, "Love God with all you heart, soul, mind, and strength," and "love your neighbor as yourself" (12:28–34). This love and trust is what Jesus calls πίστις and is usually translated "faith," but it means a lot more. However, as simple as the message is, it proves to be a great challenge not only to scribes and elders or the rich young man but also to the disciples.

How does Jesus see himself? As we have seen in the first part of the story (1:16–8:26), the other characters come up with all types of different assumptions ranging from Elijah, John the Baptist, and a prophet like the prophets of old, as well as rabbi, teacher, Lord, son of David, king of Israel, and someone who is possessed. Jesus is very interested in what others think

43. Cf. Sandra Huebenthal, "A Possible New World: How the Possible Worlds Theory Can Enhance Understanding of Mark," *Annali di Storia dell'Esegesi* 32 (2015): 393–414.

but likewise reluctant about sharing his own ideas. He never introduces himself to anyone, especially not by a particular expression or title, and he would never call himself "Son of God." The furthest Jesus goes is making use of the *sonship* metaphor in the expression "Son of Man" that he first uses in 2:10, 28 to explain where his authority (ἐξουσία) comes from. As Jesus has been revealed, his unique relationship to God in terms of sonship, using this expression, seems to be a good choice. The title makes clear, however, that he is neither God nor a divine being, only someone who is granted a share in God's power because he is granted insight into God's will. On the other hand, "Son of Man" is an expression prone to misunderstanding and results in the plot to kill Jesus (3:6). It is thus not surprising that Jesus ceases to use the expression for the rest of the first part of the story. He will eventually return to it after Peter's confession in 8:29. For the moment the reader cannot help thinking that there is something dangerous about the expression "Son of Man."

The closest we get to a self-introduction is 6:4 when Jesus complains that "a prophet is not without honor except in his native place and among his own kin and in his own house." Seeing himself as the messenger of the kingdom of God, Jesus seems to be happy with the label "prophet."[44] He never directly contradicts anyone when the title is applied to him, and he even uses it himself in the third main part of the story (11:1–15:39) in the parable of the wicked tenants (12:1–12). On this occasion, Jesus allegorically puts the *son* in line with the *prophets*, thereby marking the *son* as a *special prophet*: the *son* will be the *final, eschatological prophet*.[45] Mark 13:22 and 14:65 might just echo this idea.

For the moment, we could conclude that Jesus's own perspective on his experience describes his relationship in terms of *sonship* but that he is also much more comfortable with the term *prophet*, for it expresses his task as a messenger. After his experience in the river and the desert, Jesus sees himself mainly as a prophet—an eschatological messenger of what he has experienced of God's closeness and what he calls the "kingdom of God" in line with Second Temple Judaism and its traditions.

---

44. Cf. Goulder, "Jesus without Q," 1295–307.

45. David S. Du Toit, "Prolepsis als Prophetie: Zur christologischen Funktion narrativer Anachronie im Markusevangelium," *Wort und Dienst* 26 (2001): 165–89 (esp. 141–43).

4. Negotiating the Different Perspectives

Our reflections started with the observation that the Markan Jesus and the Markan narrator do not speak with the same voice and that their perspectives on the events differ. In addition, the ideas of the other characters as to how Jesus is best understood neither match Jesus's nor the narrator's ideas. That leads to the question as to how all these different ideas and perspectives are negotiated and what the Gospel's final statement about "Christology" is.

One strategy that Mark's Gospel uses is that it assigns different concepts and ideas about Jesus that were known in Mark's times to different characters in the narrative and has them discuss these ideas. The strategy includes evaluating the ideas, which is mostly achieved by evaluations of the characters themselves. When the narrative ends, the reader has little doubt as to how Jesus is best understood, because the characters holding the wrong opinion are evaluated negatively. It is clear to the reader that the images of Jesus that the crowds, the people in Jesus's hometown, the Pharisees and scribes, Herod, the high council, and Pilate have are wrong, because they are unreliable characters or have other issues. In addition, the disciples' ideas can be premature at times and often need correction. It seems that the only reliable interpreters of Jesus are Jesus himself and the characters of the numinous and divine sphere. The explicit and implicit evaluations of different characters and their ideas guide the reader safely through the text. The most obvious technique is the narrator's comments about the characters in the moment (e.g., Herod Antipas in 6:26; Joseph of Arimathea in 15:43), or before (e.g., the scribes in 1:22), or after they act (e.g., the disciples in 6:52, the chief priests in 15:10). Another obvious technique is the "priming" of the reader in the prologue (1:1–15) that provides all the necessary information for understanding Jesus. Although often only noticed at second glance, the author never leaves the readers to themselves nor allows them to develop their own ideas, and thus the negotiation on the part of the characters is not without a predetermined conclusion. As we have seen, the author has a clear understanding of who Jesus is and uses several literary techniques to get the message across.

This also applies to the protagonist himself. The evaluation of Jesus's perspective, too, is neither left to him nor the reader but to those who rank higher than Jesus in the hierarchy of the narrated world. In Mark's Gospel it is not only the narrator who stands above the human characters but also the characters from the numinous and divine sphere. These characters also make use of the *sonship* metaphor, and they drive home the narrator's point: the demons address Jesus as Son of God (3:11; 5:7) or God's holy one (1:24), and God himself calls him "my beloved Son" (1:11; 9:7). There can be no doubt that Jesus himself has little say when God and the narrator agree that he is the Son of God, and even the demons support that view. Though Jesus might be allowed his proclamation of the kingdom of God and the use of the expression "Son of Man," it is nevertheless clear that in the end he will be seen as the Son of God.[46] Almost as if to explicitly make the point that not only the opponents are wrong about who Jesus is but also the protagonist himself, the moment Jesus dies, the realization that he really was the Son of God is finally introduced to the world of characters by a character from the human sphere (15:39). The reader cannot but agree to this statement.

This leaves us to the question how the narrator wants the characters and the reader to arrive at his conclusions. As we have already seen, the expression "Anointed One" (Χριστός) does not occur very often. A closer look at its second occurrence is sufficient to understand the underlying scheme. Peter's confession of Jesus as the Anointed One (8:29), usually referred to as Peter's confession of Jesus as the Messiah, is sometimes understood to be a fracture of both Mark's messianic secret (*Messiasgeheimnis*) and the disciples' lack of comprehension (*Jüngerunverständnis*).[47] Both the messianic secret and the disciples' lack of comprehension are, however, modern interpretative categories, not features of the text. Paired with the historical-critical tendency of reading smaller portions or cutouts (what biblical scholars would call "pericopae" instead of longer passages), they might in fact be less enlightening and confusing. Read according to later christological categories, Peter's statement is indeed somewhat surprising. When "Markan Christology" is about the suffering Messiah who can only be adequately understood as Christ and Son of God through cross and resurrection, Peter's testimony can only be seen as

46. Cf. Jack Dean Kingsbury, "The Christology of Mark and the Son of Man," in *Unity and Diversity in the Gospels and Paul: Essays in Honor of Frank J. Matera*, ed. Christopher W. Skinner and Kelly R. Iverson, ECL 7 (Atlanta: Society of Biblical Literature, 2012), 62–63; Du Toit, "Es ist nichts Geheimes," 32.

47. William Wrede, *Das Messiasgeheimnis in den Evangelien: Zugleich ein Beitrag zum Verständnis des Markusevangeliums* (Göttingen: Vandenhoeck & Ruprecht, 1901); Du Toit, "Es ist nichts Geheimes"; Malbon, *Mark's Jesus*, 129–94.

oddly premature. Peter seems to say something that—according to the logic of the narrative—he cannot know at this point in time. Matthew seemingly "solves" this problem in his Gospel by crediting to him a divine revelation: "Jesus said to him in reply, 'Blessed are you, Simon son of Jonah. For flesh and blood has not revealed this to you, but my heavenly Father'" (16:17). Matthew's reading is comprehensible, for it allows retaining christological categories that were formed and accepted much later than the Gospels and only decided upon in the ecumenical councils. In Mark's Gospel, however, later christological categories are not at stake; rather, Isaiah's anointed-son-of-God concept is at work.

Read this way, the scene exhibits how characters (and readers) can arrive at the narrator's conclusions about Jesus. The beginning of the Gospel's middle section turns out to be the perfect example of how the narrator negotiates different ideas about Jesus. It all begins with a déjà vu: Mark 8:27–29 repeats a theme that was already discussed in 6:1–16, namely, different approaches to understanding Jesus. Following the logic of the narrative, the question is not whether Peter's insight is slightly premature but is rather, *What has Peter seen up to this point, and which experience does he verbalize by his impression?* In this moment, a rather production-oriented, diachronic reader of Mark's Gospel who is predominantly interested in the shape and origin of the smaller pre-Markan units might be lost, but a synchronic reader who is following the narrative arc will have little trouble answering that Peter has last seen that Jesus made a blind man to see. This not only releases the man from darkness but also from poverty, for with his sight restored he will be able to work and lead a normal life.[48] Peter has also seen that Jesus refuses to give signs, suggesting that Jesus shouldn't be thought of as a "signs prophet." Examples of signs prophets would include a man called Theudas, whom we know through Flavius Josephus, a Rome-based Jewish historian of the late first century (cf. Josephus, *Ant.* 20.97–98). Peter's experience also suggests that Jesus should not be identified with a "political messiah" like Jude the Galilean, whom we also encounter in Josephus's writings (Josephus, *J.W.* 2.118; *Ant.* 18.4–10). Peter has seen Jesus

48. Bernd Kollmann, "Krankheitsbilder und soziale Folgen: Blindheit, Lähmung, Aussatz, Taubheit oder Taubstummheit," in *Kompendium der frühchristlichen Wundererzählungen I: Die Wunder Jesu*, ed. Ruben Zimmermann (Gütersloh: Gütersloher, 2013), 87–93.

feeding hungry people and healing a deaf man who spoke with difficulties.[49] In 7:37, presumably non-Jewish characters even praise God in the words of Isaiah 35:5: "Then the eyes of the blind will be opened, and the ears of the deaf will be unstopped."

Peter could have seen and understood all of that. Read though the Isaianic lens as the narrator instructs, Peter's assessment that Jesus is the *Christos* (Χριστός) means that he is *the anointed Son of God*, Isaiah's eschatological messenger of the kingdom of God.[50] Peter's evaluation would thus not only be correct but almost compelling. He simply verbalizes what everybody familiar with Isaiah's prophecy could have seen and understood. This does not only apply to Peter's testimony but also to the following transfiguration scene, which is equally crucial for properly understanding Jesus. In this scene, not only the character Jesus is transformed but Jesus's perceptions, too, are taken to another level.[51]

We could thus summarize that Mark's Gospel addresses the question about Jesus in different stages. In the *first part* (1:16–8:26), which is located in and around Galilee, the characters want to know who Jesus is and how his words and deeds can be best understood. Jesus is first allowed to introduce himself in words and deeds (until 3:6), followed by a first round of "evaluations" by other characters. This first part introduces most of the images of Jesus that the text deals with, and the more political titles "Son of David" (υἱὸς Δαυίδ), "king of the Jews" (βασιλεὺς τῶν Ἰουδαίων), and "king of Israel" (βασλεὺς Ἰσραήλ) are only introduced later, closer to the passion narrative. The second part (8:27–10:52), narrating Jesus's way to Jerusalem, begins as we have just seen with Jesus's question about the different ways people understand him. They mention John the Baptist, Elijah, or another prophet as reception categories suggested so far. Jesus then asks the disciples how they themselves perceive him. Peter repeats the narrator's answer as it was introduced in the first line of the text: he believes Jesus to be "the Anointed One" (8:29). Although he is correct according to the narrator, the character Jesus commands Peter to keep silent about it.

---

49. Assuming, of course, that the disciples are present in 7:24–37, which the text does not explicitly say. In this case the synchronic reader of the story has an advantage.

50. Cf. Du Toit, "Prolepsis als Prophetie," 183–84.

51. Cf. Du Toit, "Es ist nichts Geheimes," 35–36; "Treasuring Memory," 348–53.

The scene is a reminder of the fitting, adequate perception of Jesus and indicates that the disciples have caught up in understanding. This reading is supported by the following verses. Here, Jesus returns to the expression "Son of Man" (8:31; cf. 2:10, 28), now with the extension of the prediction of the Son's suffering that will be tied to the expression from now on whenever Jesus speaks about the future way of the Son of Man. A few verses later, Jesus will return to his original message, namely, the proclamation about the kingdom of God (9:1; cf. 1:14–15). Even more striking, the subsequent transfiguration scene of 9:1–8 reminds the reader of the voice from heaven that the reader and Jesus have already heard in 1:11 (see 9:7). Other than in the baptism scene, where only Jesus and the reader hear the voice from above, the voice is now also audible to Peter, James, and John, who are introduced to the idea that Jesus is the beloved Son of the Most High (9:7). After this experience, Jesus commands them to keep silent until the Son of Man is raised from the dead (v. 9). Besides Isaiah, it seems, the second important lens for understanding Jesus is his death; otherwise the command to keep silent up to this point makes no sense.

On the way back, the disciples discuss Jesus's words, and they are concerned with the question as to what resurrection from the dead means (v. 10). This passage serves as a bridge for the reader and evaluates other ideas about Jesus. It clarifies that Jesus is neither John the Baptist nor Elijah (vv. 11–13). After the beheading of the Baptist, the multiplication of the loaves has already implicitly communicated that there is more here in Jesus than Elijah. Jesus now makes it explicit. When applying eschatological schemes, the disciples have to get it right. Indeed, Elijah must come first, although John the Baptist is the returning prophet, not Jesus. The rationale is simply that Jesus is connected to the Son of Man, and Elijah has just been seen talking to him.

In the transfiguration, Elijah and Moses appear in person (v. 4). Once more the transfiguration has the function of a turning point. Jesus, it becomes obvious, is neither the revenant of Moses nor of Elijah but the eschatological messenger of God's kingdom whom Isaiah announces. This has immediate consequences: the idea about Jesus as Elijah no longer appears after 9:13.[52] When Jesus and the disciples descend from the mountain, allusions to Jesus

52. Cf. Omerzu, "Geschichte durch Geschichten," 88–91.

as the new Moses change and become less prominent. Unquestioned by all the characters in Mark's Gospel, Moses is the authoritative giver of the law. The Moses-tradition is, however, not completely without prophetic and eschatological twists, and here pre-Markan traditions come in that Mark's Gospel happily embraces on the structural level. They provide another explanation for Jesus's miraculous deeds up to the transfiguration scene. Jesus's authority can also be seen in terms of Jesus being the eschatological prophet like Moses, announced in Deuteronomy 18:15–22 and 34:10–11.[53] The two stories of feeding the crowds and walking on the sea (Mark 6:30–52) can be read in the light of the Moses (and Joshua) traditions, as du Toit has convincingly worked out. Du Toit suggests that the idea of a "a prophet like Moses" based on Deut 18 and 34, in connection with other traditions about Moses and Joshua, provides a stable frame to structure and organize Jesus memories and Jesus traditions.[54] Though more subtle, the idea that Jesus is a prophet like Moses is much stronger than the allusions to Elijah. When this tradition is connected to Isaiah 61:1, the eschatological messenger of God becomes the dominant perception. Isaiah's anointed son of God exhibits all the features of the "prophet like Moses." In a similar way, the assignment of eschatological roles is clarified, for neither Elijah nor Moses is God's eschatological and final messenger: Jesus is the "prophet" announced by God in Deuteronomy 18:15–22.[55] This way, the *prophet* is completely absorbed by the *anointed son of God*. The same applies to Jesus's idea about himself: it is also fully absorbed by the narrator's perspective.

The section 8:27–9:13 is most intriguing regarding the proper understanding of Jesus. Unnoticed by the characters, it evaluates different possible perceptions of Jesus to the point that only three suggestions are left: Anointed One, Son of Man, and Son of God. Two of them were already established as correct by the narrator in the first line of the Gospel: Anointed One and Son of God. What about "Son of Man"? Initially Jesus uses the expression "Son of Man." As the narrative continues, however, this concept is successively linked more closely to the "Anointed One" until at Jesus's mention of the eschatological parousia both concepts apply to the same person (14:61–62).

53. Cf. Du Toit, "Treasuring Memory," 348–49; "Es ist nichts Geheimes," 37–38.

54. Du Toit, "Treasuring Memory," 348.

55. Du Toit, "Prolepsis als Prophetie," 186; "'Gesalbter Gottessohn,'" 42; Omerzu, "Geschichte durch Geschichten," 98.

Once more, the narrator absorbs the ideas of the characters. Jesus's perception has no chance; in the end, it will become apparent that he is indeed God's anointed Son. The historical Peter might not have been able to see this, but due to Mark's presentation the character Peter cannot but recognize in Jesus God's anointed Son and the eschatological messenger of God's kingdom, *as it is written in the prophet Isaiah.*

Jesus's words about the Son of Man who must suffer initiate the process of bringing the different perspectives together. Mark 9 is indeed the turning point, for the disciples have now caught up in understanding who Jesus is. Their next challenge is the more difficult step of accepting that God's anointed Son and eschatological prophet of God's kingdom will suffer and die a most disgraceful death.[56] The final answer as to whether Jesus really was, or if he really is, the Messiah, the Son of the Most High, it seems, can only be answered at the parousia of the Son of Man, the exalted Christ.[57] This answer will be given outside Mark's Gospel. The story about "the beginning of the gospel of Jesus the anointed Son of God" has a more urgent task. It must provide a satisfactory explanation for the shock of Jesus's violent death. The Son of Man title is used to address the elephant in the room—the suffering and death of the anointed Son of God.

5. Addressing the Suffering and Death of the Anointed Son of God

Mark's stories about Jesus and the beginning of the gospel are not a historical report but a theological reflection of experience narrated from a particular point of view. As Jesus's death on the cross is the most difficult and traumatizing experience, it is no surprise that learning to deal with Jesus's passion and death takes a lot of space in the narrative. This process starts early and becomes gradually more perceptible. Jesus is not remembered to have had it easy with religious leaders and authorities, and he is more or less in constant conflict with Pharisees, scribes, Herodians, and, later in the course of the narrative, elders and high priests, until the council hands him over to Pontius Pilate. The reader soon learns that there will be no happy

---

56. Cf. Robert C. Tannehill, "The Gospel of Mark as Narrative Christology," *Semeia* 16 (1979): 57–95; Du Toit, "Es ist nichts Geheimes," 43; "Prolepsis als Prophetie," 185–87.

57. Cilliers Breytenbach, "Grundzüge markinischer Gottessohn-Christologie," in *Anfänge der Christologie: Festschrift für Ferdinand Hahn zum 65. Geburtstag*, ed. Cilliers Breytenbach and Henning Paulsen (Göttingen: Vandenhoeck & Ruprecht, 1991), 183; cf. Kingsbury, "Christology of Mark," 66–69.

ending: the first plot to kill Jesus is narrated as early as 3:6, and the fate of John the Baptist signals that Jesus, who began his proclamation when the Baptist was handed over, might soon be in trouble as well (1:14; 6:17–29). On the way to Jerusalem, Jesus predicts his passion three times (8:31; 9:31; 10:33–34), and in the parable of the wicked tenants (12:1–12) he speaks about his fate allegorically, but no less clearly.

The title "Son of Man" is a lens for understanding what happens. Although Jesus's first use in 2:10, 28 does not seem to evoke anything dangerous, looking backward, the plot to kill Jesus (3:6) can be seen as a reaction to Jesus's claim about what the "Son of Man" is entitled to be and do. That is to say, stating that sins are forgiven and being Lord of the Sabbath, indicating that he claims to share in God's power (no matter how it is termed), will eventually lead to trouble. The title "Son of Man" occurs fourteen times in the Gospel of Mark: twice in the first part of the inner story (2:10, 28), seven times in the second part, six of which are connected with passion predictions (8:31; 9:9, 12, 31; 10:33, 45) and one with an eschatological time frame (8:38), and finally five times in the third part, thrice with reference to the passion (14:21 [2x], 41) and twice with an eschatological time frame (13:26; 14:62). From 9:31 on, the "Son of Man" sayings are at times additionally constructed with forms of the verb "to hand over," indicating that the moment of betrayal plays a key role for the fate of the Son of Man (see, e.g., 9:31; 10:33 [2x]; 14:21, 41). "Handing over" already occurs much earlier in the text. The Greek verb *paradidōmi* (παραδίδωμι), which literally means "to give over from one's hand," is used for passing on tradition as well as for authoritative commitment or passing someone along in a juridical process. It is used for the first time in 1:14 to make it clear that Jesus begins his own proclamation the very moment John the Baptist is arrested.

It becomes clear in the process of reading that this is not a coincidence. Quite the contrary, the narrator makes deliberate use of the verb's range of meaning and uses it several times to allude to Jesus's fate. It is interesting to see how the particular scenes where the expression is used connect the beginning of Jesus's proclamation with the fate of the Baptist (1:14), his own fate (3:19; 14:10–11; 15:1, 10, 15), the behavior of the disciples (14:18–21), and the enigmatic predictions about the Son of Man (9:31; 10:33), which can finally be seen as referring to himself in the moment of his arrest (14:41–44). There are numerous connections of word and motif between these sequences.

Perhaps the most intriguing connection is the link between 1:14–15 and 14:41–42, which brings together a couple of themes: the fulfillment of a certain time (καιρός in 1:15; ὥρα in 14:41), which denotes the arrival of something to be expected, and the "handing over" of someone. Read in the context of the overall narrative, the "handing over" of the Son of Man to the "hands of men" (9:31), the need to proclaim the gospel to all nations (13:10, also 14:9), and the fulfilment of all the predictions about the fate of the Son of Man (9:31; 10:31; 14:18–21) during the passion (14:10–11, 41–44; 15:1–10, 15) make the connection all the stronger and depict Jesus once more as the reliable prophet. Whatever he prophesied about the Son of Man did not only come true but also came true in his person.[58]

1:14–15	**14:41–42**
After John was **handed over**, Jesus came into Galilee, proclaiming the gospel of God: **The time** [καιρός] has been fulfilled, and **the kingdom of God has arrived**. Change your ways and believe this **gospel**.	And he comes a third time and says to them: Continue to sleep and take your rest. It is enough. **The hour** [ὥρα] has come: see, **the Son of Man is handed over** into the hands of sinners. Get up, let us go; see, **the one who hands me over has arrived**.

It is intriguing to see how "handing over" and the need to get up and do something—in Jesus's case, proclamation—are connected, and that the experience of handing over, even by loved ones, must not stop the process of passing on the message. The network of verbal connections is quite dense in these passages, and the only loose end, so to say, seems to be the kingdom of God. When Jesus speaks about the necessity to proclaim to the nations, it is not the kingdom of God that is to be proclaimed, but the gospel. It is further left open, whether it is the gospel of God (1:14) or the gospel of Jesus (1:1) that is to be proclaimed. The more important message seems to be that death and betrayal will not stop the gospel and its proclamation—a signal also for the reader.

58. Du Toit, "Prolepsis als Prophetie," passim.

The last verses of the inner story are crucial in this regard. The key moment immediately after Jesus's death is told in enigmatic, symbolic language: the veil in the temple is torn in two parts from top to bottom (15:38). Like the darkness that had come over the whole land from the sixth to the ninth hour and darkened the scene of the abandoned Jesus to the moment of his last cry (v. 33), the reillumination and the tearing in two of the temple's veil underline the tremendousness of the moment: Jesus's death has cosmic dimensions. It is not just any insurrectionist who dies at the cross, as immediately confirmed by the Roman centurion (v. 39). Mark 15:37–39 narrates two different reactions to Jesus's death, both highly symbolic. This becomes even clearer when we compare them to the moment after Jesus's baptism, which also prepared him for the cosmic conflict in the desert (1:10–11).

15:37–39	**1:10–11**
And Jesus uttered a loud cry and breathed his last/the **spirit**, and the veil in the temple was **torn** in two **from top to bottom**. And when the centurion who stood facing him saw how he breathed his last/the **spirit**, he said, "Truly, this man was **Son of God**!"	And immediately, ascending out of the water, he saw the heavens **torn** apart and the **spirit** like a dove **descending** upon him. And a voice came from the heavens: "You are my **beloved Son**, in you I am well pleased."

Adding a little topographical knowledge, it is obvious that no one could have possibly seen Jesus's death and the rupture of the veil taking place in close temporal sequence. Its meaning must thus be purely symbolic, which is confirmed by the structure of the material and its analogy to 1:10–11: event, rupture, comment. The phrasing of Mark 15:38 is important because it uses the same verb—σχίζω—for the rupture that had been used in the baptism scene in 1:10 to describe what Jesus saw. According to Josephus, the temple veil depicted the entire visible firmament (*J.W.* 5.241), which makes the connection even more striking. In both cases, the rupture resolves the separation between God and man, between the divine and the human sphere. What Jesus has experienced immediately after his baptism is finally open to everyone—a direct connection to God. The words of the centurion echo what Jesus has heard in 1:10; this man is special, a son of God. What has made him visibly and recognizably special was his affiliation with the Spirit. In 1:10 Jesus saw the Spirit descend on him, and as the reader knows, it remained on him up to his last moment. The verb describing Jesus's death (*exepneusen*; ἐξέπνευσεν, vv. 37, 39) does not accidently contain the Greek word for "spirit" (*pneuma*; πνεῦμα) and recalls this moment.[59]

A Roman, and thus gentile, centurion, being the one who calls Jesus "Son of God," is also significant for the narrative structure, as it introduces this idea to the world of (human) characters. Up to this point, Jesus as Son of God has only been mentioned by the Markan narrator (1:1), the voice from heaven (1:11; 9:7 ["my Son"]), and some agents from the numinous sphere who have recognized him (cf. 1:24; 3:11; 5:7). The narrative develops the right perception of Jesus in several steps. In 1:1 the narrator gives the full formula for the proper understanding of Jesus: "Anointed One" and "Son of God." Both elements of the formula are subsequently confirmed and introduced to Jesus (and the reader) by a sign (1:10) and a word from heaven (v. 11). The characters begin their way to understanding only in 1:16, when the inner story begins, and it takes a while before they get there. Instantly after Peter arrives at the right conclusion in 8:29, combining what he has hitherto experienced of Isaiah's prophecy coming to fulfillment in Jesus's ministry, Jesus changes gear and (re-)introduces the enigmatic figure of the Son of Man, who must suffer. The second and third parts of the inner narrative are dominated by this theme until the climax in 15:39.

Whether Peter and the other disciples are to blame for not understanding at that point in the narrative what could only be understood from the perspective of the narrator, namely, that the Anointed One must suffer, is an ongoing and still unresolved debate in biblical scholarship. From a narratological point of view, one cannot blame Peter. The character of Peter understands in 8:29 what he can understand at this point according to the rules of the story. If it is true that Mark's text itself is an attempt to come to terms with Jesus's suffering and death, asking that a character understands

59. Cf. Breytenbach, "Grundzüge markinischer Gottessohn-Christologie," 178.

what the narrator is presenting as the outcome of a longer process of theological reflection is asking a bit too much.

What remains is that Peter, the Jewish disciple, introduces the expression "Anointed One" to the world of characters, and after Jesus's death the gentile centurion introduces the expression "Son of God" to the world of the characters. The complete formula is now accessible. Characters and readers share the same level of knowledge: Jesus is the *anointed Son of God*. After Jesus's death, the full confession is possible—both titles have arrived in the world of characters, and Jesus's expression "Son of Man" has finally been connected to Jesus himself, showing that full awareness and full understanding are only possible after Jesus's passion and death.

After the question about Jesus is finally answered, one last issue remains open: What will happen to the message once the messenger is gone? Before the narrative is finally closed, the fate of the message about the kingdom of God comes into focus one last time. Hitherto, the concept "kingdom of God" has only been used by Jesus. Looking back to 1:14–15, Jesus started his proclamation only after John the Baptist was handed over, and he only then introduced the kingdom of God as a formula for his experience of God's closeness and unique relationship with God. The last time that the reader has heard about the kingdom of God was in 12:34 when Jesus said to a scribe that he was not far from it, and in 14:26 when Jesus indicated that he would only then have wine again. The question is what will happen to this message after Jesus is gone, as the opponent's strategy clearly was to do away with the message by doing away with the messenger.

It turns out that the seed of Jesus's message has already started to grow. A few hours after Jesus has died, just before the Sabbath begins, Joseph of Arimathea goes to Pilate and asks for Jesus's body in order to bury him (15:43). This Joseph is not only characterized as a respected member of the council but also as someone receiving and welcoming the kingdom of God. The narrator is reluctant about sharing the future destiny of the message. The words about Joseph, however, indicate that Jesus's idea has finally arrived at the level of the characters and, even more striking, becomes visible on this level in a moment of crisis. The theme has come around full circle: Jesus began to proclaim the message of the kingdom after John had been handed over, and the moment Jesus is buried, the stage is set for characters and readers to start their own proclamation of that message.

At this point, the story of the "beginning of the gospel of Jesus, the anointed son of God" (1:1) comes to an end, and it is up to the recipient whether 16:8 is the last word or whether there will be another ending, as it might be alluded to in 1:35–39. This passage in the first chapter shares surprisingly much vocabulary and ideas with 16:1–8, the very unsatisfactory open end of Mark's Gospel. Both scenes take place at the same time of day, very early in the morning on the day after the Sabbath, and they have a similar theme—people are searching for Jesus. Simon is the only one mentioned by name in both scenes, and in both cases the message is to leave and proclaim and that Jesus will eventually be found in Galilee. Taking up the summary in 1:39 and the prediction in 14:9, a conciliatory closing of Mark's Gospel would be: "And they went out and told the disciples. And they went back to Galilee where they saw Jesus. And after having seen him, they went out and proclaimed the gospel of Jesus, the Anointed Son of God, to the whole world."

Conclusions

The narrator would be fairly content with this ending. The continuation of Mark's Gospel in the lives of the early Jesus-followers, for whom this story was indeed only the *beginning*, has proven this assumption to be right: death and betrayal must not and could not stop the gospel and its proclamation. What was and is proclaimed, however, was subject to change. As said in the introduction, though the first narrative account in written form, Mark's Gospel was only one contribution to the greater early Christian discourse and had to be negotiated with other contributions in other times and places. Part of this process is preserved in the New Testament, though the larger part followed after the New Testament documents were written.

From what we have seen above in the Gospel of Mark, a group of Jesus-followers seeks to make sense of their experiences with Jesus and his proclamation. The socioreligious and cultural frames used in this text are both Second Temple Judaism, Israel's holy Scriptures, and the Roman imperial culture in which the text was written. In accordance with other Jewish groups, their most important frame of reference is the book of Isaiah, and in line with Isaiah's prophecy they understand Jesus as God's anointed Son, the eschatological messenger of the kingdom of God. This messenger suffers the fate of the prophet and the righteous: although he has done nothing wrong, he is persecuted by those in power because of his liberating message for the sick, the marginalized, and the suffering. The text works on two different levels and narrates different ideas, but in the end it invites the reader to adopt the narrator's perspective on Jesus and his message.

In the narrated world, there is no place for a divine Jesus, not even for a concept similar to what ranks today as "Christology." Jesus is granted the insight into a special relationship with God before the actual story starts. This special relationship is phrased in the language of anointing (1:1, 10) and sonship (v. 1, 11). Jesus processes his baptism in the desert (vv. 12–13), and afterward, in a moment of crisis caused by the arrest of John the Baptist, Jesus takes up his own teaching and healing activity (vv. 14–15). Its focus is on God and his reign and the implementation of God's kingdom in the world, not on Jesus himself: "The Markan Jesus consistently deflects honor away from himself and toward God."[60] When it comes to his message, Mark's Jesus is a one-hit wonder: the claim that God's kingdom is at hand seems to be his only message. This message, however, is unfolded in teaching and healing throughout the text. What does it mean that the *kingdom of God* is at hand? How does the implementation of God's principle in the world become manifest? Jesus's program is simple: whatever hinders the direct and undisturbed relationship with God must be done away with, be it hardness of heart, misunderstanding, sickness, possession, or excesses of a misunderstood religiosity.

This program leaves little space for a divine or semidivine being besides God. Only one thing can be the center of all things. Nevertheless, Jesus is the founding figure of a new religious movement, and besides telling its founding story, Mark's Gospel has to answer in which terms Jesus is best understood: teacher, prophet, heretic, or Son of Man—as Jesus seems to suggest—or anointed Son of God—as the narrator suggests?

Jesus's words about the fate of the Son of Man and what will happen at the end-time support the inference that Jesus and the narrator could agree on *Christos* (χριστός), even though it might only be applicable to Jesus after

60. Elizabeth Struthers Malbon, "The Christology of Mark's Gospel: Narrative Christology and the Markan Jesus," in *Who Do You Say That I Am? Essays on Christology (Essays in Honor of Jack Dean Kingsbury)*, ed. Mark Allan Powell and David R. Bauer, 2nd ed. (Louisville: Westminster John Knox, 2000), 41; cf. idem, *Mark's Jesus*, 135–36.

his death. Jesus himself suspends it until the return at the end of time, the parousia. Only then will the Son of Man be recognized as the Christ. The narrator only suspends it until after the resurrection and already hints at Jesus being the Christ during his lifetime. What they both leave open, however, is the nature of this figure. Is the Christ human, divine, or both? With *Christos* (χριστός) being "something of a generic umbrella term for Mark,"[61] the text is ambiguous about this question and thus open to different understandings. Both Adoptionist and Trinitarian Christologies have used it to make their case. Jesus's healing ability and his claim to divine authority suggest that there is some kind of divinity, at least a share in divine power, about him, but on the other hand his need to rest, withdraw, sleep, and eat depict him as a human among humans. He exhibits human fear, pain, and a sense of isolation during the passion.

In Mark's Gospel, calling Jesus "Son of God" expresses a unique closeness to God, a particular relationship that is not necessarily based on kinship. God's Anointed One is special to him and perceived to be special by others, even without crossing the boundaries between the human, numinous, and divine spheres. The Roman concepts of divine (*deus*) and deified (*divus*) indicate that Roman culture had a clear awareness of the distinction, and when the boundaries between god and man are transgressed, it is rather the gods who take human shape for a while rather than vice versa. It is difficult to express these differences in Greek. From the Greek expression used in Mark 1:1 alone, it is impossible to say whether it means a divine or a deified son. Mark's Gospel allows for both understandings and does not provide the reader with an easy solution. The text's ambiguity permits different interpretations and at one point explicitly states that there are other ways to follow Jesus (9:38–39).

A further development shows that the title "Son of God" took the road to the understanding of a Jesus not only as a divine agent but as a divine being, as God. Roman imperial propaganda might have added to this development. Reception history—the other canonical Gospels and the decisions of the first ecumenical councils—show where the journey went. The development of a Trinitarian faith at last solved one of the core ambiguities of Mark's Gospel. When Jesus is God and both human and divine, he himself provides access

61. Boring, "Markan Christology," 454; see also Kingsbury, "Christology of Mark," 58.

to the direct and undisturbed relationship with God. It is a relationship that sees God at the center of all things—or to phrase it with Mark's Jesus, that the kingdom of God is at hand.

At the end of our journey, let us wrap up the initial question: Does Mark assign Jesus a divine role? After a lengthy excursion into the worlds of Mark's Gospel, the brief answer is "not explicitly." In the world of the characters, Jesus is perceived as a human being and messenger of God who is granted the authority to perform exorcisms, healings, and other signs due to his special relationship with God. The Markan narrator, by carefully structuring the story and mediating different perspectives, opens a door to the possibility of seeing Jesus as a divine being. The moment the text is written, however, the jury is still out. In this respect, too, Mark's Gospel has an open ending. Its Christology is suspended until further notice. Later readers were only too keen on closing that gap.

Hurtado Response to Huebenthal

LARRY W. HURTADO

Sandra Huebenthal's essay strikes me as both novel in some of its proposals, and also problematic in a number of them. At the risk of coming across as simply critical, but in the interests of clarifying our discussion, I will turn immediately to matters that I find problematic.

The Gospel of Mark in the Ancient Christian Setting

Regarding her opening comments about how the Gospel of Mark (hereafter, GMark) might have fared in the sort of "what if" scenarios proffered by Francis Watson, I have to say that I do not see how this is strictly relevant. But in any case, the preference for the four Gospels that became canonical was not quite as much a happenstance as Watson suggests. The use of GMark by the authors of GMatthew and GLuke (and perhaps GJohn) suggests that, at least at an early stage after its composition, GMark enjoyed a wide and favourable circulation among circles of the late first-century Jesus-movement. It apparently resonated immediately with many. Granted, the authors of GMatthew and GLuke obviously thought that their renditions of the Jesus story were needed, and perhaps superior, but their demonstrable indebtedness to GMark also shows up clearly. These authors added substantially to the Markan narrative and also appear to have amended some passages in GMark, but I see no indication of a refutation of it in either text. To be sure, once these other Gospels circulated, they appear to have been more frequently cited (and also more frequently copied).[1] But there are good reasons to judge that at a surprisingly early point the familiar four Gospels, including GMark, were treated as a distinctive group of favored accounts of Jesus.[2] And, although GMark was overshadowed by the other Gospels, it remained one of the four that increasingly acquired a special significance in various early Christian circles all across the second century.[3]

The Approach

To turn now to her approach to the text, on the one hand, at a few points she acknowledges that GMark draws upon beliefs of the Jesus-movement, the matrix in which it arose. On the other hand, it seems to me that she does not really use this observation to any significant effect in her reading of the text. Instead, although she claims that the text can be understood independently of its original situation, she then repeatedly points to other external factors, such as the putative relevance of passages in Isaiah. Indeed, at one point she declares that "a thorough knowledge of Isaiah" (p. 17) is necessary to understand the text well.

Granting that Isaiah is an influence in GMark, it bears emphasizing, however, that we are not dealing with Isaiah pure and simple but with Isaiah

1. In the earliest stages, well into the second century and even later, the Gospels circulated physically as individual codices, and the manuscript evidence suggests that GMatthew and GJohn were copied far more frequently than the others, GMark apparently the least frequent. As shown by 𝔓45, however, at least by the third century the four NT Gospels were beginning to be copied in one codex. See my discussion in Larry W. Hurtado, *The Earliest Christian Artifacts: Manuscripts and Christian Origins* (Grand Rapids: Eerdmans, 2006), 15–41.

2. G. N. Stanton, "The Fourfold Gospel," *NTS* 43 (1997): 317–46; Martin Hengel, "The Four Gospels and the One Gospel of Jesus Christ," in *The Earliest Gospels*, ed. Charles Horton (London: T&T Clark International, 2004), 13–26; Charles E. Hill, "A Four-Gospel Canon in the Second Century? Artifact and Arti-Fiction," *Early Christianity* 4 (2013): 310–33. The various attempts to provide GMark with an ending beyond 16:8 (e.g., the "long ending," which likely emerged ca. 100–150 CE) all reflect the early influence of the other NT Gospels, and the attempt to align GMark with them. This in turn shows that GMark remained sufficiently important to supply it with such endings.

3. See, e.g., Oskar Skarsaune, "Justin and His Bible," in *Justin Martyr and His Worlds*, ed. Sara Parvis and Paul Foster (Minneapolis: Fortress, 2007), 53–76, who shows that Justin appears to have known and used the four familiar Gospels. Likewise, Graham Stanton, "Jesus Traditions and Gospels in Justin Martyr and Irenaeus," in *The Biblical Canons: Bibliotheca Ephemeridum Theologicarum Lovaniensium CLXIII*, ed. J.-M. Auwers and H. J. De Jonge (Leuven: Leuven University Press, 2003), 353–70; Joseph Verheyden, "Justin's Text of the Gospels: Another Look at the Citations in 1 Apol. 15. 1–8," in *The Early Text of the New Testament*, ed. Charles E. Hill and Michael J. Kruger (Oxford: Oxford University Press, 2012), 313–35. Contra the theory of Michael J. Kok, *The Gospel on the Margins: The Reception of Mark in the Second Century* (Minneapolis: Fortress, 2015), there is no evidence that GMark was particularly favored by "heretical" groups and had to be rescued by proto-orthodox Christians.

as mined and deployed in, and refracted through, the early Jesus-movement. This should be obvious from the initial example in GMark, in 1:2–3. For, although v. 3 is a quotation of Isaiah 40:3, what is ascribed to Isaiah in v. 2 is commonly recognized as more directly indebted to Exodus 23:20 and Malachi 3:1. Whether one chooses to attribute this curious Isaianic ascription of v. 2 to the author or to the early tradition on which he drew, it apparently owes more to the particular exegetical activities of the early Jesus-movement than simply to the text of Isaiah itself.[4]

Likewise, in her treatment of the term "Christ" (*Christos*; Χριστός) in 1:1, she turns to various Jewish and pagan sources about anointed figures but omits serious consideration of relevant early Jesus-movement traditions. For, it is important to note that Mark 1:1 has the formulaic expression, "Jesus Christ" (Ιησοῦ Χριστοῦ), that also appears numerous times in other Jesus-movement texts prior to GMark (e.g., fifteen times in Romans alone). To be sure, in earliest usage of this expression among Jesus-believers the messianic connotation of "Christ/*Christos*" was not lost, and several texts in GMark indicate that Jesus's messianic status is one of the author's emphases. But in all the other instances in GMark, we have the articular form, "the Christ" (ὁ χριστός: 8:29; 12:35; 13:21; 14:61; 15:32), making the term in these texts more obviously a standalone title. In 1:1, however, we see the use of what had become decades earlier a traditional christological expression among Jesus-believers, "Jesus Christ." This shows that, from the outset, GMark presupposes readers who are familiar with, and will draw upon, the terminology, beliefs, and practices of the early Jesus-movement. I submit that today's readers should do the same.

Exegesis

In addition, Huebenthal infuses the text with a good deal of what we might term "psychologizing," in various passages imputing to characters in the narrative what their thinking or feelings were, but often, so far as I can see, without support from the text. For example, she posits Jesus's supposed thought process after his baptism that led him to understand his own mission. This is, in one sense, a plausible idea, were we attempting an

4. See, e.g., the discussion in Adela Yarbro Collins, *Mark: A Commentary*, Hermeneia (Minneapolis: Fortress, 2007), 135–36.

imaginative modern life of Jesus, I suppose. But it hardly represents a strictly narrative approach to GMark. For the author of GMark shows that, when it serves his purposes, he was fully capable of ascribing feelings to characters in the narrative, as in several texts where Jesus's emotional responses are given (1:41; 3:5; 8:2). So, respecting the narrative requires that when the author does not ascribe feelings or thoughts this is intentional, and at those points the psychological processes of characters are not relevant. It is, thus, dubious to impute them.

At a number of other points, it seems to me that Huebenthal just misses the more obvious force of the Markan text. For example, she takes the blasphemy charge of the high priest in 14:61–64 as a response to Jesus claiming "a prophetic role" (p. 19). The priest's question, however, is not whether Jesus claims to be a prophet but whether he claims to be "the Christ/Messiah, the son of the Blessed," and Jesus's response is a ringing affirmation. This text, along with others, also make dubious Huebenthal's claim that the Markan Jesus "would never call himself 'Son of God'" (pp. 24–25). How else are we to take Jesus's "I am" in v. 62, in answer to the priest's question? Moreover, in the vineyard parable (12:1–12), the "one beloved son" who is the heir of the vineyard is obviously Jesus's self-characterization that echoes the phrasing of the divine voice in 1:11 and 9:7. As well, in 13:32, it appears that Jesus refers to himself simply as "the Son" of "the Father" (God). Whatever one may think was Jesus's actual use of divine sonship language, the Markan Jesus affirms it at several points in the narrative.

Linked to this is Huebenthal's curious notion that the Markan narrative shows Jesus only coming to understand his divine sonship at the end of his life, and that his use of the expression "the Son of Man" shows that, along with the other human characters in the narrative, he, too, did not initially have a correct view of himself. But "the Son of Man" does not function in GMark as an alternative claim to divine sonship or messianic status. As has been shown for several decades now, unlike "Messiah," for example, "the Son of Man" was not a known title or touted status in Second Temple Jewish tradition.[5] Instead, "the Son of Man" functions in GMark as it does in all

5. On the expression, see now the multiauthor volume: Larry W. Hurtado and Paul L. Owen, eds., *"Who Is This Son of Man?" The Latest Scholarship on a Puzzling Expression of the Historical Jesus* (London: T&T Clark, 2011). I have gathered up the evidence in the final essay, "Summing Up and Concluding Observations," 159–77.

the Gospels, as Jesus's distinctive self-designation. What makes it distinctive is the articular form, which has the effect of Jesus referring to himself with a particularity as *the/this* particular human figure.[6] This phrasing implicitly connotes a distinctive identity and role. But because this articular expression was novel in its time, the other human characters in the narratives seem unable to make anything of it, and it functions as part of the Markan emphasis that they could not perceive Jesus's true identity and status until after his crucifixion and resurrection (e.g., 9:9).

Consequently, I find it strange that in dealing with Peter's confession of Jesus as "the Christ/Messiah" (8:29), Huebenthal seems to take this emphasis that Jesus's status cannot be fully understood until after his crucifixion and resurrection as reflecting "later christological categories" ("later" than GMark?). She claims that in GMark "later christological categories are not at stake" and that it is only "Isaiah's anointed-son-of-God concept" that is relevant, contending that in its narrative context Peter's confession of Jesus as Christ/Messiah cannot be taken as deficient (p. 28). This may reflect an admirable sympathy for Peter as a human being, but it fails to grasp how the narrative character of Peter functions in the scene.

For the importance of Jesus's crucifixion and resurrection as adequately disclosing the nature of his messianic role is hardly a "later christological category"! The three well-known passion-resurrection predictions in GMark (8:31–32; 9:30–32; 10:32–34) make these events crucial, both redemptively and cognitively.[7] Jesus's demand that his disciples must not declare to others the messianic claim (8:30) surely indicates that Jesus's crucifixion and resurrection are necessary to define adequately his messianic work for disciples, and for readers. Moreover, in the immediate context, Peter's negative reaction to the first of Jesus's passion-resurrection predictions, and Jesus's immediate stern rebuke of Peter, obviously show that Peter's understanding of Jesus as Messiah is to be taken by readers as seriously faulty.

At one point, Huebenthal states that "the moment Jesus is buried, the stage is set for characters and readers to start their proclamation" (p. 37).

---

6. The expression "(a) son of man" and the plural "sons of men" are, of course, well attested in biblical and Second Temple extrabiblical texts. But neither the Hebrew nor the Aramaic equivalent of the Greek articular form is found in them. If the Gospels are correct that Jesus used the expression, the Aramaic (definite) form would be *bar 'enasha*.

7. It should be noted that what are more frequently called Markan "passion predictions" are more accurately passion-resurrection predictions.

But this is surely wrong! For in 9:9, Jesus commands the three disciples not to disclose the transfiguration until after his resurrection. And, it is the news of Jesus's resurrection and the promise that they will see him again in Galilee that the women are to convey to Jesus's other disciples (16:5–7). In the Markan narrative, a buried Jesus only invites mourning. It is the resurrected Jesus that sparks proclamation.[8]

I am similarly a bit puzzled at Huebenthal's somewhat sentimentalizing portrayal of the Markan theme of "faith" (πίστις) as a general openness to a relationship with God. For in GMark the term "faith" appears more specifically as a factor in the setting of miracles (2:5; 4:40; 5:34; 10:52; 11:22), and the various texts where Jesus exhorts people to "believe/have faith" (πιστεύω) likewise are often in reference to miracles (e.g., 5:36; 9:23; 11:23–24).

Moreover, Huebenthal's characterization of Jesus's message in such generalized terms does not seem to take account of the evidence that GMark was more specifically addressed to Jesus-believers facing (or fearing) opposition and strong persecution. For example, the parable of the seeds/soils in 4:3–20 includes warnings of the dangers of persecution (esp. v. 17). Jesus demands that his followers be prepared to give their lives "for my sake and for the gospel" (8:34–35), warns that believers will be arraigned "for my sake" and will be denounced by close relatives and "hated by all on account of my name," and urges that "he who endures to the end will be saved" (13:9–13).

Two Narratives?

Much of Huebenthal's characterization of the Markan text seems to depend upon her view that we have two narratives: an "inner" one (1:16–15:39) framed by an outer layer comprising 1:1–13 and 15:42–16:8 (with a "narrative bridge" in 1:14–15 and in 15:40–41). She posits that the opening and closing material reflect the author's view of Jesus, but that the "inner" narrative portrays a different view. In the Markan author's view, she grants, Jesus is the Christ and the Son of God. But, Huebenthal claims, the "inner"

---

8. In GMark, Jesus's suffering is certainly important, but I contend that the climatic event in the narrative is God's resurrection of the crucified Messiah. Larry W. Hurtado, "The Women, the Tomb, and the Climax of Mark," in *A Wandering Galilean: Essays in Honour of Seàn Freyne*, ed. Zuleika Rodgers, Margaret Daly-Denton, and Anne Fitzpatrick McKinley (Leiden: Brill, 2009), 427–50.

story conveys a Jesus who is almost as puzzled about himself as the other human characters and has to discover through his experiences who he is and what he is to do. I have to say that I find this all unpersuasive.

For I see no indications that the author intended us to find two, somewhat competing, narratives. Instead, so far as I can tell, from the opening through 16:8, GMark presents a continuous and ordered narrative. There are, of course, two levels of comprehension of Jesus's identity and significance: the one advanced by the author and shared, at least substantially, by the intended readers; and the other the very imperfect comprehension of all the human characters in the narrative. In all the narrative of Jesus's activities, the human characters do not perceive Jesus rightly or adequately. But as for the way the narrative depicts Jesus himself, from the divine acclamation/commissioning scene in 1:9–11 onward through the rest of the account, he seems to me to operate confidently in his mission, his authoritative status, and his divinely mandated fate.

In her concluding comments, Huebenthal poses the question of whether the Markan text portrays Jesus as human or divine. She finds GMark ambiguous on this question, and points to subsequent theological developments (whether "Adoptionist" or "Trinitarian") as formulating more definitive (but contrasting) answers.[9] But I suggest that to frame the question in these terms, with only two stark and mutually exclusive alternatives, is too simple. For in such a set of alternatives, GMark (and, for that matter, a lot of other NT writings as well) will seem ambiguous in the way they present Jesus.[10] But are we to think that the author was himself not sure what to believe, or that he wrote with only a provisional understanding, hoping that later developments would clarify matters? Surely not. None of the authors of early texts such as GMark could have been aware that there would be later

9. Actually, however, it is not clear that GMark was quite the crucial text for Adoptionists and Ebionites that is sometimes asserted. The only references to Ebionites that we do have ascribe to them a special interest in GMatthew, not GMark. See Oskar Skarsaune, "The Ebionites," in *Jewish Believers in Jesus: The Early Centuries*, ed. Oskar Skarsaune and Reidar Hvalvik (Peabody, MA: Hendrickson, 2007), 419–62. As for Adoptionists, they have been described as "a historian's abstraction, a line of thought never developed or presented complete by any one theologian" (Lionel R. Wickham, "Adoptionism," *Encyclopedia of Early Christianity*, 2nd ed., Everett Ferguson (New York: Garland, 1998), 20–21.

10. E.g., is Paul ambiguous in affirming both Jesus's human birth, historical activities, and death (e.g., Rom 5:6–11; 15:7–8; Gal 4:4–6), and his role as agent of creation (1 Cor 8:4–6) and his heavenly origin (Phil 2:5–6)? Is Hebrews ambiguous in declaring explicitly that Jesus is the unique Son who reflects God's glory and through whom the worlds were made (1:1–4), and was also genuinely human and so underwent sufferings and temptations (2:5–18)?

theological developments. In their own minds and for their own time, their views of Jesus were fully meaningful and an adequate basis on which to proclaim the gospel to all nations.

Is it not a sounder approach to GMark to recognize, first, that it was never intended as some definitive christological statement to address the particular question whether Jesus was either human or divine? Instead, I submit that GMark presupposes certain convictions about Jesus, traditional and current in the circles of Jesus-believers for whom the author wrote, and focuses more on making his earthly activities both the basis/origin of believers' redemption (e.g., 1:1; 10:45) and the pattern for their redeemed existence amid real or potential opposition.

I contend, therefore, that GMark is not ambiguous if we allow the author to pursue his own agenda, instead of posing the "human or divine" question as mutually exclusive alternatives. For the Jesus of GMark is surely and genuinely a human, albeit with a particularity as "*the* Son of Man." But this human Jesus is also the divinely exalted Lord of the circles of intended readers, who was affirmed by God on earth and then vindicated by resurrection as God's unique Son, was recognized on earth by demonic powers as such, who exercised divine power and prerogatives during his historic ministry, and whose glory will be revealed to all in the eschatological climax of history (13:26–27; 14:62). First-century Jesus-believers certainly drew upon previous conceptual categories in trying to understand and express Jesus's significance, such as "Messiah," and what I have referred to as "chief agent" traditions. But, as well, from a remarkably early point Jesus-believers modified such categories to accommodate the unique status of Jesus in their beliefs and devotional life, producing a novel "mutation" for which we do not have a true precedent or parallel.[11]

11. I first laid out the case for this in my book, *One God, One Lord: Early Christian Devotion and Ancient Jewish Monotheism* (Philadelphia: Fortress; 2nd ed., Edinburgh: T&T Clark, 1998; 3rd ed., London: Bloomsbury T&T Clark, 2015).

Kirk Response to Huebenthal

J. R. DANIEL KIRK

Sandra Huebenthal locates Jesus well, mapping the journey he has taken from divinely empowered human messiah in Mark's Gospel to divine incarnation in the later history of the church. In doing so she has provided readers with what might be the most important posture for probing the nature of Christology in the New Testament: the New Testament writers vary among themselves, and the later church's testimony is both a composite picture and a further development of what the biblical authors wrote.

Moreover, Huebenthal's deployment of narrative criticism again draws our eyes in the right direction. Jesus in the Gospel of Mark is made known within a particular story. Social, historical, cultural, religious, and scriptural contexts all inform how we read that story, but in the end the degree to which any depiction of Mark's Christology is found satisfying will have to be judged by the degree to which it makes sense of Mark's narrative as a whole.

This response to Huebenthal thus unfolds on a broad plane of agreement: Mark's Jesus is a divinely empowered human figure, an eschatological prophet, whose identity and mission are further made known by the story in which he functions. Moreover, in this narrative we must navigate among different perspectives on the person of Jesus, including those that are incomplete, wrong, and hostile as well as those that come from trustworthy sources such as the narrator and Jesus and yet differ from one another. It is this very attention to the narrative dynamics of Mark that raises a number of questions, including the nature of Jesus's mission, the content and quality of his teaching, and the viability of Peter's (and the other disciples') understanding of Jesus.

Mark's Eschatological Prophet

Professor Huebenthal summarizes her understanding of Mark's Jesus in this way: "Mark's Gospel does not visualize Jesus as a divine or preexistent being but rather depicts him in Isaianic categories as a human messenger of God with an extraordinary experience and, as a result, extraordinary abilities" (p. 5). This is a faithful representation of Mark's story.

To begin, Mark's Gospel does not depict Jesus as divine—at least, not in the sense that a modern reader would understand this term. It could well be that an ancient reader would see some sort of divinity in a being who ultimately ascends to heaven and takes a cosmic throne; however, this would be the divinity of exaltation and transformation, not the divinity of an inherent divine nature. The story provides clear indications of how Jesus comes to possess his extraordinary powers and authority. As Huebenthal suggests, the receipt of the Spirit at his baptism is when Jesus receives his empowerment. Jesus and the narrator collaborate to make this point in the "Beelzebub controversy" in chapter 3. Here, Jesus defends himself against the charge of being possessed by an unclean spirit by issuing a warning against blaspheming God's Holy Spirit (3:29), and the narrator interprets this as a rejoinder to the accusation that Jesus possessed an unclean spirit (v. 30).

Moreover, all the images of Jesus as an exalted, heavenly being (such as the transfiguration and the exalted "Son of Man" sayings) are clearly tied with Jesus's life after his resurrection. In other words, Mark does not depict Jesus as possessing or having come from preexistent heavenly glory; instead, Mark's Jesus enters heavenly glory after his resurrection (see Dan 12:3). There is no case to be made for Jesus as a preexistent being in the story Mark tells.

Isaiah is also critical background, as Mark invites readers to refer to that store of prophecy in the introduction to his Gospel. Shortly I will argue that this should steer us away from one path Huebenthal takes in her assessment of Jesus's ministry; however, Isaiah is a prophet of "good news," and Mark draws deeply from this well. At the same time, we must not allow Isaiah to totalize our view of Jesus. As Huebenthal herself notes, Psalm 2 is an important piece of background for understanding the anointing that happens at the baptism. Genesis 22 is also critical for making full sense of what that scene entails. Moreover, in coming to terms with Jesus as Son of Man we cannot collapse Daniel 7 into Isaiah without losing considerable insight into both the character of Mark's Jesus and Mark's overall storyline.

Finally, I wish to underscore the importance of the word "extraordinary" in Huebenthal's description of Jesus. One of the highest hurdles that current readers face in reading Mark's Jesus as a type of human figure is that "human" is seen as pejorative, or as something to be overcome. Too often the divine-human Christology of the church has cultivated the notion that what is good about Jesus and his ministry is divine, whereas his humanity is simply for the purpose of solidarity with humanity in weakness, sin, and death. However, this is not the story that Mark (or most any other New Testament writer) tells. The larger scriptural story on which they draw is one in which humanity is created as "son (and daughter) of God" by bearing the divine image; in which Israel as a nation plays this role as divine son; in which the Davidic kings are "begotten" into this role of divine son at their coronation. Jesus, empowered with the Spirit (like David before him), plays this role at the final turning of the ages, the time at which God's salvation arrives. In the story of Mark, Jesus is not "merely" human but perfectly and ideally human as no human had been before. The discontinuity between Mark's Jesus and his scriptural predecessors is not that he is ontologically distinct but instead that he acts at a particular time (the moment of God's eschatological salvation), with a consistent faithfulness, and with an extraordinary realization of the Spirit's power that enables him to play the role of God's Messiah.

Jesus's Hopes

The fact that Jesus plays the role of eschatological Jewish prophet in the narrative that we see unfold in Mark highlights one of the most unlikely claims one finds in Huebenthal's study, namely, that Jesus is offering a "life-changing experience with God" in hopes that others might find their way to the "direct relationship with God" that Jesus himself experiences (pp. 12, 11, respectively). The notion that such an "eternal salvation" is the outcome of Jesus's messianic mission does not square with the story Mark tells.

When Jesus expresses his exasperation with the "unbelieving generation" in Mark 9:19, there is no indication that his frustration regards the request for healing rather than a person's seeking a "deeper salvation level." Instead, Jesus's frustration is leveled where it often has been over the previous several stories: at his uncomprehending disciples who are unable to see the power and nature of the kingdom of God that they have been participating in since they began to follow Jesus (8:17–21, 33). Jesus's comment comes after it is reported to him that the disciples were unable to cast out a demon (9:18), and a discussion of their inability bookends the story as well (9:28–29).

I will return below to argue for a less sanguine view of Jesus's followers as an aid to understanding Mark's Christology. For now, it is critical to recognize that the salvation Jesus hopes to bring as Messiah is not distinct from healing and other acts of power; instead, Jesus hopes to usher his followers into precisely this kind of world-transforming performance of the coming kingdom of God. As Huebenthal notes, this is exactly what it means for Isaiah's expected salvation to arrive: "He will come to save you. Then the eyes of the blind shall be opened, and the ears of the deaf unstopped; then the lame shall leap like a deer, and the tongue of the speechless sing for joy" (Isa 35:4–6 NRSV). Indeed, in Mark's Gospel the Greek σῴζω ("to save") is regularly used to describe healing by Jesus himself (Mark 3:4; 5:34; 10:52), by those who seek it from him (5:23, 28), and by the narrator (6:56). Healing is not an alternative to the salvation Jesus offers; it is a significant, constituent part of it.

Huebenthal returns to Jesus's experience in baptism and subsequent time in the desert to explain how Jesus thought of his own relationship with God and what that might mean for his mission and message. The interpretation she offers of these texts points in two directions at once. First, there is the cosmic and communal dimension; Jesus is proclaimed to be God's anointed as he is empowered for the task with the reception of the Spirit. Then, there is the existential component of "a direct relationship with God," or a "close and special" relationship with God. This leads to the conclusion that the expression "kingdom of God" means that "the special relationship to God he has been introduced to and which he happily embraced is open to everyone" (p. 24). The focus on the cosmic battle is well-founded and is generally what we would expect from a first-century Jewish apocalyptic prophet.

The language around a close and special relationship with God strikes me as anachronistic and alien to Mark's concerns.

There is a sense in which I would be happy to say that Jesus is reflecting on his relationship to God and introduces others into a similar relationship. Jesus is given the Spirit for the purpose of initiating the rule of God on earth. That is to say, "Son of God" is a functional title, a title given to the human who has a specific role to play in mediating the words and work of God upon the earth. Through knowledge and empowerment, both from God's Spirit, Jesus serves as a stand-in for God. In this sense he is "closer" to God than other humans and indicates that their participation in God's family (i.e., to become other sons and daughters of God) is possible and comes through adherence to himself (3:33–35). Indeed, when he calls his twelve followers, he does so for the purposes of their being with him and of engaging in exactly the activities that mark his ministry: proclamation and exorcism (3:14–15; 6:7–13). In this way, Jesus and his disciples participate in the "cosmic battle" against Satan. If this is what is meant by a special relationship with God, then there are good grounds for it in Mark. Jesus as God's Son is demonstrating what it looks like to take the side of God in the conflict between the forces of life and death.

However, the phrase "kingdom of God" most certainly does not, in this Gospel, mean a personal relationship with God in terms of intimate proximity or "knowing God" and "being known by God." These concepts are well-developed in John's Gospel (though in ways that many moderns would still find surprising), but they are simply absent from Mark. Thus, in Mark's description of Jesus's temptation in the desert, there is a complete absence of reflection on Jesus's mental and emotional state, no mention of God (only angels), and very little interpretation of what the time spent means: "He was in the desert forty days, being tested by Satan, and he was with the beasts, and the angels served him" (1:13).There is, indeed, cosmic conflict here, with Jesus standing against Satan and angelic hosts at his side. In this we catch a glimpse of Mark's Christology; Jesus is the champion of God against the powers of Satan that would wound and destroy God's people. However, there is no suggestion of an intimate, existential relationship with God that all might hope to experience.

This brings us to the question of Jesus as proclaimer and teacher. What did his teaching mean, and how should we understand Jesus the teacher in Mark?

Jesus the Teacher

Before exploring specific teaching passages in depth, we do well to revisit Jesus's proclamation of God's reign in Mark 1. On the one hand, there is Jesus's apocopated teaching that "the reign of God has come near" (1:15). Its tidy words and brief invitation to repent and believe are open to almost limitless interpretation. However, in Mark's Gospel these words do not stand alone but introduce a series of stories before Jesus then teaches again. Inasmuch as these later stories are regularly taken up with the question of the authority of Jesus's proclamation, a narrative assessment of Jesus's teaching must interpret the proclamation in light of the stories that follow. When we do so, what we discover is that Jesus gathers followers: the reign of God looks like the gathering of a scattered community, even as Isaiah foretold (Mark 1:16–20). He teaches with astounding authority that coincides with his authority to cast out demons: he can speak and act for God, victorious over Satan's forces (vv. 21–28). He heals and proclaims and purifies and forgives sins (1:29–2:12). As he enters into various conflicts, Jesus offers an alternative entryway to the family of God that is not guarded by the religious establishment (2:1–3:6). This is the reign of God. It is the arrival of God's salvation for humanity here on earth as God's power and rule are embodied by Jesus for the good of the people he encounters. This is what it looks like for Jesus to be the "Son of God"; he plays the role of the king of this kingdom, the mediator of the life-giving power of God.

A further observation is in order regarding Jesus's teaching of the "kingdom of God." Huebenthal writes, "Jesus never goes beyond this expression or explains it in greater detail. The readers learn several times that the audiences are astonished . . . by Jesus's teaching or marvel at it, but they do not learn what Jesus actually said" (p. 24). While it is true that Mark much more frequently tells us *that* Jesus taught rather than narrating *what* Jesus said, there is also the significant exception of Mark 4, the parables chapter. Here we not only have teaching in general but teaching that enigmatically depicts the nature of the kingdom of God (see 4:11, 26, 30). Here we learn of glorious endings from humble beginnings (a hundredfold crop, a huge plant from a tiny grain of seed), of mysterious growth that leads to a final harvest, and of the danger that the message of Jesus will not bear fruit with everyone. These vignettes provide a grid for measuring other stories in the Gospel, where surprising abundance of food breaks out in desert places, where Jesus's teaching is celebrated but ultimately rejected in the face of persecution when he is arrested, and where, finally, life will come from the surprising source of Jesus's crucified body. This is not teaching about "a special relationship with God" but is instead about God's peculiar engagement with the world, demonstrating power and abundance in places of weakness and scarcity. It is Jesus's surprising embodiment of this power that provokes questions such as, "Who is this?" (e.g., 4:41) and "What is this? A new teaching with authority!" (1:27). These are hints at a Christology that will ultimately hold together the entire narrative of Mark. Jesus is a uniquely empowered human messiah who will come into greater power via the way of the cross.

Other teaching moments also contribute to this Christology and its narrative of salvation. Various teaching moments in Galilee may deploy "colloquial" imagery, but it is unlikely in the extreme that the point of this is to show Jesus "insecure when it comes to factual knowledge": the narrator's numerous summaries about the crowds' astonishment regarding Jesus's teaching belies this reading. For cultivating our understanding of Mark's Christology, it is far better to see that Jesus is using familiar images to place himself squarely within the unfolding of God's saving work.

Thus his words about fasting, deploying images of shrunk cloth and bloated wineskins, ultimately point to his own presence as the reason that religious laws are being transformed (Mark 2:18–22, esp. vv. 19–20). The grain-plucking episode may have a historical mistake regarding 1 Samuel 21:1–7, but it seems less likely that Mark is trying to subtly show Jesus is unlearned than that the story intends to show Jesus as one like David. He is anointed, but not yet on his throne, wandering with his followers, and therefore able to determine an instance in which he can break the law guiltlessly (Mark 2:23–28).

Much later, Jesus observes a poor widow contributing her last pennies to the sanctuary. Jesus turns to his disciples and says that she has given the most because she has placed her very life (βίος) in the treasury (12:44). This is not a simple "common sense" story indicating how unimpressive Jesus is as a teacher. Within the narrative world that Mark has constructed, there are two critical conjunctions with earlier teachings of Jesus. First, he has just accused the scribes of devouring widows' houses in their hypocritical religious zeal. Here, then, is a widow whose house is being devoured before our eyes. Second, and more importantly, in elaborating on her gift as "everything she had, her whole life," Jesus depicts her as a faithful follower. To give up one's whole life is the content of Jesus's mission throughout the second half of Mark; moreover, to be willing to lose one's life is precisely the call to discipleship that Jesus issues immediately after predicting his own death—a call his closest followers reject but that this nameless woman embodies.

The narrative approach that Huebenthal commends offers us various avenues for enriching our understanding of Mark's Christology through attention to Jesus's teaching and the narrator's commentary around it. In so doing, we find greater clarity concerning what sort of kingdom Jesus believes God is initiating and what role Jesus plays in its arrival.

You Are the Christ?

The contrast between the woman who embodies Jesus's call to self-sacrificial trust and the disciples who reject it brings us to the question of how we should measure the disciples in Mark. In particular, giving them too much credit in their understanding and following of Jesus can blunt the force of the narrative as it attempts to reframe their mistaken understandings of what it means for Jesus to be the Christ.

For readers shaped in their understanding by the fourfold Gospel tradition of the New Testament, Mark's depiction of Peter's confession is stark. "You are the Christ" does not elicit praise from Jesus or the narrator; instead, the disciples only receive a sharp command not to tell anyone about him (Mark 8:29–30). As Elizabeth Struthers Malbon points out, the character of Jesus is hesitant about the title "Christ."[1] He does not use it of himself, and when others use it of him he immediately reinterprets the title using his preferred self-reference, "Son of Man." In this case we discover that Peter's understanding of Jesus's identity does not cohere with either the narrator's (for whom, as Huebenthal points out, Christology "is about the suffering Messiah who can only be adequately understood as Christ and Son of God through cross and resurrection" [p. 27]) or Jesus's. As the unfolding story shows, this is not merely a "premature" statement of something Peter "cannot know at this point in time" but is a mistaken perception. Peter has landed

1. Elizabeth Struthers Malbon, *Mark's Jesus: Characterization as Narrative Christology* (Waco, TX: Baylor University Press, 2009), e.g., 238.

on the correct title, but he has not allowed Jesus to transform what the connotations of that title are.

Here, again, attention to the larger narrative aids the reader in parsing how it is that Peter can speak of Jesus in a way that coheres with the narrator's own judgment and yet be deeply mistaken about Jesus's true identity. Most importantly, Jesus redirects his followers away from the title "Christ" and toward the title "Son of Man." However, rather than using this to appeal to authority, as he had done in Mark 2, Jesus now uses the phrase to tell the disciples something new: "he *began* to teach them" that what he must now endure is rejection, suffering, death, and resurrection (8:31–32). As if to underscore the ignorance disguised as knowledge in Peter's confession, Peter then rebukes Jesus for saying these things, which in turn merits him a rebuke from Jesus, who names him nothing less than the Satan whose rule Jesus claims to undo (vv. 32–33). To understand Mark's Christology aright, we must learn what it is to side with Jesus's interpretations of his own mission, and God's interpretation of Jesus's mission, over against the disciples who continually misunderstand it.

Further affirmation for this posture is found when we expand our gaze from the confession scene itself to the strange story that precedes it. In Mark 8:22–26 we read a strange story of a two-stage healing. A blind man is healed so that he has sight, but it takes a second intervention before he can perceive accurately. It is no coincidence that immediately prior to this healing story Jesus had expressed exasperation at his disciples by saying to them, "Do you not consider aright or understand? Have you had your heart hardened? Having eyes, do you not see, having ears do you not hear?" (vv. 17–18). Within Mark's unfolding narrative, the two-stage healing of the blind man functions as a metaphor for the disciples, as embodied in Peter's confession. On the one hand they have eyes to see ("You are the Christ!"), but on the other hand they are hard-hearted and lack correct perception, like a blind man who perceives men as though they were trees.

If we continue to draw back our view, we see that the subsequently unfolding story underscores the ongoing failure of Jesus's closest followers. The transfiguration features the divine voice telling the disciples to listen to Jesus—a pointed rebuke for Peter's earlier rejection of Jesus's looming passion (9:7). And when Jesus tells them on the way down the mountain not to tell what they have seen until after the Son of Man's resurrection, they are completely lost and ask a question that shows their lack of comprehension (vv. 9–10). Moreover, when they arrive at the bottom of the mountain, we find the disciples are unable to perform the very sort of miracle that Jesus had enabled them to do during their earlier itinerant ministries (vv. 15–29). Moreover, it is a deaf and mute spirit they are unable to exorcize, symbolizing that their authority over words, embodied in their authority to preach, is also lost. Indeed, the disciples will continue to reject Jesus's teaching about humility (10:13–16; cf. 9:37!) and demonstrate lack of understanding about his own fate (9:30–32; 10:32–34), while seeking glory for themselves (9:33–41; 10:35–45). In this second half of the book, where the "Son of Man" title connotes suffering and death followed by subsequent heavenly reign rather than authority here on earth as in Mark 2, Jesus exorcises once and heals only one time, and the disciples perform no miracles and in the end show themselves to be rocky soil—those who fall away when danger and persecution arise on account of the word.

For the Christology of Mark, this tells us three things. First, the disciples' understanding of Jesus is not trustworthy. They become foils against which the more accurate Christologies of Jesus, God, and the narrator come into sharper relief. Second, the suffering of Jesus is itself the surprising secret of Jesus's identity: it is what unfolds in fulfillment of Jesus's "Son of Man" self-designation, and this "Son of Man" Christology in turn shows the reader what it means to call Jesus the "Christ," as the narrator does in 1:1. As Jesus redirects the title "Christ" toward one who must suffer and die before rising again in 8:31 and then redirects the high-priest's titles of "Christ" and "Son of the Blessed" toward the "Son of Man" who will be enthroned at God's right hand (14:61–62), the reader receives a rich, multifaceted reinterpretation of the title "Christ" that holds together the authoritative human on earth (Mark 1:1–8:30) who must nonetheless suffer, die, then be raised and finally enthroned (Mark 8:31–16:8) in order for the reign of God to come into full effect. Finally, in light of these corrections that Jesus offers to the misunderstandings of those around him, we do well to follow Huebenthal in acknowledging that there is no place for a "divine" Christ in this story. Divinity is not the great and scandalous secret of Mark's Gospel—the cross is.

Winn Response to Huebenthal

ADAM WINN

Though it offers a much different understanding of Mark's Christology than my own, Sandra Huebenthal's essay, "Suspended Christology," provides a careful and thoroughgoing narrative analysis of Mark's Gospel and Christology. Before I offer any critique or address our differences, I want to note affirmations and places of agreement. First, I appreciate Huebenthal's initial discussion on Christology and its history within the larger world of theological studies. She offers an important disclaimer that Christology is, technically speaking, a "theological latecomer," and one must take care when they use this term in reference to any book of the New Testament not to bring with it anachronistic dogmas. With this disclaimer properly in place, both Huebenthal and I agree that Mark's Gospel has something to say about Jesus's mission and identity, and that what Mark says about both was one voice among many in the first centuries of the Christian movement. Second, like Huebenthal, I too believe it is important to read Mark as a narrative whole and not as a loose conglomeration of Jesus traditions or as a mere window for reconstructing the historical Jesus or early church. The evangelist's crafting of a narrative generates unique meaning itself, and the Gospel is not merely the sum of its individual parts. While in my essay I did not offer a narrative analysis of Mark's Christology, I have elsewhere, and my own essay of Mark's presentation of Jesus's identity has an eye on the entire narrative and not simply isolated traditions. Other points of agreement would be the importance of Isaiah in Mark's understanding of Jesus, as well as the importance of titles such as "Messiah/Anointed One," "Son of God," and "Son of Man." Certainly there are other minor points of agreement throughout the essay. Yet, as I noted at the outset, Huebenthal's understanding of Mark's presentation differs significantly from my own, as does her reading of Mark's Gospel at many points. I now turn to these differences.

Starting Points and Presuppositions

At the outset of my own essay, I noted that one's starting points and presuppositions, particularly those about the one God of Israel, have a significant impact on how one understands Mark's Christology. I noted that there is a widely held presupposition among New Testament scholars that the Jews of the Second Temple period not only believed in one God but that they understood that one God in terms of strict singularity, that is, not only is there one God but that God is indivisibly one. Such a presupposition then becomes a major obstacle to any sort of conclusion that Jesus could be identified as divine or sharing a divine identity with Israel's God. Huebenthal's essay makes it quite clear that she shares this presupposition. Early in her essay, she quotes Eugene Boring who claims, "To ask whether the Markan Jesus is 'divine' or not is to impose an alien schema on Markan thought" (p. 2). For Huebenthal, this quote seems to communicate that questions about a divine identity for the Markan Jesus are simply foreign to the Gospel and thus presumably not to be asked. Not much later, she claims, "The idea of two gods, YHWH and Jesus, is not reconcilable with Jewish monotheism" (p. 4). Here Huebenthal seems to imply that one cannot affirm Jesus as divine without violating Jewish monotheism. Such a presupposition gives an answer to one aspect of the Markan Jesus's identity before even engaging the text itself. The Markan Jesus cannot be divine, so he must be human, a conclusion Huebenthal reaches in the essay, but one that was predetermined by her own presuppositions.

As I noted in my essay, this volume is not the place for debate on the nature of Jewish monotheism in the Second Temple period or to lay out the evidence that Jews could understand their one God in terms of complex plurality rather than simple singularity. But what is important is that there is indeed an ongoing debate, and this question is not yet resolved. To claim that recognition of two gods is a violation of Jewish monotheism seems to run contrary to Philo's claim that the Logos is the "second god" or the claim in John's prologue that the Logos, which would take on flesh in the person of Jesus, was God. Now one might argue that the Logos is just another way for Philo to speak of God, and that he does not truly envision a hypostatic being distinguishable from God. Or one might argue that Mark's Jesus looks nothing like the preexistent Jesus of John. But again, those are arguments that must be made and cannot be assumed. If Philo did understand the Logos as one with but also distinguishable from God, then there is at least a category that exists in Second Temple Jewish thought upon which Mark could draw to both affirm Jesus's divine identity and Jewish monotheism. And regardless of what one concludes about the relationship between the Gospels of Mark and John, the Gospel of John at the very least demonstrates that Christians in the late first century could affirm *both* Jewish monotheism and a divine identity for Jesus. My primary point is that Huebenthal needs to consider such a divine identity for the Markan Jesus a possibility and not dismiss it from the outset. Let the conclusion that the Markan Jesus is a mere human being come from a close reading of the Markan text and not from a presupposition.

Because of Huebenthal's presumption that the Markan Jesus is a human figure, she never gives careful attention to the places in Mark's narrative where evidence for a divine identity might be present. There is no discussion of the text's assertion that only God can forgive sins, and Jesus's subsequent claim that the Son of Man has authority on earth to forgive sins. There is no discussion of the theophanic description of Jesus in the walking-on-the-water episode. While Huebenthal gives significant weight to Isaiah for assessing the Markan Jesus's identity, she fails to note that Jesus takes the place of YHWH in Mark's opening Scripture citation. Additionally, she notes the obvious connection between Jesus healing a deaf mute and Isaiah 35, but she fails to note that in Isaiah 35, it is not YHWH's Servant that will unstop ears and loosen tongues but the God of Israel himself. These are a handful of examples where the presupposition that the Markan Jesus could not be divine prevents important analysis of the text itself, analysis that might run contrary to the presupposition.

A Narrative Approach

As I noted above, I share Huebenthal's desire to read Mark as a unified narrative whole. However, there are aspects of Huebenthal's narrative approach that I find problematic. I would first note Huebenthal's move not only to distinguish between but to set in contrast and/or conflict the voice of the narrator and the voice of Jesus (or at times, even the voice of God and the voice of Jesus). Such a move leads her to conclude that the narrator understands Jesus to be the anointed Son of God, while Jesus never seems to affirm such an identity. Instead, Jesus identifies himself as Son of Man. Such a move creates a divide between these identities, one which the narrator then must overcome: "Once more, the narrator absorbs the ideas of the characters. Jesus's perception has no chance; in the end, it will become apparent that he is indeed God's anointed Son" (pp. 31–32). While such a reading strategy might be common in modern literary criticism, I know of no evidence that suggests it was a strategy used by ancient readers. Thus, applying such a strategy to the Gospel of Mark seems to ignore and distort its identity as an *ancient* narrative. While Mark indeed should be read as a narrative whole, I would contend that readers must appreciate the *ancient* literary context in which it was written and avoid imposing foreign reading strategies on the text. No doubt Huebenthal recognizes Mark as an ancient text in many ways, but in her bifurcation of the Markan Jesus and the Markan narrator, I am afraid she does not. I am quite confident that no ancient reader of Mark, particularly ancient Christian readers of Mark, would set the perspective of the Markan Jesus against that of the Markan narrator. Instead, these readers would seek to find unity and mutual understanding between the two. For example, I do not think ancient Christian readers of Mark would perceive any tension between Jesus's use of "Son of Man" and the narrator's use of "Son of God." Instead, it seems the reader would seek to understand these two titles as mutually interpretive and overlapping. The narrator's declaration of Jesus as Messiah and Son of God at the outset of the Gospel, along with God's affirmation of Jesus's divine sonship, gives the reader a lens through which to understand both Jesus's actions and self-identification. While these titles for Jesus certainly have different nuances, I would argue that they significantly overlap, and each one affirms Jesus's identity as God's messianic agent. In the end, I would contend that the narrator, the Markan Jesus, God, supernatural opponents of Jesus, and even many human characters speak with essentially a unified voice about Jesus, and that this voice is only intended to be contrasted with the voices of unreliable or hostile characters such as the scribes, Pharisees, chief priests, Herod Antipas, and Pilate.

Another aspect I find problematic, not only of Huebenthal's narrative approach but also the narrative approach of many others, is the subjective assessments of what knowledge a reader brings to the text. Huebenthal specifically states that she wants to read the text apart from any specific historical setting, which is common to many narrative-reading strategies. She claims, "the task of a narratological analysis is not to describe the world from which the text has originated or which it seems to refer to but to depict the world of the text itself. The point is not to shed light on the historical author and the real world but on the narrator and the narrated world which comes alive while reading the text" (p. 6). But surely one can only understand the narrated world in light of the world in which the text was written, for example, its language, grammar, social customs, political figures, etc. Huebenthal's highly informed discussion of numerous aspects of the first-century Jewish and Greco-Roman world affirms the necessity of this knowledge for reading Mark. Without such knowledge, the Gospel becomes unintelligible. But what remains unclear both in Huebenthal's work and in that of other narrative critics is where one draws the line on what knowledge can be brought to bear on understanding the narrated world. Narrative critics often claim that the only knowledge one can assume on the part of the reader is what is implied by the text itself; for example, understanding of Greek, familiarity with cultural references, and knowledge of people, groups, and locations. But determining what is actually implied by the text is quite subjective, and this subjectivity leads to inconsistencies in interpreters' conclusions regarding the knowledge a reader brings to the text. Most narrative critics would assume the reader knows of certain Jewish Scriptures, has heard of John the Baptist, knows of Galilee, and is familiar with things like demon possession and leprosy. But how much does the reader know about these things and how can their level of knowledge be implied by the text? Making such assessments is highly subjective.

Let me offer an example of how I see such subjective assessments manifesting themselves in Huebenthal's assessment of Mark's Christology. Huebenthal places great importance on the role Isaiah plays in shaping the reader's understanding of Jesus. In fact, Mark's use of both the title Messiah and Son of God are for Huebenthal shaped by the Isaianic Servant tradition more than any other factor. Her conclusion is drawn from Mark's opening citation of Isaiah and the role the book seems to play throughout the Gospel of Mark. Thus Huebenthal assumes a number of things about the reader of Mark: familiarity with the text of Isaiah, recognition of the text of Isaiah as Scripture, and interpretive sophistication that allows the reader to connect the Servant of Isaiah with the concept of Son of God, which is neither an identity granted to the Servant in Isaiah nor a title that appears in the whole of Isaiah. These assumptions about the implied reader allow Huebenthal to arrive at her assessment of important christological titles in Mark.

However, the knowledge of the implied reader seems to shrink significantly when it comes to her assessment of the Markan Jesus's self-identification as the Son of Man. When treating the use of "Son of Man," Huebenthal apparently does not grant any previous knowledge or understanding of this title to the Markan reader. Though it is quite clear that the Gospel implies the reader's knowledge and familiarity with the text of Daniel, and particularly Daniel 7:13, Huebenthal does not allow for that knowledge to shape the readers understanding of Jesus's first use of "Son of Man," a use which is, without any explanation, linked with extreme authority on earth. In fact, Huebenthal does not once mention a connection between the Markan Jesus and the Danielic Son of Man, a figure that clearly evokes messianic activity and identity. Here Huebenthal evinces her selective approach to what the reader of Mark knows and brings to his or her reading of the Markan text. She allows the reader familiarity with Isaiah, and such a sophisticated understanding that lets the reader quickly connect Jesus's identity as Messiah and Son of God with the Isaianic Servant. Yet, she does not allow the same reader familiarity with Daniel, a text Mark's Gospel clearly implies the reader is familiar with. Neither does she allow the reader the sophistication that would enable connecting Jesus's use of Son of Man with the Danielic Son of Man, a figure to whom God grants a universal and everlasting kingdom—clearly a messianic notion! Just such a connection would seem quite natural when the first presentation of Jesus as Son of Man is directly linked to having the authority "on earth" to forgive sins.

Huebenthal's choice to privilege certain knowledge of the reader over against other knowledge has a tremendous implication for her reading of Mark and her understanding of Mark's Christology. By not allowing a Danielic influence on the readers' understanding of Jesus's first and subsequent self-identifications as Son of Man, she is able to treat the identification as an ambiguous and easily misunderstood reference, and one the reader associates with unexplained danger. It seems somewhat contradictory then when Huebenthal claims this *ambiguous* and easily misunderstood reference *clearly* distinguishes Jesus from God or divine identity. Later in Mark, she argues that "Son of Man" becomes a means of addressing Jesus's shameful suffering. Such a reading of Jesus's self-identification allows Huebenthal to move forward with a reading in which the Markan narrator and the Markan Jesus are in conflict over Jesus's identity. While the Markan narrator claims Jesus as both Messiah and Son of God, Jesus stubbornly holds to his claim to be the ambiguous Son of Man. In the end, he loses this fight to the narrator. This is ultimately connected to Huebenthal's notion of "suspended Christology," as she argues that for the Markan Jesus, the truth of his identity as Messiah will only be certain at the parousia of the Son of Man, but for the narrator, the truth of Jesus's identity is confirmed at his resurrection.

But this reading is significantly weakened if one allows the reader to bring their knowledge of Daniel to the Markan Jesus's self-identification as Son of Man. If Jesus is identifying himself in Mark 2 as the Danielic Son of Man, a figure to whom God grants univeral and everlasting kingship, then it is hard to avoid the conclusion that the Markan Jesus is using "Son of Man" to identify himself as God's Messiah. And if "Son of Man" is a way in which the Markan Jesus expresses messianic identity, then both the Markan Jesus and the narrator *agree* on Jesus's identity, namely, that Jesus is God's Messiah, an identity that can be communicated through the titles "Son of God" and "Son of Man." This agreement would then undercut the notion that there is any uncertainty about Jesus's identity as God's Messiah or that certainty is suspended until either the parousia or the resurrection. Instead, Mark's Gospel could be read with a unanimous voice from beginning to end claiming Jesus's identity as God's Messiah.

The Influence of Isaiah

Huebenthal is quite right to note the influence of Isaiah on Mark's Gospel. This influence is well demonstrated by her work here and other strong studies. However, it seems that in her analysis there is an overemphasis on Isaianic influence on Mark and a neglect of other voices that shape the Gospel's understanding of Jesus. Primacy is given to Isaiah in understanding the Markan Jesus's identity as both Messiah and Son of God, but the text of Mark would indicate that other Hebrew Scriptures are also being drawn on to understand these titles. God's declaration of Jesus as his Son in both Mark 1:11 and 9:7 is clearly drawing on Psalm 2:7, a royal coronation psalm. As such, it would seem this psalm plays a significant role in understanding Jesus's identity as God's Son. That is, for Mark divine sonship is understood in terms of being God's appointed ruler. The passion narrative again draws on the psalms and particularly draws on Psalm 22 for understanding Jesus's identity. As noted above, Mark's Gospel seemingly draws on Daniel for shaping the text's understanding of Jesus's identity as "Son of Man," that is, a figure to whom God grants an everlasting and universal reign. Thus, while Isaiah certainly plays a role in shaping Mark's presentation of Jesus, it is important to recognize that it is simply one of many voices from Hebrew Scripture that must be considered when assessing Mark's Christology. To be sure, Huebenthal is aware of the way in which these other texts of Hebrew Scripture influence Mark's Gospel, as she briefly notes some of them throughout the essay. Yet, in comparison to Isaiah, they seem to play little to no role in shaping her understanding of Mark's Christology. If Isaiah was read in concert with these other voices, perhaps different dimensions of Mark's presentation of Jesus would emerge.

Questionable Characterizations of the Markan Jesus

There are a number of characterizations of Jesus offered by Huebenthal that I found problematic and inconsistent with what I see in Mark's Gospel. The first of these characterizations is that Mark presents Jesus as a rather "ordinary" person. She notes that when we first find Jesus, he is seemingly an ordinary Galilean who is lined up on the shores of the Jordan with the rest of those following John the Baptist. She also notes that the narrator "deliberately depicts Jesus slightly insecure when it comes to factual knowledge, in order to present him as an ordinary Galilean who has a quick brain and is at home in his own religious tradition but is nevertheless not a learned person" (p. 12). At numerous points she notes that Jesus is a rather unimpressive teacher in Mark. Such descriptions of the Markan Jesus were quite surprising to me, and I find it hard to substantiate that from the text itself. From the outset of Mark's Gospel, Jesus appears to be anything but ordinary. John himself declares Jesus's greatness at the outset of the Gospel

(1:7–8), noting he, John, is not able to untie the thong of Jesus's sandal and that Jesus will baptize people with God's Holy Spirit—hardly an act to be performed by the ordinary! Jesus is then declared to be God's Son by the very voice of God at what appears to be his royal coronation. He comes proclaiming the kingdom of God and demonstrating its presence through the exorcizing of demons and unprecedented power to heal. He claims that his identity as Son of Man gives him the divine prerogative to forgive sins and to have lordship over the Sabbath—far from ordinary traits! He commands the winds and the waves, and they obey him. He walks on the sea, an act that Job 9:8 claims only YHWH can do. He feeds thousands with meager amounts of food, surpassing the miracle of Elisha (2 Kgs 4:42–44). While Jesus's disciples are able to heal and cast out demons (Mark 6:13), there is no indication they are able to match the power demonstrated by Jesus. I find it hard to believe any ancient reader of Mark would conclude that Jesus was merely an "ordinary" human being. Regarding Jesus as teacher, it is true that his teaching in Mark is not nearly as robust as it is in the other Gospels, and surely the Markan Jesus would not be confused for Aristotle or Seneca in his philosophical teachings. Yet, to conclude that the Gospel presents Jesus as an unimpressive teacher seems to run contrary to many features we actually find in the text. In Mark 1:22, the crowds are "astounded" by Jesus's teaching, and both here and in verse 27 Jesus's teaching is associated with "authority," a quality that amazes the people and sets him apart from the teaching of the scribes. Presumably it is not only his healing powers but also this impressive and authoritative teaching that bring the crowds to Jesus. In Mark 4, Jesus's teachings are connected to the "secrets of the kingdom of God," which he has presumably passed on to his disciples (4:11). And Jesus's teachings regularly thwart the religious leaders of Israel, demonstrating his intellectual superiority. Perhaps the Markan Jesus is less impressive than other ancient teachers (including the Jesus of other Gospels!), but it does not seem that the Markan narrative seeks to present Jesus as an unimpressive teacher—quite the contrary.

Another questionable characterization offered by Huebenthal is the repeated suggestion that the character of Jesus evolves or changes throughout Mark's narrative. She claims, "The Markan Jesus gradually learns both to understand how the encounter with God changed him and to deal with the crowds . . ." (p. 13). At a later point, she claims that "in the desert Jesus comes to realize how close and special his relationship to God is. Put to the test, Jesus experiences being drawn into the cosmic battle between God and Satan. Being with the wild animals and with the angels serving him, he realizes that God is on his side and Satan cannot harm him" (p. 22). Still later, "This is how Jesus realizes that he can do things others cannot. The anointment with God's Spirit changes him, and in the course of the narrative it also changes the way he is perceived by others" (p. 23). The problem, however, is that the Markan text never indicates that events like his baptism, experience in the wilderness, or otherwise lead him to realize anything. In Mark's Gospel, we have no access to Jesus before these events to determine whether these events bring about any particular realizations for Jesus. There is also no suggestion throughout Mark's Gospel of Jesus learning, growing, or evolving in his knowledge, actions, or character. The text simply does not substantiate such readings.

An additional characterization that I find questionable is that of the Markan Jesus both reluctant to heal and frustrated by people who merely seem to be seeking healing from him. Huebenthal claims that "Jesus is a rather unwilling healer" and that "there is no end to people seeking him for physical health rather than eternal salvation, which renders Jesus increasingly unhappy" (p. 11). She suggests that Jesus's statement, "O unbelieving generation, how long shall I be with you? How long shall I put up with you?" (9:19) reflects his frustration over people seeking physical salvation over spiritual salvation. It is certainly true that Jesus often withdraws from the crowds and to deserted places, but that he does this because he is reluctant to heal is unclear. The fact that Jesus frequently heals people throughout Mark and that it seems to be a central feature of his ministry and proclamation of the kingdom of God would run counter to seeing Jesus as reluctant to heal. I also see no evidence of Jesus being frustrated by people seeking healing (if Jesus heals a leper out of anger rather than compassion, we might have our one exception!). What actually seems to frustrate Jesus is not people seeking healing from him but people lacking faith in his ability to heal (see 5:35–36; 9:19, 23–24). It is this very lack of faith that Jesus's words to an "unbelieving generation" (9:19) seem to be addressing.

Huebenthal has provided a thoroughgoing narrative critical analysis of Mark's Christology, one that will be received sympathetically by many narrative critics. Yet I question the ability of this approach to capture the

Christology of Mark's Gospel as it would have been read by Mark's earliest Christian readers. Would any of them read the Gospel in this way? Additionally, I wonder if there are not certain readings of Mark offered by Huebenthal that even sympathetic narrative critics of Mark would find problematic, such as an "ordinary" Jesus or a Jesus who is presented as a marginal teacher.

Rejoinder

SANDRA HUEBENTHAL

As the other authors of this volume disagree with me on more than a few points, I think it might be helpful to start by distinguishing between different ways to disagree. Some of the disagreements discussed in this book are on the factual level—whether a feature of the text was overlooked, a passage was misread, or a method applied incorrectly. However, many of our disagreements cannot be broken down to right or wrong, to true or untrue but depend on more fundamental choices and beliefs.

Examples for the second type of disagreement can often be found in debates between historians on one side and economists or sociologists on the other. While one side (the historians) claim to work with facts, the other side (economists and sociologists) claim to work with theories and models, and the disagreement often ends up in polemics. Jan N. Bremmer's review of Rodney Stark's *The Rise of Christianity* can serve as an example:[1]

> With this work we enter a world totally different from our previous scholars. Both Gibbon and Harnack were experts on the ancient world, if each in their own way. Our last iconic figure has no credentials in this respect. Yet the choice of subject is typical of Stark's scholarly daring or, as some would prefer, recklessness. By his own confession he is not a New Testament scholar or a historian. His aim is to contribute "better social science—better theories and more formal methods of analysis,

1. Jan N. Bremmer, *The Rise of Christianity through the Eyes of Gibbon, Harnack and Rodney Stark* (Groningen: Barkhuis, 2010), 49, 63. Bremmer reviews Rodney Stark, *The Rise of Christianity: How the Obscure, Marginal Jesus Movement Became the Dominant Religious Force in the Western World in a Few Centuries* (Princeton: Princeton University Press, 1996).

> including quantification whenever possible and appropriate" (xii). Stark, then, is the complete opposite of Harnack, who was proud of having offered virtually no hypotheses in his work. Moreover, whereas the latter read all Christian texts in the original, Stark has to depend on translation. Whereas Harnack was mostly facts, Stark is mostly theory. Whereas Harnack was rather cautious, Stark is nothing but adventurous. Finally, with its stress on agency and rationality, Stark's favorite theoretical perspective, Rational Choice Theory, is a typical modern approach with nomothetic ambitions to override all the complicating specificities of context.
>
> It is not that easy to pass a balanced judgement on Stark's book. It is only fair to say that when I read it for the first time ten years ago, I was impressed by its bravura styles and technical expertise. However, closer inspection as shown that his treatment of subjects is often rather sketchy, his statistical exercises misguided and his knowledge of the ancient world mostly outdated. We welcome a sociologist on our turf, but a guest should also play by the rules and inform himself properly about the nature of the game.

In other words, *apply our hermeneutics and methodology or stay out. Do not bring outside experience and ideas to our field as they might challenge our beliefs or methods.* One can see in Bremmer's response that the idea of comparing the rise of Christianity to the rise of other religious movements is challenging for him. Comparing the development of Christianity to the rise of the Mormons or—*horribile dictu*—even the Moonies must be challenging to a Lutheran professor. Nevertheless, this is what Stark as a sociologist should do, and there is no benefit to be gained from polemics.

Reading experiences of others can sharpen one's own arguments, can help to see their weaknesses, and find out where your readers might have misunderstood you. As stated in Matthew 7:3–5//Luke 6:41–42, one can never exclude the possibility of being the one who has the beam in the eye and not the mote.

When evaluating an argument, the first step should therefore be trying to understand the argument in its own context, before evaluating it using your standards. When reading biblical texts, this is what I do and what I teach my students. First, you try to understand a text in its context, and only after that you start to apply your own ideas. Otherwise you run the risk of reading your own world into it. Rediscovering in a text what one has brought to it might provide a comforting sense of recognition and déjà vu, but it runs the risk of misunderstanding both text and author.

Larry Hurtado claims that he cannot see how the first part of my essay is strictly relevant. From his perspective, this might be true. This first part of my contribution provides the context in which the argument is to be read and understood. Unless you apply a third- or fourth-century canonical Christian perspective, the questions whether Mark "enjoyed a wide and favourable circulation among circles of the late first-century Jesus-movement" and whether he "resonated immediately with many" cannot be answered (p. 42). Without manuscript evidence of this period and only having Matthew (and Luke) as verified readers, such an assumption must remain speculative. It has recently been subjected to criticism by Matthew Larsen who—based on patristic evidence—claims that Mark was never intended to be published as a book.[2] Regarding the impression that there is no indication of a refutation of Mark in a text like Matthew, recent scholarship on Matthew discusses the notion that Matthew did not want to complement but rather replace Mark.[3] Since the rise of orality and memory studies in New Testament scholarship, we are gaining new perspectives on the origin and development of the Gospels in general and the fourfold Gospel in particular. The church fathers' promotion of the fourfold Gospel can be interpreted as a defensive move trying to establish a foundation narrative.

These observations are important to understand my argument. The first part of my essay outlines how christological beliefs have changed over time, and later ideas about what particular formulas and titles mean cannot be projected back into the text, which happens if you work within a hermeneutical framework that leaves little room for historical development. I do not claim that such a presupposition lies behind Larry Hurtado's claim that Christian traditions and the Christian "refraction" of Isaiah were used in Mark. The idea is still slightly odd, as it works from traditions of which we have no evidence other than what we read in the New Testament. The basic

---

2. Matthew Larsen, *Gospels before the Book* (New York: Oxford University Press, 2018).

3. Matthias Konradt, "Das Matthäusevangelium als judenchristlicher Gegenentwurf zum Markusevangelium," in *Studien zum Matthäusevangelium*, ed. Alida Euler, WUNT 1/358 (Tübingen: Mohr Siebeck, 2016), 43–68.

fact that the expression "Jesus Christ" appears frequently in Paul does not tell us that it actually was some kind of titular Christology nor what the expression means.

With this in mind, there is not so much difference between Larry's and my reading of the text. Once you subtract the idea that Paul already used "Jesus Christ" in the same or at least in a similar way as we use it today and Mark picked it up as a "traditional christological expression," we are very much on the same page. It is difficult, however, to claim that something is a "tradition" as early as twenty years later.

Using Mark's Gospel as a window into the time of its composition or into the historical events themselves is a feature of historical-critical exegesis; it is also hermeneutically debatable. This is illustrated by Hurtado's claim about "evidence that GMark was more specifically addressed to Jesus-believers facing (or fearing) opposition and strong persecution" (p. 47). The arguments that follow this claim can be seen as an exercise in speculative mirror reading, extending the world of the text into the real world without explaining how this can be done in a hermeneutically sound way. Research on New Testament epistolography warns against applying such an approach to letters, and this holds true even more for applying it to narratives.[4]

It is commonly held that according to Mark's Gospel, Jesus (and his status) cannot be understood without his crucifixion and resurrection. As J. R. Daniel Kirk puts it so well in his response, "Divinity is not the great and scandalous secret of Mark's Gospel—the cross is" (p. 59). Kirk's essay, and even more so his response, illustrates how close our arguments are regarding methodology and content. It was intriguing to learn from his ideas, and I would welcome a detailed conversation about our reading impressions, especially in places where we differ. This might start with the question about how Jesus is depicted in the episode when he is said to be walking on the lake, whether the widow's donation is an act of discipleship or of outright stupidity, and what we can learn from the Markan narrative about God's interpretation of Jesus's mission.

Reading Adam Winn's response, I found that his reflection about presuppositions might indeed "serve the purpose of preparing the stage to evaluate

4. Timo Glaser, "Erzählung im Fragment: Ein narratologischer Ansatz zur Auslegung pseudepigrapher Briefbücher," in *Pseudepigraphie und* Verfasserfiktion in *frühchristlichen Briefen*, ed. Jörg Frey et al., WUNT 1/246 (Tübingen: Mohr Siebeck, 2009), 267–94.

the other contributions through the lens of this hermeneutical approach" (p. 244), as I noted in my response to his argument. Winn concludes via an *argumentum ex silentio* that I share the presupposition that "not only is there one God but that God is indivisibly one," which then "becomes a major obstacle to any sort of conclusion that Jesus could be identified as divine or sharing a divine identity with Israel's God" (p. 61). Winn's paraphrase of my putative conclusion that "the Markan Jesus cannot be divine, so he must be human"—a dichotomy that I neither argue for nor believe in, which he terms "predetermined by her own presuppositions" (p. 61), might be logical according to his presuppositions but is nevertheless beside the point.

Reading Winn's section, "Questionable Characterizations of the Markan Jesus," I realized that we all close gaps in the text and that nobody is able to put aside their own experience, background, and belief. I assume that what Winn terms "questionable characterizations" and where he argues, "The Markan text never indicates that events like his baptism, experience in the wilderness, or otherwise, lead [Jesus] to realize anything" (p. 69), is what Hurtado described as "psychologizing" or "sentimentalizing" (pp. 44, 47). I take the point and wonder how we can ever avoid closing gaps with our own *Wirklichkeitsverständnis* ("understanding of reality") or, as Umberto Eco would call it, encyclopedia. However, half a page prior to making this point, Winn claims that "John himself declares Jesus's greatness at the outset of the Gospel (1:7–8), noting he, John, is not able to untie the thong of Jesus's sandal and that Jesus will baptize people with God's Holy Spirit" (pp. 67–68). The Markan text never indicates that it is God's Holy Spirit or that John is talking about Jesus. As I outlined elsewhere, the passage 1:8 is one of the major gaps that are never closed in the Markan text and will be closed by each reader according to his own beliefs and experiences.[5]

Reading Winn's comments about the narrative approach, I could not avoid the impression that his response betrays a lack of familiarity with the current state of narratological discourse in New Testament scholarship—a state well-documented in Elizabeth Struthers Malbon's *Mark's Jesus*.[6] My impression stems from his misunderstandings about the narratological toolkit I apply. My approach is neither about constructing implied or real

5. Huebenthal, *Reading Mark's Gospel*, 212–13.

6. Elizabeth Struthers Malbon, *Mark's Jesus: Characterization as Narrative Christology* (Waco, TX: Baylor University Press, 2009); see also Huebenthal, *Reading Mark's Gospel*, 44–52.

readers nor about reconstructing reader knowledge; it is about the analysis of the structure of the text.

If I read about Isaiah in Mark in such a prominent place as the first verses, I assume that knowledge of and about Isaiah is important to understand the text. A reference marked so clearly indicates that the text referred to is of larger importance for understanding than less clearly marked texts like Psalms 2 and 22—especially as the "prophet Isaiah" is referred to twice (Mark 1:2 and 7:6), once by the narrator and once by the character Jesus, each time followed by a direct quotation.

As there are more references to the Holy Scriptures of Second Temple Judaism, I assume that this entire framework is important, and to understand the text fully, real readers will have to be familiar with it or make themselves familiar. I say nothing about the real audiences, nor do I construct implied readers or target audiences. I also make no presumption about the ontological status of Jesus. I simply read the text and try to construct what ancient readers with a different encyclopedia than mine might have understood and how they might have reconstructed the narrated world according to their experiences. Working with a cultural-scientific approach, I apply the same methods as my colleagues, only in a different hermeneutical framework.

I would therefore underline Winn's point that "readers must appreciate the *ancient* literary context in which [a text] was written" but reject his conclusion that readers must "avoid imposing foreign reading strategies on the text" (p. 63). There is no point in claiming that we should only be working with interpretation techniques that the authors of our biblical texts could have known and used. Such an argument is flawed, as it would require knowledge about the authors themselves that we will never have.

In addition, following this prescription would end science as we know it. For example, word-statistical research about Homer's epic or about Shakespeare's plays would not be allowed, as these authors did not have computers. The insights that Homer's epic comes from oral schemes and patterns based on meter and that some of Shakespeare's plays might actually be written by different authors would neither be possible nor allowed. As biblical scholars, we would be left with Aristotelian rules and the seven Middot of Hillel for reading New Testament text. Moreover, if methods we embrace for investigating Shakespeare or Homer are excluded from research of the Bible because the Bible is supposedly different in character, there is a more fundamental issue at stake. One might not like the outcomes of my reading of Mark's Gospel, but it is not the method itself that is to blame. Other Markan scholars have reached similar conclusions with the use of the narratological toolkit.

My starting point is the New Testament text, and I try to understand it in its first-century context before transferring it to other contexts. Using social-memory theory as a hermeneutical frame, I apply models of collective remembering, of typical social processes in groups, and of media changes in intergenerational remembering as the blueprint for the processes behind the scenes of New Testament texts. The early Jesus-followers and later Christians do not differ from other groups when it comes to social processes such as remembering the crucial and founding events of their group, passing them on in different media, and negotiating (group) identity. Assuming that the growth of the Christian groups—referring to the processes, not the content—is not different from the growth of other religious movements might be challenging for those who believe that Christianity is unique and that this approach does not respect the uniqueness of the Christian gospel. The Christian message is unique indeed, but the social processes and mechanisms behind its growth are not.

Context is important for reading and understanding, and this cuts both ways: the context of the reader is as important as that of the author. A basic orientation of cultural-scientific exegesis is a sense of the cultural coinage and connection to one's own position. The contribution of cultural-scientific exegesis, which applies to all exegesis, is the awareness of the double connection to context, which has to be integrated into one's work. It is not only the artifacts under investigation that are bound to the contexts and discourses of their time but also the interpreters, for they, too, cannot operate outside the contexts and discourses of their own times.

This rule of double connection to context also applies to scholarly discourse and therefore to the responses collected in this book. Knowing my own context and presumptions, or *Vorverständnis* as Rudolf Bultmann called it, is as important as knowing the others' contexts and approaches. Winn is right when he directs our attention to presuppositions, and I am trying to extend this idea a step further.

Knowing the contexts of the four contributors helps to understand some of our differences. The most important difference between my co-contributors and myself is neither that I am female nor that I was born in Europe or that my native tongue is German. What most distinguishes the four of us is that I come from the Roman Catholic tradition and received my training at a Jesuit institution, where I studied not the Bible but Roman Catholic theology, while my fellow authors have their background in the Reformed tradition. Larry Hurtado grew up in Assemblies of God and attended Baptist services in his time in Edinburgh. Daniel Kirk considers himself a post-evangelical, agnostic, Christian humanist who is officially on the books in the Reformed Church in America (RCA), and Adam Winn comes from the Baptist tradition. In other words, all three are at least broadly rooted in the Protestant Reformed tradition and have at least at times had evangelical backgrounds.

When reading and interpreting the Bible, whether you apply the principle of the Reformation *sola scriptura* or whether you work from the principles of the Second Vatican Council's "Dogmatic Constitution on Divine Revelation," it impacts how you understand the Bible more than race, gender, or many other aspect of diversity. The Roman Catholic understanding of the Bible as God's word in human fashion and its notion of both Scripture and tradition as sources of revelation create a uniquely Catholic perspective. The growth and further development of faith after the Bible was written is central to my understanding and for my work. If the guiding principle is *sola scriptura* or verbal inspiration instead, the idea of historical growth will remain alien.

This is, of course not the whole story. However, it is more than a small part of it. One can often tell from how someone reads Paul, James, John, or Revelation which confessional background one has. I am not implying that a reader cannot decide to change the frame they use when reading, or that he or she cannot learn to apply different frames successfully. My point is that it is impossible to interpret a text without applying a frame, that different frames will lead to different interpretations, and that frames can be incompatible. Using the principle of *sola scriptura* leads to interpretations and results that cannot be reconciled with an approach for which growth and historical change are central. And finally, we need to remain aware of the fact that frames can be more or less difficult to reconcile with different confessional traditions of Christianity.

My suggestion for the reader of this book is to use this knowledge about the contributors as a hermeneutical lens and to reread the contributions and responses accordingly. I am sure the reader can gain fresh insights about the ways in which we argue and the ways in which our contexts explain many of our disagreements. Moreover, the reader might understand why some disagreements can lead into polemics.

CHAPTER 2

Mark's Presentation of Jesus

LARRY W. HURTADO

The Gospel of Mark (hereafter GMark) is all about Jesus, giving what most believe was the pioneering written narrative of Jesus's activities.[1] The account promotes beliefs about Jesus's unique significance, and so in that sense it can be thought of as a profoundly christological text. That is, GMark certainly reflects and advocates positive beliefs about Jesus. Indeed, I contend that Mark presents Jesus as having a unique relationship with God that cannot be likened to other figures, not in a class that includes any others. But it is hardly a complete statement of the author's beliefs about Jesus.[2] In fact, it is not clear to me that the author intended this account of Jesus's activities to be such a comprehensive christological statement, or in any other way a summary manifesto of his beliefs.[3] So I think it is more appropriate (and more feasible) to try to grasp the author's particular narrative "presentation" of Jesus rather than his "Christology."[4] Before I attempt this, however, I offer some comments about my approach.

1. I use "GMark" to designate the text, "Mark" to designate the putative author, and a similar distinction for the other Gospels.

2. To assume otherwise is, in logical terms, a fallacy called a *petitio principii*, that is, to assume what must first be demonstrated. (The phrase is often mistranslated as "to beg the question," a phrase in turn now often misused to mean the necessity to pose a particular question.)

3. I refer to "his" beliefs, simply reflecting the common assumption that the author was male. I may discredit myself to some postmodernist readers immediately in my reference to the author's intentions. I am, however, unrepentant.

4. See my discussion of GMark in *Lord Jesus Christ: Devotion to Jesus in Earliest Christianity* (Grand Rapids: Eerdmans, 2003), 283–316, where I refer to the Markan "rendition" and "presentation" of Jesus. For a somewhat similar stance, but on a different basis, see Adela Yarbro Collins, *Mark: A Commentary*, Hermeneia (Minneapolis: Fortress, 2007), 44, who prefers the "'interpretation of Jesus' in Mark, rather than the 'Christology' of Mark, because systematic, philosophical reflection on the

Interpretative Factors

I suggest that in trying to understand any text there are, in principle, four factors to take into account: (1) foremost, the contents of the text; (2) the author and what we may know about him/her; (3) the setting or circumstances of the composition of the text; and (4) the type or genre of the writing. I leave the first of these matters for later in this essay, and proceed to sketch the others.

In the case of GMark, the author is not identified in the text. Nevertheless, we are able to form some characterization of him. To be sure, very early, it was ascribed to John Mark, in early Christian tradition an associate of Peter, and Hengel has laid out a case that this ascription and connection to Peter may derive from the point when the text was first circulated.[5] But, for our purposes, it is sufficient that, whoever the author was, he did not consider it important (or perhaps even appropriate) to identify himself in the text. Indeed, the author of GMark never even directly "surfaces" in the first-person singular in the entirety of the narrative.

In the wider literary context in which GMark was composed, this virtual anonymity is an interesting feature of this text (and, indeed, of all four Gospels), although it has received only limited attention.[6] For in the early

---

nature of Christ had not yet begun in the movement carried on by the followers of Jesus." And see her rather extensive discussion of Jesus as prophet, Messiah, teacher, as well as of his death (44–84). Also, note Elizabeth Struthers Malbon's preference for "the characterization of Jesus" in GMark rather than "Christology," indicative of her "narratological" approach to the text (*Mark's Jesus: Characterization as Narrative Christology* [Waco, TX: Baylor University Press, 2009], e.g., 16–19). Daniel Johansson, "The Identity of Jesus in the Gospel of Mark: Past and Present Proposals," *Currents in Biblical Research* 9 (2011): 364–93, reviews various scholars' views on the matter.

5. Martin Hengel, *Studies in the Gospel of Mark* (London: SCM, 1985), esp. 64–84. I am not persuaded, however, by his claim that in GMark already the term *euangelion* designates this text. Instead, it seems to me that in GMark the term consistently refers to the gospel message familiar to the intended readers.

6. David E. Aune, "Anonymity," *The Westminster Dictionary of New Testament and Early Christian Literature and Rhetoric* (Louisville: Westminster John Knox, 2003), 35, points to the numerous anonymous writings in the OT and NT as "a striking feature" that has been "almost completely neglected." Exceptions include Michael Wolter, "Die anonymen Schriften des Neuen Testaments: Annäherungsversuch an ein literarisches Phänomen," *ZNW* 79 (1988): 1–16, who contended that the anonymity of NT narrative writings was a distinctively Christian phenomenon; but cf. Armin D. Baum, "The Anonymity of the New Testament History Books: A Stylistic Device in the Context of Greco-Roman and Ancient Near Eastern Literature," *NovT* 50 (2008): 120–42, who argued that the NT authors of these works were influenced by the anonymity of OT narrative works. But cf. also now Simon Gathercole, "The Alleged Anonymity of the Canonical Gospels," *JTS* 62.2 (2018): 447–76, who challenges Baum's arguments, contending that Roman-era authors often did not include their names in the prologues of their works. Given, however, that authors chose whether to include their names, the choice not to do so remains worth noting.

Roman period, it was a frequent (though by no means universal) practice for authors of literary texts, including especially historical narratives, to identify themselves by name, often as part of a prologue to their works.[7] They also often provided information on the aims and/or circumstances of the writing. Authors who identified themselves usually did so for credit, even possible fame, for their compositions. So, the anonymity of GMark suggests an author who had no such motive.[8] Instead, although there are obvious indications of an author exercising some management of his narrative, this author likely intended this composition primarily as incorporating, reflecting, and furthering traditions and beliefs that were shared with the intended readers. He did not write to amend central beliefs or the gospel message of his readers but instead to narrate the foundation of those beliefs and that gospel message. If this inference is valid (and subsequently we shall see further justification for it), then we have all the more reason to be suspicious about treating GMark as offering a particular (still less, a distinctive) Christology.[9] Contrast this anonymity of GMark with the assertion of a named source in the prologue to the Gospel of Thomas, for example, which also happens to assert across the ensuing logia an interpretation of Jesus over against that of more "mainline" texts such as the four New Testament Gospels.

The *Archē* of the Gospel

I think that we get confirmation of this connection of GMark to other early Christian texts and traditions in the opening words, which, with a number of other scholars, I take to be the author's original title for the work: "The beginning [ἀρχή] of the gospel of Jesus Christ" (1:1).[10] In this view, the

7. See, Baum, "Anonymity," esp. 124–27, for numerous examples.

8. I use the term "anonymity" in the technical sense. The identity of the author may have been known, even from the outset. But it remains significant that the author did not identify himself in the text.

9. Certainly, for example, the once-touted notion that GMark offered a "corrective" Christology, e.g., a "theology of the cross" over against a "divine man" Christology, has long since been laid to rest. On this, see, e.g., Jack Dean Kingsbury, *The Christology of Mark's Gospel* (Philadelphia: Fortress, 1983), 25–45.

10. On 1:1 as the title of GMark, see, e.g., the cogent discussion by Yarbro Collins, *Mark*, 130–32. Cf. J. K. Elliott, "Mark 1.1–3—A Later Addition to the Gospel?," *NTS* 46 (2000): 585 (584–88), who (with some others) takes the opening words as referring to the immediately following verses. On the semantic range of *archē* (ἀρχή), see Franco Montanari, *GE: The Brill Dictionary of Ancient Greek* (Leiden: Brill, 2015), s.v. ἀρχή. It is not necessary here to engage the text-critical question of whether "son of God" (υἱοῦ θεοῦ) is secondary or original. Cf., e.g., Adela Collins, "Establishing the Text: Mark

entire ensuing narrative of Jesus's activities relates the origin, inception, and foundation of the early Christian gospel (εὐαγγέλιον), the proclamation in which Jesus was the central topic and which the author regards as the continuing responsibility of believers. That is, the author places GMark in direct relationship to, and support of, "the gospel" message of the Jesus-movement. In the several further uses of the term in GMark, the "gospel" is first proclaimed by Jesus (1:14–15), and then is linked directly with him, commitment to the one involving the other (10:29). Moreover, "the gospel" is to be proclaimed to all nations "first" (13:10), as virtually a precondition for the future hope of God's kingdom being established. This worldwide proclamation of "the gospel" is referred to again in the story of the unnamed woman who anoints Jesus (14:9).[11]

As indicated already, I take the term "gospel" (εὐαγγέλιον) in these passages to refer to the early Christian message about God's redemption through Jesus. So, to repeat the point for emphasis, the opening words of GMark place the narrative of Jesus's ministry as foundational for the proclamation of the Christian gospel message. The author's aim, then, is not merely to present Jesus as the focus of that continuing proclamation. Jesus's own activities are also the origin, foundation, and beginning of the message about Jesus as "Lord" (κύριος), who was proclaimed and reverenced in the late first-century circles of Christians for whom the text was written. In short, this resurrected and exalted Lord is also the historical Galilean Jesus.[12] His ministry is foundational for the gospel message and instructive for believers who profess it.

As David Aune observes, "The social context of Mark, that of the Christian church, provided the original readers and auditors with a framework within which Mark was interpreted."[13] If, therefore, our aim is to try to

---

1:1," in *Texts and Contexts: Biblical Texts in Their Textual and Situational Contexts. Essays in Honor of Lars Hartman*, ed. Tord Fornberg and David Helholm (Oslo: Scandanavian University Press, 1995), 111–27; Tommy Wasserman, "The 'Son of God' Was in the Beginning (Mark 1:1)," *JTS* 62.1 (2011): 20–50.

11. In this, I differ from Hengel's view that in GMark the term *euangelion* refers to "the story of Jesus" (*Studies in the Gospel of Mark*, 82–83, and see also 54–56), and in this was "substantially different" from Paul's use of the term.

12. At various points in GMark, Jesus is referred to as the κύριος ("Lord"), reflecting the usage of this christological title among the original readers: esp. 1:3 (the Isaianic wording adapted to make Jesus the coming "Lord"); 11:3; 12:35–36; 13:35. On these instances, see discussions of these verses in, e.g., Yarbro Collins, *Mark*.

13. David E. Aune, "Genre Theory and the Genre-Function of Mark and Matthew," in *Jesus, Gospel Tradition and Paul in the Context of Jewish and Greco-Roman Antiquity* (Tübingen: Mohr

read GMark in the terms in which it was first read (the aim I pursue here), then it is appropriate to take into account other (particularly prior) evidence of early Christian beliefs and practices. It might be an interesting exercise to read GMark on its own, ignoring this evidence, but it would hardly reflect the way that the text was ever read in its ancient setting, in circles of Jesus-believers who were baptized in Jesus's name, shared a meal that was "the Lord's Supper," invoked him and acclaimed him as part of their liturgical life, and held beliefs about Jesus's exalted status.

This means that I do not share the approaches taken by some other scholars toward reading GMark. For example, Daniel Kirk's study of the Synoptic Gospels involves fitting the presentation of Jesus into a type of figure in the Jewish tradition that he terms "idealized human figures." Kirk spends some 132 pages reviewing Jewish evidence to build this category, but, curiously, effectively proposes that we read these Gospels in isolation from other early Christian texts.[14] Kirk aims "to read the text as it was meant to be read by the author, and/or as it was likely to be heard by the audience."[15] But was GMark, for example, ever read by earliest believers with the approach that Kirk takes, ignoring the four decades of Christian traditions of belief and devotional practices? I do not think so.

For similar reasons, I find Michael Peppard's analysis of GMark faulty in his method.[16] In a telling statement early in his discussion of Jesus in GMark, Peppard refers to "the resources available to Mark: his Jewish traditions and his Greco-Roman world."[17] As his discussion proceeds, however, it becomes clear that the "Greco-Roman" resources essentially represent Roman imperial propaganda, and this then becomes the real focus of his study. But conspicuously missing in Peppard's statement of the "resources" that the author of GMark drew upon is the four decades or so of accumulating beliefs, ritual

Siebeck, 2013), 47 (25–56). His essay appeared earlier in *Mark and Matthew I: Comparative Readings. Understanding the Earliest Gospels in Their First-Century Settings*, ed. Eve-Marie Becker and Anders Runesson (Tübingen: Mohr Siebeck, 2011), 145–75. Others also take a similar view, e.g., Philip G. Davis, "Mark's Christological Paradox," *JSNT* 35 (1989): 3–18.

14. J. R. Daniel Kirk, *A Man Attested by God: The Human Jesus of the Synoptic Gospels* (Grand Rapids: Eerdmans, 2016), 13.

15. Kirk, *Man Attested by God*, 40–41.

16. Michael Peppard, *The Son of God in the Roman World: Divine Sonship in Its Social and Political Context* (Oxford: Oxford University Press, 2011), 86–131 (his discussion of GMark). See my fuller engagement with the book here: https://larryhurtado.wordpress.com/2013/01/17/the-son-of-god-inand-the-roman-empire-a-review-essay/.

17. Peppard, *Son of God*, 86.

practices, and devotional stance of the early Christian movement. Peppard almost seems to imagine that GMark was intended for, and was read by, individuals with no other knowledge of Christian traditions.[18] So, Peppard contends that GMark presents Jesus by drawing (positively) upon Roman imperial notions, particularly the idea of the emperor as "son of god" (θεοῦ υἱός), and this premise guides (and at some points skews, in my judgment) the analysis thereafter. Perhaps Peppard's approach might reflect what some readers, such as the second-century pagan critic of Christianity, Celsus, would have made of GMark, but these are hardly those for whom the author wrote. As I shall argue below, there are abundant indications that the author presupposes and alludes to specifically Christian traditions.

After all, to reiterate the chronological point for emphasis, by the time of the composition of GMark, we are several decades into the Jesus-movement. By that time, beliefs and ritual practices, and behavioral standards as well, were already traditional and widely known among circles of believers in various locations. The emphasis on a worldwide mission to all nations (13:9–10) means that GMark is by no means a product of, or for, some isolated or insulated circle out of touch with the wider developments in earliest Christianity. The notion of such isolated circles of Christians is dubious. Instead, earliest Christian groups appear to have been in frequent contact with one another, exhibiting a vigorous "interactive diversity."[19] Dwight Peterson showed the disappointing (often conflicting) results of scholarly efforts to posit a geographically specific "Markan community."[20] But my argument here is not in support of (or dependent on) some specific or localized "community" behind GMark. Instead, I simply emphasize that this text both addressed and arose from the late first-century Jesus-movement. The appropriation of GMark, as reflected in GMatthew and (to a lesser extent) GLuke, and the continuing status of GMark as one of the emergent "fourfold Gospel" collection surely attest to the wide and continuing favor that the text enjoyed.[21]

18. Peppard draws on an essay by Adela Yarbro Collins, "Mark and His Readers: The Son of God among Greeks and Romans," *HTR* 93 (2000): 85–100. I have the same methodological problem with her essay.

19. Larry W. Hurtado, "Interactive Diversity: A Proposed Model of Christian Origins," *JTS* 64 (2013): 445–62.

20. Dwight N. Peterson, *The Origins of Mark: The Markan Community in Current Debate*, BibInt 48 (Leiden: Brill, 2000). He judged that every proposal for a specific Markan community "is the product of highly speculative, viciously circular and ultimately unpersuasive and inconclusive reading" (196).

21. Granted, the fewer extant copies of GMark from the earliest period (portions of only two

Indeed, in recent years there has been renewed interest in the possible relationship of GMark and Pauline Christianity in particular, with Joel Marcus claiming that "the ground appears to be shifting" toward positing a relationship.[22] For my purposes, however, the specific connection of GMark to Pauline churches is not essential. I point to the recent scholarly discussion of the matter simply as illustrative more broadly that the immediate context of GMark is early Christianity, and that taking account of other early Christian texts is essential.

The various "in-house" terms of early Christian discourse reflect this connection of GMark to its setting in early Christian circles. In addition to the use of "the gospel" in the absolute already noted, there are the references to "the word" (ὁ λόγος) as a technical term for the gospel message (2:2; 4:14–20, 33), a use of the term also well-attested in Luke-Acts (e.g., Luke 1:2; Acts 4:4; 6:4; 8:4; 10:44; 11:19; 14:25; 16:6), with early uses in Paul as well (Gal 6:6; Phil 1:14). Moreover, the account of Jesus's "last supper" obviously reflects early Christian sacred-meal practices, including the recitation of Jesus's words over the bread and the cup, a practice for which we have evidence already in 1 Corinthians 11:17–34, a couple decades earlier.

There is probably another reflection of early Christian ritual practices in the distinctive form of Jesus's response to the request of James and John for special places in Jesus "glory" (Mark 10:35–40). GMark has Jesus refer to both "the cup" and "the baptism" as images of the demands that the two disciples must face, whereas Matthew simply refers to Jesus's "cup" (Matt 20:20–23). I suggest that the Markan account here alludes to the two chief rituals indicative of participation in the Jesus-movement, baptism and Eucharist ("Lord's Supper"), making them symbolic of the full demands of discipleship.[23]

---

manuscripts dated earlier than 300 CE: 𝔓45 and 𝔓137) suggest that it may have been less frequently copied and used, in comparison with the others of this "fourfold Gospel" collection. Nevertheless, GMark obviously survived as part of this emergent Gospel canon. The early association with Peter may well have been a key factor in this.

22. Joel Marcus, "Mark—Interpreter of Paul," in *Mark and Paul: Comparative Essays. Part II, For and Against Pauline Influence on Mark*, ed. Eve-Marie Becker, Troels Engberg-Pedersen, and Mogens Müller (Berlin: de Gruyter, 2014), 29–49 (citing 30). This essay originally appeared in *NTS* 46 (2000): 473–87.

23. And is the use of εὐχαριστέω ("to give thanks") in the description of the feeding of the crowd in Mark 8:6 another allusion to early Christian ritual practice? Cf. the use of εὐλογέω ("to bless), more reflective of Jewish terminology, in the account of the feeding of the five thousand (Mark 6:41).

In addition to these indications of a positive connection with early Christian discourse and practices, there are also more specific indications of the author's concerns. In a passage that has perhaps the most transparent references to the situation of earliest readers, 13:1–37, there are warnings about being deceived by false messianic claimants and false prophets (vv. 5–6, 21–23), about persecution by authorities, and also about familial opposition (vv. 9–13). The little aside-comment in v. 14, "let the reader understand," directly widens the situation from that of the disciples in vv. 1–4 to the subsequent reading of GMark in early Christian gatherings. And the exhortations to be "on watch" in vv. 33–37 likewise overtly speak to the situation of early believers, especially in the final words in v. 37, which widen those addressed from "you" (the disciples in vv. 1–4) to "all."

As noted often, GMark places a great deal of emphasis on discipleship as following Jesus, making him the pattern.[24] In particular, there is the large central section, chapters 8–10, in which there are three passion-resurrection predictions, each one linked to teaching about discipleship. The exhortation in 8:34–38 is perhaps the most-cited passage, in which Jesus's followers are warned that they must be prepared to suffer and even die, Jesus's cross being here the example for his followers. Indeed, if one were to identify what might be the central concern in GMark, it is likely this practical matter of behavior, how to be a faithful follower of Jesus, especially in the context of opposition.

Compatible with this emphasis, some years ago Philip Davis offered the intriguing (and, to my mind, persuasive) proposal that GMark begins and ends where it does because the author intended his presentation of the story of Jesus as a pattern for the existence of believers.

> Mark's whole story of Jesus can be read as a blueprint for the Christian life: it begins with baptism, proceeds with the vigorous pursuit of ministry in the face of temptation and opposition, and culminates in suffering and death oriented towards an as-yet unseen vindication.[25]

---

24. E.g., Larry W. Hurtado, "Following Jesus in the Gospel of Mark—and Beyond," in *Patterns of Discipleship in the New Testament*, ed. Richard N. Longenecker (Grand Rapids: Eerdmans, 1996), 9–29.

25. Philip G. Davis, "Christology, Discipleship, and Self-Understanding in the Gospel of Mark," in *Self-Definition and Self-Discovery in Early Christianity: A Study in Shifting Horizons, Essays in*

So, whether GMark is to be placed in this or that geographical context, and whether it was written during or after the Jewish war of 66–72 CE, is not crucial. What is clear is that GMark both reflects and addresses the situations of believers (perhaps in various settings) that involved the threat of opposition and even judicial trials for their faith. I repeat, however, there is no indication that the author set out to correct or to lay down some particular christological stance other than that already identified. The author sought to make the narrative of Jesus a pattern for Christian existence in the troubled, eschatologically charged time for believers in which he wrote.

The Gospel of Mark as *Bios*

It is now widely agreed that the New Testament Gospels can be fitted (albeit with varying degrees of compatibility) within the broad category of *bios* writings of the Roman period. This term describes a variety of writings (of various lengths) that present in narrative form the actions and/or character of an individual, the early literary stages of what we now call "biography."[26] As the earliest of the New Testament Gospels, GMark is a landmark work in the literary history of early Christianity, giving a quasi-biographical account of Jesus. For, however much it draws on and reflects early traditions about Jesus, as a text it is the pioneering, continuous, written narrative account of Jesus, from baptism to resurrection. If, as is commonly thought, the authors of GMatthew and GLuke (and perhaps also GJohn) used GMark as a primary source and model for their own works, it was also an impressively influential text.

From earlier texts such as 1 Corinthians 15:1–7, we know that the (oral) gospel tradition had a narrative character. Likewise, we know that the gospel message focused on the figure of Jesus, and that his Jewish ethnicity

---

Appreciation of Ben F. Meyer from His Former Students, ed. David J. Hawkin and Tom Robinson, Studies in Bible and Early Christianity 26 (Lewiston: Edwin Mellen, 1990), 101–19 (citing 109).

26. See, e.g., Richard A. Burridge, *What Are the Gospels?: A Comparison with Graeco-Roman Biography*, rev. ed. (Grand Rapids: Eerdmans, 2004; orig. edition 1997); and my discussion of the literary genre of the NT Gospels in *Lord Jesus Christ*, 270–82. More recently, Justin Marc Smith, *Why Bios? On the Relationship between Gospel Genre and Implied Audience*, LNTS 518 (London: Bloomsbury T&T Clark, 2015), explores the choice to write these bios-type accounts of Jesus and contends that this genre allowed the authors to address a potentially wide readership, albeit focused primarily on Christian readers.

was explicitly acknowledged as integral to his redemptive work (e.g., Rom 15:8–9; Gal 4:4–6). Surely, the belief that God had raised Jesus from death and exalted him uniquely meant also that God had thereby vindicated Jesus of Nazareth, all that he taught and stood for, against the charges for which he was crucified. That is, this resurrection-belief was likely the initial stimulus for gathering and preserving historical tradition about Jesus.[27]

Nevertheless, GMark was a new *literary* development, a full "*bios*-shaped" narrative of Jesus's ministry with a strong historical concern: to lay out the "beginning" (ἀρχή) of the churches' proclamation of the gospel in this account of Jesus. This combination of quasi-biographical and historical concern accounts for the rich body of details of such things as places, customs, religious issues, personages, and languages pertaining to the time of Jesus. A similar body of details characterizes all the New Testament Gospels (including GJohn), but it may well be that GMark set the pattern for this.[28]

The narrative in GMark, for example, is studded with names of various geographical locations (even if the author's grasp of the physical relation of some of these places seems a bit inaccurate), including Lake Galilee, Capernaum, the Jordan River, Tyre and Sidon, Nazareth, the Decapolis, Bethany, Bethsaida, and Jerusalem. There are references to Jewish groups including the Sadducees, Pharisees, and Herodians, and for all of them GMark is an important source of information about them. The text deals with various issues in the observance of Jewish religious law, including Sabbath-observance rules, food practices, divorce and remarriage, skin diseases, female ritual impurity, and taxation. Various historical figures of the early first-century CE appear, including John the Baptizer, Herod Antipas, and Pontius Pilate.

Another interesting feature of GMark is the use of Semitic words and expressions, which appears to be another kind of "local color" in the narrative. Indeed, among the four Gospels, GMark uses Semitic terms the most.[29] They appear particularly in some accounts of miracles and in other

---

27. Larry W. Hurtado, "Resurrection-Faith and the 'Historical' Jesus," *JSHJ* 11 (2013): 35–52.

28. Hurtado, *Lord Jesus Christ*, 265–68, where I draw a contrast with the more ahistorical nature of GThomas.

29. Michael O. Wise, "Languages of Palestine," *DJG*[1] 434–44, counts some thirty instances where the NT Gospels use Semitic terms (441), and he judges most of these instances as involving Aramaic (442). On the use of non-Greek words in GMark in particular, see Alfredo Delgado Gomez, "¡Levàntate! ¡Ábrete! El Idiolecto de Marcos a La Luz de La Sociolingüistica," *Estudios*

numinous settings in the text, some of these instances unique to GMark. For example, in the account of the raising of the daughter of the synagogue leader (5:35–43), Jesus addresses the dead girl with the Aramaic expression *talitha koum* (v. 41), and in the healing of the deaf-mute (7:31–37) Jesus's actions include the Aramaic command *ephphatha* (v. 34). On the cross, the final words of Jesus in GMark are in Aramaic, *eloi eloi lema sabachthani* (15:34). These might at first seem to be the use of incomprehensible foreign words that often features in Roman-era magic.[30] But the author of GMark consistently violates a fundamental principle that magical words are not to be translated by giving the meaning of these various Semitic expressions, and the translations render the statements rather simply, even banally. For example, the author tells us that *talitha koum* simply means, "rise up, little girl," and in the dramatic scene where the deaf-mute is healed, *ephphatha* simply means "be opened." Likewise, the author translates the final words on the cross in 15:34, which shows Jesus dying with words of Scripture on his lips. So, if there is any connection to Roman-era magic, it is more likely as parody, to *disassociate* Jesus's miraculous actions from magic.[31] The point is that the rich use of geographical, cultural, and linguistic detail fits the quasi-biographical nature of the text.

Given that the early Jesus-movement got along for several decades without a work such as GMark, we might ask why the author thought it important to produce this text, in particular this kind of text. Specifically, why a *bios*-type narrative? In an earlier consideration of the matter, I suggested that there was likely a combination of factors.[32] The larger literary environment

Ecclesiàsticos 93 (2018): 29–86. An English version of his essay is now published as "Get Up! Be Opened!: Codeswitching and Loanwords in the Gospel of Mark," *JSNT* 42.3 (2020): 390–427. See also Christopher B. Zeichmann, "Loanwords or Code-Switching? Latin Transliteration and the Setting of Mark's Composition," *JJMJS* 4 (2017): 42–64, who argues that the particular way that Latin is transliterated in GMark comports more with a location in Syria or post-revolt Palestine.

30. E.g., Campbell Bonner, *Studies in Magical Amulets, Chiefly Graeco-Egyptian* (Ann Arbor, MI: University of Michigan Press, 1950), 186–95.

31. Cf. Marcus, *Mark 1–8*, 363, who (with some others) misjudges the Semitic expressions in 5:41 and 7:34 as the author's use of exotic, foreign words for magical purposes. Instead, these scenes comprise parodies of the use of magical words. For in each case, the author violates magical practice in giving the plain meaning of the utterances. I made the basic observation offered here earlier (L. W. Hurtado, *Mark*, New International Biblical Commentary [Peabody, MA: Hendrickson, 1989], 87. See also, e.g., Barry Blackburn, *Theios Anēr and the Markan Miracle Traditions*, WUNT 2/40 [Tübingen: Mohr Siebeck, 1991], 221n198). Delgado Gomez, "Get up! Be Opened!," agrees that the translation of the Aramaic terms in the miracle stories shows that "the use of the Aramaic word as a kind of magic formula is therefore avoided."

32. Hurtado, *Lord Jesus Christ*, 277–82.

provided a broad genre of *bios*-type writings that focused on individuals of great historic significance through relating (whether briefly or at length) their life in sequential narrative form. As Richard Burridge proposed, the choice to write this kind of book about Jesus likely seemed an effective way to present the person of Jesus as "a unique individual revealing God in his deeds and words, life, death and resurrection."[33] Again, in the case of GMark, the aim was clearly to relate the historical inception and foundation of the continuing activity of gospel-proclamation. The *bios* genre likely seemed a particularly useful one for making this kind of point. For it gave readers, not a treatise containing a set of christological reflections (compare, for example, the Epistle to the Hebrews) but, instead, a vivid account of Jesus himself that related his actions and words in a fast-paced narrative.

On the other hand, David Aune has argued that GMark exhibits some contrasting features in comparison with the *bios* literature of the time, such as a noticeably simpler level of Koine Greek, and, more importantly, "the counter-cultural social and religious values of first century Christians, often marked by a subversive rejection of the values of the dominant culture." These observations led Aune to propose that GMark may actually have been written "in reaction to Graeco-Roman biography rather than as a simple emulation of it. That is, Mark can be understood as an intentional parody of the hierarchy of values that typically characterized Graeco-Roman biography."[34] But, of course, even so, GMark would reflect the aim of positioning the work in light of the wider literary environment.

An additional point to make is that the choice to write a *bios* type of text both allows for and requires attention to be given to the specific historical setting of the figure about whom the book is written. We have noted that GMark exhibits this in its rich inclusion of geographical, cultural, religious, and political specifics of the early first-century CE. Moreover, in GMark there is a well-known strong distinction between the comprehension of people in the time of Jesus's ministry and the later "post-Easter" setting. In the narrative time, the human figures who encounter Jesus come to various views about him, some more negative and others more positive (e.g., prophet,

33. Richard Burridge, "Gospel Genre, Christological Controversy and the Absence of Rabbinic Biography: Some Implications of the Biographical Hypothesis," in *Christology, Controversy, and Community: New Testament Essays in Honour of David R. Catchpole*, ed. David G. Horrell and Christopher M. Tuckett (Leiden: Brill, 2000), 137–56 (citing 156).

34. Aune, "Genre Theory," 50–51.

Messiah, sorcerer). But none of them arrives at a full apprehension of his person and significance, as came to be held in the Jesus-movement in the post-Easter period.[35] In this way, too, the author preserves something of the historical specificity of the time of Jesus's ministry.[36]

In sum, given the author's aim to present Jesus's ministry as the foundation and inception of the churches' gospel message and as the role model for believers (especially in the face of opposition), the *bios* type of writing was particularly useful.

Contents

I turn now to consider the most important matter in attempting to capture the presentation of Jesus in GMark, the contents of the narrative portrait. This Markan portrait has two intertwined features: Jesus is both genuinely human, and yet also he bears and embodies a transcendent status and significance beyond any other figure in the experience of observers in the narrative or in the biblical traditions of individuals who were vehicles of divine power. As GMark is not a theological exposition, and given that early Christians over the next few centuries were trying to find and agree how to portray Jesus's relationship with God, the author does not give any definitive statement on the matter, at least not in the conceptual categories of later theologizing. Yet I think that there is a clear sense in which the Jesus of GMark transcends all other categories and precedents of its time, such as holy man, prophet, and even Messiah and embodies God's redemptive purposes uniquely.

To reiterate the point from my discussion of the genre of GMark, this is a narrative of a historical figure, a genuine human, Jesus of Nazareth. He has a family and a hometown where he grew up. He prays, gets angry, and—most indicative of his human nature—when crucified he really dies. The human Jesus is not in question in GMark. Indeed, as I have already observed, it appears that GMark presents Jesus as the ultimate role model

---

35. I include the putative acclamation by the Roman centurion in 15:39, which I take to be ironic and only hinting at the full truth, as is the case with the mocking acclamations of the other bystanders in 15:32.

36. Compare this with the bolder way that the author of GJohn narrates Jesus's ministry with more explicit reference to post-Easter beliefs, thereby merging the horizons of Jesus and early Christian readers more overtly.

for followers, specifically those for whom the author originally wrote. Jesus's humanity is, thus, religiously/theologically important in GMark, without question. The remaining question before us is whether this is all that GMark tells us about Jesus.[37]

The first thing to note is that the very first verses of GMark (1:1–3) immediately place Jesus in a larger narrative of divine promise and eschatological fulfillment. The designation of Jesus as *Christos* in v. 1 presupposes and lays claim to the notion of a divinely authorized agent who embodies hopes for redemption. Note also, however, that the phrasing "Jesus Christ" (Ἰησοῦ Χριστοῦ) reflects the widely used form in various early Christian texts and circles—some 107 times in a wide assortment of New Testament writings, including nineteen occurrences in Romans alone, and eleven in Acts. The term "Christ" (Χριστός) clearly became a standard reverential way of designating Jesus in these various circles and was linked with Jesus exclusively. The Gospel of Mark's use here is further confirmation of its context in early Christian beliefs.[38] This, plus the prophetic words that follow in vv. 2–3, frame the ensuing narrative as foretold and rooted in, and so to be recognized as, fulfillment of these hopes. In place of any other grand narrative, such as the Roman imperial one that claimed the Roman Empire as the fulfillment of history, GMark affirms the biblical narrative in which God's prophetic purposes frame history.

More specifically, in light of the verses that follow them, the two prophetic statements (both curiously ascribed here to Isaiah) are to be taken as descriptive of the place of John the Baptizer in this scheme. He is the messenger sent to prepare "your way," and the "voice" who prepares "the way of the Lord." But the one who then comes in the narrative is Jesus, who is thus to be identified here as "the Lord" in the biblical citation.[39] To be sure, Jesus and God are also distinguishable in GMark; but, in this passage and others, "the activity of God and of Jesus are intimately related."[40]

This close, indeed unique, connection of Jesus and God is further

37. For a recent and particularly robust case that GMark gives a view of Jesus that reflects beliefs in his preexistence and sharing in divine glory, see Michael Bird, *Jesus the Eternal Son: Answering Adoptionist Christology* (Grand Rapids: Eerdmans, 2017), esp. 64–106.

38. See, e.g., the survey of Pauline usage of the term by Ben Witherington III, "Christ," *DPL*[1] 95–100.

39. So, e.g., Yarbro Collins, *Mark*, 136–37.

40. Yarbro Collins, *Mark*, 137.

reflected in the portrayal of observers as amazed at Jesus's *authority* (ἐξουσία); for example, in teaching (e.g., 1:22) and in exorcism (vv. 27–28). In fact, one of the key terms in the presentation of Jesus in GMark is his "authority." Jesus claims authority to forgive sins (2:10). Still more remarkably, Jesus himself confers divine authority to his disciples, so that they too can cast out spirits (3:15; 6:7). The demand of the temple authorities is that Jesus adduce his authority, a demand that he refuses on account of their obtuseness (11:28–33).

In other scenes as well, Jesus is portrayed as acting with unique authority and power. In 4:35–41, for example, unlike Jonah, Jesus does not pray to be delivered from the raging storm; instead, he directly rebukes the wind and waves himself. As Yarbro Collins observed, noting the likely allusions to Old Testament references, Jesus does not act here "like a devout human person but like God."[41] The disciples are frightened and wonder "who therefore is this" (v. 41). They are unable to comprehend how the human figure, Jesus, is also such a direct expression of divine power and presence. But readers are expected to perceive the matter correctly.

For, over against the various inadequate (or downright incorrect) ways that human characters label Jesus in GMark (e.g., 3:22; 6:14–16), there are two scenes in particular where God expresses his relationship to Jesus explicitly. At Jesus's baptism in 1:9–11, as the divine Spirit descends upon him, God addresses him directly as "my beloved Son, in whom I was pleased [εὐδόκησα]."[42] The baptism scene is, of course, the affirmation of Jesus and the commissioning of him for what readers will see as the messianic ministry that follows. But this divine voice, which readers are surely to take as the ultimately authoritative one in the narrative, emphasizes, not Jesus's mission but his unique relationship to God as "the beloved Son" (note well the definite article). Indeed, it is important to note the specifics of the heavenly voice.

The first few words often remind commentators of Psalm 2:7, a royal coronation psalm, although the wording is not actually the same; compare "you are my beloved Son" (σὺ εἶ ὁ υἱός μου ὁ ἀγαπητός; Mark 1:11) with "you are my Son" (υἱός μου εἶ σύ; Ps 2:7 LXX). It is not, thus, a quotation but

41. Yarbro Collins, *Mark*, 260.

42. The reference in 1:10 to "the Spirit" without any further qualifying term is another example of the author's use of "in-house" terminology of the early Jesus-movement.

at most an echo of the idea of royal divine sonship.[43] Moreover, if there is an indirect allusion to the psalm, what is omitted is also interesting. The rest of Psalm 2:7 reads, "Today I have begotten you," which signals that the human personage spoken to is being inducted into a new filial status with God. If one posits an allusion to Psalm 2:7 in the words of the heavenly voice in Mark 1:11, the omission of the latter phrase suggests that the author of GMark (followed in this by Matthew and Luke) wanted to avoid precisely this notion of adoption with reference to Jesus.[44] In short, this is not an adoption scene. In Mark it is a private, divine acclamation and commissioning, described as heard by Jesus alone.[45] The divine voice affirms Jesus's divine sonship; the voice does not here confer it, as further indicated by the aorist indicative verb εὐδόκησα ("my beloved Son in whom *I took delight*").[46]

This emphasis on Jesus's divine sonship is echoed again in 9:2–10, the second scene where God speaks. Here, Jesus is portrayed as transfigured (μετεμορφώθη, v. 2) before the three disciples accompanying him, and Moses and Elijah appear, speaking with Jesus. In the immediate and larger context (prior to and following this scene), I take the vision of the transfigured Jesus to be a preview of the eschatological glory that Jesus (who refers to himself here and elsewhere in the distinctive phrase, "the Son of Man") is to receive and exhibit (9:9; and, e.g., 8:38; 13:26; 14:62).[47] Peter is presented as so impressed to see Jesus included in the company of these two great worthies that he proposes to erect three shrines in their honor.

43. I have elsewhere noted (with some puzzlement) the lack of reference to Psalm 2 in Paul's epistles in "Early Christological Interpretation of the Messianic Psalms," in Larry W. Hurtado, *Ancient Jewish Monotheism and Early Christian Jesus-Devotion: The Context and Character of Christological Faith* (Waco, TX: Baylor University Press, 2017), 559–82, esp. 569–75.

44. The view that Psalm 2:7 is an adoption scene has been disputed by others as well; e.g., Adela Yarbro Collins and John J. Collins, *King and Messiah as Son of God: Divine, Human, and Angelic Messianic Figures in Biblical and Related Literature* (Grand Rapids: Eerdmans, 2008), 19–22.

45. Despite Peppard's valiant and complex effort to establish his view that Mark 1:9–11 is an adoption scene (*Son of God*, 95–112), I am not persuaded, in part because he does not do justice to the wording of the Markan text, and also he does not take account of the state of early Christian traditions of Jesus's preexistence that had been common coinage for several decades.

46. Cf. the more exact citation of Psalm 2:7 in Acts 13:33, where this author seems to take the "today" as Jesus's resurrection and installation as "Lord and Christ" (Acts 2:34–36). Yet this must be set alongside the earlier text (Luke 1:35) where an angel declares that Mary will miraculously conceive, and her child will be called "son of God" (υἱὸς θεοῦ), which appears to mean that he is this from birth. Note also the citation of Psalm 2:7 as a variant reading in Luke 3:22, supported by several early Christian writers. See Bruce M. Metzger, *A Textual Commentary on the Greek New Testament, Second Edition* (Stuttgart: United Bible Societies, 1994), 112–13.

47. So, similarly, Stein, *Mark*, 416–17. Cf. Yarbro Collins, *Mark*, 421, who tends to align the passage with wider accounts of epiphanies.

But the text first subtly makes this an inappropriate suggestion ("he [Peter] did not know how to respond," 9:6). It then more explicitly sets the matter aright in the words of God's voice, once again declaring—this time to the three disciples—that Jesus is "my beloved Son" and ordering them to listen to *him*. If the question is whether GMark fits Jesus into an established cadre of "idealized humans," of which Jesus is one example, this text surely quashes that idea.[48] In whatever terms we are to distinguish Jesus and God and yet also link them uniquely, it will require a category that exceeds even that to which figures such as Elijah and Moses belong. Indeed, it appears that for GMark (as for much of earliest Christianity) this category is populated by Jesus alone!

Consider also the parable in Mark 12:1–12. The parable commences the final part of GMark set in Jerusalem, with Jesus in debate with Jewish religious critics. In v. 12 the author has the temple authorities recognize themselves as the disobedient tenants, and so Jesus has to be the "one beloved son" sent "last of all" (v. 6). Note again the characterization of this figure as "the beloved son," which, of course echoes similar phrasing in the two passages already discussed where God affirms Jesus's unique status. Quoting part of Psalm 118, the passage then declares that this beloved son, even though rejected now, will be made the "chief cornerstone" (vv. 10–11), a status that seems to excel that of any other figure save God.

There follows a series of antagonistic questions put to Jesus by a variety of critics (12:13–34), and then Jesus's own question in turn to these critics (vv. 35–37) about how it is that the scribes refer to the Messiah as "son of David." Without waiting for a reply, Jesus then cites Psalm 110:1 (109:1 LXX). For the argument here in GMark to work, we have to take on board the late Second Temple tradition ascribing the Psalms as a whole to David, and seeing David as prophetically inspired in writing them.[49] As well, we have to accept the premise of the argument that (at least for the intended readers) Psalm 110:1 refers to the Messiah (a view that is difficult, however, to confirm in Second Temple sources, something that cannot detain us here).[50]

48. Cf. Kirk, *Man Attested by God*, who argues that the Synoptic Gospels present Jesus as simply an "idealized human" figure (e.g., p. 13). In my view, he oversimplifies matters.

49. See, e.g., my discussion of developments in Jewish traditions about the Psalms in "Early Christological Interpretation," esp. 560–68.

50. Hurtado, "Early Christological Interpretation," esp. 575–81.

The force of the text cited is in the use of the term "my lord" in the psalm (by David) to refer to the Messiah. Jesus's concluding question is, if David refers to him as his "lord" (his superior), how then can the Messiah be David's son? Of course, this purports to challenge some Second Temple messianic ideas, but the focus of the passage is also phrased specifically in terms of sonship. Whose son is the Messiah? In the wider context of Mark 12, particularly the parable of vv. 1–12, and the preceding four decades of early Christian confession and devotional practice, the answer that the intended readers will know is that the Messiah (Jesus) is actually God's unique "beloved Son."

This raises the question of the relationship of Jesus's messianic status and his divine sonship for the author of GMark and his early readers. For some scholars, the two notions are essentially synonymous—Jesus's divine sonship is simply another way of describing him as Messiah.[51] I think that such a view is mistaken. To be sure, early believers (such as the author of GMark) ascribed both messianic status and divine sonship to Jesus, and so the two notions are linked, specifically and uniquely in the person of Jesus. Perhaps the most explicit example of this is in the question of the high priest in 14:61: "Are you the Messiah [ὁ χριστός], the Son of the Blessed One [ὁ υἱὸς τοῦ εὐλογητοῦ]?" But it seems to me that a careful analysis of the usage of the two ideas in New Testament texts such as GMark yields the conclusion that, though there is certainly a connection and a certain overlap, each also has its own significance and connotation. To be brief, GMark seems to me to use "the Messiah" to position Jesus vis-à-vis God's people and God's eschatological purposes as the unique royal agent in fulfillment of messianic hopes. The references to Jesus's divine sonship, however, are in statements that relate him to God, affirming Jesus's unique validity, authority, and intimacy with God. That is, Jesus is Messiah ("Christ") and the unique Son of God. The two claims are united in his person, but each one is a distinguishable claim.

Peter's confession of Jesus as Messiah in Mark 8:29 seems intended by the author to reflect one particular sense of this term. Peter's confession surpasses the views of Jesus offered by other human voices of the time, but

---

51. For discussion of the matter in Mark, see, e.g., Yarbro Collins and Collins, *King and Messiah as Son of God*, 123–34. Indeed, they even take "Son of Man" to be another, roughly synonymous, messianic title (133).

this confession, too, is inappropriate publicly until Jesus's full redemptive work has been completed. So Jesus forbids public use of the claim (v. 30). In their mission, Jesus's followers may be given refreshment "in my [Jesus's] name because you belong to Messiah" (9:41). The royal, messianic claim is obviously reflected in the mocking references to Jesus as "king of the Jews" (Pilate in 15:2; and his soldiers in v. 18; cf. v. 26), and still more directly in the mockery of the Jewish bystanders in v. 32, who taunt him as "the Messiah, the king of Israel." Also, we have already noted how Jesus's challenge to his critics in 12:35–37 includes reference both to the Messiah and to the question of his true sonship. Moreover, in GMark the accusation of being a royal, messianic claimant is essentially the charge that brought Jesus before Pilate, and for which Jesus was crucified. "Messiah" and "Son" are not two competing alternatives. But, I repeat, they are distinguishable claims.

In support of this, it is noteworthy that in both cases the voice from heaven acclaims Jesus as "my beloved Son," and not as Messiah. That is not a matter of contrast but of perceptible emphasis. Also, the demonic acclamations (which appear to be suppressed by Jesus "because they knew him," 1:34) declare his divine sonship (3:11; 5:7; and cf. "the holy one of God," 1:24) and never refer to him as Messiah. In the famous statement ascribed to Jesus in 13:32 about knowledge of God's eschatological timetable, he refers to himself simply as "the Son" (and this simple yet absolute expression rather obviously reflects the in-house terminology of early Christian circles).[52] Also, the oft-cited statement of the Roman centurion in 15:39 (however you take it) refers to Jesus's divine sonship. Let me emphasize again that the author of GMark certainly did not want to play off the notion of Jesus's messianic status against the ascription of divine sonship. Instead, the author affirms both notions. But each had its own usage. I repeat that, for the author, Jesus's divine sonship better captures Jesus's unique status, particularly vis-à-vis God.

Of course, divine-sonship language had a long and varied usage, both in Jewish/biblical tradition and in the wider environment, and in all instances had roughly a similar function of placing a given figure in close relation to a deity. Angels collectively can be called "sons of God" (e.g., Job 1:6), and Israel is referred to as God's son (Hos 11:1; cf. Exod 4:22). As noted already,

52. See, e.g., 1 Cor 15:28; Heb 1:8; and many uses in the Johannine writings.

in Psalm 2:7 the Judean king is acclaimed as God's son. In some cases, the devout are referred to as God's "child" or "children" (e.g., Wis 2:12–20; 5:1–8), or individually as "a son of the Most High" (Sir 4:10). Also, in ancient Jewish prayer-practice, God can be addressed as "our Father," connoting a filial status of those who offer the prayer. Moreover, as has been noted for a long time, divine sonship was also frequently ascribed to rulers, including the Roman emperor.

This wider usage of divine sonship language probably accounts for, and makes significant, the typical use of the Greek article (= "the" in English) in the references to Jesus as God's Son in GMark (1:11; 3:11; 9:7; 13:32; 14:61).[53] Jesus's divine sonship is thereby referred to repeatedly as one-of-a-kind, unique, *par excellence*. Jesus is *the* divine Son. This fits with other evidence cited earlier that GMark seems to place Jesus in a unique relationship with God that cannot be likened to that of other figures, not in a class that includes any others. So, to underscore the matter, a basic notion of divine sonship was both varied and pervasive in the ancient world, but GMark (and other early Christian texts) ascribed to Jesus a *unique* divine sonship, indicating a distinctively close and intimate relationship with God.

Notice, however, that the emphasis in GMark is placed on the *idea* of Jesus's divine sonship, not on any particular title or fixed terminology to express it. Among the seven or so references to Jesus's divine sonship in GMark, only three of them acclaim him with what might be variations on the expression "Son of God," and no two of these are the same. Actually, the only instance of the precise title "the Son of God" is the demonic acclamation in 3:11. In 5:7 another demoniac calls Jesus "Son of the Most High God," and the phrasing ascribed to the centurion in 15:39 lacks an article and so might mean "a son of [a (?)] god" (υἱὸς θεοῦ). The remaining (i.e., the majority) of references affirm Jesus's divine sonship in varying ways (as noted: e.g., "beloved Son," "the Son"). Clearly, the ascription of unique divine sonship to Jesus mattered to this author much more than the title "Son of God."[54]

---

53. Cf. 1:24, "the holy one of God"; the vocative form "Jesus, son of the Most High God" (Ἰησοῦ υἱὲ τοῦ θεοῦ τοῦ ὑψίστου) in 5:7 accounts for the absence of the article; and the centurion's comment in 15:39, "Truly, this was a son of God" (ἀληῶς οὗτος ὁ ἄνθρωπος υἱὸς θεοῦ ἦν; the textual variations in the last three words are all word order, and none features the article) seems to fall short of the early Christian emphasis on Jesus as *the* divine son.

54. This is, by the way, another reason to hesitate in accepting Peppard's bold claim that the

This is, however, by no means a peculiarity of GMark. It is worth noting that there is, for example, a similar pattern in Paul's letters.[55] Among the seventeen references to Jesus's divine sonship in the entire Pauline corpus, the expression "son of God" appears only four times, and even among these instances there are variations in the precise wording.[56] In short, just as the case in GMark, so for Paul it was the conviction that Jesus is God's unique Son that was apparently what mattered, rather than the christological title "Son of God" or any other formulaic expression of this conviction.[57] This variety of expressions to affirm Jesus's divine sonship in GMark is thus reflective of a similar and wider early Christian practice in the verbal formulations expressing this conviction. That is, we have here another link of GMark to the discourse and convictions of earlier Christian circles as reflected, for example, in Paul's letters, a further confirmation of the approach that I have advocated that we should read GMark in the context of these early Christian beliefs.

The varied expressions of Jesus's divine sonship in GMark (and in Paul) are all the more noteworthy when compared with the much more prominent use of the fixed expression "the Son of God" later in the Johannine writings (six instances in John and another seven in 1 John).[58] In these writings (for reasons that cannot be explored here), clearly the fixed title "the Son of God" had become much more prominent in faith-discourse in comparison to GMark (or Paul).

---

author of Mark intended a direct contrast between the Roman emperor's claim of divine sonship and Jesus. The imperial claims much more typically involved a fixed form of the title, "son of god" (e.g., θεοῦ υἱός).

55. Larry W. Hurtado, "Son of God," *DPL*[1] 900–906; idem, "Jesus's Divine Sonship in Paul's Epistle to the Romans," in *Romans and the People of God: Essays in Honor of Gordon D. Fee on the Occasion of His 65th Birthday*, ed. Sven Soderlund and N. T. Wright (Grand Rapids: Eerdmans, 1999), 217–33; republished in Hurtado, *Ancient Jewish Monotheism and Early Christian Devotion*, 407–24, which I cite here.

56. See Rom 1:4, "declared the son of God" (τοῦ ὁρισθέντος υἱοῦ θεοῦ); 2 Cor 1:19, "the Son of God" (ὁ τοῦ θεοῦ . . . υἱός); Gal 2:20 and Eph 4:13, "the Son of God" (τοῦ υἱοῦ τοῦ θεοῦ). For variants in Gal 2:20 and Eph 4:13, see Hurtado, "Jesus's Divine Sonship," 411n17. The remaining thirteen references variously affirm Jesus as "his [God's] Son" (Rom 1:3, 9; 5:10; 8:29; 1 Cor 1:9; Gal 1:16; 4:4, 6; 1 Thess 1:10), "his [God's] own Son" (Rom 8:3, 32), "the Son" (1 Cor 15:28), and "the Son of his [God's] love" (Col 1:13).

57. Hurtado, "Son of God," 903.

58. John 1:34, 49; 5:25; 11:4, 27; 20:31; 1 John 3:8; 4:15; 5:5, 10, 12, 13, 20. In addition, of course, there are the many references to Jesus in John as "the Son," and the well-known reference to him as "the only/unique Son" (τοῦ μονογενοῦς υἱοῦ τοῦ θεοῦ) in John 3:18. The accusation of Jewish opponents in John 19:7, υἱὸν θεοῦ ἑαυτὸν ἐποίησεν, could be translated "he made himself the/a son of God," or "he made himself a son of [a] god."

We have noted that linkage of the two convictions that Jesus is the promised Messiah and the unique Son of God is reflected in the Markan account of the demand of the high priest: "Are you the Messiah, the Son of the Blessed One?" (14:61).[59] As indicated already, it appears that Mark presents the royal, messianic-claimant charge as the basis of Jesus's arraignment before Pilate and Jesus's subsequent crucifixion. But we have noted above that in GMark Jesus's divine sonship carries its own, somewhat distinguishable, force connoting a unique relationship with God. So it seems to me likely that we are to take Jesus's specific affirmation of this claim, which includes his oracular statement that the priests would see him exalted to "the right hand of the Power, and coming with the clouds of heaven" (v. 62) as the offense that generates immediately the charge of "blasphemy" (vv. 63–64).

Conclusion

The presentation of Jesus in GMark both reflects a good deal of earliest Christian beliefs and practices, but it also represents a particular and influential literary work as well. The ministry of Jesus of Nazareth in GMark is the beginning, the foundation of the continuing proclamation of those for whom the author wrote, and Jesus is the pattern for their own life as his followers. Consequently, the story of Jesus is of an authentically human figure, to be sure. But at various points, GMark also reflects and, indeed, explicitly affirms earliest Christian beliefs that Jesus bears a unique and transcendent status, expressed particularly in God's affirmations of Jesus's unique divine sonship.

Of course, it would be anachronistic to read back into GMark the developed "two natures" formulations of later Christian thought. But that kind of later formulation did not appear out of the blue. Texts such as GMark gave later Christian thinkers a presentation of Jesus as genuinely human, and they also put him in a distinctive and unique category that exceeded any prior divine-agent figure or class. In GMark, from the opening lines, Jesus is the unique, earthly embodiment of "the Lord" promised in the prophetic texts cited there. He is God's unique "Son," whose authority exceeds even that of Moses or Elijah. For the readers of GMark, the risen and glorified Jesus was

59. Matthew 26:63 has, "Are you the Messiah, the Son of God?" whereas Luke 22:67 has here only, "Are you the Messiah," adding as a separate question (v. 70), "Are you the Son of God?"

surely included with God in their devotional and worship practices, and he held centrality in their beliefs and gospel message. GMark's presentation of Jesus reflects this high view of Jesus at several crucial points in the text, but it also makes him the foundation and pattern for the proclamation and life of believers. The combination of a narrative of the human Jesus who is also the embodiment and bearer of divine significance comprises the presentation of Jesus in GMark.

Huebenthal Response to Hurtado

SANDRA HUEBENTHAL

Larry Hurtado is known for his extensive work in the New Testament and early Christianity. Over forty years he has published a series of monographs and articles related to the question of how Jesus was received in the earliest documents of Christianity and how early groups of Jesus-followers worshiped Christ. Hurtado's approach to the biblical text can be described as "text-centered historical."

In this volume, Hurtado starts his argument with a first look at the artifact he is dealing with, that is, the text itself. As an artifact of history, without at least some knowledge of its context it is useless, and Hurtado directly addresses this issue: Mark's Gospel is the first written narrative account about Jesus and presents him as having a unique relationship with God, different from any other relationship a human being has enjoyed with God. This is what makes the text *christological*, that is, a statement about the author's beliefs about Jesus *Christ*.

As Mark's Gospel is chronologically the *first* narrative statement, Hurtado continues, it will not be a comprehensive conclusion but one that makes initial and most important points. In other words, Mark is not a complete survey; it only provides one perspective, or one *presentation* of Jesus. Hurtado suggests not thinking of Mark's textualized beliefs about Jesus as *Christology*, but as *presentation*.

Before going deeper into the matter, Hurtado introduces his hermeneutical principle for reading Mark. He deems four aspects crucial for understanding—not only biblical texts but, in fact, all texts. These four aspects are (a) author, (b) situation of the composition (i.e., historical and literary background), (c) genre, and (d) content. Hurtado mentions content first and claims that it is the most important one, but in his argument treats the other three aspects first. This approach is typical for a historical-critical reading. Although the text itself is the center of attention, the scenery must be prepared prior to reading it. In other words, we need its context: *When was the text written, by whom and in what circumstances, and what genre is used?* His goal is to undertake a reading of Mark "in the terms in which it was first read," and to achieve this "it is appropriate to take into account other (particularly prior) evidence of Christian beliefs and practices" (p. 85).

In the essay, Hurtado works his way from environment to content in order to make his argument that Mark does present a unique, distinguishable Christology, while participating in the stream of existing Christian tradition of its time. The novelty is, so to say, that *Christ* and *Son of God* are more closely linked than in the Pauline writings, but still remain distinguishable entities. It is also not entirely clear what these categories mean for Mark and the readers of the text.

Regarding the author, Hurtado makes the case that the author of what we know as the Gospel according to Mark remains opaque: he never speaks in the first person and does not otherwise give away who he is. Whatever we putatively know about "Mark" comes from later tradition and is not important to understand the text itself. Hurtado introduces an author who is invisible behind the text and has no intention of leading the reader into a certain direction by adding his own ideas. The author's goal is to narrate the foundations of his and the readers' beliefs and the foundations of the gospel message.

A narratological approach, as Daniel Kirk and I present it, goes a different way. A narratological analysis would distinguish between author and narrator and demonstrate that the narrator is not as innocent and understated as it seems. Against classic historical-critical assumptions, Mark's text is more than a collection of traditions; it is a carefully crafted, arranged, and presented work. Once one has realized how the narrator guides the reader through the text, it is obvious that this narrator has a purpose and a message, or, in other words, the text has a particular pragmatics in its presentation of Jesus.

Regarding the context of Mark's Gospel, the text is connected to other texts in the early Christian tradition. Hurtado claims that it is part of the movement that understands *euangelion* to refer to the early Christian message about God's redemption through Jesus. There is, nevertheless, a new twist to Mark's presentation of Jesus; it "is not merely to present Jesus as the focus of that continuing proclamation. Jesus's own activities are also the origin, foundation, and beginning of the message about Jesus as 'Lord'" (p. 84). The idea behind the text is thus to show that the risen and exalted Jesus is no other than the Jew from Galilee.

As mentioned above, it is important for Hurtado to provide a possible reading of Mark's Gospel as it was first read. Thus, the question of plausibility of a particular reading scenario is important for the argument. This is the reason why the context of the composition and prior traditions are important, and it explains his concerns with Kirk's argument as he presents it in the text. Hurtado is convinced that early Christianity was organized as a network with an "interactive diversity" and was not a collection of unrelated groups. This network, he argues, must have shared a common framework and tradition.

Hurtado's issue with Kirk's suggestion "to read the text as it was meant to be read by the author, and/or as it was likely to be heard by the audience" (p. 85) is that Hurtado thinks Kirk reads the Gospels in isolation from other early Christian texts. We encounter an argument of plausibility here: "Was GMark . . . ever read . . . ignoring the four decades of Christian traditions of belief and devotional practices?" (p. 85). Hurtado does not deem that likely, which does not say that it is not possible.

The expression "specifically Christian tradition" is worth a second look, as it sounds very convincing at first glance. "By the time of the composition of GMark," Hurtado argues, "we are several decades into the Jesus-movement. By that time, beliefs and ritual practices, and behavioral standards as well, were already traditional and widely known among circles of believers in various locations" (p. 86). It sounds compelling but is, unfortunately, not the case. If it were true, we would not see a struggle for a distinctive identity of Jesus-followers in texts that were written roughly at the same time as Mark, like Colossians, or the need to "correct" some of Mark's ideas a few years or decades later, as in Matthew and Luke or the Pastoral Epistles.

The approximately forty years that have passed between the Jesus event and Mark's Gospel are roughly one generation. We know from the extensive research in cultural studies and social-memory theory that one generation is not enough to establish a solid tradition. On the contrary, the so-called "generational gap" shows that after roughly one generation there is more often than not a moment of crisis when the children take over business from their parents. The moment when a tradition is becoming strong and well-established is not when the second generation takes over from the first but when the fourth generation takes over from the third. It is the great-grandchildren, who have perhaps not even met their grandparents, who prove a custom or tradition to be stable. I would describe these mechanisms in a nutshell as follows: studies of group development and how they evolve over time reveal the important influence of stories. Overall group dynamics are informed by the stories shared by the group. As groups evolve, their collectively held perception of what just happened eventually becomes "the past." At first, the event is thought of as "recent past." Members of the group will have vivid (albeit variegated) recollections of a significant event. This is especially true of experiences that serve as seminal moments for the group's identity. Eventually a group will have no living connection to such memories, only mediated memories. Recollections become more distant and move to the realm of "distant past" and even "far distant past." Individual members of the group no longer have autobiographical recollections of seminal events. Over time, connections to members of the elder generation will be lost, too, along with their direct connections to seminal events. Subsequent generations, however, continue to hold these events in storied form. Moreover, such stories (and what they mean for "today") become crucial for their collective identity. The path from vivid connection to conventionalized cultural knowledge is rather short. It usually only takes three or four generations. As I've written in a previous work,

> On the way from the vivid connection to the founding events to the conventionalized cultural knowledge, a group experiences two typical moments of crisis. The first moment is when the generation of those who have experienced these crucial moments, i.e., the grandparents, slowly hand over responsibility and retire. This usually happens 30–50 years after the events, and this crisis is called "generational gap." When the generation of the grandparents dies and the second generation of the parents moves into retirement, handing over responsibility to their own

> children, a second moment of crisis arises. After roughly 80–120 years, the group moves into what is called "floating gap." Three generations have passed since the beginning when the grandchildren are running the business as grown-ups.[1]

When the third generation (the grandchildren) assumes responsibility and raises their own children (the fourth generation), the development of their narrativized framework becomes clear. In teaching the great-grandchildren through story, the traditions and norms of the group are passed forward. But has the group passed forward fire or ashes? The group will experience a crisis of identity during such transitions as the life of the group finds itself in peril. Such periods of generational transition are especially interesting to sociological study. These periods are marked by negotiation and renegotiation of seminal stories, traditions, norms, and values. The third and fourth generations must decide if and how their "common past" will be remembered and celebrated. Such analysis is especially interesting for New Testament studies because most of these texts were composed in the wake of generational transitions.

What social-memory theory has empirically demonstrated and also crafted into theory is a helpful hermeneutical lens for reading the New Testament times as the formative period of Christianity, and we can also find hints to the mechanism in Hurtado's essay, even in the argument itself. Hurtado rightly refers to "the various 'in-house' terms of early Christian discourse reflect[ing] this connection of GMark to its setting in early Christian circles" (p. 87), but he also must admit that many of these terms were not exactly defined. Mark's text can be read as an attempt to spell out what discipleship means: "The author sought to make the narrative of Jesus a pattern for Christian existence" (p. 89). Obviously, there was a need for such a text, and it was not Mark's only innovation to present it in the shape of a narrative.

In social-memory theory, it is commonly held that the *generational gap* frequently comes with a media change within the discourses of the memory

1. Sandra Huebenthal, "Proclamation Rejected, Truth Confirmed: Reading John 12:37–44 in a Social Memory Theoretical Framework," in *Biblical Interpretation in Early Christian Gospels, Volume 4: The Gospel of John*, ed. Thomas R. Hatina, LNTS 613 (London: T&T Clark, 2020), 183–200 (185–86). For a comprehensive introduction into the underlying theory and general hermeneutical reflections, cf. Huebenthal, *Reading Mark's Gospel*, 85–178.

group. Hurtado's thoughts about Mark's Gospel as *bios* can be read in this light. Although Mark's Gospel is not a full-blown *bios* of its time, Hurtado, along with others, receives it as at least a *bios*-type, or a "quasi-biographical account of Jesus" that narrates his story "from baptism to resurrection" (p. 89). Here, too, someone who is versed in this approach detects the mechanisms and media of social-memory theory. When Hurtado writes that "again, in the case of GMark, the aim was clearly to relate the historical inception and foundation of the continuing activity of gospel-proclamation. The *bios* genre likely seemed a particularly useful one for making this kind of point. For it gave readers, not a treatise containing a set of christological reflections . . . but, instead, a vivid account of Jesus himself that related his actions and words in a fast-paced narrative" (p. 92). This sounds a lot like Mark was an identity-forming text, designed to be the founding story of Jesus-followers and providing a clear orientation for them both as individual Jesus-followers and as a group. The Gospel can be read as a first draft of a foundational text for Jesus-followers.

Part of such an attempt to provide a framework for *Christian* identity construction was to engage with the ideas about Jesus that were already current. This includes questions about the composition and organization of the groups of Jesus-followers as well as their practices and rituals, but for the sake of the argument, we stay with the ideas about Jesus. If, as Hurtado suggests, the earliest Christians were a close network with an interactive diversity, then it was all the more necessary to have a common foundation. One aspect of this would be a shared idea of who Jesus was for them and how this related to the general idea of the early Christian message about God's redemption through Jesus. As Hurtado states in somewhat lofty words, "Early Christians were trying to find and agree how to portray Jesus's relationship with God for the next few centuries" (p. 93). In such a moment, it is necessary to make a statement about this central point in a foundational text, and a narrative analysis of Mark's Gospel demonstrates that the Markan narrator is very explicit about making such a statement. It might not be a "definite statement" in the sense of a creed or a dogma, but it is difficult to argue that Mark leaves it entirely open as to what the nature of Jesus's relationship with God is. If I understand Hurtado correctly, the terms *Christology* and *nature of Jesus's relationship with God* describe basically the same thing.

Indeed, Mark makes such a statement. It is not a statement in the sense of an ultimate or final creedal decision, especially not one that answers to later theological questions, but it is a theological statement. Mark's addition to tradition, to phrase it in Hurtado's terms, is that he connects the two titles "Messiah" and "Son of God" much more closely than previous tradition and does so in the form of a narrative. *Christ* (or *Messiah*) is "a standard reverential way of designating Jesus" (p. 94), and Mark joins this conversation. Bringing it closer to "Son of God" reveals the unique nature of the Messiah's relationship with God. Since the first line of Mark's Gospel is "the beginning of the gospel of Jesus Christ, Son of God," then both titles are not brought together on the level of the characters or the narrative but on the level of the narrator. One could see it as a clear theological statement on the part of Mark. In Hurtado's words, "GMark seems to me to use 'the Messiah' to position Jesus vis-à-vis God's people and God's eschatological purposes as the unique royal agent in fulfillment of messianic hopes. The references to Jesus's divine sonship, however, are in statements that relate him to God, affirming Jesus's unique validity, authority, and intimacy with God. That is, Jesus is Messiah ('Christ') and the unique Son of God. The two claims are united in his person, but each one is a distinguishable claim" (pp. 98–99).

What this says about Jesus's divine status is a different matter. Hurtado is very careful not to read Jesus's divinity into the text: "The emphasis in GMark is placed on the *idea* of Jesus's divine sonship, not on any particular title or fixed terminology to express it" (p. 100). If this is meant to indicate that the ascription of a divine nature for Jesus is a later development, I agree with Hurtado. As I phrase it in my own essay, Mark opens doors, but the questions concerning what *Messiah* and *divine sonship* mean are not (yet) entirely sorted out. I also agree with Hurtado that we do not find a two-nature doctrine, not even its precursor, in Mark's Gospel. With *Christ* and *Son of God*, Mark brings two distinguishable claims closer together and thus contributes to the ongoing struggle to understand who Jesus is.

In this struggle, Mark's text, as ambiguous as it is, could be used by different groups and for their different ideas. As stated earlier, Mark should rather be read as a first attempt for a foundational narrative designed to provide frames for Christian-identity constructions. That does not mean that it is solving every question, and it does not mean that there are already stable traditions. With an ever-growing group of New Testament scholars, I am cautious to use the term "Christian tradition" as early as the time when Mark was written. When Acts introduces the term Χριστιανοί for the Jesus-followers in Antioch (Acts 11:26), this rather mirrors the introduction of the expression for Luke's own times. It might be time to accept that in the first and second century, *Christianity* was not the stable entity that is sometimes pictured. The notion of stable and harmonious growth as it is described in Acts is written with hindsight and provides another—and later—foundational story providing frames for identity construction.

What I like a lot about Hurtado's argument is that it works from the text and the environment of the text and apart from the early Christian stream of tradition, operating without additional assumptions from outside the text and is very clear about the danger or reading later theological developments into the text. It shares that with Kirk's approach, and one could see both essays as complementary in this regard.

I agree with Hurtado that Mark provides a model for the identity of Jesus-followers. In that regard, Mark is an identity-forming text. However, I neither agree that Mark needs to be read as a *bios* nor understand what the genre *bios* (especially the explanation that Mark can be seen within "the broad category" of *bios*) adds to understanding the text and its "christological profile."[2] A narrative from baptism to burial is hardly considered a *bios*, in my perception. It sounds more like a narrative about a particular person, his impact, and what he and his impact mean for a particular group of people.

Especially if the proclamation of Jesus and the proclamation about Jesus are closely interwoven in Mark's Gospel—and I agree with Hurtado on that, too—then the term "*bios*-shaped" seems to have little use. The claim is to have "a narrative . . . with a strong historical concern" (p. 90), which at the same time exhibits a particular pragmatics; that is, it provides a model for discipleship in memory of Jesus. Thus, is the text more about history or about Christian identity? Would a historical account provide the desired identity, or does it not rather need an interpreted version of the events and experiences to provide people with such a blueprint? Especially as regards the details Hurtado mentions. Do they not rather point into Mark's own times than into Jesus's times?

2. For a more nuanced critique, cf. Werner H. Kelber, "On 'Mastering the Genre,'" in *Modern and Ancient Literary Criticism of the Gospels: Continuing the Debate on Gospel Genre(s)*, ed. Robert Matthew Calhoun, David P. Moessner, and Tobias Nicklas, WUNT 451 (Tübingen: Mohr Siebeck, 2020), 57–76.

I am also cautious about what Mark "wanted to avoid" in his text as regards theological statements. Regarding the baptism scene, I am not convinced that "GMark . . . wanted to avoid precisely this notion of adoption with reference to Jesus. In short, this is not an adoption scene" (p. 96). If this was Mark's idea, it was at least not executed clearly enough, as we have evidence of early Christian groups doing exactly that: reading Mark's baptism as an adoption scene. Matthew and Luke made sure that this was not possible by slightly altering the scene, and especially by adding infancy narratives with clear statements about Jesus being the Son of God on a non-adoption basis. Thus, I would not say that Mark wanted to avoid this notion but that Christian tradition has in the course of time consciously decided not to understand Mark's baptism scene as an adoption and ruled out Adoptionism as heresy in Nicaea (325 CE). Conversely, this means that it is possible to read the scene that way, and that it had happened in the Christian community.

Intriguingly, these slight adjustments do not weaken but rather strengthen Hurtado's argument. Even though we can't get into Mark's head and find out what the author wanted to express and can only guess about how the text was received by its original addressees, the pragmatics carved out by the combination of historical and narratological methods used in a memory-theoretical frame are similar. Mark's Gospel, as the first narrative account of Jesus-followers, is written in a new genre and is aimed at providing a foundation for understanding Jesus and for living as a true disciple after the Lord's example, as well as providing a foundation for continuing proclamation. As a first account, it is concerned with connecting the human figure Jesus of Nazareth with the belief of the exalted Christ, without solving every question about the status and the nature of Jesus as *Christ* and *Son of God.*

Kirk Response to Hurtado

J. R. DANIEL KIRK

Larry Hurtado lays out a comprehensive approach to interpreting Mark's Gospel: an assessment of the author (unknown), the setting of the text (early Christianity with its common pool of beliefs about Jesus), and its genre (*bios*, though with significant differences). The question of context is especially important for his project, and he begins by drawing the crucial line connecting Mark's contents and the proclamation of the early church: "This resurrected and exalted Lord Jesus [of early church proclamation] is also the historical Galilean Jesus" (p. 84).

As this posture of reading Mark within the context of the early church unfolds, however, Hurtado finds himself in the unenviable position of both believing that the early church held convictions about Jesus as preexistent and having to interpret a text that demonstrates no such ideas about Jesus. The essay thus invites three lines of response. First, I will point out how carefully Hurtado has chosen his words so as not to say more than the text will allow, but in so doing leaves us with little more than a fully human Jesus. Second, I will take up the challenge of reading Mark in light of our earliest evidence regarding the church's convictions and practices; specifically, I will offer an interpretation of the baptism scene, and the divine declaration of Jesus's sonship, in light of other baptismal traditions. Third, having demonstrated the continuity between Jesus's baptism and that of early Christian baptizands, we will revisit Mark's depiction of Jesus as Son of God and see how the story Mark tells is one of a glorified human and not an eternal or preexistent Son.

Rising to Expectations?

Larry Hurtado demonstrates careful scholarship throughout his work. This includes an admirable restraint that rarely, if ever, overreaches when making a claim for a text. However, this also means that at times we find vague language that could lead a reader to draw a conclusion that Hurtado himself is unwilling to directly articulate himself.

The clearest example one finds of this tendency has been noted above. On page 96 in footnote 45, Hurtado demurs from Michael Peppard's interpretation of the baptism as an "adoption" scene in part because of "early Christian traditions of Jesus's preexistence that had been common coinage for several decades." But in Hurtado's exegesis of the passage itself, we hear "this is not an adoption scene" but a "private, divine acclamation and commissioning," and an "affirm[ation] of Jesus's divine sonship" (p. 96). Absent is any statement of what divine sonship means or when it came into effect. The reader is left to draw the conclusion that Jesus has a sonship through preexistence with God prior to the timeline of the story, but this conclusion Hurtado himself does not articulate.

Similarly, Hurtado wishes to draw a strong line of demarcation between the type of being that Jesus is and the types of beings that Moses and Elijah are, as depicted in the transfiguration scene. And yet we read in his interpretation that the glory revealed there is not one that Jesus had prior to his time on earth but is, instead, "a preview of the eschatological glory that Jesus . . . is to receive and exhibit" (pp. 96–97). In other words, this is the glory borne by the resurrected Jesus. It is a revelation of Jesus in Jesus's post-crucifixion cosmic lordship. To say that Jesus in his heavenly glory occupies a category "populated by Jesus alone" is no argument for a divine Jesus or that Jesus is something other than a particular kind of idealized human figure. Only Jesus is the Lord and Messiah—we might say, the king of God's kingdom. Only Jesus is the Son of Man who, after being given authority on earth, nonetheless is rejected, suffers, is killed, and raised again on the third day, and will then come in glory. All of this speaks to Jesus's uniqueness, which Hurtado has done well to capture for readers, and none of it speaks to preexistence or divinity, neither of which Hurtado is willing to directly ascribe to Mark's Jesus. The question is not whether Jesus is different from Moses and Elijah but rather what this difference entails.

Hurtado's exegesis does not qualify what this difference might be in any precise fashion.

This brings us to the discussion of Jesus as "beloved Son," which we will explore in greater depth below. In his discussion of Mark 12:35–37, Hurtado suggests that Mark's readers know to resolve the tension between the Messiah as David's son and the Messiah as David's lord by understanding that the Messiah "is actually God's unique 'beloved Son'" (p. 98). This is a good reading of Mark, and nothing about that title as deployed by the evangelist suggests that it entails preexistence or divinity.

So what, exactly, does Hurtado see as the content Mark gives for someone bearing this title? It is a testimony to "Jesus's unique validity, authority, and intimacy with God" (p. 98). What are we to make of these three categorizations? References to Jesus's sonship typically come from others: the narrator, God, demons, a Roman centurion. First, then, because this title is given by God, it certainly adds validity to the claims that Jesus makes for himself and that the narrative makes on his behalf. Second, it is likely that this title connotes authority since it is given alongside reception of the Spirit that is later pointed to as the source of Jesus's power to exorcise and, by proxy, to teach (Mark 3:22–30). Validity and authority are claims that Jesus makes for himself using the title "the Son of Man" (better rendered "the Human One") and that others make on his behalf by referring to him as God's Son. To be a valid and authorized agent of God's coming reign, however, is not necessarily to be anything more than a specially empowered human.

Third, Hurtado twice uses the word "intimacy" to describe what he sees as Jesus's distinct relationship with God. It is difficult to know what to make of this word or what its connotations might be for Mark's Christology. It is a word foreign to most biblical literature in depictions of divine-human relations or Jesus's unique connection to God. There are ways that John's Gospel depicts Jesus's unique knowledge of God or communion with God prior to coming to earth that may well fit the bill. But Hurtado offers no argument or conclusion regarding either what intimacy might mean or how this would stand as an argument for a divine Christ rather than a human agent possessing God's Spirit. A human empowered by God's Spirit may well know the will of God and be empowered for such works as we see unfolding on the pages of the Gospel of Mark. Readers of Mark such as myself, who see Mark's Jesus playing a unique role in God's saving work within the coming kingdom of God, can affirm along with Hurtado that Jesus has a "unique divine sonship" without drawing the conclusion that the specific thing that makes it unique is preexistence or some other quality of divinity. It is important to note that Hurtado does not articulate such a conclusion, either.

Baptism in the Early Church and Mark 1

The bulk of Hurtado's christological discussion concerns Jesus as Son of God, and the foundational text for this title in the Gospel of Mark is the baptism scene. Moreover, Hurtado has asked that we read and interpret Mark's Gospel in light of what we know about the practices and convictions of the early church. If we read Mark's baptism scene in conversation with other early discussions of baptism, we discover a network of early Christian convictions that connect divine sonship, the Spirit, and the death of Jesus. The twist, however, is that these are not depicted as the exclusive purview of Jesus but are facets of Jesus's identity that other humans share. Such data push toward the twin recognition that Jesus does have a unique role to play in establishing the story of the people of God and that he plays this role in ontological continuity with other humans and not as a preexistent divine being.

First, in Galatians 3 Paul unveils a convoluted argument that links together reception of the Spirit, baptism, and sonship.[1] The purpose of Paul's argument is to demonstrate that those who have the Spirit are God's children—which is also to say, they are Abraham's offspring—without their needing to be circumcised. At the climactic moment of his argument, Paul says that the reason all the Galatians are sons of God is that they have been baptized into Christ (Gal 3:26–27; English readers should note that the Greek of v. 27 has an explanatory conjunction, "for" (γάρ), that is left untranslated in many English versions). Moreover, this sonship is further associated with reception of the Spirit. The Spirit marks "adoption as sons" (4:5), is called "the Spirit of his [God's] Son" (v. 6), and cries out "*Abba*, Father" (v. 6), even as Jesus does in Mark 14:36. From this we learn that

1. The term "sonship" has the unfortunate disadvantage of being a male term describing a state into which both men and women would have claimed. For the purposes of this essay, retaining the word "son" is meant to help English-speaking readers hold the connection between Jesus as "Son of God" and Christians as children ("sons") of God.

reception of the Spirit and baptism are distinguishable aspects of the same reality: it is when and how the baptized come to be related to God in a way that they were not previously. Moreover, this new relationship is one of adoption. In terms of having God as a Father, this new status puts the baptizand on equal footing with Jesus in being able to call out to God, "*Abba*, Father."

Significantly, in Galatians these implications of baptism are all derivative. It is not the case that Jesus is simply the first in a series of people who all have the same experience. Instead, those who are baptized come into union with Jesus in such a way that things that belonged to and/or were true of Jesus come to be shared in by his followers. Jesus plays a unique role that the others do not play: he is the "one seed" of Abraham (Gal 3:16), the Christ (v. 16) and Lord who defines the family.

Paul thus depicts Jesus as one who has been empowered to determine and define the destiny of an entire people. Jesus is given the Spirit who ushers other people into the same sonship that he himself enjoys, so that, as Paul says in Romans 8:29, "he might be the firstborn among many brothers and sisters." What we have here is a both/and of special role alongside shared humanity that determines Jesus's place in the baptismal story of the early church. The Spirit and sonship that are Jesus's first and foremost also become the possession of those who are baptized in his name.

Within such a matrix of convictions in the early church, the most likely interpretation of the baptism scene in Mark is that Jesus is the first to receive what he comes to hold in trust for his later followers. Just as they receive the Spirit of adoption as God's children ("sons") once they are baptized, so too does Jesus receive the adoption as God's Son while he receives the Spirit's anointing. The baptism is not a declaration of what has always been the case but a true instance of "becoming" a son of God in a way that Jesus previously was not. For Mark's Jesus, this entails being the Human One; for Paul this entails Jesus being the second and last Adam.

A further critical component to early Christian convictions concerning baptism is that it is a participation in Jesus's own death. Paul opens a conversation about baptism in Romans 6:3 by saying, "Do you not know that all of us who have been baptized into Christ Jesus have been baptized into his death?" This touches off an argument about Jesus's followers having a share in the resurrection life of Jesus, thereby freed for the reign of God and freed from the reign of sin (Rom 6:3–14).

We find an allusion to this idea of baptism as a representation of death in an interchange between Jesus and his followers in Mark 10. After James and John come asking Jesus for seats at his right and left hand in glory, Jesus in turn asks them, "Are you able to drink the cup that I drink, or be baptized with the baptism I am baptized with?" (Mark 10:38). In response to their pursuit of glory, Jesus has invoked the road of suffering and death that he has just predicted for the third time (Mark 10:32–34). Mark, then, shows evidence of sharing in the early Christian conviction that baptism is a symbol of Jesus's death.

Confirmation of this is found in the most direct allusion we find to God's words, "You are my beloved Son." As Leroy Huizenga has shown, these words find their closest scriptural parallel in the description of Isaac as Abraham's beloved son in the context of Abraham being called to sacrifice his son.[2] Thus, while the "sonship" described in the baptism scene likely does carry royal connotations, what is also on display is the particular task assigned to Jesus as Christ and Son of God. The role Jesus will play is inseparable from his death on the cross.

In light of both the early Christian tradition about baptism and Jesus's death and the probable allusion to Genesis 22:2, it is likely that a first-century Christian reader would see Jesus's baptism as an anticipation of the death that they know awaits him at the end of the story. As such, the particular significance of the words spoken by the divine voice come into sharper focus: the divine delight comes from the willingness of the Son to be obedient to the point of death. And so the "Son of God" title, borne by Jesus as he is anointed to his task and empowered by the Spirit, is further delineated in terms of death, even as the readers who have been called "sons of God" through reception of the Spirit and baptism are called to take up their crosses and follow Jesus along that same road (Mark 8:34).

If we, in this way, choose to read the baptism scene by taking our cues from the early church as Hurtado has suggested, we end up with a rich christological palette that lacks any suggestion of divine ontology or preexistence. Jesus is God's beloved Son, anointed and empowered by the Spirit. As such, he is receiving in himself what he will later bestow on his followers: the Spirit and sonship. Because these are shared, it is highly unlikely that

---

2. Leroy A. Huizenga, *The New Isaac: Tradition and Intertextuality in the Gospel of Matthew*, NovTSup (Leiden: Brill, 2009).

Jesus's possession of them should be taken to indicate that he occupies a different category of being from his followers. At the same time, the fact that he is, in Mark's story and the early church, the Christ, and that he is the one from whom others partake of these identity markers, no less clearly signals that he occupies a unique category, different from his followers and those who have come before. Christ is the Messiah who must die; in so doing, he demonstrates the nature of discipleship—Paul would say of divine sonship—for those who are his "mother and sisters and brothers" (Mark 3:33–35).

Mark's Story of the Son of God

Taking stock of the baptism scene is an ideal primer for revisiting how Jesus as God's Son functions within Mark's narrative. Here, greater attention to narrative dynamics can provide a more accurate exposition of the Christology behind such references to Jesus's relationship to God.

We have said most of what needs saying about the baptism scene. However, one more point is in order. Hurtado resists the idea that sonship is in any way conferred at the baptism. While looking at the baptismal theology of the early church casts significant doubt on this conclusion, biblical precedents make it unlikely in the extreme. Hurtado does well to reference Psalm 2:7, a coronation psalm, in which the Davidic king is anointed with the divine declaration, "You are my son" (see also Ps 89:26–27). This, then, opens up to us the biblical royal theology that includes stories of Saul and David receiving the Spirit when they are anointed to their kingships (1 Sam 10:1–13; 16:13). Jesus becomes Son of God in the sense of being anointed and appointed to royal office. This is a title given for the purpose of playing a particular role that will involve his death.

With this first scene in place, we then turn to the second divine declaration of Jesus's sonship. Hurtado has rightly pointed out that the divine voice directs the disciples to Jesus with the strong admonition, "This is my Son, whom I love. Listen to him!" (Mark 9:7). In the flow of Mark's narrative, this is the first scene after Peter's confession at Caesarea Philippi. In that immediately anterior story, Peter famously does not listen to Jesus. After Peter deploys the title "Christ" to identify Jesus, Jesus prophesies his own death for the first time, after which Peter rebukes him (Mark 8:28–33). Thus, when the divine voice reprimands the disciples and tells them to listen to Jesus, it is not an indication that Peter is wrongly trying to listen to other "idealized humans," and the divine voice tells him he needs to listen to someone ontologically distinct, as Hurtado might be taken to imply. Instead, the divine voice is reprimanding Peter for not listening to Jesus's declaration about the nature of his remaining mission.

In the divine declaration at the baptism scene, we saw the peculiar conjunction of an exalted status before God ("Son of God" as Spirit-empowered royalty) and the death that awaits Jesus at the end of the story ("beloved Son" as Isaac figure). When the divine voice repeats this title, it is at the exact moment of the story in which Peter has affirmed the royalty of Jesus but rejected the call to suffering. On the Mount of Transfiguration, the divine voice not only reiterates this peculiar title of glory and suffering but directs us to Jesus as the one who understands its connotations. Those connotations, in turn, Jesus spelled out when he began to predict his coming suffering, death, and resurrection.

Further confirmation of this point is found in Jesus's next words to the three who were with him: they are not to tell what they have seen until the Son of Man has been raised (9:9). What the disciples have seen is, as Hurtado notes, an anticipation of the glory that awaits Jesus after he is raised from the dead. The divine voice confirms that this glory will be Jesus's in the way that Jesus has predicted and not in any other manner that Peter might have in mind for the kingdom of God to arrive.

These two moments of divine declaration set the stage well for the parable of the wicked tenants in Mark 12:1–12. First, we read of a series of messengers "sent" by the vineyard owner to collect what is due. It is important to recognize that all the messengers are "sent" by the owner, who is a stand-in for God. The son in the parable is not "sent" in some categorically different way that would indicate preexistence in contrast to the others who came before him. Second, Jesus is represented by the "son" in the story, in contrast to the "servants." This contrast fits the narrative of Mark exactly. We have already read of the prophet John who baptizes but does not receive any sort of Spirit-anointing or declaration of sonship. In contrast, Jesus receives such an anointing and appointment when John baptizes him. Jesus is, in fact, Son of God in a way that the others are not. Finally, divine sonship entails rejection and death at the hands of the religious leaders—but subsequent reversal of this death and glorification by God. The narrative of the parable is simply the narrative of Jesus, the Son of Man, that readers have seen implied in the "Son of God" declarations and anticipated in Jesus's "Son of Man" passion predictions.

Finally, we find Jesus called "Son of God" at his death. The entire crucifixion scene is thick with dramatic irony, as the Romans mock Jesus as "king of the Jews" in such a way as to show that, to their minds, he is no king at all. However, for the reader of Mark, the death itself is the means by which Jesus comes into his kingdom and glory. It thus comes about that over Jesus's head is an interpretive key to the whole scene that the characters themselves are too blind to apprehend, a sign that reads, "The king of the Jews" (Mark 15:26). Paradoxically, it is precisely this murder that is ushering Jesus into his kingship, affirming the prophetic claims he has made for himself. Jesus then "expires," and, upon seeing how he died, a Roman centurion declares, "Surely this man was a son of God" (or "son of a god"; Mark 15:39). The way this is framed, Jesus's death becomes the affirmation, not the denial, of his divine sonship.

Besides naming Jesus "Son of God," Mark's narrative provides us with several clues that the crucifixion should be read alongside the baptism scene. These two scenes each contain one of the two uses of the word σχίζω (meaning "to tear apart") in the whole Gospel (see 1:10; 15:38). Moreover, each scene evokes the prophet Elijah (1:6; 15:35–36). In stark contrast to Jesus receiving the Spirit in 1:10, Jesus breathes out his breath/spirit as he dies in 15:39. Thus, for the reader who sees Jesus's divine sonship conferred at his baptism as a royal title, empowering him for his work and yet mysteriously anticipating his death, the crucifixion is a perfect bookend, affirming the royal title through the paradoxical powerlessness of Spirit-losing death.

Mark's Jesus

In sum, I would invite Mark's readers to trust Mark and the story he tells. Hurtado's essay demonstrates how precarious the ground is for those who would attempt to find a Christology of divine ontology or preexistence in Mark's Gospel. We can at times find warrant for nudges beyond what we would expect to be possible for an exalted human, but at those points Mark gives us greater cause to readjust our expectations of what is humanly possible for one such as Jesus than to readjust our understanding of the character of Jesus as one who came down from above. In Mark, it is not Jesus but the Spirit of God who comes down from above. Jesus is Son of God as he is the baptized, Spirit-receiving Messiah with a mission that includes giving his life as a ransom for many. Jesus is Son of God as one whose future holds radiant heavenly glory. In light of this, we do well to see Jesus as Son of God and Jesus as Son of Man as two different perspectives on the same matrix of Jesus's messianic vocation. Empowered by God for his ministry on earth, the Christ must nonetheless be rejected by the religious establishment, suffer, die, be raised on the third day, and then ascend to the right hand of God, from which location he will return with heavenly glory. In the end, Mark's Jesus will come from above, but this is part of his eschatological future rather than his hoary past.

Winn Response to Hurtado

ADAM WINN

Let me begin by saying that it is with great sadness of heart that I respond to this fine essay by Larry Hurtado. His recent passing is a great loss of both an exemplary scholar and of a truly kind and caring person. In 2009, I presented my first academic paper to the Mark Group at the national meeting of the Society of Biblical Literature. The paper was ambitious and pushed against the grain of major trends in Markan scholarship (somewhat misguidedly, I would admit today!). It received some harsh criticism, and rightfully so. However, Larry Hurtado, a faithful participant in the group, was both kind and generous to the young scholar I was, and after the session took time to discuss ways I might improve my work. His advice was tremendously helpful, resulting in a number of publications, but his kindness to me made the bigger impact. For this kindness, I am forever grateful.

In the present essay, "Mark's Presentation of Jesus," true to form, Hurtado has provided us with a careful and thoughtful treatment of both Mark's Gospel and Christology. There is much in this essay that I agree with, and I will begin with these points of agreements. With Hurtado, I agree that it important to establish the identity of the most probable intended readers of Mark's Gospel, and that the text be read from the knowledge base that such readers would have possessed. While one can certainly try to read Mark's Gospel apart from such knowledge, as it seems the other two essays have, to varying degrees, sought to do, these strategies seem to produce readings that to one degree or another appear foreign to the first readers of Mark. With Hurtado, I agree that Mark's first readers were Christians and that they brought to their reading of Mark's Gospel a Christian understanding of terms like "gospel," "Christ," and "Son of God." They also brought to Mark's Gospel their own understanding of Jesus and the worship practices that shaped such understanding. I agree with Hurtado that Mark's Gospel itself presupposes that just such an understanding and experience will be brought to the text. I also agree with Hurtado that the evangelist chose the genre of *bios* to convey in a vivid way the beginning of the story of God's redemption through Jesus, a story with which Mark's readers were already familiar. Beyond these shared starting points, there is much in Hurtado's reading of the content of Mark itself that I also affirm. I agree that Mark clearly depicts Jesus as a human being. I agree that Jesus is rightly identified as the "Lord" in Mark's citation of Isaiah 40:3, that Jesus possesses divine authority, including the authority to forgive sins, that Jesus calms the winds and the waves not like a devout human being but like God, and that the Markan Jesus and God are linked together in an unprecedented way.

Despite these agreements, there are noteworthy places where I disagree with Hurtado's conclusions regarding various details in the Markan text, as well as a general dissatisfaction I feel with his ultimate conclusion regarding Jesus's identity in Mark. I will begin with the former and conclude with the latter. First, I disagree with Hurtado's conclusion that Jesus's transfiguration does not reveal his current identity but rather is a reflection of his future eschatological glory (a conclusion that Hurtado actually shares with Kirk). I do not see how the narrative of Mark leads to such a conclusion, and I wish Hurtado would have explained his rationale more thoroughly. A *prima facie* reading of the transfiguration seems to depict an unveiling of Jesus's current heavenly identity. This identity is closely associated with his identity as God's beloved Son, an identity that is clearly possessed by Jesus *currently* in the pericope. Many of those who understand the transfiguration as a foreshadowing of future glory often seem more motivated by a desire to overcome what appears to be an obstacle to a divine or preexistent identity for the Markan Jesus than by narrative clues from the text. Thus, it is particularly surprising that Hurtado opts for such a reading. Given Hurtado's commitment to reading Mark's Gospel within the early Jesus movement, a movement in which there is evidence that Jesus was perceived as a preexistent heavenly figure (John 1:1–5; 1 Cor 8:6; Phil 2:6–11; Col 1:15–20, etc.), I am curious why he does not bring such an understanding of Jesus to this text.

I also disagree with Hurtado's link between Jesus's affirmation of divine sonship, understood by Hurtado as communicating the unique and intimate relationship between Jesus and God, and the subsequent charge of blasphemy. There seems to be little reason to conclude that a claim to a unique or unprecedented relationship with God would so naturally and so quickly be linked to blasphemy of the one God of Israel, unless that relationship implied a claim to share in the identity of the one God. To claim unique closeness to God, as long as one is not infringing on the identity of God, is not, as far as I can tell, grounds for the charge of blasphemy. Thus, it seems there must be more in Jesus's response to merit this charge, such as Jesus's use of "I am" and his identification with the heavenly (divine?) Son of Man, both of which are brought to bear on the meaning and nature of divine sonship.

For Hurtado, the Markan Jesus acts like God, is identified as the Lord of Isaiah 40:3, and possesses an unprecedented intimacy with God. Hurtado even says in his conclusion, "For the readers of GMark, the risen and glorified Jesus was surely included with God in their devotional and worship practices" (p. 103). Those familiar will Hurtado's entire body of work will understand that Hurtado is claiming that Jesus was worshiped alongside the God of Israel by the earliest Christians. Throughout his essay, Hurtado seems to bring Jesus to the very point of being identified as divine or the God of Israel and pulls up just short of doing so. Despite the numerous agreements I share with Hurtado, it is this hesitancy that leaves me ultimately unsatisfied with Hurtado's conclusion regarding Mark's presentation of Jesus. In fact, apart from Hurtado's commitment to Mark's earliest readers being Christians who would have incorporated Jesus into their worship of the one God of Israel, the Jesus that emerges from his reading of Mark's Gospel could seemingly be fit into a slightly nuanced version of Kirk's category of an "idealized human figure." Hurtado's understanding of the Markan Jesus as a person that bears divine authority fits with Kirk's understanding of Jesus as the final, eschatological human agent of God who acts on God's behalf. Hurtado's understanding of Jesus being identified as the Lord of Isaiah 40:3 could be explained by Kirk's understanding of God being present through a human agent. Hurtado's understanding of Jesus as one unprecedented in intimacy and closeness with God may push Kirk's understanding of Jesus as an "idealized human" a bit, but even for Kirk, though Jesus fits into this category, his equal within it is hard to find.

The similarity I see between both Kirk's and Hurtado's understanding of the Markan Jesus leads me to question just how far apart these two interpreters really are in their evaluations of Mark's Christology. To pursue this line of thought, it will be helpful to look more closely at Hurtado's understanding of early Christ devotion and its origins. Throughout his work, Hurtado understands the Jewish God in terms of strict singularity ("exclusive monotheism" is language often used by Hurtado, though not in his essay in the present project),[1] and thus he sees no precedent in Judaism for the Christian practice of worshiping Jesus. For Hurtado, Christian worship of Jesus alongside the one God of Israel is a novel development in monotheism, one that arises out of Christian experience with the risen and glorified Christ. It is from this experience and subsequent practice of worship that Christian thinking about the divinity of Jesus grows and develops. Thus, for Hurtado, divine identification follows devotional practice, and not vice versa. Hurtado is reluctant to identify Jesus with or as the God of Israel, but folds Jesus into the worship of that God. What results, according to Hurtado, is a novel binitarianism rather than the worship of two gods; though in Hurtado's work the relationship between God and Jesus as well as the nature of Jesus (i.e., divine or human) remains ambiguous.

Given the ambiguity that exists regarding Jesus's identity in Hurtado's reconstruction of the Christ devotion of the earliest Christians, what precludes the Markan Jesus, as understood by Kirk, from being a recipient of Christ devotion as understood by Hurtado? It cannot be Kirk's claim that the Markan Jesus is human because Hurtado clearly affirms Jesus's humanity as well. Perhaps by placing Jesus in the category of "idealized human," Hurtado might conclude that Kirk is inappropriately placing Jesus too closely to other exalted beings that did not receive worship. Yet, if I am reading Kirk correctly, though Jesus fits in the category of "idealized human," he is the greatest within the category. Such seems evident when Kirk claims, "Following in the tradition of Jewish mediators, but with a strong claim that Jesus is the ultimate, eschatological agent of God's visitation and deliverance, Jesus stands in for God such that how one responds to Jesus is how one responds to the God who sent him" (p. 141). Additionally, for Kirk, this "idealized human" Jesus will, after his death, be resurrected, exalted to

1. For example, see Larry W. Hurtado, "'Ancient Jewish Monotheism' in the Hellenistic and Roman Periods," *JAJ* 4.3 (2013): 379–400.

heavenly glory (which is apparently God's own glory), and seated at the right hand of God. For Hurtado, it is early Christian encounter with just such an exalted and glorified Jesus that results in Christ devotion. I am having a difficult time seeing the line between Kirk's understanding of Jesus as the pinnacle of the "idealized human" who is exalted to glory and Hurtado's Jesus who was the object of early Christian devotion. If divine identification did not precede the worship of Jesus, as Hurtado argues, why could the pinnacle of "idealized human" identity not precede it? It seems to me that the readers of Mark, proposed by Hurtado, could find the Markan Jesus, as understood by Kirk, to be consistent with the Jesus of their devotional practice. Put another way, I do not see how Hurtado's insistence on reading Mark from the perspective of an early Christian produces a Jesus that is in any way significantly different from the Markan Jesus adduced by Kirk.

I am actually surprised that the essays by both Kirk and Hurtado are not altogether more different than I perceive them to be, as I anticipated that Hurtado's reading would be much closer to my own. I anticipated that Hurtado's affirmation of Christian worship of Jesus would result in his affirmation of a clear divine Christology in Mark. Yet, again, differing reconstructions of Second Temple Judaism, particularly Jewish conceptions of the one God of Israel, lead to different assessments of Mark's Jesus. I perceive a clear precedent in Judaism for Jesus's divine identity and worship, where Hurtado does not. Interestingly, it seems to me that the Markan Jesus I propose fits quite well with the Christian worship practices for which Hurtado has spent much of his career advocating; better, in fact, than the Markan Jesus that Hurtado himself presents here.

I will close by saying that I would have liked to have seen more detailed treatment of Markan pericopes that might contribute to identifying Jesus as divine; for example, the episodes of Jesus forgiving sins, walking on water, claiming that no one is good but God alone, or the various Markan uses of "Lord" in reference to Jesus. I recognize that these essays cannot be exhaustive, but I was left wanting more on these and other Markan stories. Unfortunately, with the passing of Larry Hurtado, that wanting will not be satisfied in this present age, but I look forward to the day the conversation can continue in the next.

Rejoinder

CHRIS KEITH

With sadness, I have agreed to take the place of Larry Hurtado, my *Doktorvater*, in offering a brief rejoinder to the responses to his essay on the Gospel of Mark's presentation of Jesus. Larry's passing in November 2019 was a great loss to New Testament scholarship in general and this volume in particular. To my knowledge, his essay and responses to the other contributors were his final scholarly contributions. Prior to his death, he and I discussed this project, so I can claim a limited amount of familiarity with his thoughts, though I remain acutely aware of my inadequacy when it comes to taking his place in this regard. I have learned much from the dialogue between Hurtado, Winn, Kirk, and Huebenthal. In keeping with the design of the book, I restrict my comments to the responses to Hurtado's essay.

Rejoinder to Sandra Huebenthal

Sandra Huebenthal responds to Hurtado's essay more specifically from the perspective of social memory theory. She agrees with Hurtado that Mark's Gospel is "ambiguous," that Mark's Gospel is devoid of a two-nature Christology, and thus that interpreters should avoid reading an explicit divine Christology into Mark's Gospel. Similar to Kirk, she also acknowledges that the text "opens doors" to further questions but equally that "the questions concerning what *Messiah* and *divine sonship* mean are not (yet) entirely sorted out" (p. 110). Huebenthal challenges Hurtado on the degree to which Mark's Gospel can be viewed as an established form of "Christian tradition," whether Mark should be read as a *bios*, and Hurtado's argument that Mark's Gospel may specifically avoid presenting Jesus's baptism as an adoption scene. I concentrate on the first and third of these matters.

Huebenthal argues that Hurtado's attempt to read Mark's Gospel in light of Pauline tradition, and as established gospel tradition, is not "compelling": "If it were true, we would not see a struggle for a distinctive identity of Jesus-followers in texts that were written roughly at the same time as Mark, like Colossians, or the need to 'correct' some of Mark's ideas a few years or decades later, as in Matthew and Luke or the Pastoral Epistles" (p. 106). She then enlists Jan Assmann's cultural-memory theory, and especially the idea of the "floating gap," which Assmann had borrowed from oral historian Jan Vansina, in order to argue that "solid tradition" that is "stable" does not emerge until the fourth generation of a distinct cultural identity: "We know from the extensive research in cultural studies and social-memory theory that one generation is not enough to establish a solid tradition. . . . The moment when a tradition is becoming strong and well-established is not when the second generation takes over from the first, but when the fourth generation takes over from the third" (pp. 106–7). Thus, for Huebenthal, any attempt to regard Mark's Gospel as established, solid, stable tradition is misguided when considering its status in the first-century CE.

I do not accept the apodosis of her conditional statement ("we would not see a struggle for a distinctive identity"), and I expect that Hurtado would not either. Contestation over tradition is every bit the hallmark of unestablished tradition as it is established tradition; it is often the contestation itself that "establishes" it. Regardless, the presence of conflict and correction among the tradents does not indicate that the tradition is not yet culturally "established" to some extent. But this point raises the further question of what Huebenthal means by "solid," "stable," "strong," and "well-established" tradition. What counts as "solid tradition," and how are we measuring solidity, stability, and strength when it comes to tradition?

Huebenthal's invocation of Assmann and his usage of Vansina's "floating gap" does not support her on this matter in the manner that she portrays. She is correct that Assmann enlists the "floating gap" and the related notion of a (typically generational) crisis in collective memory in order to hypothesize how group memory transitions from the "collective memory" (or "communicative memory") of a present generation into the "cultural memory" of established generations. For Assmann, the developed end of this process—a process that is not monolithic since a variety of cultural factors affect it—is the establishment of a hardened and official form of cultural memory, attested most clearly as a "canon" complete with a class of interpreters responsible for its cultivation and transmission. But Assmann does not postulate that the nascent end of that process—the group memory of the founding generation in the period of their life—was somehow totally mutable, fluid, or gelatinous to the extent that it could not be "established" culturally in some sense. To the contrary, the "collective memory" of the present has to be culturally recognized at least to the extent that it is a candidate for further cultural workings that transform it into "cultural memory." Assmann was clear that these processes are not inevitable but deliberate and thus the result of social effort. Even more to the point, though, Hurtado never argued that "early Christian tradition" had to be "solid" or "stable"—whatever we might mean by those terms—in order to be *operative*. In this case, Huebenthal has faulted Hurtado for an assumption about the nature of tradition among early followers of Jesus that he never expressed.

Huebenthal is also not convinced by Hurtado's suggestion that Mark "wanted to avoid" portraying it as an adoption scene, and I am broadly in agreement with her on whether his case has been made (p. 112). In Hurtado's defense, his original suggestion to this effect was based on the premise of identifying God's words "you are my Son" in Mark 1:11 as an allusion to Psalm 2:7. "If," Hurtado claimed, one posits an allusion to Psalm 2:7, then the omission of that psalm's further words "today I have begotten you" would suggest that Mark "wanted to avoid" an adoptionist presentation. Nevertheless, I am in agreement with Huebenthal that Hurtado's suggestion is short of convincing. It is an argument *e silentio*. However suggestive that silence may be, a firm conclusion against this narrative as an adoption scene would require more than noting what Mark did not say.

Rejoinder to J. R. Daniel Kirk

J. R. Daniel Kirk's response to Hurtado's essay comes on the heels of a much more detailed and in-depth interaction between the two, which occasionally stands in the background of Hurtado's initial essay as well. This response cannot do justice to their rich discussion that has, at least in its reciprocal nature, unfortunately come to an end. My overall reaction, however, is that these two scholars have much more in common than their rhetoric may at first reveal. Reading their interactions with each other has something of the feel of being the third person in an airplane row with them, watching them argue over who gets to put their elbow on the armrest: they are in the same plane, the same row, facing the same direction, and ultimately heading to the same destination, while disputing the fractional space that they cannot share.

With regard to this unshared space, and unless I am drastically mistaken, their differences boil down to this: for Hurtado, Mark's Gospel presents Jesus as thoroughly human, as God's special representative, and as unique *to the extent that he cannot be adequately compared* to any other such figure from Jewish tradition; whereas, for Kirk, Mark's Gospel presents Jesus as thoroughly human, as God's special representative, and as unique *to the extent that he can best be understood by comparing him* to other such figures from scriptural tradition. Both agree that Jesus is in a class of his own as "Son of God" in the Markan narrative (Hurtado: "GMark seems to place Jesus in a unique relationship with God that cannot be likened to that of other figures, not in a class that includes any others"; Kirk: "He occupies a unique category" and is "Son of God in a way that others are not"). They also agree that, in the words of Kirk, "We can at times find warrant for nudges beyond what we would expect to be possible for an exalted human" (p. 121). Even further, Hurtado and Kirk both seem to agree that we should, as scholars, explicitly say no more than does the Markan narrative itself. Yet their disagreement—at the risk of oversimplification—is one of scholarly posture toward prior examples. Hurtado believes scholars should *contrast* Jesus with prior examples of God's agents, while Kirk believes scholarship should *compare* Jesus with prior examples of God's agents.

Taking his cue from Hurtado's essay, Kirk offers a productive reading of the Gospel of Mark's narrative in light of Paul. Kirk takes as his specific example the baptism of Jesus by John the Baptist in light of Galatians 3 and Romans 6. Kirk's and Hurtado's interpretations of Mark's Gospel in light of Paul reveal the lack of clear resolution on some matters on the part of the Markan narrator and thus the crucial role of the interpreter. This matter is perhaps the biggest strength of Kirk's essay—both implicitly and explicitly it highlights the role of the reader in making christological sense of Mark's portrayal of Jesus. As Kirk notes, at some points the reader must "choose to read" in one direction or another. In rightly showing that the Markan Jesus has not "come down from above" in Johannine fashion, Kirk has shown that narratives such as the baptism of Jesus or the parable of the vineyard can plausibly be read in more than one way and thus contribute to more than one understanding of Jesus as God's "Son." I suspect that Hurtado would say that this interpretive openness is intrinsic to the Markan narrative.

Rejoinder to Adam Winn

Winn begins by observing shared ground with Hurtado. He agrees with Hurtado that one has to interpret Mark's Gospel not only in light of the claims of the text but also in light of a working knowledge of the likely audience of the text. This point was an important one for Hurtado. In contrast to reading strategies that focus strictly on the text of Mark's Gospel for its interpretation or, alternatively, assume that Mark's Gospel was akin to a missionary tract intended to convince readers who otherwise knew nothing of Jesus, Hurtado's essay argues at various points that Mark's Gospel would have been read by people who already knew the story of Jesus and likely shared theological and christological convictions that are on display prior to Mark's Gospel (evinced, e.g., in the writings of the apostle Paul). Beyond this general point, Winn also agrees with Hurtado that Mark 1:3 presents Jesus as the *kyrios* of Isaiah 40:3 and that, in other ways, the Jesus of Mark's Gospel is human but also someone more than human. In the words of Winn, but in agreement with Hurtado, "the Markan Jesus and God are linked together in an unprecedented way" (p. 124).

Winn's dissatisfactions with Hurtado's essay stem from Hurtado's (supposed) unwillingness to say more. He states that Hurtado "bring[s] Jesus to the very point of being identified *as* divine or the God of Israel" but then "pulls up just short of doing so" (p. 125). Winn thus describes him as "hesitant" ("it is this hesitancy that leaves me ultimately unsatisfied with Hurtado's conclusion") and "reluctant" (pp. 125, 126, respectively). I have little trouble imagining Hurtado responding to these charges with a statement to the effect that one person's hesitance or reluctance is another person's attention to nuance, but let us consider two examples Winn cites: the transfiguration and the Jewish trial.

Winn disagrees with Hurtado regarding the identity claims for Jesus that the transfiguration narrative of Mark 9:2–13 makes. In his essay,

Hurtado says that he understands this presentation of Jesus as "a preview of the eschatological glory that Jesus . . . is to receive and exhibit" (pp. 96–97). Winn claims, in contrast, that the narrative presents not a future identity for Jesus but a present one: "A *prima facie* reading of the transfiguration seems to depict an unveiling of Jesus's current heavenly identity. This identity is . . . clearly possessed by Jesus *currently* in the pericope" (p. 124).

Winn has overly simplified the interpretation of a narrative that deserves to be left as more complex, and has done so in at least two ways. First, the clean separation of current and future realities in this manner is precisely what apocalyptic imagery militates against since, at a general level, such imagery emphasizes the capacity for either to infiltrate the other. One could respond by saying that Hurtado's (and others') insistence on viewing this text as a claim for a future eschatological state of Jesus (presently revealed but nevertheless future) provides a similar separation, but I think that would miss a second issue.

This second issue is that a proper interpretation of this narrative must assess it not only in terms of the christological assertions that Mark makes for his reader *but the manner in which he does so* by narrating the christological assertions that Peter fails to understand. Mark's purpose, in other words, is not simply to inform readers of *exactly who Jesus is* (or even *will be*) but to inform them of exactly how Peter and company failed to grasp any such reality in full at the time of his ministry, even or especially when they should have. Mark's Gospel is written in retrospect, to state the obvious, and at more than one place enlists the *leitmotif* of the disciples' lack of understanding in order to account for the change of perspective between the narrated time and the time of narration. Just prior to the transfiguration, and in separate pericopae in the Markan narrative, Jesus rhetorically asks the disciples, "Do you not yet understand?" (Mark 8:21), and the narrator answers on their behalf, "But they did not understand what he was saying" (Mark 9:32). Positioned in the narrative between these two statements, and beyond a *prima facie* reading of the narrative but in line with the nature of apocalyptic imagery's capacity to blur the present and the future, the main point of the transfiguration is not simply to state that Jesus "had" this identity *already* or that he "had" this identity *only later*, but to state that his full identity was something that his followers were only able to come to understand after the resurrection (cf. 9:10), the perspective from which the author writes.

We have not even breached the topic of whether, in the transfiguration narrative, Mark presents Jesus as the top of a class of human eschatological figures or as a unique breaker of the mold of human eschatological figures, but these points suffice for pushing back against the notion that this narrative clearly offers a claim for Jesus's divine identity or at least that a *prima facie* reading of the narrative at this point unequivocally yields such a claim. In this case, Hurtado was correct to "pull up just short."

In another case, however, Winn is correct that Hurtado could have made more of an aspect of the Markan narrative. Toward the end of his essay, Hurtado addresses the so-called "Jewish trial" of Jesus in Mark 14 and specifically the charge of blasphemy (14:64). In accounting for the charge, Hurtado does not mention specifically Jesus's self-designation as "Son of Man" but nevertheless attributes the blasphemy charge to Jesus's claim that, as Son of Man, he would be "seated at the right hand of the Power, and 'coming with the clouds of heaven'" (v. 62). Hurtado also does not here mention Jesus's immediate response to the question of whether he was the Messiah, the son of the Blessed One (v. 61), which was, "I am" (ἐγώ εἰμι) (v. 62). Given the significance of this phrase as the Greek translation of the divine name, as well as its earlier and conspicuous appearance at Mark 6:50 where Jesus is portrayed as doing something that, at least according to some Jewish Scriptures (Job 9:8; 38:8–11, 16, 34; Pss 65:7; 77:19; 89:9), only God himself did,[1] I agree with Winn that "there must be more in Jesus's response to merit this charge" of blasphemy and that the occurrence of "I am" is a contributing factor (p. 125). I suspect Hurtado would agree on this matter as well since he elsewhere draws attention to this feature of the text.[2]

Conclusion

Huebenthal, Kirk, and Winn have all helpfully and critically engaged with Hurtado's presentation of the Gospel of Mark. It has been an honor to listen in on this conversation, and even more of an honor to be allowed a word here at the end of this particular part of it. As a means of nudging the conversation forward, there are several matters that I might have liked to

1. Cf. however, J. R. Daniel Kirk and Stephen L. Young, "'I Will Set His Hand to the Sea': Psalm 88:26 LXX and Christology in Mark," *JBL* 133.2 (2014): 333–40.

2. See, e.g., his responses to Huebenthal and Kirk in this volume.

have seen discussed more by Hurtado and his interlocutors. For example, Hurtado and Kirk both read the scene of Jesus's baptism against Pauline formulations of baptism and understandings of Jesus as Son of God. How might the Markan narrative location of Jesus's baptism immediately after John the Baptist's proclamation of a baptism "for forgiveness of sins," as well as the distinction between the Baptist's baptism with water and Jesus's baptism with the Holy Spirit (Mark 1:4, 8) disrupt or contribute to Pauline understandings of baptism and Jesus that such readers might bring to Mark's Gospel? It also strikes me that Hurtado and his interlocutors did not give the scribes' question, "Who can forgive sins but God alone?" (Mark 2:7), quite the attention it deserves, though I trust that this text will feature in the discussion elsewhere in this volume. Winn might have buttressed his argument with further explication of this passage, but it also illustrates a point shared by Hurtado, Kirk, and Huebenthal, which is that the text may hint at, or ask questions about, the possibility of a "more than human" Christology while nevertheless not expressly claiming one. In the very least, this question placed on the lips of Jesus's enemies demonstrates conclusively that the Markan narrative is interested in such questions, even if it is less interested in answering them clearly. This point, however, brings us back to the need for this book and its helpfulness in allowing us to think further about such matters.

CHAPTER 3

Narrative Christology of a Suffering King[1]

J. R. DANIEL KIRK

Mark's Gospel opens with the words, "The beginning of the good news about Jesus the Messiah" (Mark 1:1).[2] It continues, "as it is written in Isaiah the prophet: 'I will send my messenger ahead of you, who will prepare your way'—'a voice of one calling in the wilderness, "Prepare the way for the Lord, make straight paths for him"'" (Mark 1:2 NIV). This introductory flourish enables readers to plot a course for understanding the Christology of Mark.

First, any Christology we discover in the Gospel will be a narrative Christology.[3] When analyzing any one aspect of a story, we are confronted with the challenge Flannery O'Connor captured when she wrote, "A story is a way to say something that can't be said any other way, and it takes every word in the story to say what the meaning is."[4] In order to know Mark's Jesus, we have to know Mark's story through and through. We cannot study

1. The material in this essay is by and large an abbreviation of the argument I make more fully in J. R. Daniel Kirk, *A Man Attested by God: The Human Jesus of the Synoptic Gospels* (Grand Rapids: Eerdmans, 2016). I will spare the reader a footnote to myself after every sentence, trusting that this initial disclosure will be enough to point the curious to where they might read more.

2. Some manuscripts include "the Son of God." This will be a critical facet of Mark's Christology to explore, but, given its doubtful originality at this point in the text, I leave it aside for the present.

3. Elizabeth Struthers Malbon, *Mark's Jesus: Characterization as Narrative Christology* (Waco, TX: Baylor University Press, 2000), 1–19.

4. Flannery O'Connor, *Mystery and Manners: Occasional Prose*, ed. Sally Fitzgerald and Robert Fitzgerald (New York: Farrar, Straus and Giroux, 1970), 96.

titles in the abstract, and we cannot simply bring in previously existing scriptural or Jewish ideas and expect them to carry some prior meaning into the Gospel unchanged. We cannot even look at one of Mark's own pericopes removed from the flow of the narrative. When Mark says that this is "the beginning," it means at very least that we have to follow the story of Jesus in Mark from beginning through middle to end.

Second, the story is about Jesus the Messiah. For the interpreter of Mark, there are two dangers here. On the one hand, twenty-first-century Christians might fall into the trap of bringing their own, more developed ideas of who Jesus is and reading them into the text. Many Christians have an instinctive notion that to be Messiah, for instance, is to be divine. But this would not have been the assumption of a first-century Jewish reader, and may not have been the conviction of the earliest Jesus-followers. We have to let Mark's own story tell us what *Messiah* means in this case.

On the other hand, Mark's Jesus does not neatly fit into any preexisting boxes of Jewish expectation for a messiah.[5] By and large, if someone ends up crucified by the Romans, this proves that the person is not the deliverer for whom the Jewish people have been waiting! So we have to allow that this story is going to both make sense to its first-century audience and also make claims for Jesus that would have been genuinely surprising to Jews who were awaiting God's deliverance.

Messiah simply means, God's "anointed." It is a title that might have royal implications. It might have priestly connotations. From what we know from early Jewish texts, it is not likely to have carried suggestions of divinity. When we probe the Christology of Mark, we are asking what kind of Messiah Mark's Jesus might be. Mark telegraphs to his readers in 1:1 that this is the very question that his story sets out to answer.

Third, the citation of Scripture indicates that this story of Jesus the Messiah has its primary interpretive grid in the Scriptures of Israel and their reception by the Jewish people.[6] Mark was written in Greek within the bounds of the Roman Empire. However, the Gospel's opening verses suggest to Mark's readers that this Jewish world with its texts and practices is the

---

5. See Adela Yarbro Collins and John J. Collins, *King and Messiah and Son of God: Divine, Human, and Angelic Messianic Figures in Biblical and Related Literature* (Grand Rapids: Eerdmans, 2008).

6. See Rikki E. Watts, *Isaiah's New Exodus in Mark* (Grand Rapids: Baker Academic, 2001), esp. 29–52.

primary conversation partner for making sense of the story that is to come, rather than the broader Greek and Latin cultural corpora.[7]

Of course, this third point has to be held with the first two still firmly in place. Mark is not simply transferring Jewish ideas onto a person he believes to be a messiah. He is telling a story about how Jesus, as the Messiah, fulfills, transforms, and even rejects the expectations of many of his contemporaries—not least of all the expectations of his closest followers.

Mark's Narrative

To understand Mark's christological narrative, we first must have a basic understanding of Mark's Gospel and its flow.

First, modern readers of Mark might need to remind themselves that Mark contains no birth, infancy, or childhood narratives, and no resurrection appearances. Jesus arrives on the scene as a fully grown man, first seen at his baptism. His final words in the Gospel are his cry of dereliction from the cross, "My God, my God, why have you forsaken me?" (Mark 15:34). A young man (likely an angel) will announce the resurrection, but Jesus himself does not appear (16:5–8).

Such a beginning and ending underscore the fact that Mark's Jesus is known within the bounds of his earthly life. In Mark, Jesus does not possess the sort of hidden identity that one can only find by peering into an eternal past in heaven from which the Messiah had eternal origins. As far as the reader knows, Jesus is not ontologically different from other humans by virtue of preexistence, supernatural conception, or divine parentage.

Second, readers should be aware of the large divisions in the story, because Jesus and his disciples are dynamic characters who develop over the course of the narrative. Mark divides roughly in half, with the confession of Peter at Caesarea Philippi (8:27–33) as the most significant dividing line between the first and second parts of the book.[8]

---

7. It is worth noting that first-century Judaism was itself "Hellenized," which is to say that it did not exist in some hermetically sealed sphere, untouched by the radical imposition of Greek culture that began with the fourth-century BCE conquests of Alexander the Great and continued to influence the Greek-speaking East of the Roman Empire.

8. It may well be that the previous story, in which Jesus heals a blind man in two stages, is the more precise point at which to draw the line between the first and second halves of the book. For our purposes, however, Peter's confession will be a convenient shorthand for this transitional stage in

Mark's Gospel before and after Peter's confession is a study of contrasts. Prior to Peter's confession, Jesus's ministry is marked by authority. This authority is associated with teaching, countless miracles, and exorcisms in particular (1:22, 27, 34; 2:10–12; 3:10; 3:20–30; 6:5, 55–56). The first half of the book contains two miraculous feeding narratives (6:33–45; 8:1–9) and two instances of Jesus exercising control over the sea (4:35–41; 6:46–52). In stark contrast to all this, subsequent to Peter's confession Jesus performs only one exorcism (9:14–29) and heals only one blind man (10:46–52).

Why this disparity? The first half of Mark establishes Jesus as the authoritative Messiah, empowered by God's Spirit to speak and act for God. Peter understands this much. When asked who Jesus is, he can answer for the twelve disciples, "You are the Messiah" (8:29). Readers of Mark know that this is an accurate title: its only prior appearance was in the voice of the narrator when it identified Jesus as Messiah in 1:1. But there is a surprise in store for the disciples: what it means for Jesus to be Messiah is not, finally, about acclamation, power, and glory.[9] To be Messiah, Jesus has to be rejected, suffer, and die before being raised by God (8:31; 9:30–31; 10:32–34). While the first half of the Gospel establishes Jesus as the authoritative, powerful Messiah, the second half represents a steady march to the cross.

This broad overview of the story captures the most basic contours of Mark's Christology: Jesus is the authoritative, Spirit-empowered Christ who, despite (because of!) this empowerment can only take his messianic throne by way of rejection, suffering, crucifixion, and death. The mystery of Mark's Jesus is found in the conjunction of his messianic authority and his need to suffer and die.

Jesus has one potent ally who stands by his side, affirming both portions of his messianic identity. That character is God. God directly participates in Mark's Gospel only twice. One appearance is at Jesus's first public appearance (his baptism in Mark 1), the other comes in the scene immediately following Peter's confession (the transfiguration in Mark 9). God speaks nearly identical words each time, with at least one important difference. At the baptism, the Spirit comes upon Jesus as God says, "You are my Son, whom I love; with you I am well pleased" (1:11 NIV). After Peter's confession

---

Mark's Gospel. See Joel Marcus, *Mark 1–8: A New Translation with Introduction and Commentary*, AB 27 (New York: Doubleday, 2000), 62–64.

9. See Malbon, *Mark's Jesus*, 204.

of Jesus as the Messiah, he subsequently rebukes Jesus for claiming that he must suffer and die; this is where we hear from God a second time. This time, God addresses Jesus's followers: "This is my Son, whom I love. Listen to him!" (9:7). Listening to Jesus is precisely what Peter had failed to do moments earlier. We will dive into these passages in more detail below. For now it is enough to recognize that the voice of God undergirds each leg of Jesus's journey through Mark as Messiah, interpreting Jesus's empowering reception of the Spirit at his baptism, and confirming his need to suffer, die, and rise again after Peter's confession and Jesus's first passion prediction.

This brief overview of Mark is a reminder that the Gospel tells a dynamic story. The reader's knowledge of Jesus's vocation shifts as Jesus himself reveals it to his followers. The disciples around Jesus, and even Jesus himself, are dynamic characters who change as they encounter the various challenges before them. God is a character whose participation within the narrative itself is limited yet indispensable. Other characters, such as supplicants, opponents, and unnamed women, all play a part in helping Mark's Gospel disclose the identity of Jesus.

Standing in for God

Though Mark begins by giving Jesus a quite human title in the word *Messiah*, it is no less striking in its indication that Jesus represents and stands in closest possible relation to Israel's God. The advent of Jesus the Messiah is what divine visitation looks like on earth: not God being personally present as Jesus but God's presence and work being enacted in and through him. Following in the tradition of Jewish mediators, but with a strong claim that Jesus is the ultimate, eschatological agent of God's visitation and deliverance, Jesus stands in for God such that how one responds to Jesus is how one responds to the God who sent him. Such close proximity reflects how Jewish writers depicted a vast number of idealized human figures.

These elements of (a) divine visitation, (b) through a mediator, (c) at the time of final salvation are all suggested in the opening scriptural citation: "As it is written in Isaiah the prophet: 'I will send my messenger ahead of you, who will prepare your way'—'a voice of one calling in the wilderness, "Prepare the way for the Lord, make straight paths for him"'" (1:2–3 NIV). In Mark, these verses speak most directly about John the Baptist, who arrives on the scene as the forerunner. Significantly, however, this selection of Old Testament passages is deployed in such a way that God is speaking not about himself as the one for whom John prepares the way, but Jesus instead. In Isaiah 40:3 we read, "make straight in the desert a highway for *our God*" (NIV, emphasis added). In Mark, God is the speaker, and rather than say "for me" or "for your God," as though God were referring to himself, the reference is changed to someone who, though representing God, is a different person.[10]

On the one hand, by situating the entirety of Jesus's ministry under the umbrella of such a prophetic text, Mark indicates that the narrative world of the Hebrew Bible is the place we must look if we are to answer such basic questions as who is God, what has happened in the story before, and what goal is this narrative trying to reach. On the other hand, by transforming the biblical verse in its new context, we are made aware that only Mark's own story can show us what God's "arrival" for salvation actually looks like.

We also learn that both John and Jesus are agents in God's eschatological visitation of Israel. The phrase, "who will prepare your way" (1:2) likely comes from Malachi 3:1, a passage which, paired with Malachi's subsequent expectation that Elijah would come before the Lord's own return (Mal 4:5), created one of the early Jewish frameworks for God's final arrival for both judgment and deliverance. In Malachi 3:1, as in Isaiah 40:3, God is the one whose way is prepared. But here, too, the divine speaker refers to Jesus as a different character, saying that "your" way rather than "my" way will be prepared.

This does not mean that Jesus is being identified *as* God, though we might well say that it means Jesus is being identified *with* God.[11] Other Jewish writers made similar moves: when they believed that their hero was the eschatological agent who was to lead God's people into final salvation (and the world into final judgment), they might replace God as the subject of a biblical citation with this leader. In the Dead Sea Scrolls, we find at

---

10. See the illuminating discussion in Joel Marcus, *The Way of the Lord: Christological Exegesis of the Old Testament in the Gospel of Mark* (Louisville: Westminster John Knox, 1992), esp. 38–41.

11. For a divine interpretation of Jesus's identity based, in part, on this scriptural citation, see Herman C. Waetjen, *A Reordering of Power: A Socio-Political Reading of Mark's Gospel* (Minneapolis: Fortress, 1989), 63–67; Richard B. Hays, *Reading Backwards: Figural Christology and the Fourfold Gospel Witness* (Waco, TX: Baylor University Press, 2014), 20–21.

least three examples of this.[12] Each displays an interpretive move that we might call "eschatological transformation." That is to say, the meaning and referent of the verse is transformed in light of what the author believes to be the final ("eschatological") and climactic activity of God in salvation and/or judgment. Each of these Jewish writers no doubt believed that God was, in fact, at work through the human figures who became the subjects of these verses that previously spoke directly of God. However, replacing God as the biblical reference with the human hero did not entail a conviction that the person involved was God incarnate. We might say that the actions of these human agents show us what it looks like when God acts as promised in these prophetic texts.

Mark's scriptural citation works the same way. It invites the reader, in conversation with the Scriptures of Israel, to recognize that the actions unfolding in the subsequent narrative are the promised eschatological activity of God. By assigning the role of God to Jesus, it invites us to see Jesus as the human agent through whom God is exercising this visitation.[13] Throughout Mark's Gospel, Jesus and God remain distinct characters, even as the "Lord Jesus" acts in God's spirit, name, and power to such a degree that following him is the only sure way to honor "the Lord God."

The Story of God's Son

Declarations of Jesus as God's Son structure the entire narrative of Mark.[14] They occur at three critical junctures in the story: the first time we meet Jesus (his baptism, Mark 1:11), at his transfiguration immediately after Peter's confession (9:7), and the last time we see Jesus (after his death, 15:39).[15] These three declarations are the only times in the story when a character

12. See 1QpHab VIII where Hab 2:4 is interpreted as referring to the people's faith in the Teacher of Righteousness, the application of God's role, "I will be like a lion" in Hos 5:14 to "the priest" in 4Q166–67, and the application of Isa 61:1–2 to Melchizedek in 11QMelchizedek 2.9 where "the year of the Lord's favor" becomes the year of Melchizedek's favor. Cf. Maurice Casey, "Chronology and the Development of Pauline Christology," in *Paul and Paulinism: Essays in Honour of C. K. Barrett*, ed. M. D. Hooker and S. G. Wilson (London: SPCK, 1982), 128; John J. Collins, *The Scepter and the Star: Messianism in Light of the Dead Sea Scrolls*, 2nd ed. (Grand Rapids: Eerdmans, 2010), 133; Carl Judson Davis, *The Name and Way of the Lord: Old Testament Themes, New Testament Christology*, JSNTSup 129 (Sheffield: Sheffield Academic, 1996), 47–48.

13. Cf. Adela Yarbro Collins, *Mark: A Commentary*, Hermeneia (Minneapolis: Fortress, 2007), 135–38.

14. See Collins, *Mark*, 134–35.

15. See Philip G. Davis, "Mark's Christological Paradox," *JSNT* 35 (1989): 3–15; Donald H. Juel,

other than a demon identifies Jesus as God's Son: twice the person so naming Jesus is God, and once it is a Roman centurion. The first and last passages also bookend the Gospel by containing the only uses of the Greek word σχίζω, "to rend," once referring to the tearing open of the heavens (1:10) and once referring to the tearing of the temple curtain (15:38). Such narrative markers demonstrate that to understand Mark's Jesus is to see him as God's Son. What, then, does *Son of God* mean in this story?

Contemporary Christians once again have to take special care that the history of the title as it developed in Christian theology not overrun the meaning of the phrase in its biblical context. *Son of God* has become a way of speaking of the eternal, second person of the Trinity. But long before it carried this connotation it was a way of depicting humans who stood in special relation to God, such as Adam (Gen 1:26; 5:1–3), Israel (Exod 4:22–23; Hos 11:1), and Davidic kings (2 Sam 7:14; Ps 89:26–27).[16] Since Mark's readers already know that Jesus is Messiah when they come to the first declaration that Jesus is God's Son, it is this connotation we should explore first.

Baptism

The first time Jesus appears as a character in the action of Mark's Gospel, he comes to be baptized by John (Mark 1:9). "Just as Jesus was coming up out of the water, he saw heaven being torn open and the Spirit descending on him like a dove. And a voice came from heaven: 'You are my Son, whom I love; with you I am well pleased'" (1:10–11 NIV). Many commentators recognize here an allusion to Psalm 2.[17] Psalm 2 was likely an enthronement psalm, sung at coronations or annual reenactments. Thus, God says in the psalm, "I have installed my king on Zion" (Ps 2:6 NIV). The king then declares, "I will proclaim the LORD's decree: He said to me, 'You are my son; today I have become your father'" (v. 7 NIV). Similarly, the voice from heaven declares to Jesus, "You are my Son," in Mark 1:11, in what may well be an anointing of Jesus to kingship.

The reception of the Spirit is another indication that this is an anointing

"The Origin of Mark's Christology," in *The Messiah: Developments in Earliest Judaism and Christianity*, ed. J. H. Charlesworth (Minneapolis: Fortress, 1992), 449–60; and Kirk, *Man Attested*, 179–82.

16. See Collins and Collins, *King and Messiah*, 1–24.

17. E.g., Collins, *Mark*, 150; Marcus, *Mark 1–8*, 162.

to office.[18] Israel's first kings were inaugurated into their offices by being anointed with oil and receiving the Spirit (1 Sam 10:1, 6, 10; 16:13). Receipt of the Spirit is a sign of the sonship and kingship that come with being anointed to rule on God's behalf.[19]

Another aspect of this scene lurks just beneath the surface, a secret hiding in plain sight for Mark's readers to discover as they work their way through the story and reflect on the Scriptures of Israel. The words of God, "You are my Son whom I love," echo God's words to Abraham in Genesis 22:2 when he tells the patriarch to take his son whom he loves, Isaac, and offer him as a sacrifice.[20] Here we have a hint at the dark turn that Jesus's messianic tale will take; Jesus will have to die.

This suggestion that the baptism scene foreshadows Jesus's death finds confirmation several chapters later. When James and John come to Jesus asking to sit at his right and left hand in glory, he replies, "Can you drink the cup I drink and be baptized with the baptism I am baptized with?" (Mark 10:37–38 NIV). This is an allusion to Jesus's looming death on the cross, as the subsequent discussion makes clear (esp. vv. 43–45). In early Christianity, baptism became a symbol of Jesus's death (cf., e.g., Rom 6:3).

If we hold these two dynamics of the scene together, we find ourselves with a "Son of God" Christology that perfectly matches the story of Mark as I outlined it above. Jesus is, paradoxically, (a) the Spirit-empowered Messiah who (b) must suffer and die in order to enter his glory. The baptism scene thus tells the story of Mark in nuce.

Transfiguration

The second time God declares Jesus's sonship is at his transfiguration (Mark 9:2–13). The words are nearly identical to the baptism, only this time the words are in the third person, speaking about Jesus to those who are present, rather than second person, speaking to Jesus himself: "This is my Son, whom I love. Listen to him!" (v. 7 NIV). This twofold divine

---

18. See Collins, *Mark*, 150; Marcus, *Mark 1–8*, 160.

19. See also Robert D. Rowe, *God's Kingdom and God's Son: The Background of Mark's Christology from Concepts of Kingship in the Psalms* (Leiden: Brill, 2002), 242.

20. See Leroy A. Huizenga, *The New Isaac: Tradition and Intertextuality in the Gospel of Matthew*, NovTSup 131 (Leiden: Brill, 2009); Thomas R. Hatina, "Embedded Scripture Texts and the Plurality of Meaning," in *Biblical Interpretation in Early Christian Gospels*, vol. 1, *The Gospel of Mark*, ed. T. R. Hatina, LNTS 304 (New York: T&T Clark, 2006), 81–99.

affirmation of Jesus as God's Son, the only direct actions God performs in the Gospel, underscores the centrality of this facet of Jesus's identity for understanding Mark's Christology.

Why does the divine voice tell the disciples present on the mountain (including Peter), "Listen to him"? The answer is likely found in the immediately prior interaction between Jesus and his followers.[21] In Mark 8, at Caesarea Philippi, Peter had correctly identified Jesus as Messiah, but he had vehemently objected to the notion that Jesus, as Messiah, was going to have to die (vv. 29–33).[22] Peter had rightly apprehended half the truth about Jesus's identity: he is the Messiah. But he rejected the other half: that Jesus as Messiah would have to die. The divine voice comes in to take Jesus's side in this dispute. Yes, Jesus is the Messiah ("my Son"), and Jesus knows that his destiny is rejection, suffering, and death prior to resurrection glory ("listen to him").

When Jesus is on the Mount of Transfiguration, two heavenly companions appear: Moses and Elijah (9:4). These heavenly humans stand as markers of Israel's prophetic past, but also of heavenly human life. In line with Jesus's predictions about his future, the glory he bears in the transfiguration is not the disclosure of a divine glory that was always his (i.e., before coming to earth); instead, it is a preview of the glory that Jesus will bear when, as the human Messiah who faithfully suffers and dies, he is then raised from the dead.[23]

The denouement of the transfiguration story confirms this interpretation. Jesus tells the disciples not to tell of the scene until he is raised from the dead (v. 9). And while the confused disciples puzzle about why the scribes say Elijah must come first (v. 11), Jesus wants them to turn their query to the question of why it is written that "the Son of Man must suffer much and be rejected" (v. 12 NIV). These are not random, disconnected words of Jesus. The allusions to resurrection, suffering, and rejection are the interpretive keys to the scene on the mountain top from which they are departing. This second critical divine proclamation confirms that Mark's "Son of God" Christology is a Christology of suffering followed by resurrection glory.

---

21. Cf. Rowe, *God's Kingdom and God's Son*, 259–60.

22. Adela Yarbro Collins, "Mark and His Readers: The Son of God among Jews," *HTR* 92 (1999): 393–408; esp. 401.

23. Joel Marcus, *Mark 8–16*, AB27A (New Haven: Yale University Press, 2009), 637, 640–41.

Crucifixion

Only one human ever acknowledges Jesus as "Son of God" in Mark's Gospel. It is the centurion who watches him die (15:39).[24] Paired with God's own words at the baptism, this declaration of Jesus's sonship forms a bookend to the Gospel. A number of connections stitch the two passages together: in both, Jesus is called God's Son (1:11; 15:39), and the passages contain the only two uses of the Greek word σχίζω: to "rend" or "tear" (the heavens are torn in 1:10; the temple curtain is torn in 15:38). Both scenes also evoke Elijah (1:6; cf. 9:12; 15:35–36). Finally, in the baptism scene, the Spirit (πνεῦμα) comes into Jesus (1:10), while Mark chooses to describe his death as expiring (ἐξέπνευσεν, 15:37). Thus, the first appearance of Jesus and his final departure from the Gospel form a literary *inclusio* that includes Jesus's identity as "Son of God" as the climax of each scene and the Gospel of Mark as a whole.

Above I argued that the baptism functions as a sort of anointing to kingship. In parallel with this, Jesus is crucified under the banner, "The King of the Jews" (15:26). While the Romans bestow this title in mockery (see vv. 16–20), knowing that anyone who is being killed can be no king, the readers of Mark know that the title finds its fulfillment precisely through Jesus surrendering himself to death.[25] Suffering-king Christology is pointedly enacted in the crucifixion scene as the climax of the story as a whole and of the "Son of God" Christology in particular.

Mark 15:39 reads, "And when the centurion, who stood there in front of Jesus, saw how he died, he said, 'Surely this man was the Son of God!'" (NIV). Notice that the very reason that the narrator gives the reader for the centurion's confession of Jesus as Son of God was that the Roman had seen how Jesus died. The great paradox of Mark's Gospel, and the heart of his "Son of God" Christology, is that Jesus's divine sonship is disclosed through his death.

Parable of the Vineyard

There is one more piece of evidence that points toward a suffering-messiah Christology as the significance of Jesus as God's Son in Mark:

---

24. See Davis, "Mark's Christological Paradox," 4–5. Davis's claims for a divine Christology here rest on a doubtful interpretation of Mark 1:11.

25. Cf. Collins, *Mark*, 728.

the parable of the vineyard in 12:1–12. It tells of a vineyard owner sending servants to collect fruit from vineyard tenants (v. 2). The tenants beat and kill the servants, sending away empty-handed any who live (vv. 3–5). Finally, there is "one left to send, a son, whom he loved" (v. 6 NIV). The language of a "beloved son" is nearly identical to God's words at the baptism (1:11) and transfiguration (9:7). In the parable, the vineyard owner clearly stands for God, and the beloved son is Jesus. The tenants kill this final emissary, hoping to usurp the son's inheritance (12:7–8). In keeping with Mark's divine-son Christology, this is a story of a son who is killed and subsequently glorified.

The story of the vineyard illustrates some ways in which Mark's Jesus is similar to and differs from other agents who represent God to Israel. First, the parable shows us that being "sent" by God within Mark's narrative world does not evoke the notion of preexistence.[26] Many servants are sent by the vineyard owner to the people. The same language is used of the son and the earlier servants, with no differentiation articulated between the place from which they come or the way in which they were sent.

Second, the parable suggests a few ways in which the figure of the son is distinct. Most importantly, the son is the final messenger, the one whose rejection will at last bring God's judgment to bear on the tenants. In addition, the son is "the heir" in a way that the other messengers are not. Jesus stands in a unique relationship to God, which means that he has a unique claim to the "vineyard."[27] The parable of the vineyard underscores that Jesus is the eschatological fulcrum of God's dealings with Israel. In the enthronement psalm echoed at the baptism, God says to Israel's king, "Ask me, and I will make the nations your inheritance, the ends of the earth your possession" (Ps 2:8 NIV). The king of Israel is the "heir" through whom the people take possession of God's promises. Mark's Jesus stands in this place. Finally, the rejection and death of the son is the occasion for God to glorify what the people have spurned (Mark 12:10–11). The hope hinted at in the transfiguration—that suffering and death are not the end but instead are the very means for the son of God to come to his throne—is corroborated here.

---

26. Simon Gathercole, *The Preexistent Son: Recovering the Christologies of Matthew, Mark, and Luke* (Grand Rapids: Eerdmans, 2006), argues that "I have come" sayings indicate Jesus's preexistence; however, he acknowledges that in this parable being "sent" by God is common currency for all the agents in this parable (187–88). It seems to me that if prophets can be described by others as "sent by God," then they might say of themselves, "I have come."

27. Cf. Marcus, *Mark 8–16*, 810.

For a Roman

A final note might be added here about what "son of God" might mean to a Roman reader. A Roman lacking a deep knowledge of the Jewish Scriptures and traditions of interpretation would nonetheless have some ready frames of reference by which to understand the notion.[28] More often than not, it was a way to claim that a human (such as Octavian) had been adopted by someone else who had once been human (such as Julius Caesar), the latter of which was now thought to be divinized. To be "son of god" was to be chosen for rule and for inheritance by one's adopted father.[29] Thus, while a Roman no less than a Jew would have been jarred by the notion that one's work as a son of a god entailed suffering and death, both would equally have understood such sonship as adding a supernatural imprimatur to a human being's claims to kingship.

Son of God as Suffering King

Mark contains a coherent "Son of God" Christology that is consistent with the contours of the Gospel as a whole. It depicts a Messiah who will have to come to his throne by way of rejection, suffering, and death. Through its placement in the beginning, middle, and end, it helps structure the narrative, and through its articulation by the divine voice it takes a prominent, defining role in telling Mark's readers who Jesus is. As Son of God, Jesus is Israel's Spirit-empowered Messiah who must nonetheless suffer and die.

The Story of the Human One

There is one other title that can anchor our study of Mark's Jesus because it reflects the narrative shape of the Gospel as a whole and develops alongside it. That title, often translated "the Son of Man," is more literally rendered, "the son of the human," but its force might be best captured in the rendering of the Common English Bible: "the Human One."

The Human One is a title that has vexed scholars for generations, especially as they have attempted to understand the origins and developments

28. See Michael Peppard, *The Son of God in the Roman World: Divine Sonship in Its Social and Political Context* (New York: Oxford, 2011).

29. Peppard, *Son of God*, 3–5.

of the phrase and how it might have been used by the historical Jesus.[30] However, if we confine our attention to Mark's Gospel, then several orienting points can be made with some confidence. Jesus is the only one who uses this phrase, he uses it as a title, and he always deploys it in reference to himself.[31] The phrase is used to depict three different aspects of Jesus's life: his current authoritative power on earth (Mark 2:10, 28), his looming rejection, suffering, death, and resurrection (8:31; 9:9, 12, 31; 10:33, 45; 14:21, 41), and his future heavenly glory (8:38; 13:26; 14:62). In this last category, Jesus's deployment of the phrase "the son of the human" echoes the more general "one like a son of a human" from Daniel 7:13 (Mark 13:26; 14:62).

Also, the claims Jesus makes for the Human One align with the plot development of Mark's narrative. In the first half of the Gospel, in which Jesus is demonstrating his authoritative messianic status, he claims that the Human One has authority (2:10, 28). After Peter's confession, Jesus uses this title in his prediction of rejection, suffering, and death (8:31), and it is only then that Jesus speaks of the Human One in heavenly glory (v. 38). So Mark's readers know that the way Jesus attains to this heavenly glory is not a straight line from earthly authority to enthronement; nor is it the case (as far as Mark's readers know) that the Human One is preexistent in glory. Heavenly glory is his only after he dies and is raised.

Claiming Authority

The first two times Jesus refers to himself as the Human One, he is claiming unique authority. Opening a string of controversy stories, the healing of the paralytic finds Jesus transgressing the scribes' understanding of what a human can rightfully assert when he forgives the man's sins (2:3–7). Jesus's opponents accuse him of blasphemy, saying, "Who can forgive sins but God alone?" (v. 7). Thus, the story confronts the reader with the christological question in a pointed fashion: What is Jesus claiming for himself by his forgiveness of sins?

---

30. For a recent attempt at cutting through this nettle, see Maurice Casey, *The Solution to the 'Son of Man' Problem*, LNTS 343 (New York: T&T Clark, 2007).

31. The fact that nobody else uses the title in the story plays into the role of this phrase in the story; it is Jesus's own way of talking about his identity and mission, an identity and mission that are not rightly understood by almost any other character within the narrative. Even though he uses "the Human One" as a title, it was not a preexisting title that Jesus could deploy because it was in circulation previously with a set of assumptions about what it meant. Instead, it holds the mystery of Jesus's identity in such a way that only the Gospel story itself can accurately depict its significance.

One way that scholars have attempted to answer this question is to take their cue from the scribes: to forgive sins is to claim divine prerogative; therefore, Jesus is staking a claim to divinity.[32] But this approach fails at the level of Mark's story. First, in this story the scribes are the opponents of Jesus, the antagonists whom the readers know to be untrustworthy. This makes the scribes unreliable guides to Jesus's identity and to the validity of his actions. Second, the readers of Mark know that the eschatological moment of which Jesus is a part includes humans entrusted with the task of proclaiming and even administering forgiveness of sins. This is the substance of John the Baptist's ministry (1:4–5).

Rather than assent to the scribes' interpretation, we should look to Jesus's rejoinder to guide our interpretation of his authority to forgive.[33] The first thing to note is that Jesus ties his authority to forgive with his authority to heal (2:10–11). Healing, in turn, is a gift that Jesus shares with other humans in this Gospel (6:13). This suggests that Jesus can heal and forgive because he is a certain type of God-authorized human, not because he is "the one God."

Second, Jesus tells the scribes that his healing of the paralyzed man demonstrates "that the human one has authority on earth to forgive sins" (2:10). It would seem that Jesus is providing an alternative explanation to the scribes' charge of unjustly infringing on the divine prerogatives; he is claiming to have heavenly authority delegated to himself in the earthly sphere. "Authority" (ἐξουσία) has already been a hallmark of Jesus's ministry, something that distinguishes his teaching from that of the scribes (1:22, 27). The reason that exercising such authority is not blasphemous is that God has bestowed this authority on Jesus (cf. 1:11; 3:29–30). "On the earth" distinguishes what has been currently delegated to Jesus (authority on the earth, 2:10) from what has not (authority in heaven). Moreover, this phrase may evoke the realm over which God gave humanity authority in Genesis 1:26–28, such that "the Human One" is laying hold of the authority that God gave human beings in the beginning.[34]

The second time Jesus claims authority for himself as the Human One (Mark 2:28), it is even more clear that his special status comes from being a

32. Daniel Johannson, "'Who Can Forgive Sins but God Alone?' Human and Angelic Agents, and Divine Forgiveness in Early Judaism," *JSNT* 33 (2011): 351–74.

33. Malbon, *Mark's Jesus*, 151–52.

34. See Morna Hooker, *Son of Man in Mark: A Study of the Background of the Term "Son of Man" and Its Use in St. Mark's Gospel* (Montreal: McGill University Press, 1967), 91–93.

particular kind of human. The story begins with Jesus's disciples plucking heads of grain on a Sabbath (v. 23). When the Pharisees ask why the disciples do what is unlawful (οὐκ ἔξεστιν, v. 24), Jesus recalls a scriptural story in which David provided food for his followers that it was not lawful (οὐκ ἔξεστιν, v. 26) for them to eat. For precedent, Jesus cites a human who is God's anointed, not-yet-enthroned king whose immediate exigencies override what is strictly legal in terms of provision of food for his followers. Jesus does not dispute that the law has been broken; he claims a particular human role in the life of God's people that allows him to break the law guiltlessly.[35]

After invoking the David story, Jesus makes a second argument in response to the charge of unlawful activity: "The Sabbath was made for humanity, not humanity for the Sabbath. So the Human One is lord even of the Sabbath" (vv. 27–28). The threefold repetition of the word "human" (ἄνθρωπος, NIV "man") places Jesus's self-identification as "the son of the human" squarely within the realm of the "humanity" for whom the Sabbath was made. The logic of the claim only works if Jesus is claiming to be a member of the group for whom the Sabbath is a gift. Indeed, when exploring the historical roots of the "Son of Man" sayings, this particular claim is sometimes thought to point to Jesus's use of the phrase to speak about humans in general: people are masters of the Sabbath. Such arguments show that the force of Jesus's statement rests on the humanness of the one who is lord of the Sabbath. In this particular context, however, Jesus is making a claim about his own authority as the Human One.

From these first two deployments of the Human One title, we see a claim to authority on earth. It is possible that both stories echo creation, with God giving humanity to rule on the earth and God implementing the Sabbath on the seventh day. It may well be that in deploying "the Human One" as a title, Mark's Jesus is evoking the primal role of humanity to rule the world on God's behalf.[36] Additionally, Jesus draws a parallel between David's incipient royal authority as his own. Thus, these early indicators of Mark's "Human One" Christology fall within the broader scope of the narrative force of Mark 1–8 in establishing Jesus's powerful authority as the

---

35. On the idea of breaking the law guiltlessly, see Matthew's rendering of the story, in which Jesus draws attention to the priests who work in the temple on the Sabbath and yet are guiltless (Matt 12:5).

36. Cf. Joel Marcus, "Son of Man as Son of Adam: Part II: Exegesis," *RB* 110 (2003): 370–86.

Messiah. They demonstrate that Jesus is a kind of human agent who has been specially authorized by God to exercise discernment and control over matters that otherwise would have been governed by God through law and tradition.

Passion and Resurrection

As Mark's Gospel shifts from depicting Jesus as wonder-worker to tracking his path to the cross, the connotations of the "Human One" title develop accordingly.[37] Jesus speaks of his cruciform fate under the rubric of the Human One: each time that Jesus predicts his death, he does so by telling his disciples that "the Human One" must suffer and die (8:31; 9:12, 31; 10:33, 45; 14:21).

The first such deployment of the title comes immediately after Peter's confession of Jesus as Messiah. Readers familiar with Jesus's praise of Peter in Matthew's version of the story ("Blessed are you, Simon son of Jonah!" Matt 16:17) might be surprised by Jesus's response to Peter in Mark: "Jesus warned them not to tell anyone about him" (Mark 8:30 NIV). There is no praise here. Indeed, it seems that the most important thing is that Jesus reinterprets the disciples' Christology. After Peter affirms that Jesus is the Messiah, Jesus "began to teach them that the Son of Man must suffer many things and be rejected . . . be killed and after three days rise again" (v. 31 NIV).

Here is a critical point in Mark's Christology: as with the scribes in Mark 2:7–10, so here also, "the Human One" is what Jesus says of himself *instead of* what the other characters in the story say about him. The disciples are poor guides to the Christology of Jesus in Mark's Gospel. The disciples are confused by and reject the notion that Jesus must suffer and die. Thus, Peter's reaction to the first passion prediction is to take Jesus aside and rebuke him (8:32). Jesus, in turn, rebukes Peter and calls him "Satan" for so rejecting Jesus's vocation (v. 33).

The "Human One" Christology articulates what is not inherent in the confession of Jesus as Messiah: Jesus is both specially authorized to speak and act with divine power as well as set on a trajectory of rejection, suffering, and death. The passion predictions clearly articulate this, and just as clearly the

---

37. Edwin K. Broadhead, *Naming Jesus, Titular Christology in the Gospel of Mark*, JSNTSup 175 (Sheffield: Sheffield Academic 1999), 133.

disciples remain confused as they hope for a more traditional path to glory (9:30–37; 10:33–45).[38]

In Mark's narrative world, Jesus discloses his cruciform fate using the "Human One" title, and then he begins to move geographically from far in the north (Caesarea Philippi), through Galilee, and then south to Judea and Jerusalem, with the geographical progression marked by passion predictions at each point. He then enters Jerusalem (11:1) for the final week of his life. And, as this part of the story develops, he attempts to teach his disciples that this paradoxical suffering en route to glory is not simply about himself (Christology proper) but is suggestive of an entire alternative economy in God's kingdom in which his followers must participate (see below). The development of Christology, the narrative itself, and broader literary themes all coalesce around the Human One as a suffering Messiah.

One more component of Mark's suffering "Human One" Christology is worth probing. Jesus says that it is necessary (δεῖ) for the Human One to be rejected, suffer, and die (8:31). Later, on the way down from the Mount of Transfiguration, he asks his three disciples, "How is it written about the Human One that he will suffer many things and be despised?" (9:12). Such statements raise the questions, "Why is it necessary?" and "Where, exactly, is it written?" In this case, the answers would come together: being "written" in Scripture creates a sort of divinely ordained necessity. But what Scripture might Jesus have in mind?

There is one scriptural passage that Mark clearly invokes as precedent for Jesus as the Human One: Daniel 7:13 (Mark 13:26; 14:62). Jane Schaberg has made a compelling case for the idea that this provides the scriptural precedent for Mark's "passion-resurrection predictions."[39] Daniel 7 recounts a vision of four beasts who successively defeat each other and rule the world until a heavenly throne is set for judgment and "one like a son of a human" (i.e., a human being in contrast to the beasts) is given all authority. But the final victor is first subjected to cruel treatment at the hands of the fourth beast: "The holy people will be delivered into his hands for a time, times and half a time" (Dan 7:25 NIV). In the Greek translation of Daniel 7:25, the

38. See Osvaldo Vena, "The Markan Construction of Jesus as Disciple of the Kingdom," in *Mark*, ed. Nicole W. Duran, Teresa Okure, and Daniel M. Patte, Texts @ Contexts (Minneapolis: Fortress, 2010), 71–99, esp. 86.

39. Jane Schaberg, "Daniel 7, 12 and the New Testament Passion-Resurrection Predictions," *NTS* 31 (1985): 208–22.

word "be delivered" (παραδοθήσεται) is the same word Jesus uses to speak of the Human One being "handed over" to people (παραδίδοται, Mark 9:31), specifically the high priests and scribes (10:33; cf. 14:41). In addition, both Daniel 7:25 and Mark 9:31; 14:41 describe this handing over using the prepositional phrase, "into the hands of" (εἰς [τὰς] χεῖρας). Finally, Mark's Jesus strangely predicts his resurrection "after" the third day, despite his resurrection on the Sunday subsequent to a Friday killing. The source for this appears to be a literal rendering of Daniel 7:25, which indicates deliverance after three and a half days.[40] Mark's Jesus adopts Daniel's corporate narrative as his own, claiming for himself the story of the beleaguered and slaughtered faithful ones who are subsequently given kingship, authority, and even resurrection life (see Dan 12:2–3).

Exalted to Glory

Perhaps nowhere is the narrative embedding of Mark's "Human One" Christology more important than in its depictions of the exalted Human One who comes to earth in glory (Mark 8:38) and sits enthroned at God's right hand (13:26; 14:62). The narrative flow is critical because each of these heavenly indications comes only after Mark's Jesus has predicted his death and resurrection.[41] That is to say, none of these scenes suggests that Jesus was enthroned at God's right hand, as Son of Man, prior to his life and death on earth. Instead, they speak of a heavenly exaltation that comes only after Jesus is raised from the dead.[42]

Mark 8:38 contains the first glorified Human One saying in the Gospel: "If anyone is ashamed of me and my words in this adulterous and sinful generation, the Son of Man will be ashamed of them when he comes in his Father's glory with the holy angels" (NIV). Context is critical. Jesus has predicted the Human One's rejection, death, and resurrection (v. 31), exchanged rebukes with Peter (vv. 32–33), and called a crowd to follow him on his downward path to glory (vv. 34–37). Thus, Jesus links his own fate as the suffering Human One, his call to follow him in cross-bearing, and the

40. Schaberg, "Daniel 7, 12," 210.

41. A point missed by Sigurd Grindheim, *Christology in the Synoptic Gospels: God or God's Servant?* (New York: T&T Clark, 2012), 55, that leads to a misunderstanding of what sort of heavenly being Jesus is.

42. See James D. G. Dunn, *Christology in the Making: A New Testament Inquiry into the Origins of the Doctrine of Incarnation* (Grand Rapids: Eerdmans, 1996), 88.

Human One's posture toward a person when he returns in a full reflection of the Father's glory. The coherence of the saying is made complete by the glorious appearance being the culmination of Jesus's own willingness to endure a fate that would be considered deeply shameful. Here again the Human One Christology paradoxically joins suffering with glory.

The saying contributes one critical piece to our understanding of Mark's Christology: the exalted Jesus bears a glory that is not, properly speaking, his own native possession but, instead, is the glory of the Father (v. 38). This saying dovetails with our interpretation of the transfiguration story (Mark's next pericope), that the glory with which Jesus shines is a glory he receives at his resurrection, not a once borne, now hidden glory poking its way through. Mark's Christology is dynamic. Mark's Jesus enters different phases of his messianic role not only during his life on earth (from authoritative agent to suffering servant) but also in his move from his earthly ministry to heavenly exaltation.

The heavenly, exalted Human One is the theme of two sayings that directly allude to Daniel 7:13 (13:26; 14:62). In the first, the Human One is a cosmic eschatological redeemer who gathers in the people of God in the final days (13:26). Mark 13 contains its own narrative about the fall of Jerusalem, a time of great tribulation, and a climactic moment of revelation when the Human One appears on the clouds with power and glory. The context suggests a few points about Mark's Human One Christology.

Immediately prior to his description of the appearance of the Human One (13:26), Jesus warns his followers against false messiahs (vv. 21–22). These will perform deceitful wonders (v. 22). In this context, the signs of a darkened sun and falling stars (vv. 24–25) form the true sign of the Messiah's advent in contradistinction to the deceptive signs of the false messiahs and prophets. Thus, when these signs are accompanied by the glorious appearance of the Human One, readers should connect the dots and see that the Human One is the true Messiah. The "Human One" designation articulates Jesus's vision of what the true Messiah's appearance will look like at this eschatological moment (in contrast to what the Messiah's appearance entailed when Jesus first walked the earth and had to endure suffering and death).

Because of the point at which the Human One comes from heaven in Mark's overall story and the narrative of Mark 13, there is no case to be made here for divine preexistence prior to Jesus's life on earth. Instead, the human Jesus is looking to the future, when the Human One will come with the glory that he has received after his death and resurrection. Putting this together with the previous observation, Mark 13:21–27 does not contrast a divine deliverer with a human deliverer but instead shows us what kind of human rescuer it is that comes at the moment of Israel's great eschatological crisis.

Though Mark does not use any citation formula to signal to readers that this Human One saying refers to Daniel 7:13–14, its depiction of his being seen coming with the clouds with power and glory is evocative of that scriptural antecedent: "Look! Upon the clouds of heaven, one like a son of a human came . . . and authority was given to him and every nation of the earth according to its kind, and all glory was rendered to him" (Dan 7:13–14, my translation of the LXX). Mark's Jesus says, "They will see the Human One coming with the clouds, with great power and glory" (Mark 13:26). Daniel's vision tells the story of a climactic moment in Israel's story when its own great tribulation (Dan 7:25) comes to an end with God overthrowing a wicked king and establishing God's own people in an everlasting kingdom, ruling over all the nations of the earth (vv. 26–27).[43] The narrative in Mark 13 follows the board contours of Daniel 7 in expecting Jerusalem's climactic persecution to be resolved by the advent of the Human One (paralleling Daniel's "one like a human") and the deliverance of God's people.

Some have argued that the Human One's traveling on a cloud is a signal that he is some sort of heavenly being, inasmuch as such locomotion is typically God's own in the Hebrew Bible (e.g., Ps 68:4). There are strong arguments against reading divinity into this reference, however. First, in Daniel itself the human-like being comes into the presence of God on a cloud and is clearly distinguished from the deity. Second, in Daniel's interpretation of the vision the human-like being stands for the people of Israel, not a literal heavenly figure such as an angel or other divine being (Dan 7:27). Third, elsewhere in the Christian tradition we find a vision of human martyrs who rise after three days and are carried into heaven on a cloud (Rev 11:11–12)—a clear indication that the imagery of the cloud-traveling, resurrected Human One was being read as the sort of story in which other humans could participate. It is thus better to read the idea of coming with clouds in tandem with

43. See also Marcus, *Way of the Lord*, 94–97.

what Mark's readers already know: the glorified Human One comes with the Father's glory (Mark 8:38), and presumably from the Father's presence. His arrival demonstrates his own heavenly exaltation and power, but these are aspects of his identity as the exalted Human One after his resurrection from the dead.[44]

We have already seen that Daniel's human-like being is a visionary representation of the beleaguered people of God who are subsequently vindicated. The vindication, moreover, entails reception of what might well be called royal power inasmuch as God bestows an eternal kingdom on his people: "Then their kingdom and authority and the splendor and the domain of all the kingdoms under heaven will be handed over to the holy people of the Most High, for them to rule over an eternal kingdom" (Dan 7:27, my translation of the LXX). If Daniel 7 adds anything to our understanding of the Christology of Mark 13, it may simply be that the glorified Human One has been exalted to a place of rule over the kingdom of God that he has been proclaiming and enacting since his first public proclamation of the gospel (Mark 1:15).

Jesus's final deployment of the Human One phrase about himself comes at his trial before the Sanhedrin (Mark 14:55–65). The carefully crafted narrative of Mark's Human One Christology becomes evident here, as the last usage of the title in the Gospel parallels the first, with Jesus being accused of blasphemy (2:7; 14:64). Just as importantly, in Jesus's exchange with the high priest, the three major markers of Jesus's identity in the story (Messiah, God's Son, and Human One) are drawn together as mutually interpreting titles.

The climactic moment of the trial comes as the priest asks Jesus, "Are you the Messiah, the Son of the Blessed?" "Son of the Blessed," that is, Son of God, is in an epexegetical relationship with the first title, "Messiah." In other words, for this character in the story, to be Messiah is to be God's Son. This coheres with the argument made above, that the declarations of divine sonship are indications of Jesus playing the role of the anointed one, not indications of divine ontology.[45] Because the query is in the mouth

44. Cf. Dunn, *Christology in the Making*, 88.

45. E. Earl Ellis, "Deity-Christology in Mark 14:58," in *Jesus of Nazareth: Lord and Christ: Essays on the Historical Jesus and New Testament Christology*, ed. Joel B. Green and Max Turner (Grand Rapids: Eerdmans, 1994), 196, reads this exchange as a challenge and affirmation of Jesus's deity, a move that

of Jesus's opponent, the reader might hold this equivalence with caution. Jesus, though, immediately allays any such concerns, responding with the unequivocal, "I am." However, he does not stop there and once again speaks about the Human One to reinterpret these other titles: "I am, and you will see the Human One seated at the right hand of power and coming with the clouds of heaven" (14:62). Christ, Son of God, and Son of Man can all mean the same thing—but only if they are all interpreted through Jesus's own description and embodiment of the Human One.

Two aspects of Jesus's response invite comment, as they might touch on Mark's Christology. First, the phrase "I am" (ἐγώ εἰμι) is sometimes read as an identification with the God of the Old Testament. Two pieces of data speak against this. One is that Jesus's response is simply the first person singular response to the question put to him by the priest in the second person: the appropriate response to "Are you?" is either "I am" or "I am not." The other is that in the most often cited biblical antecedent, Moses at the burning bush in Exodus 3:14, the Greek version does not have God say "I am" (ἐγώ εἰμι) as a substantive to refer to himself.[46] Instead, God says, "I am [ἐγώ εἰμι] the one who is [ὁ ὤν]. . . . Say to the sons of Israel, '*The one who is* [ὁ ὤν] has sent me'" (Exod 3:14, my translation of the LXX). When Jesus says, "(Yes) I am," he is affirming his identification with the titles Christ and Son of God, not claiming a share in God's own divinity.[47]

Second, the allusion to Daniel 7:13 is here mixed with an allusion to Psalm 110:1, as Jesus inserts, "seated at the right hand of power" (Mark 14:62). Jesus has previously invoked this psalm in a dispute in the temple (12:36). Both Jesus and his opponents take the psalm to be a depiction of the Messiah (12:35–37), even as Jesus uses it to question whether "son of David" is an appropriate title for the Christ. The psalm, and Jesus's deployment of it, speaks of the Messiah being enthroned at God's "right hand." In Daniel 7:9, prior to the appearance of God or the one like a human, thrones (plural) are set in place. This suggests that the human-like being will be enthroned next to God. Mark's Jesus, by blending the two citations, indicates that Jesus's Human One Christology is a heavenly enthronement Christology. In this

comes hand in hand with his unlikely interpretation of the "Son of God" language as indicators of a divine Christology.

46. A mistake made, e.g., in Grindheim, *Christology*, 48.

47. See also Rebecca Scharbach Wollenberg, "אני יי רפאך: A Short Note on ἐγώ εἰμι Sayings and the Dangers of Translation Tradition," *NovT* 59 (2017): 20–26.

story, to be the Christ, the son of the Blessed, is to be the Human One who takes his messianic throne through exaltation to God's right hand.[48]

The Human One in Mark's Story

God's words for Jesus (the beloved Son) and Jesus's words for himself (the Human One) provide a strikingly coherent framework for Mark's Christology as a whole. These so structure the story and so define Jesus that they create a strong presupposition against any significant variation being introduced elsewhere. If someone wants to argue for a divine Christology in Mark, it will not be sufficient to point to ad hoc moments in the story that might be read as a theophany or other such association of Jesus as God. The whole narrative will have to be reread to argue for an identification of Jesus with the divine in these particular christological ideas and in the overarching narrative of the whole, and in such a way as to substantively contribute to that story. Given that neither Jesus, nor any of his followers, nor God, nor any other character in the story, nor the narrator ever articulate divinity or preexistence for Jesus, it is highly unlikely that such an argument would be successful.[49]

The Story of Power and Weakness

Having established some major overarching christological contours for Mark's Gospel, we can take a few soundings to explore how well the map we have drawn anticipates the more detailed terrain of the story. Jesus's proclamation and enactment of the kingdom of God should help us understand more clearly Jesus's part in God's reign over the earth.

Authoritative Power

The first few chapters of Mark show us both that Jesus has unique authority and that responding appropriately to Jesus's ministry is inseparable from recognizing the arrival of God's own reign. Jesus proclaims this reign the first time he speaks in the Gospel: "'The time has come,' he said. 'The

---

48. For such exaltation being the cause for the blasphemy charge, cf. Marcus, *Mark 8–16*, 1008–9; Richard B. Hays, *Echoes of Scripture in the Gospels* (Waco, TX: Baylor University Press, 2016), 60–61.

49. I am indebted to James McGrath for this observation.

kingdom of God has come near'" (Mark 1:15 NIV). Mark's Jesus does not preach about the kingdom of God for the next three chapters; instead, we find an enactment of this kingdom, with hints that Jesus is the king who reigns over it.

His eschatological announcement is immediately followed by Jesus summoning his first followers, so that Mark's story depicts a Jewish expectation of what E. P. Sanders has labeled "restoration eschatology." This is the notion that God's people would be gathered together as part of God's final act of salvation.[50] The surprise is that the narrative will not develop smoothly from gathering to glory but will be interrupted by the crucifixion and only finished when the Human One sends out his messengers to gather all the elect from the ends of the earth (13:27).

Jesus's authority is put front and center in his first public action: teaching in a synagogue in Capernaum and exorcising a man's demons (1:21–27). His authority is astounding to the people (vv. 22, 27), particularly for its being different from that of the scribes. That same authority to speak authoritatively in teaching is pegged as the power Jesus has to command evil spirits (v. 27). The spirits also know who Jesus is. He is "God's holy one," an indication that Jesus and God are distinct and yet God is the source of the extraordinary authority Jesus embodies.[51]

The authority to teach and exorcise is then coordinated with the authority to heal more generally, as Jesus heals many at the house of Simon Peter, including the latter's mother-in-law. A final healing in Mark 1 is of a leper, adding the nuance of "cleansing" to Jesus's authoritative power. Both of these latter two scenes end with Jesus withdrawn from the people in wilderness places, the second time against his will (vv. 35, 45). These are the first hints that the power of Jesus will not lead him straight to glorious acclamation and enthronement.

Mark 2:1–3:6 contains a series of conflict stories. The value of these is that they show us the point of contention between Jesus and his countrymen as understood by the author of Mark. We have already covered two of these. The first conflict takes place when Jesus heals the paralytic and forgives his sins, claiming the right to do so as "the Human One." The penultimate

50. E. P. Sanders, *Jesus and Judaism* (Minneapolis: Fortress, 1985), 61–119.
51. See Vena, "Markan Construction of Jesus," 77–80.

conflict in this series is the grain-plucking episode, in which Jesus deploys the same title to validate actions of his followers that fall beyond what law and tradition have circumscribed. In these the peculiar authority of Jesus is in dispute.

In the second conflict narrative, Jesus is chastised for eating with sinners and tax collectors (2:15–17), as he appears to be skewing traditional narratives about the identity of the faithful, gathered people of God, and claiming to have the authority to create such a people (cf. 3:31–33). Next, he is called out for his disciples not fasting like others and identifies his own current presence and future absence as the hallmarks to which his followers' religious behavior is attuned (2:18–22). Moreover, in using the image of a bridegroom in his response, Jesus invokes eschatological narratives that suggest he himself is the marker of Israel's age of fulfillment (2:19; cf. 1:15). In the final story, Jesus heals a man in front of spying eyes that were waiting to see if he would heal on a sabbath (3:1–6). His healing authority and life-giving work are set in contrast to killing and destroying—the very things his opponents then go out to plot against him. In this final scene, the die seems to be cast; it is precisely Jesus's authority as healer and teacher that ensures his paradoxical, cruciform fate.

These conflict stories represent Jesus as the one to whom people must look to learn what faithfulness to God entails, not because he is telling people "what was right all along," nor because he has some inherent divine status or being in himself, but because he is the decisive agent in the eschatological moment of Israel's deliverance. This reading coalesces with the last pericope in Mark 3, the Beelzebul controversy (3:20–35). Here, Jesus's opponents ascribe his great power to his being in league with Satan (vv. 22–23). In response, Jesus indicates that his work is "binding" the satanic "strong man" so as to pillage his house (v. 27). But as for the true source of his power, it is the Holy Spirit whom he received from God (vv. 28–30).[52] In terms of Christology, we learn here that Jesus plays a role in the downfall of God's satanic opponent, and we are reminded that his power and authority are not inherent to himself but come from the Spirit he received at his baptism.

52. Overlooking this exegetical detail is what allows Grindheim, *Christology*, 43–44, to marshal the story as evidence for a divine Christology.

Royal Authority

The paradoxical nature of Jesus's mission finds hints in Mark's first lengthy teaching text, the parables of Mark 4. The story of the sower shows a profligate spreading of "the word," but a much more stingy taking root. Extraordinary abundance comes, however, from the few seeds that do yield a harvest. The kingdom of God itself (see v. 11), like Mark's Christology, rises from below, amid conflict and failure, rather than descending from above with power and glory.

The parable chapter is rounded off by the first of two stories that depict Jesus's control over waters, this one being a storm-stilling episode (vv. 35–41; see also 6:45–52). The pericope concludes with the disciples' lingering question, "Who is this man that the wind and sea obey him?" thus inviting the reader to probe its christological significance (4:41). The first time Jesus teaches, the authority of his teaching is confirmed by his exorcising a demon (1:21–27). Mark 4 makes a similar move in much greater detail, providing the reader with the content of the teaching and a greater show of authority.

The stilling of the sea and the exorcism are closer to one another than a modern reader might see. When the disciples cried out to Jesus, he "rebuked" the wind and said to the sea saying, "Silence! Shut up!" (4:39). The same Greek words for "rebuke" and "shut up" are deployed when Jesus exorcises that first demon in 1:25: Jesus "rebuked him saying, 'Shut up and come out of him.'" The sea is depicted as a hostile spiritual force, in keeping with hostile renderings of the sea in much ancient Near Eastern literature, such that the whole scene is like a grand exorcism. The upshot is that Jesus stills the storm with the same authority he has to exorcise demons—an authority empowered by the Spirit that he has received from God.

Such a notion fits well enough into the suggestion that Jesus is a divinely empowered messiah figure. Psalm 89 depicts the relationship between God's great power and that with which God imbues an idealized Davidic king. This king is God's son, calling God "Father" (Ps 89:26 [88:27 LXX]). God bestows on this king the power to control the "cosmic enemies"[53] that are sea and river: "I will set his hand over the sea and his right hand over the rivers" (v. 25 [26 LXX]).[54] The Hebrew Bible thus has a very good answer for

53. Mark S. Smith, *Priestly Vision of Genesis 1* (Minneapolis: Fortress, 2010), 21.

54. See J. R. Daniel Kirk and Stephen L. Young, ""I Will Set His Hand to the Sea": Psalm 88:26 LXX and Christology in Mark," *JBL* 133 (2014): 333–40.

the disciples' query, "Who is this?" It is an answer that fits the mold of the "Son of God" Christology explored above. The one who can call on God as Father is the Messiah to whom God has given earthly authority over all the enemies of God's people. As if to confirm such a reading, the next pericope, the exorcism of the many-demon "Legion," depicts Jesus under the rubric of "Son of the Most High God" (Mark 5:7) and ends with the demons joining the depths of the very sea that Jesus conquers here.

Shared Scripts

The feeding narratives provide another angle on Mark's Christology. Both depict the surprising economy of God's work in Jesus (i.e., the kingdom of God) through the appearance of abundance out of apparent lack, which reflects the expectations of the parable of the sower and anticipates the second half of the narrative when life and glory come out of suffering and death. As dramatic feeding narratives, these scenes reflect both the feeding of Israel in the desert and Elisha's miraculous feeding of a hundred men (2 Kgs 4:42–44). The feeding of the five thousand in Mark 6 provides us with a christological cue at the beginning: Jesus has compassion on the people because they are like sheep without a shepherd, and so he meets their need by first teaching the people and then by feeding them through the hands of other shepherds.

The shepherding image is one that the Scriptures use of both God and Israel's kings (see Ezek 34). Mark's introduction of the shepherding imagery seems to echo scriptural precedents; talk of sheep without a shepherd appears in both Numbers 27:17 and 1 Kings 22:17. In the former, Moses's prayer that Israel not be shepherdless is met by the appointment of Joshua. In the latter, the prophet Michaiah prophesies the death of the king of Israel. The role Jesus plays here is the role of a human shepherd, stepping into the void of faithful leadership—a void perhaps best exemplified in the immediately preceding story of "king" Herod's murder of John the Baptist (6:14–29).

The idea that the feeding story shows that a specially empowered human can be the agent of a feeding miracle is confirmed by a close reading of the story's details. It is not Jesus who feeds the five thousand but the disciples.[55] He commands the disciples to give the people something to eat (6:37), they

55. See Suzanne Watts Henderson, *Christology and Discipleship in the Gospel of Mark*, SNTSMS 135 (Cambridge: Cambridge University Press, 2006).

find out how much food they have in their own stores (v. 38), they have the people sit in banqueting groups (v. 39), and after Jesus blesses the bread he gives it to the disciples to set before the people (v. 41—all of this can be contrasted with the Gospel of John's telling in John 6:5–11). Jesus as shepherd empowers other shepherds, just as his first act of gathering fishermen was to make them fishers of people (1:16–17). The shared work underscores that the Christology operative in the feeding narratives is not one in which Jesus is a different type of being from his followers.

This brings us to another narrative thread that confirms Mark's Christology as a richly textured, high, and human Christology: Jesus's disciples do, or are called to do, most of what Jesus himself does. As we just saw, Jesus gathers followers who will, in turn, gather (1:16–17). Jesus's ministry of power is typified by teaching, healing, and exorcising (e.g., 1:39). When he appoints the twelve apostles, the purpose is to be with Jesus and be given authority to preach and exorcize (3:14–15). Jesus later sends them out with these specific authorizations, and the editorial note that they healed as well (6:7, 12–13).[56] As we saw above, it is the disciples who mediate the feeding of the five thousand (6:30–44); they feed the four thousand as well (8:1–10). In the narrative world of Mark, what makes a person capable of speaking authoritatively for God, healing a sick body, exorcising a demon, or exercising power over nature is not being divine but is instead having appropriately delegated authority conferred upon oneself.

When the narrative turns toward the cross, the involvement of Jesus's followers in the tasks assigned to Jesus is no less acutely expected. Immediately after predicting his death for the first time, Jesus turns to the crowds to let them know that discipleship means participating in his cruciform fate: "Whoever wants to be my disciple must deny themselves and take up their cross and follow me" (8:34 NIV; see also 9:35–37; 10:35–45).With this, Jesus's followers are incorporated into the second half of his story. Unlike John's Gospel (e.g., John 10:17), there is no special divine power that enables him to embrace the cross and enact his own resurrection. Instead, Jesus goes to the cross, completely entrusting himself to God, and his followers must trust that they, too, will be vindicated by God and the glorified Human One if they follow the same path.

56. Vena, "Markan Construction of Jesus," 70–82.

Mark's Christology is a human Christology, at least in part, because it is showing Jesus's human followers what their faithful human lives should look like on the earth through both prongs of Jesus's messianic identity (i.e., authority and suffering), narrated over both halves of Mark's Gospel.[57]

Christology in the Kingdom Economy

Jesus's ability to bring abundance out of apparent lack is evidence of a kingdom in which apparent lowliness or emptiness is the point at which fullness and glory are discovered. Jesus's vocation to die and be raised is defined as messianic within such a kingdom. We see these threads woven together after Jesus's passion predictions. After the second passion prediction (9:30–32), his disciples begin to dispute about greatness, a debate Jesus reframes by telling them greatness is found in servanthood (nearly the bottom rung of the patriarchal ladder of power) and by putting a child (another contender for least of all in a patriarchal power structure) in front of them as the picture of greatness (vv. 35–36). The christological connection is not left to the reader's imagination, as Jesus identifies himself with the child: "Whoever welcomes one of these little children in my name welcomes me" (v. 37 NIV). Jesus's cruciform Christology is part and parcel of a humble, upside-down economy of greatness and power in the kingdom of God. At the same time, and paradoxically, Jesus says that to receive him is to receive the one who sent him (i.e., God, v. 37); thus, receiving God is a matter of receiving God's agents, and receiving God's agents is a matter of looking "down" rather than "up." Thus, the functional, suffering, humble Christology that marks the narrative of Mark as a whole, and the Son of God and Son of Man Christologies more particularly, finds perfect concord with the broader narrative of the kingdom of God and Jesus's identity within it.

A parallel interaction takes place after the third passion prediction, when the confusion of the disciples about Jesus's having to die (10:32–34) is further expressed in James and John's desire for seats of glory (vv. 35–37). The connection with Jesus's death is made clear in his response about the need to drink his cup and endure his baptism (vv. 38–39). Unlike gentile

57. Jin-Young Choi, "The Misunderstanding of Jesus's Disciples in Mark: An Interpretation from a Community-Centered Perspective," in Duran, Okure, and Patte, *Mark*, 55–69, argues that the disciples' participation is a signal of a horizontal, kinship relationship of mutuality rather than a vertical, patron-client type relationship of dependence.

greatness, greatness among Jesus's followers is found in servanthood and slavery and even giving of one's life (vv. 43–45).

More subtly, Mark encodes this upside-down quality of the kingdom in its depictions of unnamed women. These characters dance in the margins of the narrative; they are unnamed, female, and with no extended participation in Mark's Gospel. However, in a narrative that claims a status of greatness for those at the bottom of the social hierarchy, triple-marginalization should be a paradoxical hint that these characters might be the greatest of Jesus's followers. Indeed, we find in them qualities and actions that the named men who follow Jesus often lack or reject: service (1:31; cf. 9:33–35), faith (5:34; cf. 4:40), recognition of abundant bread (7:28; cf. 6:36, 42; 8:4, 8, 14–21), laying down one's life (12:44; cf. 8:32; 9:30–34), and the ability to conjoin anointing/messiahship and death in the person of Jesus (14:3–9; cf. 8:32).[58] The notion that greatness is found in lowliness is not simply spoken and enacted by the person of Jesus but is embedded in the broader narrative as well. The unnamed women are part of a narratival infrastructure that gives meaning to the person of Jesus, whose ultimate greatness is found through a willingness to serve and lay down his life as a ransom for many (10:45).

As we pursue the question of Mark's Christology, it is worth exploring whether efforts to find a divine Christology in Mark trade on the notion that true value and significance can only come from an exalted, otherworldly glory. Such readings cut against the grain of Mark's narrative as they pursue some clue other than the notion that humble, self-giving humanity (even to the point of death) is the location where ultimate greatness is found in God's kingdom.

Human Limits

The limits of Jesus's humanity appear at several junctures in Mark's Gospel, sometimes to the embarrassment of later Christian interpreters. In Mark 6 Jesus goes to his hometown but could not do many miracles there because of their lack of faith (vv. 1–6). In the apocalyptic discourse in Mark 13, Jesus says that the hour of the great consummation is unknown to the Son; only the Father knows (v. 32). The distinction between Jesus and the Father is underscored in Gethsemane when Jesus prays to God as Father,

58. Cf. Malbon, *Mark's Jesus*, 221, 225–26.

asking for the cup to be taken away and differentiating and subordinating his own will to that of God (14:36).[59] The final moment of differentiation between Jesus and God is at the cross, where Jesus cries out, "My God, my God, why have you forsaken me?" (15:34). This is the critical piece of narrative evidence that Mark's Jesus and Mark's God are distinct and separate characters. Any "divinity" one might claim for Jesus in Mark must be not only that of a different person but also of a different substance from God.

Christology of the Passion

Over a century ago, Martin Kähler described Mark's Gospel as "a passion narrative with an extended introduction."[60] Such a claim finds some validation in what we have seen thus far. Jesus's first appearance, at his baptism, foreshadows a messianic death, and the movement of various stories and sayings from humility and lack to abundance and honor creates a wide-ranging mold that also shapes Jesus's movement from death to resurrection. Not only this, but the way the storytelling becomes increasingly slow and detailed as we approach the last day of Jesus's life makes the passion narrative the focal point of the story. We should thus expect that the Christology of Mark as a whole would make itself visible here.

We can observe two facets of the passion narrative to confirm the notion that Jesus's identity is found in the paradoxical juxtaposition of kingship and suffering (with resurrection and glory following only afterward). One facet is on the surface of the narrative, as royal indicators are peppered throughout the story of Jesus's suffering. If we begin our survey with the plot to kill Jesus in Mark 14:1, there immediately follows a dinner party at which Jesus is anointed with oil on his head (v. 3), an action that recalls Jesus's messianic identity. Yet he then interprets the action as preparation of his body for burial (v. 8) and declares that this action will be told wherever the gospel is proclaimed (v. 9). The juxtaposition of suffering and messianic office is the summary of Mark's Gospel.

The Lord's Supper itself depicts Jesus's suffering as the core aspect of his identity that he shares in order to give life to his followers (14:22–25). At that

---

59. Grindheim, *Christology*, 51, badly misreads Mark's story when he claims that Jesus's "authority is second to none, not even that of God."

60. Martin Kähler, *The So-Called Historical Jesus and the Historic, Biblical Christ*, trans. and ed. Carl E. Braaten (Philadelphia: Fortress, 1964), 80.

meal Jesus also predicts that the disciples will abandon him by quoting Zechariah 13:7: "I will strike the shepherd, and the sheep will be scattered" (Mark 14:27 NIV). The "shepherd" language likely refers to Jesus's role as king, one he plays out, in part, by submitting to rejection, suffering, and death. The first-person language of the biblical citation, "'I' will strike," appears to indicate God as an active agent in the passion. Jesus's prayer in Gethsemane does the same. In addressing God as "Father" (v. 36), Jesus evokes the two divine affirmations of his own sonship (= kingship). And his prayer is for the removal of the suffering and death (cf. v. 34) that is besetting him. The prayer thus reflects the broader Christology of the Gospel in binding together Jesus as Messiah with the role of the righteous sufferer.

Jesus's suffering at the hands of the Romans provides an ironic confirmation of Mark's suffering Messiah Christology. Here, the charge has been couched in such a way as to raise Roman ire: Jesus as "king of the Jews" (15:2, 9, 12, 18, 26). Jesus is coy about this title (v. 2), not owning it as directly as he did the title "Messiah, Son of the Blessed" (14:61). But it becomes the mantra for the Romans as they fulfill his messianic destiny. Turning Jesus's fate over to the crowd, Pilate asks what is to be done with "the king of the Jews," to which the crowds reply, twice, "Crucify him!" (15:12–15). The soldiers mock Jesus as would-be king, dressing him in a "royal" purple robe and a "crown" of thorns, bowing before him and hailing him as king prior to stripping him and leading him away to be crucified (vv. 16–20). Finally, Jesus is hung on the cross with "king of the Jews" as the charge placarded above his head. In this, Pilate adopts the charge articulated by Jesus's opponents, and the force of the Roman actions is to disprove the would-be royal pretender's claims to such authority.

In a twist of dramatic irony, however, Mark's readers know that it is precisely through this suffering and death that Jesus's royal claim is made good. This suffering lies, paradoxically, at the heart of Mark's messianic Christology. The connection between suffering and Jesus's royal status is confirmed in the end by the centurion's proclamation that Jesus is God's Son upon seeing how he died (v. 39). In all of this, Mark's Jesus is being shown to be a particular kind of human person, playing a particular role in Israel's story, and not only distinct from God as a character but finally separable from God as well. The cry of dereliction, "My God, my God, why have you forsaken me?" (v. 34; cf. Ps 22:1) underscores the dependence of the human

Jesus on the divine God for deliverance, and that Mark's Christ is a messiah who cannot be placed on the divine side of the creator-creature divide.

Jesus's cry of dereliction brings us to the other facet of the passion narrative worthy of consideration. This stretch of the Gospel regularly alludes to Scripture, and the psalms in particular.[61] One such instance is the allusion to Psalm 40:10 during the Last Supper: one who eats my bread will betray me (Mark 14:18). The voice of the psalm is David's, thus applying to Jesus a story of a betrayed royal figure. Similarly, Jesus's statement in the garden that his soul is anguished to the point of death (v. 34) is widely seen as an allusion to a refrain in Psalms 42:5, 11; 43:5. This is a psalm of a righteous sufferer who looks to God for deliverance. As alluded to above, Jesus's cry of dereliction (Mark 15:34) echoes Psalm 22:1. This is a psalm of David, in which the royal figure complains of being abandoned to his death-dealing enemies. Finally, the offer of vinegar to Jesus (Mark 15:36) echoes Psalm 69:21, located in another Davidic psalm of lament and complaint. The upshot of these various allusions to Scripture in the passion narrative is to deepen the color of the portrait already sketched of Jesus as a suffering messiah and, perhaps, to hint that Jesus, too, like anointed ones of old, can expect deliverance from God.

Conclusion

To ask about the Christology of Mark is to ask about a narrative Christology, how a character is depicted and developed within a story that gets told in one of the biblical Gospels. If Mark is a well-written piece of literature, then its Christology should cohere with the overall thrust of the narrative, and the character of Jesus should be developed in such a way as to fit smoothly within the broader sweep and shape of the story. That is what I have attempted to show in this essay. The narrative and the titles depict the paradoxical authority of Jesus as residing in and springing up out of lowliness: the authoritative Messiah only comes to his throne through suffering and death. Mark gives us a coherent yet multivalent portrait of an idealized human figure.

61. See Marcus, *Way of the Lord*, 174–75; Stephen P. Ahearne-Kroll, *The Psalms of Lament in Mark's Passion: Jesus's Davidic Suffering*, SNTSMS 142 (New York: Cambridge University Press, 2007), 61–77.

Mark's narrative is one in which Jesus who appears in the wilderness is empowered and declared God's Son with the gift of the Spirit. The authority he bears creates a following and impacts the religious life, physical bodies, and natural world wherever he goes—a ministry that unfolds under the rubric of the near-drawing kingdom of God. Having thus established his messianic credentials, Jesus predicts his death at the midway point in the story. He then is on a steady road to the cross, with the promise of resurrection and exaltation to follow. This overall narrative forms the backbone for Mark's narrative Christology as well. We find a remarkable cohesion between the movement from authority to suffering and thence to exaltation captured in Mark's story as a whole, its Son of God Christology, and its Human One Christology. In all of this, there is no hint of a preexistence Christology or a Christology of divine nature; there is simply the affirmation that Jesus scandalously exercises divine functions as God's anointed and/or appointed human agent.

Mark's story loses much and gains little more than insubstantial gilding by attempts to read Mark's Jesus as in some way identified as Israel's God. Most importantly, it loses its internal coherence, in which Jesus and God are clearly distinct characters. Jesus constantly points his followers back to God as the appropriate object of praise, and God shows up only to affirm that Jesus is the one who understands how God is at work at the great eschatological fulcrum of Israel's history. Indeed, so distinct are the two characters that in the end the crucified Jesus can be abandoned by the God whom he has served and proclaimed throughout (Mark 15:34).

This is why, in looking to Mark's Christology, we do well to set aside expectations created by the more developed theology of the later church. It simply does not reflect the story that Mark has told. And, in setting such a Christology aside, we discover a rich alternative in the story of an idealized human Messiah who comes to glory along the way of the cross.

Huebenthal Response to Kirk

SANDRA HUEBENTHAL

J. R. Daniel Kirk's essay is an abbreviation of the argument he makes in his book *A Man Attested by God: The Human Jesus of the Synoptic Gospels*. The book, originally published in 2018, aims to preserve and propagate a reading that does justice to the Synoptic Gospels, while pushing back biased interpretations and fostering the development of a theological focal point for those readings and their impact on the understanding of Jesus as well as the self-understanding of today's faithful. In this brief summary, the trained theologian and exegete hears echoes of Paul Ricœur's hermeneutics and—knowing about Kirk's other work—assumes a narrative approach, which reads each New Testament text individually and independently in order to understand its unique contribution to the discourses of the Jesus-followers of the late first century.

As I understand it, such an enterprise is not meant to be a confessional statement or even an attack on the foundations of Christian faith. It is rather what I would call the prevalent task of the New Testament scholar, that is, an etic reading of a New Testament text as an externalization of collective memory, as opposed to an emic reading of a New Testament text as part of the Christian cultural memory, which is the prevalent task of a theologian. Both ways of reading are not exclusive but complementary and can be distinguished by their research questions. While the theologian with the emic perspective looks from the inside and asks, "How do we understand the New Testament texts today and how do they inform our faith?" the New Testament scholar with the etic perspective looks from the outside and asks, "How does a particular New Testament text reflect the events, and what frames does it provide for understanding and identity construction of its audiences?"[1]

It is not difficult to see that Kirk asks the questions of the New Testament scholar with the etic perspective. He starts his reflections about Markan Christology not with an exploration of the context, as Larry Hurtado, or a theological assumption, as Adam Winn, but with the text itself. In order to find out what Mark is about and what awaits the reader in this Gospel, he starts like the readers themselves and turns to the first lines of the text.

As is usually the case in ancient texts, the beginning of a text, that is, its headline and first paragraphs, serves a similar purpose as our book covers, blurbs, and other paratexts today. Thus it makes perfect sense to start the essay with Mark 1:1–2. The book cover, if we stay with this image for a moment, reads, "The beginning of the good news about Jesus the Messiah, as it is written in Isaiah the prophet: 'I will send my messenger ahead of you, who will prepare your way'—'a voice calling in the wilderness, "Prepare the way for the Lord, make straight the paths for him."'"

This glance at the cover reveals three points for Kirk: (1) the book will present a narrative Christology, (2) the story is about Jesus the Messiah, and (3) this story has its primary interpretive grid in the Scriptures of Israel and their reception in Second Temple Judaism. As the story is about Jesus, the Messiah, Kirk also issues two warnings upfront. One concerns the modern reader; the danger is that today's faithful will bring their own beliefs about *Jesus* to this text and try to read them into the text in order to find their developed beliefs already in a first-century text. The other warning concerns the ancient reader, as the story might not necessarily fit into the expectations for a *messiah*, as they were current in Second Temple Judaism.

To avoid falling into either trap, Kirk suggests to "allow that this story is going to make both sense to its first-century audience and also makes claims for Jesus that would have been genuinely surprising to Jews who were awaiting God's deliverance" (p. 138). Thus, both ancient and modern audiences might be in for surprises. The story will indeed turn out to be quite unexpected, as the unbiased reader will be introduced to "an idealized

1. Cf. Sandra Huebenthal, "Frozen Moments: Early Christianity through the Lens of Social Memory Theory," in *Memory and Memories in Early Christianity*, ed. Simon Butticaz and Enrico Norelli, WUNT 398 (Tübingen: Mohr Siebeck, 2018), 17–43 (esp. 41–43).

human messiah who comes to glory along the way of the cross" (p. 171). It is unsurprising, then, that this story can be somewhat explosive not only to modern Christian and late first-century Jewish ears but also for Roman readers, if there were any. Roman audiences do not, however, seem to be the primary target group. The opening verses state in no uncertain terms that, even though the text was written in the Roman Empire and in Greek—the *lingua franca* of those days, the "Jewish world with its texts and practices is the primary conversation partner for making sense of the story that is to come" (p. 139).

This does not mean that there might not be allusions and references to the broader Greek and Latin encyclopedia, but it is just not the focus. I have observed the same in my own analysis of Mark's text and concluded:

> Each of the different stories considered here can be read and understood both with a Jewish and a pagan encyclopedia. Especially for the healing and miracle stories, there are reference texts from both the Jewish and the pagan environment that can be used for comparison. It is obvious, however, that inscription—engagement with the tradition—takes place only in Jewish frames of reference, which is especially striking with gentile characters. . . . The fact that the prophetic Jewish tradition is made use of continuously, while the pagan tradition is recalled only at individual points, indicates that the former is preferred as the adequate frame of reference against the latter. To put it differently: the traditions of Torah and the prophets, especially Isaiah, are the main and dominant voices in the intertextual echo chamber, while resonances of the pagan tradition are audible but do not essentially influence the sound.[2]

The argument Kirk makes in this essay is based on a narrative approach that starts with analyzing the story and the plot, before it turns to the question as to how audiences in the late first century might have received the text. Kirk's reading strictly rules out additional assumptions and concentrates on what is explicitly in the text, rather than pondering what might have been in the background and could or even should be read into the text: "Mark's Jesus is known within the bounds of his earthly life. In Mark, Jesus does not

2. Huebenthal, *Reading Mark's Gospel*, 346.

possess the sort of hidden identity that one can only find by peering into an eternal past in heaven from which the Messiah had eternal origins. As far as the reader knows, Jesus is not ontologically different from other humans by virtue of preexistence, supernatural conception, or divine parentage" (p. 139). Later in the essay, Kirk concludes: "Given that neither Jesus, nor any of his followers, nor God, nor any other character in the story, nor the narrator ever articulate divinity or preexistence for Jesus, it is highly unlikely that such an argument would be successful" (p. 160). This is a quite refreshing way to read the text: it neither requires a package of additional knowledge nor an expert who guides the reader through the text and points out what secret allusions the reader might have missed. In fact, Kirk might agree that the Markan narrator is already enough of a guide.

I would further assume that Kirk has similar hermeneutical issues with "accompanied (or supervised) reading" approaches that require a lot of additional knowledge. In my own doctoral thesis about the reception of Zechariah 9–14 in the New Testament, I have pointed at this as an important hermeneutical problem:

> The question is whether it makes sense to assume an interpretation for a particular text, which the readers are not pointed to by appropriate signals in the text itself. In the example I investigated, exclusively extra-textual knowledge would have been necessary to understand a particular section in John, which makes no sense given the cohesion and coherence of that text. Due to the form and structure of John, one has to assume that such an important statement as the defenders of the hypothesis in question suggested would be clearly marked and pointed out to the readers. With all fascination for intriguing exegetical constructions and hypotheses, whenever an intra-textual solution is possible to solve a problem of understanding, it has to be favored over an extra-textual hypothesis. This is especially applicable when an extra-textual solution runs the risk of obscuring an intra-textual or intertextual solution.[3]

In other words, whenever a particular reading that requires additional extra-textual knowledge is suggested to be the predominant or even only

3. Sandra Huebenthal, *Transformation und Aktualisierung: Zur Rezeption von Sacharja 9–14 im Neuen Testament*, SBB 57 (Stuttgart: Katholisches Bibelwerk, 2006), 294.

possible understanding of a text, my hermeneutical alarm goes off. It would be contrary to the general idea of the *gospel* that it required secret knowledge for proper understanding.

If we read Mark that way—and this is what Kirk does—the reader is safe following the narrative flow, as all necessary information will be provided in due course. As far as the story is concerned, "Jesus is the authoritative, Spirit-empowered Christ who, despite (because of!) this empowerment can only take his messianic throne by way of rejection, suffering, crucifixion, and death. The mystery of Mark's Jesus is found in the conjunction of his messianic authority and his need to suffer and die" (p. 140).

The story has several parts and dynamic characters, and I am sure that Kirk would agree with Larry Hurtado that it is "fast-paced." As the Gospel narrates the story of the Messiah, Jesus, it goes without saying that the presentation of what it means that Jesus is the Messiah takes a lot of space. Even though Jesus is presented as a human among humans, or "an ordinary Galilean," as I say in my essay, he displays a special relationship with God, which Kirk calls "standing in for God." Jesus is presented as the "ultimate, eschatological agent of God's visitation and deliverance" (p. 141). Kirk reads the introduction of this agent in Mark's Gospel as modeled after idealized human figures: he is not identified *as* God but *with* God. "In the narrative world of Mark," Kirk argues, "what makes a person capable of speaking authoritatively for God, healing a sick body, exorcising a demon, or exercising power over nature is not being divine but is instead having appropriately delegated authority conferred upon oneself" (p. 165). Due to the Jewish tradition as primary conversation partner, the network of references to Israel's Scriptures and tradition "invites the reader, in conversation with the Scriptures of Israel, to recognize that the actions unfolding in the subsequent narrative are the promised eschatological activity of God" (p. 143).

After these initial considerations, the essay concentrates on three focal points: the story of God's Son, the story of the Human One (aka the Son of Man), and the story of power and weakness.

As declarations of Jesus as God's Son occur at three key moments in the narrative, Kirk first concentrates on the question what "Son of God" means in Mark's story. Limiting the interpretation to Mark's narrative universe and the conversation partner that the text itself introduces, that is, Israel's tradition, allows for intertextual reading. This intertextual reading understands

"Son of God" as presenting a human who stands in special relationship with God without having to go into details about the exact nature of this relationship. The synopsis of the key moments with other texts allows for conclusions about the narrator's perception or the narrator's world: Mark "depicts a Messiah who will have to come to his throne by way of rejection, suffering, and death" (p. 149). In other words, Jesus is a suffering king. The humiliation is a significant part of being Son of God, as Jesus's teaching after the transfiguration and especially the words of the centurion (15:39) disclose. This Roman soldier has no idea who Jesus is and how he can be read in a Jewish frame of reference, but the very way he sees this putative royal pretender die discloses to him whom he is dealing with. Even though he is a Roman soldier and thus a non-Jew, the centurion's statement about Jesus having been a son of God is in line with the Jewish understanding. In both frames of reference, sonship was understood "as adding a supernatural imprimatur to a human being's claims to kingship" (p. 149). In other words, this title would have been understood by both groups—and would, in connection with humiliation and suffering, been equally offensive to both groups.

Kirk hints at but does not explicitly say that no Jewish character uses the title "Son of God" for Jesus. One might consider the high priest alluding to it in 14:61 ("Son of the Blessed One"). This would also make for a very interesting coincidence, as it would be the only instance where "Messiah" and "Son of God" are mentioned together by one speaker within the narrative proper. (They are also found together in the text-critically difficult first verse of Mark.) This might be of some importance for the perception of the title, as well as the fact that demons and unclean spirits also call Jesus "Son of God" on two occasions (3:11; 5:7).

The other title that Kirk deems as equally important for the narrative is "the Human One"—Kirk's preferred translation of the υἱὸς τοῦ ἀνθρώπου. The title Human One is only used by Jesus and always in reference to himself, yet with different connotations. Kirk rightly demonstrates that "the claims Jesus makes for the Human One align with the plot development of Mark's narrative" (p. 150): it is first used to claim authority, then to predict rejection, suffering, and death and then finally to allude to heavenly and eschatological glory. In this section, Kirk provides another very good close reading of the Markan text, connecting the motif with overall narratological observations.

I am especially impressed by the intertextual connections Kirk provides and carefully unfolds without ever leaving the level of the text. The temptation to do so is indeed fairly high, and as a trained reader I found myself several times looking at the historical context or the other Synoptic Gospels. As I concluded in my own essay, the suffering of the Messiah is the elephant in the room: it runs counter to the ideas of both Jewish and Roman tradition and still has to be integrated into the narrative. It has to be assigned meaning, or, in Kirk's words, "this suffering lies, paradoxically, at the heart of Mark's messianic Christology" (p. 169). The notion that it is necessary for the Human One to be rejected, suffer, and die needs a confirmation or a point of reference in Israel's Scriptures if the narrative arc and the primary conversation partner are to be taken seriously. A side-glance to Luke shows that the same question is also addressed there, and the answer is also said to be in Scripture (Luke 24:26–27). Seen from an extratextual point of view, this is quite striking: even though the temple has been destroyed and there are more non-Jewish than Jewish Jesus-followers, Israel's Scriptures are still the point of reference at the turn of the century, and the success of the proclamation of the gospel is still judged by it being in accordance with the Scriptures.

However, back to the Markan narrative, as difficult as it might initially be. The payoff of Kirk's resistance to the temptation to read literary, historical, and theological contexts other than those referenced by Mark itself into this text is the rediscovery of a consistent and well-written piece of literature. It might come with somewhat disturbing claims, such as "the affirmation that Jesus scandalously exercises divine functions as God's anointed and/or appointed human agent" (p. 171), but it nevertheless remains a coherent story with a coherent Christology. I do agree with Kirk that Mark's story loses much and gains little when Jesus is identified with God in order to assign a divine nature to him. This does require, however, that the reader reads Mark on its own terms and accepts the Gospel as a coherent narrative and an independent theological contribution. A canonical reader might easily fall into the trap of reading Mark through the lenses of Matthew, Luke, and John and thus overlook its original theological ideas, which have greatly influenced different Christian groups in the second and third centuries.

As regards method and results, our arguments are quite close. In my own readings of New Testament texts, I might go a step further than Kirk by using narratology to understand a text like Mark's Gospel as the foundational story of the group behind it. Reading Mark that way provides an additional layer of dealing with a text, one that provides a frame for identity constructions in memory of Jesus and thus has a clear pragmatics. When it comes to Mark's pragmatics, I might be closer to Hurtado; when it comes to methodology, closer to Kirk.

By way of conclusion, for me the most important point about Kirk's essay is that he distinguishes his reading of Mark from a theological statement about his own faith; that is, he sticks with the etic perspective on a text from the late first century. This text is indeed part of Christian cultural memory and foundational for our own beliefs today. Nevertheless, the question as to how the Gospel of Mark and its presentation of Jesus informs our own faith is on a different level and would require a different essay.

Hurtado Response to Kirk

LARRY W. HURTADO

I have some questions and critical comments in response to Kirk's essay, to be sure, but his emphasis that in GMark Jesus is presented as a genuinely human figure who is uniquely empowered and authorized by God is, I think, basically correct.[1] So, before offering my questions and critical comments, allow me to elaborate further as to where I think that Kirk and I agree.[2]

Agreements

As I say, in the narrative of GMark, Jesus is a genuinely human and historical figure. Most indicative of this, when crucified, he dies! More specifically, he is a Jewish male from Nazareth in Galilee whose adult activities are set chronologically in the rule of Herod Antipas in Galilee and the Roman governor, Pontius Pilate, in Judea. He has a mother and siblings (Mark 6:3). Indicative of his Jewish identity, he observes Sabbath and goes to synagogue wherever he is (e.g., Capernaum, 1:21; Nazareth, 6:1–2), and he wears the fringes that Jewish males wore at the four corners of their garments (6:56).[3] Further indicative of his first-century Jewish context in Galilee, and giving

1. Again, I use "GMark" to designate the text, and "Mark" to designate its author by the traditional name.

2. As Kirk notes, his essay is dependent on his book, *A Man Attested by God: The Human Jesus of the Synoptic Gospels* (Grand Rapids: Eerdmans, 2016). I gave an invited response to the book in a panel discussion held in the 2016 annual meeting of the Society of Biblical Literature, and I posted that response on my blog site: https://larryhurtado.wordpress.com/2017/03/11/a-man-approved-by-god-a-review/.

3. As discussed by Joel Marcus, *Mark 1–8: A New Translation with Introduction and Commentary*, AB 27 (New York: Doubleday, 2000), 437. The fringes of holy individuals were often thought to mediate divine power, as also likely reflected in the Markan account of the woman with the bloody flux in 5:28.

the narrative a linguistic "local color," Jesus is portrayed making utterances in Aramaic, as I note in my own essay in this volume.

Furthermore, whether one classifies GMark (with Helen Bond) as a biography, or more loosely (with Richard Burridge) as a kind of *bios* writing, or (with Adela Yarbro Collins) as "an eschatological historical monograph," the author's account of Jesus is rich with historical and cultural details.[4] I have cited examples in my essay and need not repeat them here. In short, to underscore an observation from my own essay, this emphasis on Jesus as a genuinely human and historically located individual is not in dispute here.

Kirk, however, seems to operate with a curious binary set of categories: Either Jesus is human (albeit a special type) or he is "God." But this may be a false dilemma. I agree with Kirk that GMark does not present Jesus in terms of the Nicene Creed and the theological categories of divine "essence" and "persons" that emerged later in the developing Christian view of God as a "Trinity." How could we expect otherwise? Kirk rightly urges Christians not to read into GMark the developed doctrines and connotations of terms that *later* became traditional. Certainly, the deity of GMark and Jesus are two distinguishable characters in the narrative and are set in a fixed relationship: Jesus sent, affirmed, empowered, authorized, given over to death, and resurrected/vindicated by God. Indeed, such a distinction between God and Jesus is in fact characteristic of the many writings that make up the New Testament, from the letters of Paul on through the latest of these texts, even GJohn.[5] But it is another question whether this distinction is all that GMark affirms about Jesus, or whether the only alternatives are choosing between "Jesus as God" or Jesus simply as one "idealized human" among others in Jewish tradition.

I also agree that GMark does not present any overt reference to Jesus's preexistence. In today's scholarly discussion, Kirk's argument about the matter seems to be directed particularly at Gathercole's claims that the Synoptic Gospels reflect a belief in Jesus's preexistence.[6] I think that Gathercole's case

---

4. Helen K. Bond, *The First Biography of Jesus: Genre and Meaning in Mark's Gospel* (Grand Rapids: Eerdmans, 2020); R. A. Burridge, *What Are the Gospels? A Comparison with Graeco-Roman Biography*, SNTSMS 70 (Cambridge: Cambridge University Press, 1992). Cf. Yarbro Collins, *Mark*, esp. 33–44. Yarbro Collins laid out her case more fully in an earlier small book, *Is Mark's Gospel a Life of Jesus? The Question of Genre* (Milwaukee: Marquette University Press, 1990).

5. See, e.g., Larry W. Hurtado, *God in New Testament Theology* (Nashville: Abingdon, 2010).

6. Simon J. Gathercole, *The Pre-Existent Son: Recovering the Christologies of Matthew, Mark, and Luke* (Grand Rapids: Eerdmans, 2006).

has more support from passages in the other Synoptics, such as Matthew 23:37–39/Luke 13:34–35, but I agree that we do not have equivalent texts in GMark.[7] We may differ over what to make of this.

Kirk is anxious to refute Gathercole's claims, but was the author of GMark similarly anxious to refute the idea of Jesus's preexistence? I fear that Kirk's own refutation-agenda may skew somewhat his view of Mark's agenda. Is the absence of direct assertions of Jesus's preexistence in GMark evidence that the author was ignorant of such a belief, or wished to deny it? Kirk does not directly make such a claim, so far as I can tell. But one could infer something like this from the tone of his argument. Put another way, Kirk wishes to correct certain readings of GMark, but did Mark likewise seek to correct or refute "high" christological beliefs, such as the idea of Jesus's preexistence? I see nothing in GMark to justify an affirmative answer to the question. Given the readiness of early Christian authors to state disagreements and refute what they regarded as errors of belief, the absence of any such an effort in GMark is surely noteworthy.

If, as I have proposed in my essay, one of the aims in GMark is to present Jesus's ministry as effectively a pattern for readers (another matter on which Kirk and I agree), this accounts for why the narrative has its shape, which is the shape of Christian existence as called for in the narrative. It begins with a baptism, continues with mission focused on the gospel, and a mixture of success and opposition, leading to death and the hope of resurrection. With such a purpose, referring to Jesus's preexistence and/or a miraculous conception would have been extraneous. Disciples don't have preexistence and aren't miraculously conceived.

The Approach

That GMark is so obviously directed to fellow Jesus-believers leads me to comment on what I regard as the most surprising thing about Kirk's approach. I elaborate here an observation made also in my essay. As in his

7. Curiously, in his book on which his essay in this volume is based, he makes no reference to Matt 23:34–39, and in his reference to Luke 13:34–35 he mentions only that Jesus aligns himself with previous prophets, with no consideration of the question of whether this text implies something like preexistence. In Matt 23:34, Jesus appears to speak as having sent prophets, wise men, and scribes, not as one of them himself. Certainly, the lament in these verses seems to echo laments of God about Israel's obduracy. Cf. Kirk, *Man Attested by God*, esp. 562.

book, so also in his essay, his reading of GMark is set within the context of Old Testament and Second Temple Jewish tradition, and he works hard to fit the Markan portrayal of Jesus firmly into what he calls the "idealized human" category in that tradition. I do not question the usefulness of taking account of the sort of traditions that Kirk cites. In my 1988 study *One God, One Lord*, for example, I surveyed ancient Jewish evidence through several chapters and proposed that earliest Jesus-believers drew upon what I termed a "chief agent" category in their efforts to accommodate Jesus next to God. But I also noted major distinctions in the early adaptation of "chief agent" tradition by Jesus-believers, contending that they produced a novel "mutation," especially evident in the place of the risen Jesus in their devotional practices.[8]

Conspicuously lacking in Kirk's analysis, however, is any serious attention to what was surely the immediate context and matrix in which GMark arose: the first-century Jesus-movement. As I have noted in my essay, numerous features of GMark confirm that it both reflects and addresses adherents of the Jesus-movement, commencing with the opening words that form the title of the text: "The gospel of Jesus Christ." To cite another example, 13:1–37 is commonly seen as directly addressing Jesus-believers in the "post-Easter" period, with its warnings that deceivers will come "in my [Jesus's] name" (vv. 5–6), and "false messiahs and false prophets" will arise (vv. 21–23), and that believers will be arraigned before Jewish and gentile authorities "for my sake" (v. 9) and will be hated "on account of my name" (v. 13). The centrality of Jesus in all this is obvious. Believers are addressed in the repeated exhortations to be on guard, as they cannot know when the promised world-redemption and judgment will come (vv. 33–37). In 13:10 Jesus calls for the international proclamation of the gospel. In 13:14, "let the reader understand" reflects the intended reading of GMark in assemblies of Jesus-believers. As also noted in my essay, wording and gestures in the Last Supper scene in 14:22–25 rather clearly reflect the eucharistic practices of early circles of believers, as evidenced earlier in 1 Corinthians 11:23–25.[9]

So, I suggest that GMark is most cogently read when we take account of its immediate context in the early Jesus-movement. After all, by the likely

8. Larry W. Hurtado, *One God, One Lord: Early Christian Devotion and Ancient Jewish Monotheism* (Philadelphia: Fortress; London: SCM, 1988; 2nd ed., Edinburgh: T&T Clark, 1998; 3rd ed., London: Bloomsbury T&T Clark, 2015).

9. Note, e.g., that both the Markan account and its parallels echo the use of εὐχαριστέω and the liturgical actions involving the cup and bread recounted earlier in 1 Cor 11:24.

date of GMark, that movement was some four decades old, and in Paul's letters (some two decades or so earlier than GMark) we already see reflected christological beliefs and Jesus-centered devotional practices that likely erupted earlier still in the first circles of the Jesus-movement. These beliefs include Jesus's preexistence (e.g., Phil 2:6), his agency in creation (1 Cor 8:6), his unique status "at God's right hand" (e.g., Rom 8:34), and his universal rule (1 Cor 15:25–28). The devotional practices include the eucharistic meal in which Jesus is the presiding *Kyrios*, baptism in his name, and the ritual acclamation and invocation of the risen Jesus as the identifying mark of believers (e.g., Rom 10:9–13; 1 Cor 1:2).

In short, believers did not have to wait for GMark to learn what to think about Jesus! Nor would early Jesus-believers have expected the author of GMark to affirm explicitly a checklist of christological beliefs of his time or present his text as a full-scale christological statement. Instead, the evidence indicates that he wrote GMark more specifically as an encouragement to fellow Jesus-believers, and to emphasize that the risen *Kyrios* at the center of their devotional life is Jesus of Nazareth, whose earthly ministry is important as the pattern for their own earthly discipleship. I submit that if we read GMark in the context of the early Jesus-movement, the context in which the author obviously was situated, and in light of the author's particular purposes and emphases, we do not have an effort to posit an alternative to "high" views of Jesus. Instead, we have an essentially complementary effort to underscore the importance of Jesus's earthly activities as the origin of the gospel and a pattern for believers, especially those facing persecution, without denying or rejecting the high views of Jesus's relationship to God and the centrality of Jesus in devotional practice.

Results

I think that Kirk's approach of ignoring the context of the early Jesus-movement leads him to miss how GMark signals a view of Jesus's status that exceeds the "idealized human" category. This produces what one might call a certain tone-deaf reading of relevant passages. I will illustrate this and show how these passages portend more than Kirk allows. This will, unavoidably, require me to deal with some texts also noted in my own essay.

The passages that underscore Jesus's authority (ἐξουσία), for example, do not liken him to others but rather emphasize Jesus's distinctiveness. In 1:22 the synagogue congregation is startled and declares Jesus's authority in his teaching to exceed that of the scribes, and then in 1:27–28 his power over unclean spirits produces bewilderment as to what to make of him. This bewilderment is contrasted, then, with the demonic recognition of Jesus as "the holy one of God" in 1:24 and the statement in 1:34 that Jesus did not permit the demons to speak "for they knew him."[10] Note that in these texts Jesus is not hailed as one of a class but, as the article indicates in 1:24, as *the* uniquely favored one, as by far "the holiest of God's elect."[11] Similarly, the demonic acclamation in 3:11, "you are *the* Son of God," reflects the uniquely high significance of Jesus that eludes the human characters in the account.

In 2:5–12, Jesus does not simply declare the paralytic's sins forgiven but himself forgives his sins (as explicitly claimed in v. 10), as well as healing the man. For readers, the scribes' allegation of blasphemy is incorrect, not because Jesus's actions are to be seen as indicative of some "idealized" category but because he has a unique authority to act on the earth in a capacity that is properly God's.[12] Jesus does not entreat God to forgive but "presumes to speak for God," and in the eyes of the scribes Jesus's action "calls the unity of God into question."[13] Surely, however, the intended readers of GMark saw in this scene a valid reflection of Jesus's unique standing as the vehicle of God's purposes, and in his action an anticipation of their own experience of forgiveness in Jesus's name.

This scene is one of two in GMark where Jesus is accused of blasphemy, the other one being 14:60–64, where the high priest declares (v. 64) that Jesus's claim for himself in v. 62 is blasphemous. As Yarbro Collins judged, Jesus's claim here that he will be seated in heaven at God's right hand "implies being equal to God, at least in terms of authority and power," which

---

10. The variant reading, "they knew that he was the Christ," supported by a number of manuscripts, is surely to be taken as a harmonization of the statement to the parallel in Luke 4:41.

11. As noted by Yarbro Collins, *Mark*, 170.

12. I cannot here address the much-discussed matter of Jesus's self-referential use of the expression, "the Son of Man." Suffice it here to note that the articular form is without precedent or parallel in biblical and Second Temple Jewish texts, and it is never treated by others in the Gospel narratives as a title claimed by Jesus. It is best understood, thus, as a distinctive idiolect on the lips of Jesus that expresses a particularity, not simply as affirming Jesus's general humanity. See my fuller discussion in Larry W. Hurtado, "Summing Up and Concluding Observations," in *Who Is This Son of Man? Latest Scholarship on a Puzzling Expression of the Historical Jesus*, ed. Larry W. Hurtado and Paul Owen (London: T&T Clark, 2011), 159–77.

13. Yarbro Collins, *Mark*, 185.

is portrayed as blasphemous from the perspective of the council in the scene, but is a fully valid claim in the eyes of the intended readers of GMark.[14] For early Jesus-believers, the high priest's accusation of blasphemy is invalid, not because he exaggerates the import of Jesus's claim but because they know that the full force of Jesus's claim is true. Once again, to read the text aright requires us to view it through the eyes of Jesus-believers of the author's time, for whom Jesus is not simply an "idealized human" but is the exalted *Kyrios* who shares uniquely in God's glory and the exercise of his power.

In other scenes as well, Jesus's high significance is signaled in terms that would be recognized by intended readers. In 3:13–15, to be sure, the Twelve are empowered also to preach and cast out demons, but their appointment and authority come from Jesus! He does not pray for their empowerment but confers it himself. He is not presented as one of a larger class of "idealized humans" but as singular in his status, mediating to the disciples the sort of divine authority that he exercises.

The two sea-storm scenes give us additional examples of this. In the first account (4:35–41), in response to the disciples' distress about the storm, Jesus does not pray for God's help but directly himself rebukes the wind and waves. Thereby, to cite Yarbro Collins, Jesus is not portrayed as behaving "like a devout human person but like God . . . not so much as a human being who has trust in God's power to save, but as a divine being." And the amazement of the disciples in v. 41 makes sense because "they have God manifest in the boat with them."[15] Joel Marcus suggests that earliest readers may have seen the storm-tossed boat as reflecting the persecution that some Jesus-believers experienced, and the story may also reflect "one of the causes of that persecution, namely, a high Christology that goes a long way toward equating Jesus with the OT God and thus lays the community open to Jewish charges of blasphemy." Marcus further notes that the exchange between Jesus and the disciples in vv. 40–41, culminating in their fearful question, "Who is this?" "reinforces the impression of his awesomely high identity."[16]

The other story set on Lake Galilee (6:45–52) is commonly taken as an epiphany narrative. Echoes of YHWH's power over the sea, and his

14. Yarbro Collins, *Mark*, 706–7.
15. Yarbro Collins, *Mark*, 260. Similarly, Marcus, *Mark 1–8*, 338.
16. Marcus, *Mark 1–8*, 339.

self-revelation to figures such as Moses, are regularly noted by commentators in Jesus walking on the waves and other elements of the account. And, as Marcus observes, in this scene Jesus is not being compared to figures such as Moses but, instead, to the God who revealed himself in the Old Testament theophanies. Indeed, although he also sees Jesus's humanness reflected in the story, Marcus judges that "the overwhelming impact made by our narrative is an impression of Jesus's divinity."[17] The passage echoes phrasing from Old Testament theophanic narratives, such as the reference to Jesus wishing to "pass by them" (v. 48), and the sonorous "It is I" (ἐγώ εἰμι, v. 50) would confirm to readers familiar with the Old Testament accounts a certain "assimilation of Jesus to God in the passage."[18] Again, this is not Nicene Christology, but Jesus is clearly something more than an "idealized human."

Conclusion

Kirk is correct to emphasize that GMark presents an account of a genuinely human Jesus. I repeat that this is not in dispute here. But the author's purpose was not to pose a human Jesus over against the "high" views of Jesus already well developed by the time that GMark was composed. Instead, the contours of the Markan account of Jesus's activities (from baptism to resurrection) are shaped to make Jesus the authoritative role model for Jesus-believers, especially those facing the threat of persecution. The examples of "idealized human" figures cited by Kirk illustrate how Second Temple tradition could accord to certain figures, such as Moses, a remarkable divine favor. But I think that Kirk errs in trying to squeeze the Markan account of Jesus into that category, making Jesus one of a class of such individuals. Instead, various passages in GMark seem to me to place Jesus in a unique status or category vis-à-vis God, the repeated acclamation of Jesus's divine sonship being the author's favored way of expressing this. For example, in the parable of the vineyard (12:1–9), in contrast to the various servants (δοῦλοι,

17. Marcus, *Mark 1–8*, 432.

18. Yarbro Collins, *Mark*, 334–35, although she grants that it is not necessary to recognize the intertextual references to OT accounts to see that in 6:45–52 "Jesus is being portrayed here as divine in a functional, not necessarily in a metaphysical sense" (335). I am unsure what "a metaphysical sense" would have meant for the author or other early Jesus-believers, and this may be a red herring. The absolute "It is I" (ἐγώ εἰμι) in the story finds multiple parallels in YHWH's self-references in Isaiah (e.g., 43:10, 25; 45:19; 46:4; 51:12), and, given other indications of the importance of Isaiah in GMark, the phrase likely signals that Jesus identifies himself similarly in a theophanic form.

who must be taken as prophets and other "idealized human" figures), Jesus is clearly the one beloved son, who is thereby uniquely the heir and in a category of his own.

Kirk is likewise correct to urge today's readers to avoid viewing the text through the theological developments of the centuries after GMark. And I agree that the rhetoric of some scholars seems to elide the distinction between Jesus and God that is reflected in GMark (and other NT writings). Jesus is not "God" in some flat equivalence in GMark (or in any other NT writing), and the sort of ontological categories of the Nicene era are also not in view. But I contend that GMark does reflect a view of Jesus as uniquely and intimately linked with God, such that it is blasphemy to outsiders but is the high truth for the Jesus-believers for whom Mark wrote. Christians struggled across the ensuing centuries to work out how best to accommodate their "high" views of Jesus in relation to God. Yet part of the reason for that struggle was that, already in texts such as GMark, I think that we see Jesus-believers according to Jesus a status in beliefs and devotional practices that represents an innovation in the context of ancient Jewish traditions.

Kirk's emphasis that GMark draws on biblical and Second Temple traditions is valid. But I think that his methodological error in failing to read GMark in its immediate context in later first-century circles of Jesus-believers leads him to miss (or misconstrue) the various indications in the text that reflect and affirm a view of Jesus that cannot be described adequately by the "idealized human" category.

Winn Response to Kirk

ADAM WINN

In his essay, "Narrative Christology of a Suffering King," Daniel Kirk has offered a careful and knowledgeable reading of the Markan narrative and the Christology found therein. Due to our different conclusions regarding the divinity of the Markan Jesus, it might surprise readers that there is a great deal that I agree with in Kirk's essay. First, I agree with Kirk that Mark's Gospel needs to be read as a narrative whole and that understanding Mark's Christology requires attention to the entire narrative. My own narrative reading of Mark agrees with Kirk on many points. I agree that the Markan Jesus is indeed presented as both God's Messiah and Son, and that as both, the Markan Jesus is God's ultimate eschatological agent. I agree with his assessment that Mark emphasizes Jesus's great power in the first part of the Gospel, and then turns his attention to Jesus's suffering and death in the second. Like Kirk, I affirm that the confession of Peter at Caesarea Philippi reflects only partial seeing, as Peter gets Jesus's identity correct but remains blind to Jesus's need to suffer and die. I agree with Kirk that the christological goal of Mark's Gospel is to bring the messianic power and authority of Jesus together into a coherent whole with his suffering and death. In addition to these points of agreement, I could note many more. Yet despite such agreements, Kirk and I come to radically different conclusions about the divinity of the Markan Jesus. Our differences come both at the level of our starting points (about both narrative criticism and ancient Judaism) and the way we read certain Markan pericopes and narrative trajectories. I will begin by addressing the former, which will then be brought to bear on the latter.

Starting Points and Presuppositions

At the outset of his argument, Kirk states, "First, any Christology we discover in the Gospel will be a narrative Christology" (p. 137). Here he echoes the claim of Robert Tannehill who was one of the pioneers of narrative criticism in Gospel studies. Such a claim offers us an important corrective to studies of the Gospels that often lost the forest for the trees in their interpretation of the Gospels by giving disproportionate attention to the parts (e.g., christological titles) and not enough attention to the way in which those parts functioned in the narrative whole. But while this correction offered by narrative critics is an important one, it can be applied to the Gospels in an overly rigid way. I think such a rigid application is evinced in Kirk's citation of Flannery O'Connor: "A story is a way to say something that can't be said any other way, and it takes every word in the story to say what the meaning is."[1] It is also evinced later when Kirk says the following about those who seek to advance a divine Christology in Mark: "The whole narrative will have to be reread to argue for an identification of Jesus with the divine in these particular christological ideas and in the overarching narrative of the whole, and in such a way as to substantively contribute to that story" (p. 160). While this strict understanding of narrative might be held by the great storyteller O'Connor, it seems it would be a mistake to apply this to every storyteller, particularly an ancient one. Such an approach denies the ability of authors to include details that reflect or convey beliefs or commitments that are not directly related to their narrative aims. Authors, especially ancient ones, often convey in narratives commitments that are not strictly tied to their narrative purposes. With that said, I think it is quite plausible that Mark's Gospel can reflect christological commitments that are not part and parcel of its narrative aims. I would agree with Kirk that presenting a divine Christ is not a primary narrative aim of the Gospel; the pieces of the narrative are not woven together with the purpose of telling the reader that Jesus is the God of Israel. But I would argue that Mark's narrative of the Messiah Jesus could reflect in ancillary ways the evangelist's commitment that the Messiah Jesus is also YHWH of Israel. Put another way, the belief that Jesus is YHWH

1. Flannery O'Connor, *Mystery and Manners: Occasional Prose*, ed. Sally Fitzgerald and Robert Fitzgerald (New York: Farrar, Straus and Giroux, 1970), 96.

of Israel could be a foundational belief of the author that manifests itself explicitly at many points in the narrative, without being a claim the author is using the narrative to convey. Now clearly, if the narrative itself presented a view that conflicted with such a divine identity of Jesus, it would undermine a case that the author held such commitments. Thus, I will endeavor to demonstrate not only that Kirk's reading of the Markan narrative (one in which Jesus is presented as human from beginning to end) is not the only possible reading, but also that it does not adequately address certain aspects of Mark's presentation of Jesus.

Another challenge related to a narrative-critical approach, and one that leads to significant differences between both Kirk's and my reading of Mark's Christology, is determining what knowledge one can assume that the reader possesses. Assessments of such knowledge vary drastically, and as a result, so do narrative readings of Mark. Some try to mitigate this problem by using the concept of the implied reader and allowing the reader to know as much as the text implies. Yet, as I note in my response to Sandra Huebenthal, determining what the text implies that the reader knows is also highly subjective. Clearly some implied knowledge is easy to assess, such as the reader knows Greek, is familiar with the existence of Jerusalem and Galilee, and other such basic narrative elements. But what about the term "Messiah" (Χριστός) and other such christological titles? Kirk claims, "We have to let Mark's own story tell us what *Messiah* means in this case" (p. 138). But does this mean the reader is starting from ground zero and comes with no more knowledge than the meaning of the Greek word "Christos," translated "anointed one"? Mark clearly never defines the term, so without some basic understanding of this word as it is used in Second Temple apocalyptic and eschatological expectation, would the reader understand what it means strictly from the Markan narrative? That they would is highly questionable in my estimation. Thus, I think Kirk and other narrative critics overstate the case. The word "Messiah/Christ" in a Jewish and early Christian context had a fairly well-established meaning, despite their being variety in messianic expectation. Thus, Mark's narrative does not, strictly speaking, tell the reader what Messiah means, but it takes a term or concept that is already familiar to that reader and shapes, challenges, and transforms that concept through a narrative. Thus, previous knowledge and the narrative work together to generate meaning.

The question of what knowledge the reader brings to the text will, therefore, always be a pressing one, and the way one answers that question can dramatically change the way one reads Mark's narrative. A number of examples can be provided to illustrate how both Kirk and I differ in our understanding of the knowledge that Mark's readers bring to the text. We can begin with the concept of *messiah*. Both Kirk and I agree that for Mark, the Jewish world is the primary context in which the term should be understood and that the term conveys the idea of a final eschatological agent of God. Where we disagree is in the possibility that this final eschatological agent of God could be understood as divine or in a real sense as YHWH of Israel. I grant that Kirk is in line with most New Testament scholars when he claims that the title *messiah* did not suggest divinity in Second Temple Jewish literature. However, as I note in my essay, that position is being challenged. The Jewish philosopher Philo may have understood the messiah in terms of the divine Logos. The Son of Man figure in the "Parables of Enoch" (1 En. 37–71) is clearly identified as messiah and is arguably depicted as a divine being. I am not contending that all Jews thought of the messiah as divine but that there is evidence that some in fact did. And even if Kirk is right that Second Temple Jews did not conceive of the messiah as a divine figure, there is very strong evidence that first-century Jewish Christians did. Numerous Pauline texts are widely recognized as depicting Jesus the Messiah as a divine figure (e.g., 1 Cor 8:6; Phil 2:6–11; Col 1:15–20). And the Gospel of John clearly depicts Jesus as both Messiah and divine. Thus, at the very least, we must allow for the possibility that early Christian readers of Mark could have brought to their reading of the Gospel the notion that the Messiah of God was also in some way God himself.

Another important example of where Kirk and I disagree regarding the knowledge that Mark's readers bring to the Gospel is our understanding of the title *Son of Man*. For Kirk, this title is better translated as "the Human One," and with this title Kirk limits his understanding of this title to what can be inferred from the Gospel of Mark alone. That is, it seems Kirk denies that the readers of Mark might already bring some sort of understanding of this title to their reading of the Gospel. With such boundaries on the readers' knowledge, Kirk reaches a number of conclusions about the meaning of this title in Mark's Gospel, including that as "the Human One," Jesus bears great divine authority, embraces the cruciform mission of God's Messiah (a mission that is the prophetic fulfillment of Dan 7), and experiences exaltation to God's right hand after his death and resurrection. But Kirk also makes claims about what "the Human One" is not, namely, that he is not depicted as a preexistent figure who had a heavenly existence, he does not have his own glory but only possesses the glory of the Father, and he does not possess his own divine authority but only that of God. While I agree with many aspects of what Kirk claims the Gospel of Mark affirms about Jesus's identity as Son of Man, I disagree strongly with what Kirk concludes the Son of Man or "Human One" is not. The primary source of this disagreement is our starting point regarding what knowledge of the "Son of Man" Mark's readers bring to the Markan narrative.

As noted, Kirk restricts himself what we find in the text of Mark itself. However, I find it highly implausible that Mark's first readers came to the text of Mark with such a blank slate or that the author of Mark expected the reader to construct the meaning of this title from nothing but the unfolding narrative. The fact that Mark's first reference to the Son of Man comes with no explanation and also claims for him the tremendous power to forgive sins suggests, in my estimation, that his readers have some framework for understanding this identity and the power that accompanies it. Within Second Temple Judaism, there were existing interpretive traditions related to the Son of Man figure in Daniel 7 that Mark alludes to explicitly on two occasions. Such traditions exist in the Dead Sea Scrolls and the Parables of Enoch, both of which link the Son of Man to either the messiah explicitly or to messianic ideas. As I noted in my essay, a number of Markan interpreters see Mark's Gospel influenced by the Son of Man tradition in Enoch, one in which a heavenly Son of Man is preexistent, sits on God's throne, forgives sins, is arguably worshiped by creation, and is arguably active in creation itself. If the readers of Mark bring this understanding of the Son of Man to Mark's Gospel, it radically changes the way in which one understands Mark's Christology. In fact, such a preunderstanding of the Son of Man fits remarkably well with my proposed reading in which the Markan Jesus is rightly identified as YHWH of Israel.

Related to the issue of what knowledge the reader brings to the text regarding the titles Messiah and Son of Man, and perhaps an even more significant source of the divergence in Kirk's understanding of Mark's Christology and that of myself, is what we conclude regarding Jewish conceptions of the one God of Israel. While Kirk does not explicitly state such a commitment, there are indicators that he understands the Jewish commitment to one God in terms of strict singularity. Such an understanding is communicated through a consistent effort to show the distinction between Jesus and God in Mark's Gospel, a distinction which is only problematic for a divine Christology if there is an underlying presupposition that the one God of Israel exists in strict singularity. But such a distinction is not problematic if the reader of Mark understands the one God of Israel in terms of complex plurality. As noted in my essay, I argue that at least some Jews understood the one God of Israel in terms of plurality, more specifically in terms of an utterly transcendent YHWH and an immanent YHWH. Thus, this difference in Kirk's and my own starting points regarding Jewish understanding of the God of Israel contribute significantly to different estimations of Mark's Christology.

Addressing Divergent Assessments of Markan Content

After noting the significant differences in the presuppositions held by both Kirk and myself, I now turn to the text of Mark itself, in order to assess both how these presuppositions impact our different readings of certain Markan pericopes as well as the compatibility of our presuppositions with the content of Mark's Gospel.

Jesus as YHWH of Isaiah: Mark 1:2–3

First, I want to consider Kirk's treatment of the opening Scripture citation in Mark 1:2–3. Kirk notes that in this passage, the evangelist has engaged in exegetical maneuvers in order to distinguish between God and Jesus. He first notes that in the citation of Malachi 3:1, the evangelist has changed "I am sending my messenger ahead of me" to "I am sending my messenger ahead of you." He then notes that the citation of Isaiah 40:3 has been changed from "make straight the way for our God" to "make straight the way for him." I certainly recognize that in the first editorial move (in Malachi) the evangelist does indeed create a distinction between God and Jesus, a distinction that I will address momentarily. Yet I dispute that a distinction is being created between God and Jesus in the citation of Isaiah 40:3. First, contra what Kirk seems to be claiming, the speaker of the words,

"Prepare the way of the Lord, make straight the way for our God" is not necessarily God himself. The phrase "for our God" would seem to indicate that the voice crying out these words is someone other than God. Second, the move from changing "for our God" to "for him" in no way makes a distinction between God and Jesus. The antecedent of "for him" is clearly the "Lord" or YHWH of Israel referenced in the first clause. The move to "for him" is still a reference to the God of Israel. Thus, the only move that distinguishes God and Jesus is found in Malachi, as far as I can tell. Not only does this analysis remove the distinction between Jesus and God that Kirk has proposed, but it also creates a problem that Kirk does not address, namely, that in this passage Mark is seemingly identifying Jesus with the God of Israel. As I noted in my essay, the "voice of one calling in the wilderness" that is "preparing the way for the Lord" is clearly John the Baptist for the Markan evangelist, and he is clearly paving the way for Jesus. But the Lord of Isaiah 40:3 is none other than the God of Israel. Thus, here the Markan evangelist seems to be equating the Lord of Isaiah 40:3, YHWH of Israel, with Jesus himself, the one for whom John the Baptist is preparing the way. Perhaps Kirk would argue that Jesus is merely standing in the place of YHWH here, but if so, the Markan evangelist has been rather careless and has certainly allowed his readers to conclude that the Lord of Isaiah 40:3, YHWH, is rightly identified with Jesus. And if Kirk is right that the evangelist has made a distinction between God and Jesus in the use of Malachi 3:1, why would the evangelist not make a more careful distinction in the citation of Isaiah 40:3?

But what then is to be made of the distinction between Jesus and God that is clearly created in the evangelist's work in the citation of Malachi? As I argue in my essay in the present volume, a "two-powers" understanding of the one God of Israel makes perfect sense of this move. The evangelist could be envisioning the transcendent YHWH sending to his people the immanent YHWH, and thus the editorial move from "me" to "you" is quite a natural one. Such an explanation also then fits with the identification of Jesus as the Lord or YHWH in the evangelist's citation of Isaiah 40:3.

The Forgiveness of Sin: Mark 2:1–12

Kirk rejects the notion that Jesus's forgiveness of sin in Mark 2:1–12 functions to establish a divine identity. Against such a conclusion, Kirk first considers the claim of the scribes that only God alone can forgive sins. According to Kirk, the scribes in Mark's Gospel are unreliable characters, and thus the reader cannot trust what they say about God. I would push back against this interpretive move on several grounds. One, this is the first time in Mark's Gospel that the scribes have appeared, and thus they have not yet been established as negative characters in the narrative. Second, simply because the scribes are enemies of Jesus throughout Mark, it does not hold that all they say is untrustworthy. In fact, a scribe is used in Mark 12:28–34 to establish the greatest and second-greatest commandments, and he even claims that following these commandments is more important than any burnt offering. Because of this answer from the scribe, Jesus claims that he is not far from the kingdom of God (v. 34). Third, there is nothing in the text that definitively demonstrates that their claim is misguided. Yet, beyond the claim that the scribes are unreliable, Kirk looks to the response of Jesus in 2:10–11 to support his position further. Kirk argues that Jesus links his power to forgive sins with his power to heal. He then notes that it is not Jesus alone that heals in the Gospel, but that this power is shared by Jesus's disciples (6:13). Kirk is certainly correct that Jesus establishes a connection between the power to forgive and the power to heal, with the power to heal being given as evidence for Jesus's power to forgive. But these two powers are not necessarily equated. That is, Jesus is not saying anyone with the power to heal has the power to forgive. It is noteworthy that while Jesus does give his disciples the power to heal, he never gives them the power to forgive sins on behalf of God. There seems to be a clear distinction between the prerogative to wield these two powers. Finally, Kirk notes Jesus's response in 2:10, "But so that you may know that the Son of Man has the power on earth to forgive sins." He interprets this passage in terms of God granting Jesus, God's eschatological agent, the power to forgive sins. This interpretation is certainly a common and possible one. It would imply that Jesus is offering a corrective to the scribes' claim, one Kirk regards as misguided. However, another interpretation is also possible. As I argued in my essay, Jesus could be claiming that the Son of Man is in fact divine and thus has the very power that the scribes have *rightly* attributed to God alone. If the reader brings to the text of Mark an understanding of "Son of Man" similar to that found in the Parables of Enoch, such a reading is made even stronger, as the Son of Man in Enoch is depicted as forgiving sins.

Lord of the Sabbath: Mark 2:23–28

Kirk uses Jesus's teaching on the Sabbath in Mark 2:23–28 to argue for a human identity of the Son of Man. He treats as mutually interpretive Jesus's response in both verse 27 and verse 28. In verse 27 Jesus claims that the Sabbath was made for human beings (ἄνθρωπος, which is translated "man" or also "human") and not human beings (ἄνθρωπος) for the Sabbath. Since these two uses of ἄνθρωπος in verse 27 clearly refer to human beings, Kirk then concludes that Jesus's lordship over the Sabbath as "the son of the human" (again, "son of ἄνθρωπος") in verse 28 places the title "squarely within the realm of the 'humanity.'" But I would contend that it is misguided to equate the humanity for whom the Sabbath was made with the Son of Man/Humanity who is identified as lord of the Sabbath. The claim in verse 27 should not be understood as establishing humanity's lordship over the Sabbath. Simply because the Sabbath was made for humanity does not give humanity dominion over it. If such were the point of verse 27, then why would we not see in verse 28 the claim that *all humanity* is lord of the Sabbath? The text seems to make a distinction between humanity and "the Son of Man/Humanity," with the latter having lordship over what was made for the former. I would argue that verse 28 offers the reader the justification for the teaching offered in verses 25–27. Jesus can give this authoritative teaching on the Sabbath because he himself is the Lord (YHWH) who established the Sabbath.

The Transfiguration: Mark 9:2–8

Regarding Jesus's transfiguration, Kirk claims the following: "The glory he bears in the transfiguration is not the disclosure of a divine glory that was always his (i.e., before coming to earth); instead, it is a preview of the glory that Jesus will bear when, as the human Messiah who faithfully suffers and dies, he is then raised from the dead" (p. 146). As I note in my essay, Kirk is not alone in such a reading, as other Markan interpreters have proposed as similar understanding. Yet I see nothing in the narrative of Mark that directs the reader to conclude that this episode conveys something about Jesus's future identity rather than his present identity. Kirk sees such evidence in Jesus's command not to speak of the scene until his resurrection, but how does such a command communicate what Kirk is claiming? I simply do not see a clear or necessary connection. Why would the reader not simply understand Jesus to be telling his disciples not to speak of his current identity until the resurrection? Such a reading seems more straightforward. Kirk also sees Jesus turning the disciples' attention from Elijah to the death of the Son of Man as another indicator that the transfiguration was a glimpse of Jesus's future glory. Yet, again, I do not see a clear or necessary connection between these two pieces of the narrative. Why would the reader not simply conclude that this powerful heavenly/divine figure must suffer and die? The more natural conclusion would seem to be that this transfiguration of Jesus, during his ministry, reveals something about his *current* identity. Immediately following this transfiguration, the divine voice declares, "This *is* my Son," a declaration that speaks to Jesus's current identity and is directly related to the transfiguration that has just taken place. Why would one conclude that the words of God declare Jesus's current identity, but the transfiguration is only a glimpse of some future reality? Reading this episode as a future glimpse of Jesus's post-resurrection glory seems forced and motivated by the interest to explain away an obstacle to establishing a fully human Christology in Mark. Would an ancient reader of Mark, not motivated by such a christological concern, really assemble the pieces of Mark's narrative this way? I find it highly unlikely.

Mark's Use of ἐγώ εἰμι, "I Am": Mark 6:50 and 14:62

Along with most Markan interpreters, Kirk argues that the Markan Jesus's use of ἐγώ εἰμι ("I am") should not be understood as a reference to the divine name of Israel's God. Kirk only deals with the use of this title in Mark 14:62. He offers two arguments in favor of this position. First, he notes that Jesus is asked a question in the second person about his identity, "Are you?" to which a first-person response of "I am" or "I am not" would be normal and expected. He also notes that the common claim that ἐγώ εἰμι is a citation of the name that YHWH give to Moses at the burning bush is a misguided one, as YHWH does not simply say his name is ἐγώ εἰμι ("I am") but rather ἐγώ εἰμι ὁ ὤν ("I am the one who is," Exod 3:14). Certainly, Kirk is right that understanding Jesus's reply as a simple affirmation is natural, but this should not exclude the possibility that the response might be multivalent. To some readers not well acquainted with the LXX, the response might be read only on the level of a positive response to the posed question. But for the reader that knows the LXX well, an intentional reference to the name of

YHWH could be perceived. Kirk is also right regarding the reply of YHWH at the burning bush, and that ἐγώ εἰμι is not the entirety of YHWH's self-identification. Yet there is still reason to believe that ἐγώ εἰμι could be used to evoke not only this tradition of YHWH's self-identification, but others as well. Ἐγώ εἰμι is used throughout much of the LXX in the context of YHWH's self-identification. In Leviticus, YHWH uses the phrase ἐγώ εἰμι κύριος ("I am the Lord") twenty-four times to identify himself. And in Ezekiel, the same phrase is used thirty-two times by YHWH to identify himself. But perhaps most importantly for Mark is the use of the phrase in Isaiah 40–53 as a prominent way in which YHWH identifies himself. In these thirteen chapters, YHWH uses ἐγώ εἰμι in self-identification formulas seventeen times. While in some of these formulas, ἐγώ εἰμι is accompanied by a modifier, such as "I am God," "I am the Lord," or "I am the first and I am the last," at other times there is no modifier at all, and ἐγώ εἰμι alone is YHWH's means of self-identification: "I am and there is no other" (Isa 45:18); "Until old age, I am, and until you grow old, I am" (Isa 46:4). On three different occasions, the phrase is repeated twice in a row, closely associating the phrase with YHWH's identity. For example, "I am, I am the one who comforts you" (Isa 51:12; see also 43:25; 45:19). Also noteworthy is the use of the phrase in describing the arrogance of the king of Babylon. At three different points, the king of Babylon is accused of saying "I am and there is no other," a phrase that clearly parrots the claims of YHWH himself (Isa 47:8, 10 [twice]). Thus, "I am" seems to function as a claim to divinity, one the king of Babylon uses that only rightly belongs to YHWH. Thus, it seems that beyond the connection between ἐγώ εἰμι and the name of YHWH at the burning bush, there is an extensive tradition in the LXX that brings ἐγώ εἰμι together with YHWH's self-identification. There are even times when the phrase stands alone as such an identification. We should therefore not be surprised to see New Testament authors draw on the tradition. Many contend that the Gospel of John draws on such a tradition, and the possibility of doing so should not be denied the Markan evangelist.

But is Mark drawing on such a tradition? Or is Kirk right that Jesus's response is nothing more than a simple affirmation? If there were no other indications of a divine identity in Mark or indications in this text itself, I would be inclined to agree with Kirk. But as I have argued in my essay, I see numerous indicators of Jesus's divine identity both in the entire Gospel and in texts where Jesus uses the phrase ἐγώ εἰμι. There is one such indicator in this very text, an indicator that Kirk fails to address, namely, the charge of blasphemy that follows Jesus's use of ἐγώ εἰμι and his self-identification as a heavenly Son of Man. As I noted in my essay, this charge of blasphemy has troubled Markan interpreters who contend that Jesus is only identifying himself as a human messiah, as there is no evidence that such a claim would rise to blasphemy in the Second Temple period. Yet this charge of blasphemy makes perfect sense if ἐγώ εἰμι is understood as a form of self-identification with the one God of Israel.

I believe the case for understanding ἐγώ εἰμι as a form of divine self-identification in Mark 14:62 is strengthened by the Gospel's previous use of the phrase in Mark 6:50, in the episode of Jesus walking on water. Jesus's first words to his terrified disciples are ἐγώ εἰμι. While the use of this phrase could be understood as a simple affirmation of Jesus's identity—"It is I"—there are, as I argued in my essay, a number of details in the story that suggest the phrase is drawing on the tradition of divine identification noted above. First, Jesus is walking on the waves, a detail that Mark conveys through a virtual citation of Job 9:8, in which YHWH alone is said to walk on the waves of the sea. Second is the odd insertion of Jesus's intention to pass the disciples by, language that finds strong parallels with two of the most significant theophany stories in Israel's tradition (Exod 33:17–34:6; 1 Kgs 19:11–15). I was surprised that Kirk did not address this episode more thoroughly in his essay, as in my estimation it is one of the strongest presentations of Jesus as the God of Israel in Mark's Gospel. No doubt he will address it in his own response to my essay.

Arguments against the Divinity of the Markan Jesus

Kirk notes a number of details in Mark's Gospel that, in his estimation, preclude the Markan Jesus from being identified as the divine or the God of Israel. Kirk notes that at several points Jesus and the God of Israel are clearly presented as distinct. This is a point that I noted above, I will gladly grant. But does such a distinction deny the possibility that Jesus could also be identified as the one God of Israel? I believe that such a distinction finds an explanation in what I have called a "two-powers" theology of the one God of Israel. Such a theology accounts for the distinction between

God and Jesus in the baptism episode and the transfiguration. But Kirk offers a couple of examples that require a bit more nuanced application of this "two-power" theology. He notes that in Mark 8:38, the Son of Man is described as "coming in the glory of his Father." Kirk argues that if Jesus is rightly understood as divine, would he not then come in his own divine glory? Why would he be clothed in the glory of the Father? I would contend that the basis for the "two-power" understanding of the one God of Israel offers us a good explanation for this Markan detail. As I argued in my essay, this "two-power" theology finds its origins in the tension between the transcendence and immanence of the God of Israel. A growing belief in God's transcendence demanded a means through which this God could also be immanent. Thus, immanent expressions of God emerge as a second distinct power; for example, the Word of God, the Wisdom of God, and, I would contend, the heavenly Son of Man. While these second powers are rightly understood as the God who interacted with Israel throughout her history, they are also representing the transcendent God. The authority and glory they bear is that of the utterly transcendent God. Thus, as the immanent expression of the one God of Israel, the Markan Jesus bears the glory of the Father, the transcendent expression of Israel's God.

Such reasoning would also help explain Jesus's claim from the cross, "My God, My God, why have you forsaken me?" Kirk contends that this text demands that Jesus is distinct from the God of Israel and that he even be of a different substance than that of God. Yet I would contend that a two-power theology, particularly one combined with Jewish messianism, provides the way forward. It must be recognized that this two-power theology I propose for Second Temple Judaism and find manifest in Mark's Gospel remains a significant distance from Nicea. Thus, there seems to be some implicit sense of subordination between the immanent and transcendent YHWH. For example, we see the transcendent God of Israel creating through his Wisdom. We see the same God calling his Word his only begotten Son, through whom he reigns and creates. It should not be surprising to see the immanent expression of YHWH refer to the transcendent God of Israel as "his God." Such an expectation increases when that immanent expression of YHWH has taken on human form, as the Markan Jesus clearly has, and must relate to the transcendent God while in such form. This understanding of Jesus as the immanent YHWH in relation with the transcendent YHWH also helps us understand Jesus's limited knowledge regarding the eschaton and the parousia (13:32), as the knowledge of the former need not be entirely shared with the latter.

What is to be made of Jesus's inability to heal (6:5), a Markan detail that Kirk finds problematic for a divine identity? I think it is important to note that even the Markan text itself corrects the claim that Jesus "could do no deed of power" in his hometown of Nazareth, as it goes on to say that he healed a few sick people. Thus, the point seems to be that human lack of faith *limited* the scope of Jesus's healing ability rather than prevented him from all such ability. But does such limitation speak against a divine identity for Jesus? I would argue that this Markan episode is part of a larger theme, namely, the necessity of human faith for divine action. We see this theme communicated in a number of Markan pericopes. Faith is demanded of Jairus in order to see his daughter healed (5:36). Faith is demanded of the father of the demon-possessed boy (11:22–24). And quite remarkably, the woman with the issue of blood is presumably healed by her faith alone, without the will of Jesus even being necessary (5:27–29). In Mark's Gospel, human faith is the key to accessing divine power, and the absence of faith has real implications for experiencing divine power. Thus Mark 6:5 really says nothing about Jesus's ability and conveys rather the reality that limited faith has for divine encounter.

A Divine Christology and a Christology of Suffering

Kirk questions whether seeking to find a divine Jesus in Mark betrays a belief that true value and significance can only be found in glory, a belief that contradicts the very claims about greatness in the Gospel of Mark. He claims that readings that promote a divine Christ "cut against the grain of Mark's narrative as they pursue some clue other than the notion that humble, self-giving humanity (even to the point of death) is the location where ultimate greatness is found in God's kingdom" (p. 167). I think Kirk's concern is valid. The pursuit of a divine Christology could undermine the very values of Mark's narrative Christology, a Christology that surely promotes humility, suffering, and sacrifice on behalf of others. But I do not think that finding a divine Christ in Mark need undermine a narrative Christology of suffering. I would say that it may in fact enhance a Christology of suffering, as Mark's

Gospel presents the very God of Israel embracing humility, service, suffering, and even death on behalf of his people. It is then again Israel's God that models the way for them to live as his people. In this way, Mark's Gospel is a sort of narrative reflection of the Christ hymn of Philippians 2:6–11.

I close by saying that if Kirk's presuppositions are largely correct and mine are not, the reading he proposes of Mark's narrative and Christology is quite strong. There may be Markan details that push against his reading or create tension with these presuppositions, such as Jesus being identified with the YHWH of Isaiah in Mark 1:3 or the depiction of Jesus walking on water; but, on the whole Kirk offers a reading that can explain well the Jesus of Mark's Gospel. But if my presuppositions are correct, Kirk's reading runs into challenges and requires reconsideration at a number of points. At the end of the day, certainty regarding presuppositions will ultimately remain elusive, and thus what we are left with is two possible yet quite different readings of Mark's Christology.

Rejoinder

J. R. DANIEL KIRK

A roundtable discussion such as the one contained in this book has the potential for both heat and light, as people passionate about their ideas come together to debate a text they all know well. And, indeed, there is much light to be had here. It is worth pointing out that all of us agree that the Jesus of Mark's Gospel is fully and truly human, and that this is a critical component of his identity. It is also important that none of the contributors to this volume think that Mark is arguing against a divine Christology. Another important point is that not only Sandra Huebenthal and myself, but also Larry Hurtado, are unwilling to say that Mark's Jesus is depicted *as* God.

Huebenthal and I have the broadest agreement in our readings. And it is worth noting that this arises from the shared commitment to allow the text of Mark to tell its own story. Hurtado's uneasiness about Mark's being the story of an idealized human comes from his understanding of what early Christians believed at the time when Mark was written. Winn's more ambitious reading finds its justification in a Second Temple theological thread together with a conviction about early Christian beliefs similar to that of Hurtado. To my mind, this increases the likelihood that Huebenthal and I are on the right track, and that divine Christology in Mark is more in the eye of the beholder than it is on the pages of the Gospel.

I would like to generally address the issue of what we know about the earliest Christian beliefs at the time that Mark was written. In all likelihood, Mark represents the second youngest witness to early Christian belief. There are Paul's letters, and then there is Mark. Mark must be read as an independent witness to the early churches' beliefs before it is subsumed under Pauline terms, if for no other reason than that it is only the second voice to speak. To read Paul as determinative of the Christology of Mark is a question-begging response to the query of New Testament Christology. The idea that Paul represents normative first-century Christianity is deeply problematic, not least because his letters bear strong evidence of deep rifts in the early Christian movement centering around Paul himself. This is all beside the fact that Paul himself does not likely hold a divine preexistence Christology and makes strong, consistent distinctions between Jesus and God. Reading material into Mark in light of "earliest Christian beliefs" is shaky ground at best, precisely because Mark is one of the earliest witnesses to those beliefs.

I turn now to address a few lingering points at issue between myself and my respondents. I will start with Hurtado.

I found a number of Hurtado's attempted rejoinders puzzling, precisely because he thought they were rejoinders rather than points of agreement. For instance, Hurtado concludes his remarks under the heading of "The Approach" by saying that Mark's depiction of Jesus as human model does not any way undermine "the high views of Jesus's relationship to God and the centrality of Jesus in devotional practice" (p. 184). He states this as though it is a contradiction of my reading of Mark. However, the whole point of my reading of Mark is to discover why and how it is that Jesus has a unique relationship to God that lands him in the middle of early Christian devotional practice. Similarly, he speaks of Jesus having a uniquely high status that eludes other humans in Mark's account. And, again, yes! While they are all human, Jesus is the Human One, the quintessential embodiment of God's plans and purposes for humanity. As I have argued elsewhere, this is roughly equivalent to Paul's Second Adam Christology: Jesus is the unique, eschatological human agent through whom other humans are able to enter into the new humanity God is creating.[1] Or, again, in discussing the healing of the paralytic, Hurtado says that what the readers know is that "he has a unique authority to act on the earth in a capacity that is properly God's" (p. 185). It would, indeed, be difficult to find a better way to articulate my own view of the matter.

Winn offers some similar missteps in his engagements with my work.

1. J. R. Daniel Kirk, "Mark's Son of Man and Paul's Second Adam," *HBT* 37 (2015): 170–95.

I think especially of his reading of the grain-plucking episode. It is a bad misreading of both my interpretation and of the syntax of Mark 2:27–28 to say that Jesus's association with humanity as the reason for his authority implies, in fact, that all persons have authority over the Sabbath. No, Jesus says that he has this authority as *the* Human One. Importantly, Winn's idea that Jesus offers in verse 28 a claim for YHWH-lordship that is unrelated to his humanity loses its punch once we realize that the Greek particle ὥστε ("so that") connects the two verses. What Jesus says in verse 27 about the Sabbath being made for humans is the reason he can claim his authority as the Human One in verse 28.

In Mark's Gospel, Jesus is the Christ, the Human One, the Son of God. The question is not *whether* Jesus occupies a unique role in the story (the impression one might get from reading Hurtado's rejoinder). The question is *what kind of person* plays this role. The story is developed in this matrix of titles, showing us that what makes Jesus unique is the position he holds, the work he does, and the Spirit with which God has endowed him. Jesus is the eschatological deliverer, the long-awaited Messiah, who acts with God's power and authority on the earth, who inaugurates the reign of God by being obedient to God to the point of death, and who is finally exalted to the right hand of God.

I find it puzzling that Hurtado and other modern scholars so often cannot grasp that Jesus as Messiah would be a unique, celebrated, exalted figure. This speaks to the profound lack of cultivation of Christian theology around the humanity of Jesus and attests to how little regard we have for Jewish messianic expectation. If we think that when we have said, "He rules from the throne at God's right hand," that we have contradicted the thesis that we are talking about a certain kind of human, we have simply demonstrated the degree to which traditional Christian theology about a divine Christ has impoverished our theological imagination with respect to Jesus's humanity. Moreover, if we think that when we say, "Jesus can do what he does because he is God's eschatological agent," we have denied Jesus the possibility of truly being thought of as Lord and Savior, then we have failed to attend to the Jewish world of expectation and belief that creates the very possibility of Jesus's life as depicted in the Gospels.

Winn also misleads readers by suggesting that I ignore the Jewish context of Mark in my attention to the story. The 132 pages I devote to demonstrating how my thesis fits within Second Temple Judaism in *A Man Attested by God* should be evidence enough of this. Moreover, my reading of the opening verses of Mark highlights that the Jewish biblical text, as received and interpreted in Second Temple Judaism, is where Mark invites its readers to look for interpretive cues. And, it is Mark's story itself that will show us how the Jewish precedents are or are not adequate to accommodate what, as Mark believes, God has actually done in and through Israel's Messiah. There is a significant difference between how Winn and I handle the Jewish sources from the Second Temple period. I have offered a wide-ranging explanation, covering both biblical and postbiblical Jewish sources over a span of centuries, to provide a framework to see someone such as Mark's Jesus being a special, unique, God-empowered human agent doing just the sorts of things that Mark's Jesus does. Winn, by contrast, leans on a minor subcurrent of Jewish theology backed by what is likely a misinterpretation of the one document of 1 Enoch.

The "son of man" background material illustrates this difference. Reading Daniel 7 in tandem with Mark makes excellent sense of otherwise peculiar claims for Jesus as the Human One, including suffering, death, resurrection, and enthronement at God's right hand. Moreover, a good reading of 1 Enoch, which recognizes the "son of man" there as Enoch, whom God exalted to heaven, provides excellent precedent for Mark's holistic depiction of Jesus's authority and power, as well as of his exaltation to a heavenly throne of power after a life of faithfulness on earth.

In the end, "two-powers" theology is just so much wishful thinking when it comes to reading Mark. While it is one thing to recognize ideas of immanent embodiments of divine power, such as Wisdom in the Jewish tradition, it is king David who cries out, "My God, my God, why have you forsaken me?" (Ps 22:1). This is a true cry of dereliction, of abandonment. It is possible for us to find any number of ways to rationalize this so as to make it fit into preconceived notions of Jesus's divinity, but that is simply not Mark's story.

In the end, this is where the judgment of the story must be allowed to have the final say. Winn helpfully points out his desire to distance himself from Mark as a storyteller. This is clear in a number of his interpretive decisions. The idea that Jesus at his transfiguration is having his own divine glory revealed is only possible if we will not attend to the narrative flow in which we have heard for the first time that Jesus will rise from the dead (Mark 8:31) and return in the Father's glory (v. 38). It is possible to hold this divine interpretation of God's words ("this is my beloved Son," 9:7) only if we have failed to attend to the significance of those words at his baptismal anointing, which anticipates his death. And the conversation going down the mountain, where Jesus's attention turns to his resurrection, is the final piece that fits the puzzle. If we will allow Mark to tell his own story, the transfiguration is a preview of the glorification of the Human One (9:9, 10, 12).

The invitation of my essay is simply this: to take Mark's telling of the Jesus story as an opportunity to enrich our understanding of what it means for Jesus, as the Human One, to be Israel's Messiah. This exercise will not be able to fall far from the next question of what it means for those who would follow Jesus to come into the fullness of their God-given humanity. Hurtado recognizes that just such fruit in understanding the nature of Christian discipleship is endemic to Mark's laser-like focus on the human aspects of Jesus's christological identity.

In closing, let me offer a few reflections from within the Christian tradition about how the human Jesus of Mark's Gospel might prove to be theologically enriching.

1. Because the Human One has come, suffered, died, and been raised, we know that God has visited God's people to begin the great work of final salvation.
2. Because God was able to save the world through a human being ruling the world on God's behalf, God's power to redeem the world by fulfilling God's original intentions for it (Gen 1:26–28) is greater than the power of evil to impede that plan and purpose.
3. Because Jesus extends his unique authority through his closest followers, we know that Jesus is not only the ideal Human One but is also ushering others into the renewed humanity he has inaugurated.
4. Because resurrection glory came to the Human One, other humans who take up their cross and follow Jesus can expect to be raised in glory as well.
5. Because the Human One becomes Son of God with the reception of the Spirit in a manner that is both relational and functional, all who receive the Spirit can also know that they are newly related to

God and given a share in the work of bringing God's reign to bear on the earth.

6. Because salvation has truly come "from below," we can expect that the ongoing transformative and saving work will arise from the same place: from those who are carrying their crosses, from the oppressed, from those whose own liberation is wrapped up in the salvation of the people they are serving. Salvation does not come from powerful crucifying empires, and to claim that the cross is the sign by which an army will conquer is the height of blasphemy.

The theological grammar of each of these claims rests on Jesus as the Human One. And they are claims that can only be fully apprehended if we are willing, with Mark and, yes, with Paul, to sit with the human Jesus and his story in not only its authority, power, and glory but also its humiliation and suffering. In an ironic twist, we most enrich our theology and practice when we withstand the impulse to race to affirm, with the church, the preexistent divine Christ. Because such a move leaves us devoid of the stories of the human Messiah that hold together not only the Gospel of Mark but the narrative that runs from Genesis to Revelation.

CHAPTER 4

A Case for Jesus as the YHWH of Israel in the Gospel of Mark

ADAM WINN

What does the Gospel of Mark tell us about the identity of Jesus *vis-à-vis* the God of Israel? Does this Gospel present Jesus as merely a human agent of God—one unprecedented in power, but still decidedly human? Or does Mark's Gospel present Jesus as more than human? Does the Gospel, though written long before the Council of Nicaea, have a view of Jesus that would be commensurate with the later orthodox confession that Jesus is rightly identified as the God of Israel? I should say that I do not believe answering such a question was an intended aim of the Gospel. I do not think that the Markan evangelist was, at least not primarily, seeking to answer this question for readers.[1] But I do believe the author of Mark's Gospel had convictions regarding the identity of Jesus as it relates to this question and that such convictions do manifest themselves within the Gospel of Mark. What follows is my position on how those convictions are rightly understood.

1. I have thoroughly addressed my understanding of the *intentional* christological message of Mark elsewhere; see Adam Winn, *Reading Mark's Christology under Caesar: Jesus the Messiah and Roman Imperial Ideology* (Downers Grove, IL: IVP Academic, 2018).

The Importance of Starting Points

Before beginning any analysis of Mark's understanding of Jesus's relationship to the God of Israel, it is crucial to consider one's starting points, particularly one's position on the range of possibilities that existed in the first century CE for understanding the one God of Israel and his messiah. A commonly held assumption within both the academic field of New Testament studies and larger popular thought is that first-century Jews understood the one God of Israel in terms of strict singularity, or something quite close to it.[2] That is to say, not only did Jews believe there was one God but that this one God existed as a single, indivisible entity. Such a belief has strong implications for understanding Jesus's relationship to this one God of Israel, as any suggestion that Jesus was identified with or as the one God of Israel quickly runs into the criticism that such an identification was not possible in a first-century Jewish context. Because of this presupposition, evidence that might otherwise lead a reader to the conclusion that a New Testament author aims to identity Jesus with or as the God of Israel becomes subject to alternative explanations.[3] Even Larry Hurtado, who argues strenuously that the worship practices of early Christians demonstrate their belief that Jesus is properly identified with the God of Israel, concludes that such a belief was unprecedented within the context of strict Jewish monotheism.[4]

Another commonly held assumption, this one held primarily by scholars, is that Jews, though diverse in messianic thought, understood any sort of messiah figure to be an agent of their God and not a divine being, that is, not the God of Israel. This assumption also has implications for the

2. A good example of such an assumption at work can be found in James Dunn's treatment of God's "Wisdom" in his well-known work *Christology in the Making: A New Testament Inquiry into the Origins of the Doctrine of Incarnation* (Grand Rapids: Eerdmans, 1980), 174: "In short, if we attempt to give clearer definition to the figure of Wisdom within the monotheism of Israel's religion, we seem to be shut up to two alternatives. Either Wisdom is a being clearly subordinate to Yahweh, like the angels, or the heavenly council in Job 1 and 2 . . . or else, and this seems more plausible, the Wisdom passages are *simply ways of describing Yahweh's wise creation and purpose*" (italics original). That Dunn fails to offer the possibility that "Wisdom" could be a distinct hypostatic being that coexists both with and as the YHWH of Israel demonstrates his assumption that the God of Israel must be understood in terms of singularity rather than plurality.

3. Examples of such alternative explanations of evidence will be addressed below in my treatment of the Markan text.

4. See Hurtado, *Lord Jesus Christ: Devotion to Jesus in Earliest Christianity* (Grand Rapids: Eerdmans, 2003), 27–78.

question of Jesus's relationship to the one God of Israel. Early Christians clearly understood Jesus to be the long-awaited Messiah of Israel. If a divine identity was not a category that first-century Jews had within their diverse set of messianic expectations, how then could early Christians who affirmed Jesus as God's Messiah also affirm his identity as the God of Israel? Such an understanding of Second Temple Judaism has led many interpreters to conclude that the earliest Christians believed that Jesus was nothing more than a human Messiah and that recognition of his divine identity came much later (a development often, though not always, associated with Hellenistic influence).

Yet recent studies have offered significant challenges to these commonly held assumptions. James McGrath has argued that Jewish monotheism was far more flexible in the first century than many modern interpreters have allowed, and that at least some Jews found divine intermediaries to be compatible with their commitment to the one God of Israel.[5] Richard Bauckham allows for hypostatized divine aspects of God, such as God's Word and Wisdom, to be understood as distinct realities that are rightly identified with the God of Israel. In this regard, Bauckham says that "Jewish writers envisage some form of real distinction within the unique identity of the one God" and that "Second Temple Jewish understanding of divine uniqueness does not define it as unitariness and does not make distinctions within the divine identity inconceivable."[6] Along with Alan Segal, Daniel Boyarin has argued that the belief in "two powers in heaven"—a belief that the one God of Israel existed in a plurality of powers that was deemed a heresy in the Mishnah—finds its origins in the Judaism of the late Second Temple period (the first century CE).[7] Though against Segal, Boyarin argues that this belief in "two powers in heaven" was not deemed a heresy in the Second Temple period but rather was an acceptable and common way for Jews to conceive of the one God of Israel.[8] According to Boyarin, this form of Judaism in the Second Temple period was only later deemed a heresy

5. James F. McGrath, *The Only True God: Early Christian Monotheism in Its Jewish Context* (Champaign: University of Illinois Press, 2012).

6. Richard Bauckham, *Jesus and the God of Israel* (Grand Rapids: Eerdmans, 2008), 17.

7. Alan F. Segal, *Two Powers in Heaven: Early Rabbinic Reports about Christianity and Gnosticism*, SJLA 25 (Leiden: Brill, 1977), 182–219, 260–67; Daniel Boyarin, *Border Lines: The Partition of Judaeo-Christianity* (Philadelphia: University of Pennsylvania Press, 2004), 112–27.

8. Boyarin, *Border Lines*, 128–47.

by the rabbis in the second century as a response to both Christianity and Gnosticism. This Second Temple belief in two powers finds its origins in a growing commitment to the utter transcendence of Israel's God, a commitment that requires explanation of Scriptures in which the God of Israel engages his creation. In order to explain this divine engagement, one sees the emergence of concepts such as God's Word and Wisdom, which are often depicted as distinct hypostatic beings who accomplish God's purposes vis-à-vis creation (see Bauckham above). Philo of Alexandria is an example of such an understanding of Israel's God. For Philo, it is through God's Word (λόγος) that God creates, mediates divine-human encounters, and reigns over creation (creates: *Sacr.* 8; mediates: *Her.* 205; *QE* 2.94; reigns: *Conf.* 146; *Cher.* 36). Philo even refers to the Logos or Word as the second God and firstborn son of God (*Agr.* 51; *QG* 2.62). Yet similar depictions of God's Word and Wisdom can be found in the wisdom literature of Sirach and Wisdom of Solomon (e.g., Sir 24; Wis 7–9), as well as apocalyptic texts like 1 and 2 Enoch, Jubilees, 2 Baruch, and 4 Ezra. The Palestinian Targum Neofiti contains a thoroughgoing "word" theology.[9] Consistently when an Old Testament text identifies the YHWH of Israel engaging creation, the Neofiti Targum replaces YHWH with "the word of YHWH." Thus, it is the "word of YHWH" that creates the world, that walks with Adam and Eve in the garden, that meets Moses in the burning bush, and that received cultic worship. While the dating of targumic traditions is difficult, Boyarin makes a strong case that the "word" theology of Targum Neofiti finds its origins in the Palestinian synagogues of the Second Temple period.[10] In light of this evidence, both Boyarin and others have argued that many Jews of the Second Temple period were perfectly comfortable understanding the one God of Israel in terms of a duality of powers, one which was utterly transcendent and others that were particularly immanent.

One possible expression of this "two-powers" theology that is of particular importance for understanding the Christology of the canonical Gospels is the "Son of Man" found in the Parables of Enoch (also known as the Similitudes, chapters 37–71 of 1 Enoch). In the Parables, two figures feature prominently. The first is clearly the God of Israel, who is called both the

---

9. For discussion of the Palestinian Targum Neofiti and its "word" theology, see Martin McNamara, *The Aramaic Bible: Targum Neofiti 1 Genesis* (Collegeville, MN: Liturgical Press, 1992).

10. See Boyarin, *Border Lines*, 112–27.

"Lord of Spirits" and "Head of Days."[11] The Parables attribute a variety of titles to the second figure, which include the "Righteous One," "Chosen One," "Messiah," and "Son of Man." This second figure is presented as both ruler and judge over all of creation (1 En. 46.4–5; 48.4; 49.2–4; 52.4; 55.4; 61.8; 62.6). He is also depicted as sitting on God's glorious and heavenly throne (45.3; 51.3; 55.4; 61.8; 62.6; 69.29). Not only does this figure sit on God's throne, but he is also the object of human worship (46.5; 48.5; 61.7; 62.6, 9). Finally, this figure is presented as preexistent, predating creation itself. It is possible this figure is even connected with the very act of creation.[12] In a Second Temple Jewish context, many of these descriptors are only appropriately applied to YHWH, and as such one might conclude that Enoch is presenting this Son of Man as YHWH. But such a conclusion would run strongly against the widely held assumption that Second Temple Jews understood their God in terms of strict singularity.[13] On the basis of such an assumption, because the Parables clearly present the Lord of Spirits/Head of Days (clearly the God of Israel) and the Son of Man as two distinct beings, then the Son of Man cannot be rightly identified with YHWH, the God of Israel. This assumption has led many interpreters to seek alternative interpretations of these descriptors of the Son of Man. A few examples can be given: (1) the Son of Man does not actually sit on God's throne but on a human one;[14] (2) the Son of Man does not receive true worship from human beings, merely reverence through obeisance;[15] (3) the Son of Man is not actually preexistent but was only appointed or named before creation.[16]

11. The title "Lord of Spirits" is seemingly derived from the title "Lord of Hosts," a title commonly used for YHWH in the Old Testament. The title "Head of Days" is likely derived from the title "Ancient of Days," which is found in Dan 7. This connection to Dan 7 is made virtually certain by the physical description of the "Head of Days" as one with a head covered in white wool, a description also given to the "Ancient of Days" in Dan 7:9.

12. I have recently argued that the narrative logic of the Parables links the "Son of Man" with the act of creation itself. Adam Winn, "Identifying the Enochic Son of Man as God's Word and Wisdom," *JSP* 28.4 (2019): 290–318.

13. Even some interpreters who are open to the possibility that Jews could understand the one God in terms of plurality or divisibility are reluctant when it comes to identifying the Enochic Son of Man with the YHWH of Israel. Richard Bauckham notes how unique this figure is in Second Temple Judaism and allows that he in some way takes part in the divine identity of YHWH. However, Bauckham somewhat hedges his bet by claiming that this Son of Man's participation in the divine identity is equivocal. See Bauckham, *Jesus and the God of Israel*, 16.

14. For such an argument, see Hurtado, *Lord Jesus Christ*, 38–39.

15. Hurtado, *Lord Jesus Christ*, 38–39.

16. For such an argument, see James C. VanderKam, "Righteous One, Messiah, Chosen One, and Son of Man in 1 Enoch 37–71," in *The Messiah*, ed. James H. Charlesworth (Minneapolis: Fortress,

Such explanations allow interpreters to understand the Enochic Son of Man as an exalted messianic and human figure—and, as such, the singularity of YHWH is preserved.

While there is not space to offer rebuttals to such arguments here, such rebuttals have been made by myself and others.[17] Ultimately, I contend the *prima facie* reading of the Parables has the better support of the existing evidence, and the proponents of the arguments noted above are primarily motivated by their presuppositions regarding the nature of Jewish monotheism, namely, that it understood the YHWH of Israel in terms of strict singularity, a singularity that has no room for a figure like the Enochic Son of Man. Yet if this presupposition regarding Jewish monotheism is abandoned and we allow for the possibility that Second Temple Jews could understand the one God of Israel in terms of plurality or "two powers," the Parables' description of the Son of Man is no longer problematic. One can conclude that the Parables depict the YHWH of Israel in terms of plurality, with the Lord of Spirits representing the transcendent YHWH and the Son of Man representing the immanent YHWH. In fact, as I have argued elsewhere, a strong case can be made that the Enochic Son of Man is best identified as an apocalyptic embodiment of God's word and wisdom, entities that in other Jewish literature are understood as means by which YHWH is immanent.[18] If one reads the Parables of Enoch from the perspective of a "two powers in heaven" paradigm, then the "Son of Man" figure is rightly identified as the YHWH of Israel. But perhaps even more importantly, the Parables offer an example in which this "two-powers" theology extends into the realm of Jewish messianism. Not only is the "Son of Man" rightly understood as YHWH, but he is also rightly understood as Israel's Messiah! Such blending of Jewish monotheism and messianism, I will henceforth refer to as "YHWH Christology."

A "two-power" understanding of Jewish monotheism in general, and the application of that monotheism to the Parables of Enoch in particular, has tremendous implications not only for the Christology of Mark but for the entire New Testament. The analysis I offer of Mark's Christology will

---

1992), 179–82; See also J. R. Daniel Kirk, *A Man Attested by God: The Human Jesus of the Synoptic Gospels* (Grand Rapids: Eerdmans, 2016), 153–54.

17. See Winn, "Identifying the Enochic Son of Man"; Crispin Fletcher-Louis, *Jesus Monotheism* (Eugene, OR: Cascade: 2015), 172–86.

18. Winn, "Identifying the Enochic Son of Man."

no doubt overlap at certain points with my fellow contributors. Yet our analysis will also differ in significant ways. I contend that the primary reason for the majority of our disagreements is our reconstruction of both Jewish monotheism and messianism. My fellow contributors bring to the text of Mark something akin to the presupposition that Jews of the Second Temple period understood the YHWH of Israel in terms of singularity, while I bring to the text of Mark a presupposition that many Jews of that same period understood the YHWH of Israel in terms of complex duality—or, more precisely, in terms of two powers in heaven, both of which are rightly identified as YHWH. This volume is not the arena for resolving the differences we will share in this regard, but it is the arena for demonstrating the implications that one's reconstruction of Second Temple Judaism has for assessing the christological development and commitments of the early Christian movement.

Jesus and the God of Israel in the Gospel of Mark

Over last fifty years, Mark has been widely regarded as having the lowest Christology of the four canonical Gospels.[19] Mark's "secret"-keeping Jesus seems strikingly different than the Johannine Jesus, who boldly proclaims both his own preexistence and his divine identity. Most interpreters perceive in Mark's Gospel both a Jesus and a narrator that never makes such claims. Even when compared to Luke's Jesus, the Jesus of Mark's Gospel appears to be in less control, more vulnerable, and perhaps, simply put, more human and thus presumably less divine.[20] Jesus is clearly Messiah in Mark, as well as Son of God and Son of Man, but most Markan interpreters understand these

19. For a review of scholarship on Mark's Christology, see Daniel Johansson, "The Identity of Jesus in the Gospel of Mark: Past and Present Proposals," *CurBR* 9.3 (2010), 371–82. For examples of those who promote a "low" Christology in Mark, see Donald Juel, *Messiah and Temple: The Trial of Jesus in the Gospel of Mark*, SBLDS 31 (Missoula, MT: Scholars Press, 1977), 78–82, 108–14; Frank Matera, *The Kingship of Jesus: Composition and Theology in Mark 15*, SBLDS 66 (Chico, CA: Scholars Press, 1982); J. D. Kingsbury, *The Christology of Mark's Gospel* (Philadelphia: Fortress, 1989), 32, 65, 142; Paul J. Achtemeier, "Mark, Gospel of," *ABD* 4:541–57; D. Rhoads and D. Mitchie, *Mark as Story* (Philadelphia: Fortress, 1982), 105; E. Broadhead, *Teaching with Authority: Miracles and Christology in the Gospel of Mark*, JSNTSup 74 (Sheffield: JSOT Press, 1992), 125–26.

20. Cf., e.g., Mark's depiction of Jesus in the garden of Gethsemane to that of Luke. On the kiss of Judas, Mark depicts Judas kissing Jesus, but the Lukan Jesus preempts the kiss by asking Judas if intends to betray him with a kiss. The Markan Jesus speaks of being grieved to the point of death, while this is omitted from Luke. In Luke, Jesus stops his disciples from violence and heals a man's wounded ear, while this material is not found in Mark.

titles to present Jesus as God's appointed eschatological agent and conclude that they do not carry divine implications. Even recent analysis of the contours of Mark's narrative concludes that there is seemingly nothing explicit in the narrative that would necessarily direct the reader to understand Jesus to be identified as divine.[21]

But with the emergence and growth of the early high-Christology movement, a handful of interpreters have turned their eyes back to Mark and have challenged the widely held conclusion regarding its low Christology. Such studies on Mark focus not on the Gospel's christological titles or even its explicit narratival claims but rather focus on the subtext of the Gospel and the subtle and/or implicit claims that might be found there.[22] These interpreters contend that if certain first-century readers (particularly those with strong familiarity with the LXX) paid close attention to the subtext or intentional ambiguity of Mark, an implied high Christology would emerge, one that would lead the reader to conclude that Mark's Gospel was identifying Jesus as the God of Israel.

The following analysis of Mark will build on the works of these previous interpreters and will consider the many texts that play a central role in their argument. However, I will augment their work with insights from the reconstruction of Jewish monotheism and messianism described above, as well as with consideration of additional texts in which a "two-powers" theology or YHWH Christology might also be found. I will begin by analyzing texts that I think make the clearest statement regarding Jesus's identity as the YHWH of Israel and then will consider the implications these texts have for texts in which Jesus's identity as YHWH is more ambiguous.

The Son of Man Has the Power on Earth to Forgive Sins (Mark 2:1–12)

In the story of Jesus healing a paralytic, Jesus's initial response to the man, "Son, your sins are forgiven" (Mark 2:5), is surprising for multiple reasons. Presumably the man was brought to Jesus in order to be healed, and not in

21. See, e.g., Elizabeth Struthers Malbon, *Mark's Jesus: Characterization as Narrative Christology* (Waco, TX: Baylor University Press, 2009), 72, 134.

22. See, e.g., Timothy J. Geddert, "The Implied YHWH Christology of Mark's Gospel: Mark's Challenge to the Reader to 'Connect the Dots,'" *BBR* 25.3 (2015): 325–40; Daniel Johansson, "'Kyrios' in the Gospel of Mark," *JSNT* 33.1 (2010): 101–24.

order to be forgiven of his sins (the reference in 1:32 to people bringing their sick to Jesus for the purpose of healing strongly supports this conclusion). As such, Jesus's response is disruptive and surprising given the narratival expectations of the reader; the expectation was that Jesus would heal the man.[23] Also surprising, at least to the characters in Mark's narrative, is the implication of Jesus's statement, namely, that he has the prerogative to forgive sins.[24] This surprising element is highlighted in the narrative by the response of the scribes, who ask the question, "Who is able to forgive sins but one, God?" a question seemingly grounded in texts like Exodus 34:6–7 and Isaiah 43:25 (which are about YHWH's role in forgiving sins). While there may be some examples of other human beings exercising forgiveness in Jewish traditions, such exceptions do not seem to be in the purview of the evangelist.[25] The text itself seems to imply that the thinking of the scribes indeed reflects conventional wisdom, conventional wisdom that Jesus's ability to forgive sins challenges. Jesus responds by questioning their reasoning (questioning for which the impetus is presumably supernatural power) and then asking which is easier to say, "Your sins are forgiven" or "Stand up take your mat and walk?" (Mark 2:9). While interpreters have debated the implied answer

23. See Francis J. Moloney, *The Gospel of Mark: A Commentary* (Peabody, MA: Hendrickson, 2002), 61; M. Eugene Boring, *Mark: A Commentary*, NTL (Louisville: Westminster John Knox, 2006), 76; Bas van Iersel, *Mark: A Reader Response Commentary*, trans. W. H. Bisscheroux (London: T&T Clark, 1998), 146.

24. Some have argued that because Jesus's declaration uses the passive voice that it implies God as the one who forgives sins, and that Jesus is simply conveying to the man that God has forgiven his sins; see Adela Yarbro Collins, *Mark*, Hermeneia (Minnesota: Fortress, 2007), 185; Boring, *Mark*, 76; R. T. France, *The Gospel of Mark: A Commentary on the Greek Text*, NIGTC (Grand Rapids: Eerdmans, 2002), 125. But such a reading does not fit with either the thoughts of the scribes, who clearly understand Jesus to be attributing forgiveness to himself rather than to God (see van Iersel, *Mark*, 148), or Jesus's own claim in v. 10 that the Son of Man has authority to forgive sins (see Morna D. Hooker, *The Gospel according to Saint Mark*, BNTC [Peabody, MA: Hendrickson, 1991], 86). See van Iersel, who argues for the presence of ambiguity regarding the use of the passive voice (*Mark*, 147).

25. See Joel Marcus, *Mark 1–8: A New Translation with Introduction and Commentary*, AB 27 (New York: Doubleday, 2000), 217; Yarbro Collins, *Mark*, 185. Collins argues that while some holy men and prophets were credited with the ability to win forgiveness for others, there is no precedent for a human being doing what Jesus does, namely, declaring that God had forgiven someone. For a similar argument, see Daniel Johansson, "'Who Can Forgive Sins but God Alone?' Human and Angelic Agents and Divine Forgiveness in Early Judaism," *JSNT* 33.4 (2011): 251–74. Daniel Kirk argues that even within Mark's Gospel, sins are able to be forgiven by human mediators. He gives examples such as John the Baptist (1:4), and even Jesus's disciples (11:25), who are likely representative of the Markan community (Kirk, *Man Attested*, 177–81). But it seems Kirk makes more of these examples than is necessary. While both examples present means through which divine forgiveness is brought about (i.e., repentance and baptism, and forgiving the sins of others), in neither of these examples are human beings directly exercising the divine prerogative of forgiveness; rather they are facilitating a means or condition through which God forgives. These examples seem decidedly different from Jesus's claim to directly forgive sins.

to this question, Jesus's final declaration ultimately makes the question irrelevant, as he says, "But so that you [the scribes] might know that the Son of Man has power on earth to forgive sins . . . I say to you [the paralytic], arise, take your mat and go to your home" (vv. 10–11). The subsequent obedience of the man decisively demonstrates that Jesus has the power to heal, but this supernatural power to heal also indicates that Jesus has the power to forgive sins as well. Of the many surprises in this pericope, perhaps one of the greatest is the oft-missed lack of clarity regarding the answer to the question of the scribes, namely, "Who can forgive sins but God alone?" (v. 7).

In the estimation of most interpreters, the scribes have asked a question that, while true in a sense, lacks the necessary nuance that Jesus provides. While the scribes are correct, they have failed to recognize that God has granted Jesus, the Son of Man, the divine prerogative to forgive sins; the Son of Man can forgive sins on behalf of God.[26] The pericope then functions to expand the powers of Jesus's messianic mission to include the forgiveness of sin. But it is noteworthy that the text never makes this answer explicit and never directly claims that the scribes' perspective is lacking in any way. The above reading presupposes a distinction between the Son of Man and the divine identity of Israel's God. But those who argue for an implicit high Christology in Mark point out that the text itself never makes such a distinction.[27] The absence of such a distinction allows another possible reading of the text to emerge.

One could conclude that the scribes have indeed made a fully accurate statement regarding who is able to forgive sins, namely, God alone, and Jesus's response does not in any way address or even qualify this true claim. Instead, Jesus's response could be read as a response to the charge of blasphemy alone. In response to this charge, Jesus does not claim that God has granted Jesus, as the Son of Man, the authority to forgive sins but rather claims that the Son of Man is in fact divine and so forgives sins, and as such he is not guilty of blasphemy.[28]

---

26. For such an interpretation, see Marcus, *Mark*, 223; idem, "Authority to Forgiven Sins upon the Earth: The SHEMA in the Gospel of Mark," in *The Gospels and the Scriptures of Israel*, ed. C. A. Evans and W. R. Stegner, JSNTSup 104 (Sheffield: Sheffield Academic, 1994), 196–211; Kirk, *Man Attested*, 272–81; Moloney, *Mark*, 60–63; France, *Mark*, 127–29; Boring, *Mark*, 76–78.

27. See Geddert, "YHWH Christology," 330.

28. For such a reading, see E. Earle Ellis, "Deity-Christology in Mark 14:58," in *Jesus of Nazareth: Lord and Christ: Essays on the Historical Jesus and New Testament Christology*, ed. J. B. Green and Max Turner (Grand Rapids: Eerdmans, 1994), 192–203; see also Geddert, "YHWH Christology," 329–31.

Both of these readings are clearly possible, but both share the same weakness. Both have to rely on a presumption of what the text in fact implies. Does it imply that Jesus forgives sins as God's agent, the Son of Man, or does it imply that Jesus the Son of Man is in fact God? Proponents of the first reading will claim that Mark's understanding of the Son of Man is one of a divine agent who acts on God's behalf and is not God himself.[29] Mark's depiction of Jesus as God's Messiah, a figure commonly understood in terms of God's agent, seems to support such a conclusion. Support can also be found in Mark's use of "Son of Man" being informed by Daniel 7:13, in which the heavenly Son of Man figure is seemingly the royal agent of the Ancient of Days. But proponents of the second reading can argue that the narrative logic stipulates that only God can forgive sins and then presents Jesus as forgiving sins! Thus, they claim it is difficult to avoid the conclusion that the text seemingly equates Jesus with God, and however one understands Jesus as a divine agent one must also account for the divine identity communicated in this pericope. It is at this interpretive impasse that I turn to my reconstruction of Jewish monotheism and messianism, that is, a two-powers theology in general and its application to the Parables of Enoch in particular, for a possible way forward.

Many interpreters have been reluctant to consider the Enochic Son of Man as a background for understanding Mark's Son of Man, a reluctance that is largely predicated on the belief that the Parables of Enoch should be dated to the end of the first century or later, and thus the Parables postdate Mark.[30] But such a position has received significant critique in the last two decades and is not held by the majority of Enochic interpreters, most of whom date the Parables prior to the destruction of the Jerusalem Temple and many as early as the Herodian period.[31] As such, the belief in a late date

---

This is the general understanding of this passage among its earliest extant interpreters; e.g., Irenaeus, *Haer.* 5.17.1; Novatian, *Trin.* 13 (this list could easily be expanded if considering the early Christian comments on the parallels in Matt 9:1–8 and Luke 5:17–26).

29. For interpreters who offer such a conclusion, see Yarbro Collins, *Mark*, 186; Kirk, *Man Attested*, 273–81; and Marcus, "Authority to Forgive Sins upon Earth," 196–211.

30. See, e.g., the conclusions of Dunn, *Christology in the Making*, 77–82; Hurtado, *Lord Jesus Christ*, 296; Delbert Burkett, *The Son of Man Debate: A History and Evaluation* (Cambridge: Cambridge University Press, 1999), 68–70.

31. For a brief overview of recent trends in the dating of the Parables of Enoch and for an outline of relevant evidence, see Winn, "Identifying the Enochic Son of Man," 291–92. For a more thorough treatment of the dating of the Parables, see D. L. Bock, "Dating the Parables of Enoch: a Forschungsbericht," in *The Parables of Enoch: A Paradigm Shift*, ed. D. L Bock and James H. Charlesworth (London: Bloomsbury T&T Clark, 2013), 58–113.

for the Parables is losing its grip on New Testament interpreters, and thus the Parables are being considered as a legitimate text for understanding the thought world from which the New Testament emerged.[32] Leslie Walck notes a number of details in Mark and the other Synoptics that "show the very strong possibility and probability that the Synoptic writers knew of, and used, the Parables of Enoch for its concepts and theology of the end-time judge."[33] Walck suggests that direct Markan dependence on the Parables is evinced in Mark 14:21, in which it is said of the one who betrays the Son of Man, "it would have been better for that one not to have been born." This verse is strikingly similar to Parables 38.2, which says of those who deny the Lord of Spirits (depicted in this context with his "Righteous One," later identified as the Son of Man), "it would be good for them if they had never been born."[34] Walck also notes a number of other features that at the very least demonstrate theological influence from the Parables on Mark, including a Son of Man granted divine and judicial authority, a Son of Man opposed by rulers and authorities, a Son of Man who gathers the elect from around the world, a Son of Man linked to divine glory, a Son of Man seated in heaven and in close proximity to the throne of God, and a Son of Man accompanied by angels.[35] Though Gabriele Boccaccini does not see direct dependence of the Parables on Mark, he does perceive theological influence and even argues that Mark's depiction of Jesus forgiving sins can be read as a midrash on Parables 50, in which eschatological forgiveness of the repentant is depicted.[36] Likewise, Adela Yarbro Collins, in her commentary on Mark, argues strongly that the Parables of Enoch offer an important interpretive lens for understanding the Markan secrecy motif.[37]

---

32. See Loren T. Stuckenbruck and Gabriele Boccaccini, eds., *Enoch and the Synoptic Gospels: Reminiscences, Allusions, and Intertextuality*, EJL 44 (Atlanta: SBL Press, 2016); Gerbern S. Oegema, "The Coming of the Righteous One in Acts and 1 Enoch," in *Enoch and the Messiah Son of Man: Revisiting the Book of Parables*, ed. Gabriele Boccaccini (Grand Rapids: Eerdmans, 2007), 250–59; Darrell L. Bock and James H. Charlesworth, eds., *Parables of Enoch: A Paradigm Shift* (London: Bloomsbury T&T Clark, 2013), esp. the essays in part 3, "*The Parables of Enoch* and New Testament Theology"; Fletcher-Louis, *Jesus Monotheism*, 171–205.

33. See Leslie Walck, "The Parables of Enoch and the Synoptic Gospels," in Bock and Charlesworth, *Parables of Enoch*, 267.

34. Walck, "Parables of Enoch and the Synoptic Gospels," 245–46.

35. Walck, "Parables of Enoch and the Synoptic Gospels," 239–46.

36. Gabriele Boccaccini, "Forgiveness of Sins: An Enochic Problem, a Synoptic Answer," in Stuckenbruck and Boccaccini, *Enoch and the Synoptic Gospels*, 153–67, esp. 166–67.

37. See Yarbro Collins, *Mark*, 58–72; idem, "The Secret Son of Man in the Parables of Enoch and the Gospel of Mark: A Response to Leslie Walck," in Boccaccini, *Enoch and the Messiah Son of*

Thus, there is reason to consider the influence of the Parables on Mark's presentation of Jesus in general and on Mark 2:10 in particular. In Mark 2:10, Jesus's identity as Son of Man is directly linked to divine power and prerogative, a striking similarity to the Enochic Son of Man who is consistently depicted possessing both divine power and prerogative. But an even more specific link can be made between Jesus's power to forgive sins and the Enochic Son of Man. Boccaccini notes Parables 48–50, in which the Son of Man is God's eschatological instrument to administer divine judgment to the righteous and the sinners.[38] In Parables 48, the righteous and the unrighteous receive their corresponding fates, but in Parables 50 a third group is introduced, a group that is repentant and, as such, is saved from God's judgment.[39] Thus, the Enochic Son of Man oversees the repentance of sinners. While there is no explicit statement that the Son of Man does indeed forgive sins in the Parables, his involvement in such forgiveness seems to be clearly implied. Thus, there is a unique link between the powers of the Markan Son of Man and the Enochic Son of Man, a link that strongly suggests the influence of the latter on the former.

When Mark 2:10 is read in light of the Enochic Son of Man, the reader is given a lens for understanding the identity of the Markan Jesus. As I contended above, the Enochic Son of Man figure is best understood as a second divine power in heaven, one who can be identified as the immanent and knowable YHWH of Israel. Jesus's answer to the question of the scribes comes into sharper focus when this understanding of the Son of Man is granted. Jesus the Son of Man is able to forgive sins not because he is YHWH's agent or representative but because he himself is the immanent and knowable YHWH. Additionally, the reader does not have to make an implicit leap to Jesus's divine identity based on the truth of the scribe's assertion alone. Rather, through Jesus's own self-identification as the Son of Man, an explicit claim to divine identity is made.

If Mark 2:1–12 is read in this way, not only does the divine identity of Jesus come into sharper focus, but Jesus's claim to have power to forgive sins "on earth" takes on greater significance. The Enochic Son of Man is clearly

---

Man, 338–42. It should be noted that Yarbro Collins is uncertain whether Mark is dependent directly on the Parables or is simply familiar with the oral traditions reflected in the Parables.

38. Boccaccini, "Forgiveness of Sins," 158–62.

39. Boccaccini, "Forgiveness of Sins," 158–62.

a heavenly figure who exercises divine authority from the heavenly sphere. Jesus's qualification of the sphere of the Son of Man's power being "on earth" could be understood in terms of an intentional contrast with the sphere of power normally associated with the Son of Man figure, namely, the heavenly sphere. Thus, with the words of verse 10, not only does Jesus boldly declare his divine identity, but he claims that a transfer of the Son of Man's authority from heaven to earth has taken place, a transfer that exists in his very presence.

Narratively, this pericope answers the questions about Jesus's authority that arise in the preceding chapter (1:22, 27), questions that are inseparable from that of Jesus's identity in Mark's Gospel. It is not surprising then that the answer comes with Jesus's first statement about his own identity, that he is the Son of Man who exercises divine authority. With this declaration, Jesus's identity and the source of his authority are clearly and boldly stated. Jesus is the immanent and knowable YHWH who has come from heaven to earth, and his authority, which is clearly derived from this identity, is now manifest on earth. In light of such a reading of Mark 2:10, I agree with previous interpreters who have seen in this pericope a high Christology but reject the assessment that this Christology is only implicit. When read against the backdrop of a Second Temple Judaism that affirmed two powers in heaven, one utterly transcendent and the other immanent, this pericope offers an explicit claim to Jesus's identity as the Son of Man, the Righteous One, who is also the YHWH of Israel.

The Son of Man Is Lord of the Sabbath (Mark 2:23–28)

Shortly after Jesus's declaration about the Son of Man's authority to forgive sins, another declaration addressing the Son of Man's authority follows. Jesus's disciples are criticized by certain Pharisees for plucking heads of grain on the Sabbath, an act these Pharisees deem to be unlawful. Jesus's reply is multidimensional, and it can be difficult to assess how all the pieces of his response fit together—such that it has caused many interpreters to conclude that Mark has simply brought together several Sabbath-related teachings of Jesus together in this pericope.[40] It is not my intention to offer analysis of

40. See Yarbro Collins, *Mark*, 201, 203; Boring, *Mark*, 90; for discussion, see also, Marcus, *Mark*, 243.

each part of Jesus's response but instead to focus on Jesus's culminating statement, "So the Son of Man is Lord even of the Sabbath" (2:28). The majority of interpreters understand this statement in much the way they understand Jesus's declaration regarding the Son of Man's authority to forgive sins. Just as Jesus as God's agent is able to forgive sins on God's behalf, so also this agency gives Jesus authority over the Sabbath.[41] But Daniel Johansson has argued that the identification of Jesus as "Lord of the Sabbath" implies a divine identity.[42] For any Jew literate in the Septuagint, the "Lord [κύριος] of the Sabbath" would be understood as none other than YHWH himself, that is, the YHWH of the Sabbath or YHWH identified with the Sabbath. While it must be granted that the Septuagint never uses the phrase "Lord of the Sabbath," the idea is clearly implied in the fourth commandment of the Decalogue (Exod 20:8–10; the third commandment by the Catholic count). It is YHWH (translated as κύριος in the Septuagint, the Greek translation of the Old Testament) that institutes the Sabbath. The seventh day is a Sabbath to YHWH (κύριος), and YHWH (κύριος) both blessed and hallowed the Sabbath. It seems the most natural way in which Jesus's declaration would be understood by a first-century Jew is that Jesus is identifying himself with the YHWH of Israel.

But here we would point out that the Markan text specifically equates the "Son of Man" with the "Lord [κύριος] of the Sabbath." That is, it is the Son of Man who is being equated with YHWH. Again, this declaration comes into sharper focus and in fact moves from an implicit to an explicit claim when read against the backdrop of the Enochic Son of Man figure. I have argued that this figure is best understood within a two-powers theology as the embodiment of the immanent and knowable YHWH. For readers familiar with the tradition of the Son of Man found in Enoch, the meaning

---

41. For such an interpretation, see France, *Mark*, 148; Moloney, *Mark*, 69; van Iersel, *Mark*, 159–60. Some have sought to understand Jesus's claim that "the Son of Man is Lord of the Sabbath" as simply a claim that "human beings" (a plausible idiomatic reading of the phrase "son of man" in the Old Testament) are to benefit from the Sabbath rather than be a servant to it (see Julius Wellhausen, *Das Evangelium Marci übersetzt und erklärt*, 2nd ed. [Berlin: G. Reimer, 1909], 20; Rudolf Bultmann, *Die Geschichte der synoptischen Tradition*, 2nd ed. [Göttingen: Vandenhoeck & Ruprecht, 1931], 14–15; cf. Yarbro Collins, who notes this interpretation even though she ultimately concludes that "Son of Man" conveys Jesus's messianic identity and authority in this text [*Mark*, 204]). But as Boring astutely argues, for the Markan evangelist, "Son of Man" clearly refers to Jesus himself and communicates the vast power that Jesus possesses (*Mark*, 90–91).

42. Johansson, "Kyrios in the Gospel of Mark," 112. For a similar conclusion, see France, *Mark*, 147, and Boring, *Mark*, 206.

of Jesus's words is straightforward: the Son of Man is the immanent and knowable YHWH who instituted the Sabbath and for whom the Sabbath is celebrated. Thus, the point of Jesus's teaching would be obvious for such readers. Jesus is not limited by the regulations of the Sabbath because he is the very YHWH who created the Sabbath and hallowed it.

Jesus Walking on the Water (Mark 6:45–52)

In Mark 6:45–52 Jesus allows his disciples to go ahead of him while he dismisses the crowds and then goes up on a mountain to pray. During the evening he can see that his disciples are facing a strong wind and struggling to row the boat. Jesus comes out on the sea and walks on the water. His disciples are terrified and think he is a ghost. Jesus identifies himself and tries to calm their fears. He gets into the boat and the winds cease, with the result being astonishment and lack of understanding by his disciples.

Many interpreters understand this story to be yet another example of God's appointed Messiah exercising extreme power over nature (cf. Mark 4:35–41). But there are a number of details in this story that could lead the reader to a strikingly different conclusion. The first detail is that of Jesus walking on the water. Walking on water (not through water) is a function attributed to YHWH alone in the Jewish Scriptures. In describing the YHWH of Israel, Job 9:8 (LXX) says, "[God] alone has stretched out the heaven and walks on the sea as firm ground." Here it is claimed that God alone walks on the seas. It is noteworthy that Mark 6:48 uses virtually the same words to describe Jesus walking on the sea (περιπατῶν ἐπὶ τῆς θαλάσσης) that are used in Job 9:8 LXX (περιπατῶν ὡς ἐπ᾽ ἐδάφους ἐπὶ θαλάσσης) to describe YHWH walking on the seas, with the only difference being the Septuagint's inclusion of the phrase "as on firm ground" and the omission of the article before "sea." An intentional allusion to Job 9:8 seems highly plausible here. Similar traditions about YHWH walking on the sea can be found in Job 38:16 and Sirach 24:4–5. Thus, with this detail, Mark depicts Jesus doing something that Jewish Scripture claims only YHWH can do.[43]

The second significant detail is the rather obscure Markan comment

43. For a similar conclusion, see Boring, *Mark*, 189; Geddert, "YHWH Christology," 332–34.

that Jesus "intended to pass them [his disciples] by" (ἤθελεν παρελθεῖν αὐτούς; 6:48).[44] At first glance, such a detail seems to suggest that Jesus never intended to help his struggling disciples and only does so when they see him and are terrified.[45] It is noteworthy that in both Matthew and John, this detail of Jesus intending to pass by is omitted, and the intended purpose of Jesus walking on the water is to come to his disciples' aid (see Matt 14:22–33; John 6:16–21). But this obscure detail takes on significance when considering the motif of "passing by" in the Old Testament.

In two of the most significant theophanies of the Old Testament, the language of "passing by" is present. In the description of Moses's encounter with God in Exodus 33, YHWH allows Moses to see his glory, but only through a glimpse of God's back. To protect Moses, YHWH places Moses in a crack within the mountain and places his hand over Moses as he passes by him. In three verses describing this event, God "passing by" Moses is referenced four times (33:19, 22 [2x]; 34:6). Similarly, when God encounters Elijah on Mount Horeb, Elijah is told to go stand before YHWH on the mountain, and YHWH will "pass by" him (1 Kgs 19:11). These texts create a significant theophanic tradition that involves the God of Israel "passing by" his appointed messengers.[46] In each of the passages noted above, the Septuagint uses the same verb (παρέρχομαι), which is the same verb used in Mark 6:48 to describe Jesus's intent to pass by his disciples. In light of this information, what appears at first glance to be a rather obscure and perhaps irrelevant detail in Mark's story takes on great significance. Language prominent in Septuagint theophanies is being borrowed by Mark and applied to Jesus. Like the YHWH of Israel, the Markan Jesus intends to reveal himself to his appointed messengers by "passing them by."

The third and final detail to consider is Jesus's manner of self-identification to his disciples. To calm their fears, Jesus says, "Take courage," but immediately following these words he identifies himself by using the

44. See Yarbro Collins, who notes that many commentators find this detail to be odd (*Mark*, 334); e.g., see Marcus (*Mark*, 426), who identifies this detail as "strange," and Boring (*Mark*, 190), who calls it a "difficult expression."

45. Note France (*Mark*, 272), who argues that even though the verb "pass by" does convey intention, this clause does not convey Jesus's intent but rather the disciples' *perception* of his intent. Such a reading seems unnatural, forced, and is not widely accepted. Regardless, it is perhaps evidence of the difficulty this detail in the text presents to Markan interpreters.

46. Such intertextual connections have been noted by many commentators; e.g., Yarbro Collins, *Mark*, 334; Boring, *Mark*, 190; Marcus, *Mark*, 426, etc.

phrase ἐγώ εἰμι (Mark 6:50). This can and does regularly function as a simple form of self-identification in Greek, and thus it is often translated, "It is I." However, this phrase has tremendous theological significance for anyone familiar with the Septuagint, as ἐγώ εἰμι is part of the response that YHWH gives to Moses when Moses asks God whom he should tell Israel is sending him (Exod 3:14). Thus, while one might read this text and simply conclude that Jesus is saying, "It is I," those readers well-versed in the Septuagint would no doubt see a striking parallel in Jesus's reply to that of YHWH's self-identification at the burning bush.

When taken all together, these details make a compelling case that Mark is intentionally communicating to the observant reader something significant about Jesus's identity. First, the Gospel presents Jesus walking on water, using the language from Old Testament passages that declare YHWH alone can walk on the sea. Then, using language that directly parallels that of two significant Old Testament theophanies, the Gospel declares that Jesus intended to "pass by" his disciples. Again, Mark depicts Jesus doing something that YHWH does, revealing himself to his messengers through "passing by." This series of events in which Jesus does what only YHWH does in the Old Testament culminates in Jesus's identifying himself as ἐγώ εἰμι, a partial citation of the way in which YHWH identifies himself to Moses at the burning bush. These last two details find additional significance when they are read in light of Exodus 33:19, where YHWH tells Moses that he will pass him by, and that as he does so he will call himself by his own name. The Markan Jesus parallels this passage in a striking way, as he intends to pass by and then identifies himself as ἐγώ εἰμι as he does so. Note that Jesus says ἐγώ εἰμι before he enters the boat; he is in the process of passing his disciples by when he speaks the divine name. Thus it appears that Mark has presented Jesus as doing the very action that YHWH performs in Exodus 33:19. Proponents of a high Christology in Mark argue that these striking parallels between Jesus and YHWH would not be missed by the observant reader, particularly a Hellenistic Jew familiar with the Septuagint.[47] So the most natural conclusion for such a reader to draw from these parallels is that Mark is indeed identifying Jesus as YHWH of Israel.

Many interpreters who have recognized these details refuse to conclude

---

47. See, e.g., Geddert, "YHWH Christology," 332–34.

that Mark is presenting Jesus as the YHWH of Israel and instead conclude that Mark is presenting Jesus, God's appointed agent, as one acting like YHWH.[48] While such an explanation could make sense of the detail of Jesus walking on the water, it does not make sense of Jesus "intending to pass by" or his speaking the divine name as he does so. The language of "passing by" is theophanic language and thus is used in the context of YHWH's self-revelation. How then can the language of "passing by" be used to present Jesus as merely acting as YHWH, when the very action he is engaged in is action directly connected to the self-revelation of YHWH? The same logic applies to the use of the divine name for self-identification. One cannot use such a name to act like YHWH but can only use it to *identify* oneself as YHWH.

Mark's presentation of Jesus as the YHWH of Israel in this pericope is completely consistent with my proposed readings for Mark 2:1–2 and 2:23–28, passages in which Jesus uses the title Son of Man to identify himself as the immanent and knowable YHWH. Interestingly, if Jesus is understood in this way by the Markan reader, the theological significance of this pericope's theophanic language increases. For a Jew committed to two divine powers in heaven, it would be the immanent and knowable YHWH that partook in Old Testament theophanies. For Mark, therefore, the language of such theophanies is quite appropriately attributed to Jesus, as he is the knowable YHWH who revealed himself to Moses, Elijah, and the people of Israel.

There Is No One Good but God Alone (Mark 10:17–31)

In Mark 10:17–31, Jesus is approached by a rich man who asks Jesus, "Good teacher, what must I do to inherit eternal life?" (v. 17). Jesus's response, "Why do you call me good? No one is good but God alone" (v. 18), is odd in a number of respects.[49] Jesus's answer raises implications about his own identity, an issue that is seemingly unrelated to the question that is posed to him and fails

48. Yarbro Collins's treatment of this passage is exemplary of just such a position (*Mark*, 333–38).

49. See France, who notes the oddities of this response from Jesus (*Mark*, 401); see also Boring on the lack of clarity regarding the significance of Jesus's initial response (*Mark*, 294). Van Iersel considers the surprise that Jesus's answer creates for the reader (*Mark*, 323).

to become explicitly relevant throughout the pericope.[50] Furthermore, Jesus's statement about only God being good seems, on the surface, to be a pedantic critique of what, for all intents and purposes, is a simple attempt by the rich man to honor Jesus.[51] These oddities suggest that Mark has constructed this response of Jesus for a reason, one likely related to Jesus's identity.[52]

Many have argued that in this text, the Markan Jesus distances himself from the one God of Israel and thus rejects any notion that he himself is divine or to be identified as that God.[53] In this reading, the man's affirmation of Jesus as "good teacher" is a misguided one. But as Timothy Geddert has pointed out, such a reading pushes against the logic of the narrative, a narrative in which Jesus is clearly presented as good![54] Thus, in light of the narrative's presentation of Jesus being good, a point that is hardly debatable, the Markan Jesus creates a logic that the reader is unable to escape: Jesus *is* good, and thus by Jesus's own declaration one must conclude that Jesus is God. While such a conclusion chafes against readings of Mark that understand Jesus as solely God's agent and not God himself, it is completely consistent with the three Markan pericopes we have already considered. Thus, Jesus can rightly be called good because he is indeed the immanent and knowable YHWH of Israel.

The Markan Jesus as the Immanent YHWH: Bringing Clarity to Additional Markan Texts

With our analysis of these four pericopes, we have argued that Mark presents Jesus as the immanent and knowable YHWH of Israel, and that such an

50. Moloney argues that in some way God's goodness is a basis for the answer that Jesus will give to the man's question; that is, God's goodness is the basis for following the commandments prescribed in the Torah (*Mark*, 198–99). Such a connection is certainly not made clear in the text itself, and this explanation seems to be an attempt to makes sense of a Markan detail that evades easy explanation.

51. Some commentators have argued that Jesus's response is intended to address insincere flattery (see A. Plummer, *The Gospel according to St. Mark* [Cambridge: Cambridge University Press, 1914], 238; A. E. Rawlinson, *The Gospel according to St. Mark*, 7th ed. [London: Methuen, 1949], 139), but such a conclusion does not seem supported by the text (see France, *Mark*, 401–2; Boring, *Mark*, 294; Craig A. Evans, *Mark 8:27–16:20*, WBC 34B [Nashville: Thomas Nelson, 2001], 95).

52. See van Iersel, *Mark*, 323–24.

53. See Vincent Taylor, *The Gospel according to St. Mark*, 2nd ed. (London: Macmillan, 1966), 427; Yarbro Collins, *Mark*, 477; Hooker, *Mark*, 241; Malbon, *Mark's Jesus: Characterization as Narrative Christology* (Waco, TX: Baylor University Press, 2009), 134. Such a reading seems implied by Evans, *Mark* 8:27–16:20, 95.

54. For this argument, see Geddert, "YHWH Christology," 328–29.

identification is not merely implicit, as others have argued, but explicit. In addition to the texts addressed above, a number of other Markan texts have been used to argue for a high Christology in the Gospel. Here we bring the concept of a "two-powers" theology and "YHWH Christology" to bear on these Markan texts and demonstrate how such a theological commitment brings both greater clarity to these texts and also at times resolves long-standing tensions related to them.[55]

Prepare the Way of the Lord (Mark 1:3)

The Markan incipit (1:1) is immediately followed by a composite citation of at least two Old Testament texts: "See, I am sending my messenger ahead of you, who will prepare your way; the voice of one crying out in the wilderness: 'Prepare the way of the Lord, make his paths straight'" (1:2–3). Verse two is a citation of Malachi 3:1 (and Exod 23:20), and verse three is a citation of Isaiah 40:3. In their Old Testament contexts, both of these texts (Mal 3:1 and Isa 40:3) refer to a messenger who prepares the people for the coming of YHWH. But here Mark appears to be using these YHWH texts to describe John the Baptist preparing the way for Jesus. Clearly John the Baptist is rightly identified with the Isaianic voice in the wilderness that is preparing the way of the Lord, and within the Markan narrative, John is preparing the way for Jesus. As such, it seems that Mark understands the "Lord" (κύριος) of Isaiah 40:3 (LXX), which is clearly a reference to YHWH, to be appropriately applied to Jesus. But such a conclusion is complicated by Mark's use of Malachi 3:1. This text is a quotation in which God states that he will send a messenger ahead of *himself* to prepare *his* way. Yet in the Markan citation of the passage, the pronouns have been changed from first person to second person ("me" to "you" and "my" to "your").[56] With this

55. Here I am not attempting to be exhaustive but am trying to focus on the evidence in Mark that I believe to be most significant for my position. My omission of certain texts should not be taken as a rejection of their value. Numerous examples can be given, and for the interested reader I direct you to the sources that discuss these examples. We do not discuss the parable of the bridegroom (2:18–20), in which Michael Tait perceives an implied high Christology (*Jesus, the Divine Bridegroom, in Mark 2:18–22: Mark's Christology Upgraded*, AnBib 185 [Rome: Gregorian University Press, 2010). We also do not discuss Jesus's curing of fever (1:30–31) or leprosy (vv. 40–45), both healings that David Garland argues support a high Christology (David E. Garland, *A Theology of Mark's Gospel: Good News about Jesus the Messiah, the Son of God*, Biblical Theology of the New Testament [Grand Rapids: Zondervan, 2015] 108–9). We also do not discuss a number of the texts put forward by Geddert ("YHWH Christology").

56. The change in pronouns is possibly related to a blending of Mal 3:1 with Exod 23:20, in which messenger is sent in front of Israel, and the second-person pronoun is used.

editorial revision, it seems the Markan evangelist has intentionally created a distinction between God and the one for whom the messenger will prepare the way.[57] Thus, while the Isaianic citation seems to equate Jesus with YHWH, the Malachi citation seems to undermine such a conclusion. The result is ambiguity regarding the way in which Jesus should be identified with the YHWH of Israel.

Johansson has argued that such ambiguity is intentional, and that Mark purposefully created it in order to affirm both the God who sends Jesus and Jesus himself as the YHWH of Israel.[58] Johansson's proposal gains greater support and clarity if this Markan citation is read with the commitment that Jesus is the Son of Man who was understood to be one of two divine powers in heaven, namely, the immanent and knowable YHWH. Mark's choice to change Malachi's first-person reference, a reference to YHWH, to a second-person reference, a references to Jesus, makes strong exegetical sense if the evangelist understands both God and Jesus to be rightly identified as the YHWH of Israel—one being the transcendent YHWH and the other the immanent. Additionally, as the immanent and knowable YHWH, Jesus can also quite naturally be the Lord/κύριος of Isaiah 40:3. There is no need to argue that Mark has inserted God's Messiah into texts where he did not originally belong, a move many interpreters have made.[59] Instead, Mark has applied a "two powers in heaven" hermeneutic to these Old Testament texts, one that allows the evangelist to naturally make the changes evident in his citation. Recognizing such a hermeneutic in Mark alleviates a tension in the Markan text that interpreters have long sought to resolve.

Who Is the Lord? (Mark 5:19–20; 7:28)

Much attention has been given to Mark's use of the title Lord (κύριος) and whether he applies the title to Jesus.[60] It is often claimed that the only explicit place where the title is used of Jesus comes in the pericope of the

57. Daniel Kirk relies heavily on this statement in his case that Jesus is not understood as the YHWH of Israel in this Markan citation (*Attested by God*, 182–83).

58. See Johansson, "Kyrios in the Gospel of Mark,"103–4.

59. E.g., see France, *Mark*, 63–64; Joel Marcus, *The Way of the Lord: Christological Exegesis of the Old Testament in the Gospel of Mark* (Edinburgh: T&T Clark, 1993), 37–41; John R. Donahue and Daniel J. Harrington, *The Gospel of Mark*, SP 2 (Collegeville, MN: Liturgical Press, 2005), 60–61; Boring, *Mark*, 36–37.

60. For a thorough treatment of this title in Mark's Gospel, see Johansson, "Kyrios in the Gospel of Mark," 101–24.

Syrophoenician woman, where a woman addresses Jesus with the title Lord (7:28; here in the vocative, κύριε). Most interpreters conclude that this use of Lord is best understood as a respectful form of address, much like the use of "sir" in English, though some interpreters have seen the combination of the title Lord and the woman's act of obeisance as a signal that the title evokes the Septuagintal use of κύριος for the YHWH of Israel.[61] As we have argued above, Mark uses this title to identify Jesus as the YHWH of Israel in his opening citation of Isaiah 40:3, and thus such an identification is quite possible here in Mark 7:28. Johansson offers the plausible solution that the title can be read on both a secular and religious level.[62] From the narrative perspective, the woman is best understood as simply addressing Jesus as "sir," but for the Markan reader who to this point has understood Jesus's identity as the immanent and knowable YHWH, the title κύριος conveys this same divine identity.

A well-known instance in which Jesus may be linked with Lord/κύριος as a reference to YHWH comes at the close of the episode of the Gerasene demoniac, where a man who has been freed of demon possession desires to go with Jesus and his disciples (5:18). Jesus refuses the man's request and instructs him to "go home to your friends and tell them how much the Lord [κύριος] has done for you, and what mercy he has shown you" (v. 19). Here it seems on the surface that Jesus's use of "Lord" is a reference to someone other than Jesus himself, namely, to God, and that there is thus a distinction between the Jesus and the "Lord" to which he refers. However, the following verse creates ambiguity, as it says, "And he departed and began to proclaim in the Decapolis all that Jesus had done for him; and all marveled" (v. 20). This disparity between Jesus's instructions and the man's actions has been interpreted in a variety of ways. Joel Marcus sees this as a move by the Markan evangelist to make the point that where Jesus acts, God is also acting, but Marcus is also adamant that this does not mean that Jesus is God in Mark—he remains only an agent of God.[63] Norman Petersen concludes that this verse contributes to the theme of incomprehension in Mark

---

61. Johansson, "Kyrios in the Gospel of Mark," 113; Rudolf Pesch, *Das Markusevangelium*, 2 vols., HThKNT (Freiburg: Herder, 1976), 1:389n17; Joachim Gnilka, *Das Evangelium nach Markus*, EKKNT (Zürich: Benziger, 1978), 293; Robert H. Stein, *Mark*, BECNT (Grand Rapids: Baker Academic, 2008), 353.

62. Johansson, "Kyrios in the Gospel of Mark," 113.

63. Marcus, *Mark*, 354. See similar conclusions in France, *Mark*, 233; Hooker, *Mark*, 147.

and parallels the incomprehension of Jesus's disciples.[64] Elizabeth Struthers Malbon uses this as an example of Jesus pointing to God and the narrator pointing to Jesus.[65] However, Timothy Geddert turns Malbon's logic on its head and asks if the narrator might be pointing out that Jesus is indeed God.[66] Johansson similarly argues that Mark is intentionally identifying Jesus with the title Lord, a title that Jesus shares with YHWH.[67] Both approaches to understanding this Markan use of "Lord" have merit, but the tension seems to fade quickly when one reads Mark in light of a theological commitment to "two powers" in heaven. Jesus is able to speak of what "the Lord" (κύριος) or transcendent YHWH has done in verse 19, and in verse 20 the man is able to tell people how much Jesus has done because Jesus is also rightly identified as "Lord," or the immanent YHWH.

The Deaf Hear and the Mute Speak (Mark 7:31–37)

Timothy Geddert has argued that in Mark's account of Jesus healing a deaf mute, one can find an implicit high Christology. He first demonstrates a strong intertextual relationship between Mark's account of Jesus healing a deaf mute and Isaiah 35.[68] In this text, Isaiah contains the promise of the Lord (YHWH) himself coming to save Israel (Isa 35:4), and that salvation will include the ears of the deaf being opened and the tongue of those who cannot speak singing for joy (vv. 5–6)—both occur as a result of Jesus healing in this Markan story. The fact that both this text from Isaiah and the account in Mark 7 are the only two texts in the Old and New Testament to use the word μογιλάλος ("impeded speech," Isa 35:6 and Mark 7:32), strongly supports an argument for intentional intertextuality. Given such a relationship, the natural conclusion is that Mark understands this story to be the fulfillment of Isaiah 35. The observant reader, familiar with the Septuagint, is intended to pick up on such intertextuality. But such intertextuality would

64. Norman R. Petersen, "The Composition of Mark 4:1–8:26," *HTR* 73 (1980), 213. See Boring, who links this textual detail to the Markan secrecy motif (*Mark*, 154).

65. Malbon, *Mark's Jesus*, 72n47. Here Malbon acknowledges that the narrator of Mark is likely seeking to identify Jesus as "lord," though Malbon does not equate such an identification with YHWH.

66. See Geddert, "YHWH Christology," 326.

67. Johansson, "Kyrios in the Gospel of Mark," 106.

68. Certainly other interpreters have noted connections to Isaiah 35 (see Markus, *Mark*, 472–73; Boring, *Mark*, 216; Moloney, *Mark*, 149–51), but few emphasize its significance to the degree of Geddert (Timothy J. Geddert, *Mark*, Believers Church Bible Commentary [Scottdale, PA: Herald, 2001], 192–93; idem, "YHWH Christology," 338; cf. William Lane, *The Gospel according to Mark*, NICNT [Grand Rapids: Eerdmans, 1974], 268n81).

also seem to have implications for Jesus's identity. Isaiah 35 explicitly speaks of YHWH coming to save his people and the people rejoicing at seeing the glory of YHWH, but in Mark it is Jesus who brings about these acts of salvation (i.e., healing the deaf and giving speech to the mute), acts which result in the rejoicing of the people. While many simply interpret Jesus as the messianic agent through whom God is present, a two-powers hermeneutic offers a more straightforward explanation. The evangelist understands the Lord of Isaiah 35:4 to be the immanent manifestation of YHWH, the YHWH who comes and interacts with his people, much like the YHWH of the burning bush or the pillar of fire. For Mark, Jesus is this revealed and immanent YHWH, and thus it is no surprise that Jesus performs the actions of YHWH in Isaiah 35:4. The evangelist has employed this hermeneutic not only in the opening citation of Malachi 3:1 and Isaiah 40:3, where it is the transcendent YHWH who speaks of a messenger that will prepare the way for the immanent YHWH, but at numerous points throughout the Gospel.

The Transfiguration (9:2–8)

Jesus's transfiguration in Mark 9:2–8 is surely a significant moment in Mark's presentation of Jesus's identity, a point recognized by virtually all Markan commentators. But what significance this event has for Jesus's identity is at times unclear among these commentators. In verse 2, the reader is told that Jesus himself is transformed in front of his disciples, which indicates that Jesus's human form is changed into something different.[69] As a result of this transformation, his clothes become "dazzling white," the otherworldliness of which is conveyed by claiming that such a white could not be achieved on earth (v. 3). Parallels between Mark's description of the transformed Jesus and the description of YHWH in Daniel 7:9 are often drawn. Additionally, the clear theophanic elements woven into the pericope suggest that the pericope intends to depict the revelation of the divine. These details lead virtually all recent commentators to concur that this transformation reveals Jesus to be, at the very least, a heavenly being if not a divine one.[70] Interpreters vary as to whether this transformation reveals

69. For a similar conclusion, see Boring, *Mark*, 262; Donahue and Harrington, *Mark*, 269; France, *Mark* 350–51.

70. See Boring, *Mark*, 262; France, *Mark*, 351; Yarbro Collins, *Mark*, 421. For those who claim this transformation reveals Jesus as a divine figure, see Hurtado, *Mark*, 145; Donahue and Harrington, *Mark*, 269; Garland, *Mark*, 301. It should be noted that Yarbro Collins seems rather noncommittal

Jesus's true present identity as a heavenly/divine figure currently walking the earth, or as a temporary glimpse of a future, post-Easter identity.[71] Most recent interpreters opt for the former reading, and Adela Yarbro Collins even goes so far as to claim that Mark is relying on Greco-Roman traditions in which gods take on human form.[72] But regardless of recognizing Jesus as a divine being, very few interpreters conclude that this transformation is rightly understood to equate Jesus with the YHWH of Israel.[73]A perceived obstacle to such a conclusion is the apparent distinction in the pericope between the God of Israel and Jesus, as it is the voice of God that declares Jesus to be his beloved Son (Mark 9:7).

At this point, there is a potential problem. If Mark is revealing Jesus to be a divine being, how is such a being to be understood within the boundaries of Jewish monotheism? Within which category does he rightly fit? Such a tension lies unresolved in most treatments of Mark's transfiguration account. However, the tension is easily resolved when one reads Mark's Gospel from the theological commitment to the existence of two powers in heaven. The natural conclusion that Mark is presenting Jesus as a divine being and that Jesus's divine form is being revealed to his disciples makes perfect sense if Mark understands Jesus as the Son of Man who is the immanent and revealed YHWH. The theophanic elements of the story fall perfectly into place when one understands that *Jesus* is the divine being that is revealed to his disciples—Jesus is revealed to be the YHWH of Israel. The presence of Elijah and Moses also takes on greater significance, as they have both already experienced similar revelations of the immanent and revealed YHWH, Moses on Mt. Sinai and Elijah on Mt. Horeb. Both are encountering YHWH on a mountaintop again! One might even conclude that the entire event takes on even greater significance with the declaration,

---

on whether Jesus is being revealed as a divine being here. She does conclude that this is a plausible interpretive option and that those in a Greco-Roman context would no doubt read the text in such a way (*Mark*, 421, 426–27).

71. See these two interpretive options clearly outlined by Yarbro Collins (*Mark*, 421).

72. See Yarbro Collins, *Mark*, 416–19. For recent commentators that opt for the former, see Garland, *Mark*, 301; Hurtado, *Mark*, 145; Boring, *Mark*, 268; France, *Mark*, 351. For those who opt for the latter, see D. E. Nineham, *The Gospel of St. Mark*, Penguin Gospel Commentaries (Baltimore: Penguin, 1963), 234; John Paul Heil, *The Transformation of Jesus: Narrative Meaning and Function of Mark 9:2–8, Matt 17:1–8, and Luke 9:28–36*, AnBib 144 (Rome: Pontifical Biblical Institute, 2000), 260.

73. Perhaps Hurtado (*Mark*, 145) and Garland (*Mark*, 301) come the closest to making such an identification.

"This is my Son," a declaration that can come from none other than the transcendent YHWH. The pericope might not only function to reveal Jesus's divine identity as the immanent YHWH but also offer the reader a glimpse of how Jesus provides experiential access to the otherwise inaccessible God of Israel.

The Son of Man Coming in the Clouds of Heaven and the Charge of Blasphemy (Mark 14:61–62)

When Jesus stands before the high priest Caiaphas, he is asked, "Are you the Messiah the Son of the Blessed One?" (14:61). To this question Jesus answers, "I am, and you will see the Son of Man seated at the right hand of power and coming in the clouds of heaven" (v. 62). To most Markan interpreters, this appears to be a direct response from Jesus to the high priest's question, with Jesus essentially saying, "Yes, I am the Messiah, the Son of the Blessed One." Jesus's statement regarding the Son of Man adds another dimension to this positive affirmation, as interpreters conclude that it looks forward to Jesus's future vindication as well as the universal judgment that he, as God's messianic agent, will exercise at the parousia.[74] But such an understanding of Jesus's words is complicated by the charge of blasphemy brought by the high priest. If Jesus is merely claiming to be God's Messiah, this sort of claim does not fit traditional understandings of blasphemy, which, according to rabbinic tradition, required one to speak the divine name.[75] To solve this problem, interpreters have argued that not all Jews agreed on the definition of blasphemy, and that some Jews of the Second Temple period held to a broader understanding of blasphemy than those of the rabbinic period. It is then proposed that such broader notions of blasphemy might include Jesus's claim to be the Messiah.[76] But while one must grant that there is evidence to support a broader understanding of blasphemy among Second Temple Jews, there is no evidence that a messianic claim alone fell under that broader understanding. Thus, the high priest's

74. For such a conclusion, see Boring, *Mark*, 414; Yarbro Collins, *Mark*, 705; Evans, *Mark 8:27–16:20*, 450–51.

75. For discussion, see Adela Yarbro Collins, "Charge of Blasphemy in Mark 14:64," *JSNT* 26.4 (2004): 379–401; also Yarbro Collins, *Mark*, 705–7.

76. Again, see Yarbro Collins, "Charge of Blasphemy"; Boring, *Mark*, 414–15; Evans, *Mark 8:27–16:20*, 453–55.

accusation of blasphemy against Jesus leaves the interpreter with a problem that has yet to be adequately resolved.

Yet this interpretive problem is instantly resolved when one applies to the text a "two powers in heaven" paradigm, one in which Jesus is the immanent and knowable YHWH. If Jesus is claiming to be the second power in heaven, the one who sits at God's right hand and comes in the clouds to judge the world, then the charge of blasphemy makes perfect sense. And there is reason to conclude that Jesus's response to the high priest communicates this very identity. First, there is Jesus's use of ἐγώ εἰμι (v. 62), a phrase that is a partial citation of YHWH's self-identification given to Moses at the burning bush at Exodus 3:14 (LXX). As noted above, Jesus used this very phrase to identify himself to his disciples as he walked on the water, a scene in which Mark seems to be depicting Jesus as YHWH. Second, Jesus identifies himself with the Son of Man, and for the third time in Mark he explicitly links this identity with the figure of Daniel 7:13. But Jesus's description of the Son of Man also bears a striking resemblance to the Enochic Son of Man, a figure that we have argued is best understood as a second divine power or the immanent YHWH. That Mark has already connected the Son of Man to such a divine identity twice, both in attributing to the Son of Man the divine prerogative to forgive sins and the identity as Lord of the Sabbath, makes it all the more likely that the Gospel does so again at this point. Thus, we contend that the most natural way to read Jesus's response to the high priest is as a claim to be the second power in heaven, the immanent and knowable YHWH. Such a reading fits the narrative context perfectly, as the high priest clearly recognizes what Jesus is claiming for himself and levies the charge of blasphemy against him (Mark 14:63–64). This solution make sense of all the pieces of Jesus's verbal exchange with the Jewish high priest, and it is consistent with our analysis of Mark's presentation of Jesus throughout the Gospel.

Considering Objections

The present argument that Mark's Gospel explicitly presents Jesus as the immanent and knowable YHWH of Israel will no doubt raise numerous objections. Though I cannot anticipate all such objections, I seek to address two anticipated objections here.

If Mark Presents Jesus as God's Messiah, How Can He Also Be the God of Israel?

From the outset of Mark's Gospel, Jesus is clearly presented as God's Messiah. Given the virtual consensus that Jews understood God's Messiah to be an agent of God and not God himself, a natural question arises. How can Mark present Jesus as both God's Messiah and God? This objection is certainly a problem for those who argue for a simple high Christology in Mark, in which Jesus is in some way being mapped on to a divine identity, but it is not a problem when Mark is read in light of a "two-powers" theology and a YHWH Christology. When Mark is read in light of such a context, a clear answer to this objection emerges. While some expressions of messianism during the Second Temple period certainly understand God's messiah in terms of a human agent of God, I have argued that others understood God's messiah in terms of a "two powers in heaven" schema, in which God's messiah was directly identified with a second power in heaven, or the immanent and knowable YHWH of Israel. The best example of such messianism is found in the Parables of Enoch, where the Son of Man is clearly identified as a divine figure in heaven but is also identified as God's messiah. If Mark is influenced by the Parables as I and others have argued, then Mark has no trouble conceiving of God's Messiah as a second divine power that comes from heaven. And as we read Mark's Gospel, such an understanding of Jesus both as God's Messiah and as the immanent and knowable YHWH, the second power of heaven, emerges.

How Can Jesus Be God and Pray to and/or Be Distinct from God?

On the surface, it might appear that Jesus's praying to God or Jesus talking about God as a distinct being are problematic for concluding that the Markan Jesus is rightly identified with the YHWH of Israel.[77] Again, this objection could truly be a problem for anyone offering a simple high Christology. However, if one understands the Markan Jesus in terms of a "two-powers" theology, the answer to this objection is no different than the answer to the previous objection. If the God of Israel is understood in terms of two powers, and Jews could conceive of YHWH in terms of both

77. Such a question seems implicit in Kirk, *Attested by God*, 501.

a transcendent power in heaven and an immanent one, then it should not be difficult to conceive of these two powers interacting and communicating with each other. For example, in the Parables of Enoch, the Lord of Spirits names, chooses, and hides the Son of Man. Similarly in Philo the Logos (or Word), whom Philo can identify as the "second God" and as the divine power that Moses encountered on Sinai, is presented as a mediator between creation and the transcendent YHWH (*Conf.* 95–97; *QG* 2.62). As noted above, the Logos is even called the firstborn son of YHWH (*Agr.* 51). Such a theological framework would make it quite easy for the Gospel of Mark to present Jesus, the knowable YHWH, as God's Son who communicates and lives in relationship with his Father, the unknowable YHWH. It is only through adherence to the singularity of the one God of Israel that Jesus's distinction from and interaction with God is problematic for understanding Jesus as divine. If the one God of Israel is understood in terms of plurality—in terms of two powers in heaven, the problems of Jesus praying to and interacting with the God of Israel quickly disappear.

Huebenthal Response to Winn

SANDRA HUEBENTHAL

Adam Winn is known for his work at the intersection of the New Testament and the Greco-Roman world with an emphasis on imperial Rome. He has contributed several works in this area, including *Reading Mark's Christology under Caesar and the Purpose of Mark's Gospel* (2018); *Mark and the Elijah-Elisha Narrative: Considering the Practice of Greco-Roman Imitation in the Search for Markan Source Material* (2016); and *The Purpose of Mark's Gospel: An Early Christian Response to Roman Imperial Propaganda* (2008). He has also edited the volume *An Introduction to Empire in the New Testament* (2016). With this background, my expectation was that his essay in this volume would go into the same direction. I was wrong.

According to Adam Winn's perception, Mark had no intention to make a statement about Jesus's nature—or in his own words, "I do not think that the Markan evangelist was, at least not primarily, seeking to answer this question for readers. But I do believe the author of Mark's Gospel had convictions regarding the identity of Jesus as it relates to this question and that such convictions do manifest themselves within the Gospel of Mark" (p. 211).

The essay aims to provide a reading of Mark based on these convictions and to demonstrate how Mark has to be understood when these convictions are rightly understood. We are dealing with a staged set of criteria: *If (a), what must be the solution to (b)?* In this case, (a) encompasses the convictions, and (b) is the proper understanding of Mark. The convictions, our (a), can be narrowed down to the claim that in Mark's Gospel, Jesus is presented as the YHWH of Israel, what Winn calls a "YHWH Christology." Thus the question is how Mark must be read and understood if one accepts this assumption.

The starting point of Winn's reading is thus neither the Markan text itself (as in Daniel Kirk's and my approach) nor the historical setting of its composition (as in Larry Hurtado's approach), but "one's position of the range of possibilities that existed in the first century CE for understanding the one God of Israel and his messiah" (p. 212). In other words, we are dealing with a theological reading, or a reading through the lens of a theological assumption.

This prerequisite is crucial for following and evaluating the argument of the essay; consequently, Winn opens his essay with this question and provides three different possible answers that necessarily lead to different readings of Mark's Gospel and its christological claim. The first possible understanding of the one God of Israel and his messiah is that "first-century Jews understood the one God of Israel in terms of strict singularity, or something quite close to it" (p. 212). The second understanding is that "Jews, though diverse in messianic thought, understood any sort of messiah figure to be an agent of their God and not a divine being, that is, not the God of Israel" (p. 212). The third understanding is that "many Jews of the Second Temple period were perfectly comfortable understanding the one God of Israel in terms of a duality of powers, one which was utterly transcendent and others that were particularly immanent" (p. 214).

The second and the third possibility sound very similar. Winn's point is that the third possibility allows for the claim of Jesus being YHWH already in the first century, while the second possibility assumes the understanding of Jesus as divine to be the result of a historical development, perhaps even associated with external influences, such as Hellenism. The crucial issue is at which point Jesus's divine identity was recognized and communicated in texts. Did this occur already in the first generation of Jesus-followers, or did it occur later, perhaps even as a result of the mission to the gentiles?

Winn opts for the third possibility. Jesus's divine identity was recognized already in the first generation, and Winn claims that the belief in "two powers in heaven" was an "acceptable and common way for Jews to conceive of the one God of Israel" in the Second Temple period and "only later deemed a heresy by the rabbis in the second century as a response to both Christianity and Gnosticism" (pp. 213–14). To make his case for the presentation of Jesus as YHWH of Israel, Winn uses the Parables of Enoch (1 En. 37–71), a part of a book of intertestamental literature that is much discussed among Second Temple and New Testament scholars, especially as it relates to our understanding of Jesus and the Gospels. In the Parables of Enoch, a figure called the "Son of Man" features, and according to Winn, "a strong case can be made that the Enochic Son of Man is best identified as an apocalyptic embodiment of God's word and wisdom, entities that in other Jewish literature are understood as means by which YHWH is immanent" (p. 216). He concludes: "If one reads the Parables of Enoch from the perspective of a 'two powers in heaven' paradigm, then the 'Son of Man' figure is rightly identified as the YHWH of Israel. But perhaps even more importantly, the Parables offer an example in which this 'two-powers' theology extends into the realm of Jewish messianism. Not only is the 'Son of Man' rightly understood as YHWH, but he is also rightly understood as Israel's Messiah" (p. 216).

The Parables of Enoch, read this way, provide the bridge to read the use of "Son of Man" in Mark's Gospel in the same way, that is, to understand him both as YHWH and as Israel's Messiah. Winn's reading of Jesus as the YHWH of Israel in Mark is thus entirely possible. This does not imply, however, that it is necessary or that it is likely that this is what Mark's Gospel aimed to achieve. The theological reading Winn presents is intriguing; nevertheless, as a possible way to read and understand the text, it is a reception scenario, not a production scenario. In other words, just because the text can be read within a particular theological framework does not mean that it was produced in this very framework.

The connection with Enoch is somewhat vague. There is no proof that the author of Mark's Gospel thought in these categories or held these convictions, just as there is no proof that the faithful behind this Gospel knew the Book of Enoch at all. It remains, in fact, unclear in Winn's essay how he imagines the audience (as a historical approach would ask) or the implied reader/model reader (as a narrative approach would ask) of Mark. The claim that the "two powers in heaven" was predominant in Second Temple Judaism, as plausible as it may sound, is nothing more than a hypothesis. It still bears the burden of proof that this was indeed so, *before* one can speculate whether it is likely that the author and the audience of

Mark—whoever they were—were indeed part of that movement. I have my reservations about turning this kind of hypothesis into the hermeneutical key to understanding the christological claim of Mark's Gospel.

Before Winn turns to the execution of his hermeneutical approach, that is, a reading Mark's Gospel as a case for Jesus as the YHWH of Israel, he leaves the level of argument and sneaks in a comment on the meta-level. He assumes that "my fellow contributors bring to the text of Mark something akin to the presupposition that Jews of the Second Temple period understood the YHWH of Israel in terms of singularity, while I bring to the text of Mark a presupposition that many Jews of that same period understood the YHWH of Israel in terms of complex duality—or, more precisely, in terms of two powers in heaven, both of which are rightly identified as YHWH" (p. 217).

Such a comment on the meta-level is surprising. It might be understood to serve the purpose of preparing the stage to evaluate the other contributions through the lens of this hermeneutical approach; in other words, whether the other contributors subscribe to Winn's favored (re)construction of Second Temple Judaism or not? One could read this meta-comment as the attempt to turn this four-views project into a question of faith, which would be surprising and very unusual for a scholarly argument. In a less-charged reading, one could say that the comment discloses Winn's *Vorverständnis* ("preconception") and aims to drive home the point that the stance one takes on (re)constructing both Jewish monotheism and messianism in the Second Temple period is crucial for understanding Mark's Gospel and its presentation of Jesus. No matter how you turn it, Winn's starting point is an additional assumption that is brought to Mark's Gospel externally and introduced as the key criteria for an adequate interpretation—before one has read a single word of the text.

As pointed out, this additional assumption is based on a constructed historical scenario, or a hypothesis. This also means that if this construction proves to be unreliable or weak, the whole argument might collapse. This is not the place to engage in an argument about the underlying assumption itself. It might be sufficient to ask a question historical-Jesus scholarship regularly finds itself confronted with, namely, *How much do we really know?* In her first challenge of the criteria approach, as early as 1970 Morna D. Hooker made a statement that is still valid fifty years later and should be a solemn warning to cases using hypothetical historical scenarios:

> As far as Judaism is concerned, the discovery of the Qumran material should be sufficient warning against over-confidence in supposing that we know the whole truth about first-century Judaism. Any comparison between the beliefs of Judaism and the teaching of Jesus, which claims to find ideas in the latter unparalleled in the former is inevitably an argument from silence, and should be treated as such. If our knowledge of Judaism is only partial, so, too, is our knowledge of early Christian belief, and here, too, we must tread with caution. The traditio-historian is the first to recognize that the material as we have it today in the New Testament represents only part of the picture; there may have been other beliefs about Jesus and Christological statements which are not now represented in our canonical material.[1]

After the section, "The Importance of Starting Points," Winn's essay engages in an analysis of Mark's Gospel with the introduced hermeneutical lens, building on previous work on high and low Christology. Four passages are analyzed thoroughly (2:1–12; 2:23–28; 6:45–52; 10:17–31), and five additional texts are engaged with in an abbreviated way (1:3; 5:19–20 + 7:28; 7:31–37; 9:2–8; 14:61–62). These analyses are synchronic theological readings, that is, there is no engagement with text production, and the aim is to show how the Parables of Enoch can shed additional light on the understanding of these passages. The sample readings are carried out with great care to detail, and the interpretations are convincing, as long as one accepts the underlying hermeneutical assumption.

The conclusion of the essay deals with possible objections and names two: (1) If Mark presents Jesus as God's Messiah, how can he also be the God of Israel?; and (2) how can Jesus be God and pray to and/or be distinct from God? Both possible objections are objections within the hermeneutical framework that Winn has established.

As a critical reader trained in theology, hermeneutics, and narratology, my questions come from a different angle. I am interested in Winn's image of the addressees or intended audiences of Mark's Gospel. Do we have to picture a predominantly Jewish, a predominantly gentile, or a mixed-body audience? At one point, Winn mentions "the observant reader, familiar with

1. Morna D. Hooker, "Christology and Methodology," *NTS* 17 (1970): 482.

the Septuagint" (p. 234), which would rather point to Jesus-followers with a Jewish background.

For the evaluation of the argument, the question of model reader or target audience is of no minor importance, as Jesus-followers coming from a gentile background might have issues getting some of the points. When it comes to Jesus's divine identity, gentile audiences would not have had any problems understanding the title "Lord" in either a secular or a religious way. The ambiguity of the text, on the contrary, offers them something like a barrier-free access to the Jesus-movement and its Jewish Messiah and Son of God.

This brings me to the question as to whether the first-century audiences and readers of Mark's Gospel would have had any of the questions that we bring to the text today. As this is a question that can never be answered in a satisfying way or with any certainty, New Testament scholarship has done well in changing perspectives. Many of today's readings cease to ask about production scenarios—when and where did Mark write his Gospel for what target audience and what message did he try to get across—and instead engage in reception scenarios, like how might the Gospel have been received in a particular historical situation and context. As Mark is usually the test case for this type of reading, there are many different approaches in this area, and they are very often quite intriguing as they reveal deeper insights into the potential of the text.

Reading Mark through the "Jesus as YHWH of Israel" lens is one of these readings. It demonstrates the potential of reading Mark's Gospel in this perspective. This perspective works very well for twenty-first century New Testament scholars, and it is altogether plausible for first-century Jesus-followers with a Jewish background, but it comes with difficulties for first-century Jesus-followers from a gentile background. The last group will have no issues making sense of Mark's text but surely miss the point about the divine identity of Jesus based on the "two powers in heaven" paradigm, as it is not part of their cultural heritage, while sons of gods are part of their daily experience.

Jesus-followers from a gentile background, especially those who lived in Rome in the late first century, might have had different associations when they heard *anointed one*, *son of god*, or *gospel* (*euangelion*). What they might or might not have heard and understood has been thoroughly explored in empire studies. As initially mentioned, Adam Winn has himself contributed studies in this area, and in his book *The Purpose of Mark's Gospel: An Early Christian Response to Roman Imperial Propaganda*, he claims that the primary purpose of Mark's Gospel was to respond to Flavian imperial propaganda that caused christological problems in the Roman church. Without going into details here, it seems that this is the opposite of what is argued in this essay. If the burning issue for the Roman groups of Jesus-followers is how to deal with Flavian imperial propaganda, can we really assume that the stance one takes on (re)constructing both Jewish monotheism and messianism in the Second Temple period is the hermeneutical key for understanding Mark's Gospel and its presentation of Jesus?

The best way to defuse this problem is to change perspective and take these readings for what they are: reception-oriented approaches that investigate how readers might have read and understood Mark's Gospel in particular locations and particular points in time. As I have argued elsewhere, while a particular reading may make sense in a particular context, that is an inadequate basis to argue for a particular construction of the text's origins. There is a difference between claiming that "we will never be able to understand Mark if we do not enter imaginatively into its first-century world" and insisting that the text can only be adequately understood as a counter-gospel to Vespasian.[2] The former indicates that a certain encyclopedia is necessary to do the text justice, while the latter provides a hypothetical production scenario and authorial-intention conditions for proper interpretation.[3]

As I read it, the "Jesus as the YHWH of Israel" hypothesis is very much the same thing: a reception scenario, which is turned into a production scenario. Its purpose seems to be a theological: The recognition of Jesus's divine identity as early as Mark. Read this way, it is not a historical and theological development, but already tangible in the earliest narrative layers of the New Testament. To me, the most intriguing question is: why would this be desirable or necessary?

---

2. Joel Marcus, *Mark 1–8: A New Translation with Introduction and Commentary*, AB 27 (New York: Doubleday, 2000), 37.

3. Huebenthal, "Anti-Gospel Revisited," 157.

Hurtado Response to Winn

LARRY W. HURTADO

It would be difficult to imagine a stronger contrast between the views of Daniel Kirk and Adam Winn on how the Gospel of Mark (GMark) presents Jesus in relation to God. In my response to Kirk's essay, I have indicated where I find it unpersuasive. But I also find Winn's essay seriously problematic. In my view, if it is inadequate to portray GMark as presenting Jesus as simply an "idealized human" figure, it is also dubious to characterize the Markan Jesus as "the God of Israel" in the way that Winn does. So I shall lay out my reasons here for the latter judgment. Because Winn's case rests heavily on his claims about Second Temple Jewish tradition and the relevance of the messianic figure of the Parables of 1 Enoch, I shall address these matters first, before turning to GMark.

"Two Powers"

Winn builds his case by relying in part on the claims by Boyarin in particular that Second Temple Jewish tradition widely held the view that there were two expressions of God, one transcendent and one immanent, and that these were thought of as two distinguishable divine beings. Winn accepts Boyarin's further claim that this was actually an accepted view that only later came to be condemned by rabbinic authorities as the "two powers in heaven" heresy. In what is still the best treatment of the matter, however, Alan Segal showed that, in Second Temple Jewish evidence, we do not really see two distinguishable deities.[1] Philo's hundreds of references to the Logos, for example, show a complexity of expression. But careful analysis of his references to the Logos as a "second god" (e.g., *QG* 2.62) shows that this is a figurative expression, the Logos serving to designate God conceptually as revealed to the finite world of creation. This allowed Philo to affirm the biblical narratives where God acts in the world and reveals himself to humans, and at the same time to address Philo's philosophical concern to maintain that the biblical deity transcends all human thought and was greater than the created order.

As for other Second Temple Jewish evidence, I contend likewise that there is no indication that Jews thought of and reverenced two gods or modes of God as separate beings.[2] In my own analysis of the evidence several decades ago, I showed instead that there was what I termed a "chief agent" conception, in which this or that figure is portrayed as God's principal servant, like the vizier of oriental potentates.[3] This figure is sometimes a principal angel (perhaps the originating chief-agent figure), sometimes an ancestral human such as Moses or Enoch, and sometimes a personified attribute of God is described in this role. Whatever the identity, the figure is typically described in remarkably exalted terms, sometimes, for example, even bearing the divine name (e.g., Yahoel in Apocalypse of Abraham), or chief among the heavenly beings and even called "Elohim" (e.g., Melchizedek in the Qumran text *11QMelchizedek*). This figure can be portrayed as presiding in the eschatological judgment and redemption (e.g., the Elect One of the Parables of Enoch), or as God's preexistent companion in creation (as, e.g., Lady Wisdom in Proverbs 8:22–31).

Yet despite the exalted descriptions of these figures, in none of these or other instances is the chief-agent figure accorded a place in the worship

---

1. Alan F. Segal, *Two Powers in Heaven: Early Rabbinic Reports about Christianity and Gnosticism*, SJLA 25 (Leiden: Brill, 1977; repr., Waco, TX: Baylor University Press, 2012), esp. 159–219.

2. Contra J. E. Fossum, *The Name of God and the Angel of the Lord* (Tübingen: Mohr Siebeck, 1985); and C. C. Rowland, "The Vision of the Risen Christ in Rev. 1.13ff.: The Debt of an Early Christology to an Aspect of Jewish Angelology," *JTS* 31 (1980): 1–11. I have given my reason for rejecting these claims in Hurtado, *One God, One Lord*, 37–39, 85–90.

3. Hurtado, *One God, One Lord*. More recently, see my discussion of the matter, with a focus on Qumran evidence, in Larry W. Hurtado, "Monotheism, Principal Angels, and the Background of Christology," in *The Oxford Handbook of the Dead Sea Scrolls*, ed. Timothy H. Lim and John J. Collins (Oxford: Oxford University Press, 2010), 546–64.

of Israel.[4] In the Jerusalem temple, there was no altar or sacrifice to Logos or Wisdom or Melchizedek or Yahoel or the others. There are no rites of devotion to these figures in the evidence of the practices of any known circles of Second Temple Jews. Moreover, the evidence of Second Temple Jewish prayer shows that it was directed to God, not to any of these chief-agent figures, even (particularly) in those texts that reflect an interest in them.[5] So, however one chooses to view the vivid language of Second Temple Jewish texts in the descriptions of the various chief-agent figures, the evidence of the religious practice of Jews of the time shows that these figures were not regarded as God, part of God, or a being equal to God.[6]

As for the deployment of the Memra in Targumic texts (and the similar term, Shekinah in rabbinic texts), these too are rightly taken as reverential terms that designate the activities of God in the world of creation.[7] And, contrary to Boyarin (on whom Winn relies), early rabbinic Judaism seems to have been quite comfortable with these terms and the conceptions that they represent. Actually, the personification of divine activities and attributes in biblical and later Jewish tradition also includes God's glory (*kābôd*), name, voice, word, arm, face, power/powers, justice, truth, righteousness, mercy, and law (*tôrāh*).[8] But none of these terms designated an alternate or second deity that had to be suppressed. Instead, as H.-F. Weiss wrote, for Philo and for rabbinic Judaism, "Wisdom, Torah and Logos are only the sides of God turned toward the world."[9]

Actually, Segal proposed that the most likely candidates for the first-

4. I reserve discussion of Winn's claim that the messianic figure of the Parables received worship for a subsequent section of this essay.

5. E.g., Norman B. Johnson, *Prayer in the Apocrypha and Pseudepigrapha: A Study of the Jewish Concept of God*, SBLMS 2 (Philadelphia: SBL, 1948); Agneta Enermalm-Ogawa, *Un langage de prière juif en grec: Le témoignage des deux premiers livres des Maccabées*, ConBNT 17 (Uppsala: Almqvist & Wiksell, 1987); Daniel K. Falk, *Daily, Sabbath, and Festival Prayers in the Dead Sea Scrolls*, STDJ (Leiden: Brill, 1998); Tessel M. Jonquiere, *Prayer in Josephus*, AJEC 70 (Leiden: Brill, 2007).

6. Again, I refer readers to my discussion of these matters in *One God, One Lord*, esp. chs. 1–4.

7. E.g., Martin McNamara, "The *Logos* of the Fourth Gospel and the *Memra* of the Palestinian Targum (Ex 12.42)," *ExpTim* 79.4 (1968): 115–17; Robert Hayward, *Divine Name and Presence: The Memra* (Totowa: Allanheld, Osmun & Co., 1981); Andrew Chester, *Divine Revelation and Divine Titles in the Pentateuchal Targumim* (Tübingen: Mohr Siebeck, 1986); A. M. Goldberg, *Untersuchungen über die Vorstellung von der Schekhinah in der frühen rabbinischen Literatur*, Studia Judaica 5 (Berlin: de Gruyter, 1969); E. E. Urbach, "The Shekina—The Presence of God in the World," in *The Sages: Their Concepts and Beliefs* (Cambridge: Harvard University Press, 1987), 37–56.

8. For discussion, see G. Pfeifer, *Ursprung und Wesen der Hypostasenvorstellungen im Judentum* (Stuttgart: Calwer, 1967).

9. Hans-Friedrich Weiss, *Untersuchungen zur Kosmologie des hellenistischen und palästinischen Judentums*, TU 97 (Berlin: Akademie, 1966), 330 (my translation).

century "heretics" who said "there are two powers in heaven" are the early Jewish believers in Jesus, who went beyond merely exalted descriptions of their chief-agent figure and incorporated him programmatically into their distinctive devotional practices, treating him as a distinguishable recipient of their devotion alongside God.[10] It is in the early Jesus-movement that we have a distinctive "mutation" in Jewish thought and devotional practice, in which Jesus is accorded the full range of roles in creation and redemption that derive from various Jewish chief-agent speculation. More significantly still, he is accorded a programmatic place in the devotional life of believers that has no precedent.[11]

So the "lens" (to use Winn's own term) through which Winn proposes that we read texts such as the Parables of 1 Enoch and GMark seems to me (and to most others who have considered the evidence) to be a misunderstanding of matters. It is, in short, a dubious distortion and not a clarifying conception. Second-century Jewish tradition was not rife with genuinely di-theistic notions, and it is a mistake in method to read the Parables of 1 Enoch or GMark controlled through such a notion.

The Elect One

This leads me to offer a brief critique of Winn's handling of the Elect One, the messianic figure in the Parables of 1 Enoch. Winn claims that this figure functions as "the God of Israel," which I find to have no support from the text. Winn makes his case for his reading of this figure by invoking his prior view that ancient Jewish tradition was quite familiar with a bifurcation of God. But I have indicated why I find this view to be dubious. So I proceed now to examine some matters specific to the Parables and the remarkable messianic figure.[12]

Before doing so, however, anyone dealing with the Parables should exercise some caution in using 1 Enoch as evidence of Second Temple Judaism, especially those parts for which we have no Aramaic or Greek portions extant.

10. Segal, *Two Powers*, 205–19.

11. I first referred to a distinctive "mutation" in the early Jesus-movement in *One God, One Lord*, 93–124.

12. See esp. Darrell D. Hannah, "The Elect Son of Man of the *Parables of Enoch*," in *"Who Is This Son of Man?" The Latest Scholarship on a Puzzling Expression of the Historical Jesus*, ed. Larry W. Hurtado and Paul L. Owen (London: T&T Clark, 2011), 130–58.

It is well to remember that what we have is an Ethiopic translation (fourth to seventh century CE) of a Greek translation of an Aramaic (and/or Hebrew) original (the various portions dated third to late first century BCE?). Moreover, the extant Ethiopic copies of 1 Enoch date variously from the fourteenth to the twentieth century CE. As Loren Stuckenbruck noted recently, reporting on his intensive effort to locate and analyze manuscripts of 1 Enoch, "there is no question that the evidence witnesses to the vicissitudes of transmission during a period of a thousand or more years," and he cautioned that

> the complicated Enochic journey from Aramaic to Greek to Ethiopic, with so many unknown variables, challenges the use of the last as a repository of material that can be straightforwardly analyzed as though it existed in essentially the same form around the turn of the Common Era.[13]

This is a particularly important cautionary note in using the Parables. For, among the remnants of Aramaic and Greek manuscripts of portions of 1 Enoch, there is nothing of the Parables, and we have only the Ethiopic with which to work, copies from a thousand years later than the originating Ethiopic translation (which was a translation from a Greek translation), and centuries further still chronologically from the originating composition.[14] Anyone familiar with the vagaries of the translation and textual transmission of ancient writings will accordingly take heed.

But let us turn to the remarkable figure that features in Winn's essay, and in a good deal of other New Testament scholarship on the Gospels. In crucial defense of his claim that this figure is to be understood as God manifest on the earth, Winn (with some others) posits that the Elect One/Messiah is pictured as receiving worship, citing several texts in the Parables. But a careful inspection of each text gives one pause to accepting Winn's claim. For in none of these passages, and nowhere else in the Parables, is the

---

13. I cite from Stuckenbruck's paper given at the meeting of the International Organization for the Study of the Old Testament, August 5, 2019, Aberdeen, Scotland. I thank him for kindly sharing his paper with me. It will be published in the proceedings of that meeting. (Editor's update: the paper is being revised, coauthored with Ted Erho, titled "The Significance of Ethiopic Witnesses for the Text Tradition of 1 Enoch: Problems and Prospects," and published in the Vetus Testamentum Supplement Series [Leiden: Brill].) The editions of 1 Enoch on which our translations depend rest on a small handful of manuscripts. Stuckenbruck's views rest on analysis of over a hundred manuscripts.

14. Hannah also drew attention to the gaps in the textual history of the Parables ("Elect Son of Man," esp. 131–33).

Elect One actually given cultic worship by the human righteous ones whom he is sent to rescue and lead. In 46.5 and 62.6, 9, those who bow to the Elect One and beseech and bless him are the "kings and mighty ones" who ruled the earth and whom he puts down, ending their oppression of the righteous. These are simply futuristic scenes of the submission of the conquered to their eschatological conqueror. In 48.5, "all who dwell upon the earth" will prostrate themselves before the Elect One, but their hymns and praise are directed not to him but to "the Lord of the Spirits" (a frequent epithet for God in the Parables). The messianic figure in this text is the occasion for their worship, but not so clearly its object. In 61.7–8 the heavenly host are apparently commanded to bless the Elect One, recognizing his supremacy over them, and this figure, notably seated with God on the heavenly throne, participates with God in judging "all the works of the holy ones in the heights of heaven." This is impressive and will remind readers of the reference in Hebrews 1:6 where God commands the angelic host to reverence Jesus, "the firstborn."[15] Both texts affirm the supremacy of the respective figure over all other heavenly beings. But what we lack is any reference to the worship of the Elect One by circles of the righteous, on the earth.

I fear that in the understandable effort to find precedents and parallels for the rich devotional phenomena reflected in the New Testament, Winn (granted, with some others) has ascribed to the texts that he cites in the Parables more than is there.[16] In any case, it bears remembering also that the Parables give visions of future scenes of eschatological triumph and judgment and do not reflect the actual worship practices of Jewish circles of the time of the composition of the text. This contrasts sharply with the New Testament writings, which directly arise from and reflect the beliefs and real devotional practices of actual circles of the Jesus-movement.

To turn to a related matter, one of the attractions of the Parables for New Testament scholars is that it features a messianic figure that is regularly referred to in English translations as the "Son of Man." But we should note that this capitalizing and fixity of translation in English translation give a

15. On the image of sharing a divine throne in antiquity, see Christoph Markschies, "'Sessio ad Dexteram': Bemerkungen zu einem altchristlichen Bekenntnismotiv in der christologischen Diskussion der altchristlichen Theologen," in *Le Trône de Dieu*, ed. Marc Philonenko, WUNT 69 (Tübingen: Mohr Siebeck, 1993), 252–317.

16. Perhaps each generation of scholars needs to note Samuel Sandmel's classic essay, "Parallelomania," *JBL* 81 (1962): 1–13.

somewhat misleading impression. As Darrell Hannah noted, the expression "'son of man' is not used as a title comparable to 'Messiah' or even the 'Elect One.'"[17] This should be evident from the different Ethiopic phrases that lie behind the English translation of "son of man." In contrast to the other epithets applied to this figure ("Messiah," "Righteous One," "Elect One"), each of which is consistently rendered by one Ethiopic expression, there are three Ethiopic phrases used to refer to the figure as a human(like) being.[18] Also, in contrast, note that the Ethiopic Bible consistently renders "the Son of Man" phrase in the Gospels with the one expression, *walda 'egʷāla 'emma-heyāw*. Clearly, the translators saw the fixity of the Greek phrase in the Gospels, "the son of man" (ὁ υἱὸς τοῦ ἀνθρώπου) as requiring an equivalent fixity in translation. But, whatever the underlying phrasing(s) of the Greek in the various passages of the Parables, the use of various Ethiopic expressions likely means that the translators did not see it as indicating a title. It would be misleading, therefore, to take the Parables as a precedent or source for the fixity of "the son of man" expression in the Gospels.[19] Instead, the most that can be claimed is that both the Parables and the Gospels show (probably independent) appropriations of Daniel 7:13–14, with its depiction of "one like a son of man" who receives rule over the whole earth.[20]

In sum at this point, the messianic figure of the Parables of 1 Enoch is not the earthly form of the God of Israel and so does not provide us with a "lens" through which to view Jesus in GMark.

Mark's Jesus

Because Winn's exegesis of passages in GMark is so heavily dependent on his dubious claims about a widespread bifurcation of God in Second Temple Jewish tradition and about the divinity of the messianic figure in the Parables of 1 Enoch, this renders his exegesis of the Markan texts in turn problematic too.

17. Hannah, "Elect Son of Man," 143.

18. The three Ethiopic expressions are *walda sab'* (46.2, 3, 4; 48.2), *walda be 'si* (62.5; 69.29); and *walda 'egʷāla 'emma-heyāw* (62.6, 9, 14; 63.11; 69.27). I omit references to chs. 70–71, which are disputed among scholars as an original part of the text of the Parables. See the discussion of these terms in Hannah, "Elect Son of Man," 137–41.

19. I have elaborated further on the expression "the son of man" as used in the Gospels in Larry W. Hurtado, "Summing Up and Concluding Observations," in Hurtado and Owen, *"Who Is This Son of Man?"*, 159–77.

20. Cf., e.g., 1 En. 46.1–6; Mark 14:62.

But perhaps the first thing I should note, to speak for myself as someone associated with what is now often referred to as the "early high Christology" emphasis, I think it exceeds the warrants of the Markan text (and the other NT writings too!) to claim that it identifies Jesus flatly as "the God of Israel." This can suggest an ontological claim that seems to me excessive, at least as worded that way. To be sure, well before GMark, Jesus-believers were confessing Jesus as the God-vindicated Messiah whose death was the decisive redemptive event, the preexistent agent of creation, the unique Son who is the image of the one God, who reflects God's glory and shares God's throne, and (crucially) the God-appointed *Kyrios* to whom the cultic reverence of believers is due, and to whom all creation is to give obeisance. As I have contended in my own essay in this volume, GMark emerged several decades into the Jesus-movement and should be read as contributing to that movement, the author presuming those widely shared beliefs and devotional practices and seeking to make his own emphasis in his pioneering account of Jesus of Nazareth.[21]

With other first-century texts of the Jesus-movement, GMark in my judgment reflects a view of Jesus as having a unique relationship with God that exceeds any other category in Jewish tradition of the time. Jesus's actions indicate this, especially the sort of actions described in the Markan passages discussed in Winn's essay. For example, unlike Moses or Elijah, Jesus does not pray for God to act in healings or settling the sea or forgiving sins, but acts himself in divine power and authority. Certainly, the opening lines of GMark make Jesus's appearance the coming of the Lord prophesied in Isaiah 40:3. This is, unarguably, a remarkable claim. But in light of the way that Second Temple Jewish texts can describe some of those I have referred to as chief-agent figures, the Markan text is not so readily to be taken as a flat identification of Jesus *as* "the God of Israel."[22] I think it would be more accurate to say that the text (with others, such as those cited by Winn) links or identifies Jesus uniquely *with* the God of Israel, as the ultimate agent of redemption, the unique/beloved "Son" and heir of all things who is sent

---

21. For a recent contribution to the "early high Christology" discussion, see David B. Capes, *The Divine Christ: Paul, the Lord Jesus, and the Scriptures of Israel* (Grand Rapids: Baker Academic, 2018), who focuses on texts that show Jesus sharing the divine name.

22. E.g., the Melchizedek figure in Qumran texts is identified as the "Elohim" of Ps 82:1 and as the one who fulfills prophecy of YHWH's eschatological vindication of the righteous. See, e.g., Hurtado, "Monotheism, Principal Angels, and the Background of Christology."

to accomplish God's purposes. In GMark, in sum, one could say that the human Jesus embodies in his person and activities the purposes and powers of YHWH, holds a unique relationship with YHWH, and has a transcendent significance and status. The "tension" that Winn seeks to resolve in GMark is a deliberate one, reflecting the dual emphasis characteristic of a number of first-century writings of the Jesus-movement on Jesus as genuinely human and also uniquely linked with God. In these texts, Jesus's full significance and identity can be described only with reference to God, and God can be described adequately only with reference to Jesus.[23]

23. For fuller discussion, see Larry W. Hurtado, *God in New Testament Theology* (Nashville: Abingdo, 2010).

Kirk Response to Winn

J. R. DANIEL KIRK

Adam Winn has offered a brave and far-reaching thesis regarding theological beliefs about Israel's God in the first century and how these beliefs might impact our understanding of the Gospel of Mark. Parting ways with other scholars who have argued for the robust singularity of God, he offers a paradigm that is less open to falsification than "divine identity Christology" (and its various permutations), which depends on isolating certain characteristics for YHWH alone, claiming that these are uniquely applied to Jesus in the New Testament, then concluding that Jesus is, in some way, identified with or as the God of Israel.

If someone adopts Winn's perspective, they are afforded a reading of the Gospel that coheres with Winn's interpretation of the "two powers in heaven" theology of Second Temple Judaism. In fact, it provides a Jewish basis for interpreting Mark's Gospel in ways that have been commonplace throughout the Christian era. In such readings, buried nuggets and hints about Jesus's identity came to be read as referring to a divine messiah whose origins are, literally and ontologically, in heaven.

Perhaps the most important contribution Winn makes to the ongoing conversation about Mark's Christology is his thoroughgoing insistence that the singularity of Israel's God has been theologized in ways that are not conducive to making sense of Israel's diverse sacred texts. This is undoubtedly true. However, where his paradigm falls short is in its failure to recognize that the most persistent being to share in the divine identity in both biblical (Old Testament) and postbiblical Judaism is not a second "hypostasis" of God but representative, idealized human figures such as Adam, Moses, David, and, supremely, the Son of Man.

Son of Man

Winn looks to the "two powers in heaven" theology as an interpretive lens for understanding 1 Enoch and the latter, in turn, as a Jewish precedent for a YHWH-as-Son-of-Man Christology in Mark. This approach leads the reader astray for four interrelated reasons. First, Mark allusively informs his readers that the background from which his Son of Man Christology derives is Daniel 7, not 1 Enoch. Second, the deployment of Mark's Son of Man Christology follows the development of Jesus's career on earth in such a way as to make clear that Jesus's heavenly presence comes only after his resurrection, while his earthly authority is part of the renewal of humanity that Jesus both embodies and imparts to his community. Third, the phrase "son of man" means "human being," a fact we must account for in both Mark and its precedents. Fourth, in light of this third point, we can revisit 1 Enoch to see that the two-manifestations-of-YHWH interpretation is not the *prima facie* interpretation but is, instead, a misreading based on a theology that 1 Enoch does not appear to share. In light of these concerns, which I will now elaborate, it is unlikely that a "Jesus is YHWH" Christology is narrated through the Gospel of Mark's "Son of Man" texts.

First, Mark's Gospel invites the reader to consider the Son of Man texts in concert with the sole biblical appearance of this figure: Daniel 7. This happens most clearly in Mark 13:26 and 14:62. The former reads, "Then they will see the son of the human coming with the clouds," which echoes Daniel 7:14: "And behold! With the clouds of heaven, one like a son of a human was coming." Moreover, as Jane Schaberg observes, when Jesus predicts the death of the Son of Man, he repeats verbiage found in Daniel 7, including the phrase "*after* three days," which is a peculiar way for Mark to describe a resurrection that takes place two days (or on the third day) after death.[1]

If we look to Daniel, rather than 1 Enoch, as our primary conversation partner for Mark's authority-wielding Son of Man, what do we learn? Daniel 7, like 1 Enoch, is an apocalyptic vision: symbolic, cosmic creatures represent earthly realities. The reign of three horrific beasts finds its end when God takes the throne and renders judgment, removing their dominion (Dan 7:2–12). It is then that one like a human being ("like 'a son of man'") enters

1. Jane Schaberg, "Daniel 7, 12 and the New Testament Passion-Resurrection Predictions," *NTS* 31 (1985): 208–22.

on clouds and is given dominion over all the people of the earth (vv. 13–14). This symbolic story is an anti-creation, re-creation narrative. In Genesis 1, humans are created to rule the beasts of the earth, but here the beasts rule. When things are put to rights, a human-like figure rules the world with the beasts displaced. This is the meaning at the level of symbol, but what does it actually refer to? In Daniel 7 the seer asks this question and is given an answer.

The beasts are four foreign kings (Dan 7:17). But then, "the holy ones of the Most High will receive the kingdom" (v. 18): the "one like a human being," the "son of man," is a symbol standing for the people of God, that is, for Israel. We further learn that the fourth beast was a persecutor of the people of God, who prevails over them until God rescues them (vv. 19–26). Subsequently, the "people of the holy ones of the Most High" receive all the kingdoms under heaven and an everlasting dominion that will not be taken away (v. 27).

In Daniel 7, then, there is a power alongside God, a power that rules the world on God's behalf, a power that is identified with God in the everlasting, righteous rule over the world. That power is God's human representative on earth: Israel. This itself is an elaboration on the theme of Genesis 1:26–27, that humanity, being identified with God (through bearing the divine image), should rule on God's behalf in the sphere where God is not tangibly present.

Daniel Boyarin, whose work on two powers has influenced Winn's work, confirms this interpretation of Daniel 7. He first argues that Daniel 7 preserves ancient Near Eastern narratives about an elder god, El, investing a younger god, Baal, with power. However, he then goes on to argue that Daniel has been rewritten, such that Israel becomes the inheritor of divine rule.[2] Daniel in its current form is about God sharing God's power of rule, not with another heavenly figure or second person in the godhead but with a representative *human* collective. Given Mark's allusions to Daniel 7, the most likely conclusion is that Mark's Jesus is assuming the surprisingly exalted role of the representative, ruling people of God, the humans whom God empowers to enact God's reign on God's behalf.

Second, when we trace the use of the "Son of Man" title in Mark,

2. Daniel Boyarin, "Daniel 7, Intertextuality, and the History of Israel's Cult," *HTR* 105 (2012): 139–62.

we discover that it follows Mark's unfolding story. Indeed, it is a story that at points follows the story of Israel in Daniel 7. In Daniel, the "one like a human being" symbolizes a people who suffer, who are even martyred, and who then are exalted to rule the nations. These elements are critical components of Mark's Son of Man story as well.

Mark divides roughly in half, with the confession of Peter ("You are the Messiah!" Mark 8:29) marking the turning point. Prior to this, Jesus's ministry was marked by preaching and innumerable miracles, and the disciples themselves were empowered to embody both the teaching and the miracles (including exorcisms and healing). It is here that we find the two "Son of Man" expressions that claim authority for Jesus: healing and forgiving of the paralytic and the "Lord of the Sabbath" claim—both of which Winn discusses. Based on Daniel 7, we would expect that these claims represent the authority that God has given to a human representative to act on God's behalf.

We find confirmation of this claim along several lines. First, Jesus's claim that as Son of Man he has authority "on the earth" to forgive is likely an allusion to the sphere over which the first humans were given authority in Genesis 1.[3] Second, Jesus links his power to forgive with his power to heal, the latter of which is embodied by other humans in the story—Jesus's followers.[4] Third, in the "Lord of the Sabbath" story, Jesus compares his authority to do what is otherwise unlawful with the unlawful activity of King David (Mark 2:25–26). Moreover, in that same story, his basis for claiming that as "the son of the human" he has authority over the Sabbath is that "the Sabbath was made for humans" (vv. 27–28). In other words, it is precisely his identification with, and embodiment of, humanity, *not* a distinction from humans through some claim to divinity, that provides Jesus the authority to do what is unlawful.

If the first half of Mark's Gospel is about Jesus as present, authoritative power, the second half is about Jesus's road to the cross. It begins with Peter's confession, after which Jesus says something shocking about the Son of Man: "He began to teach them that the Son of Man must suffer many

---

3. Morna Hooker, *The Son of Man in Mark: A Study of the Background of the Term "Son of Man" and Its Use in St. Mark's Gospel* (Montreal: McGill University Press, 1967), 91.

4. For further elaboration, see J. R. Daniel Kirk, *A Man Attested by God: The Human Jesus of the Synoptic Gospels* (Grand Rapids: Eerdmans, 2016), 278–79.

things and be rejected . . . and killed and after three days rise" (8:31). As mentioned above, this prediction contains some precise verbiage from Daniel 7, underscoring that Jesus as one who suffers is replaying the martyrdom of Israel's holy ones from an earlier era and that Jesus will be raised even as Daniel's martyrs were expected to be (see Dan 12:2–3).

Recognizing that Jesus as "the Son of Man" is, in fact, the ideal human who represents God and God's rule to the world is critical for making sense of Mark's Gospel. It is why Jesus can bestow authority on other humans to do precisely the same things that he does, including forgiving sins (Mark 11:24–25; see also John the Baptist, 1:4–5). In the first half of the Gospel, where authority is paramount, Jesus bestows such authority on his followers. In the second half of the Gospel, where the suffering Son of Man is paramount, Jesus calls his followers to follow him on the way of humble service to the point of death after every prediction of the Son of Man's suffering (8:34–38; 9:30–35; 10:32–45). Mark's Son of Man Christology is not a way to distinguish Jesus from his followers as a different sort of being; it is instead a way to depict the new humanity into which Jesus's followers are being ushered, and in which they participate as they embody his ministry.

For the purposes of understanding Mark's Christology, it is critical to note that it is only after Jesus predicts the Son of Man's resurrection that we encounter any idea of Jesus having a glorious, heavenly existence. Mark's Son of Man is a human figure who, because of his faithfulness, is raised to heavenly glory and given reign over the kingdom of God that he proclaims.

Third, any Christology built on Jesus as Son of Man has to deal with the fact that what these words literally mean is, "the son of the human being." In other words, the phrase speaks and lends particular significance to the fact that Jesus is human. This can be seen clearly in the book of Ezekiel, in which the divine voice regularly addresses the prophet as "son of man" (or, perhaps, "son of Adam," e.g., Ezek 2:1, 3, 6, 8; 3:1, 3, 4). "Son of man" is a phrase used to distinguish a human being from God, and in Daniel it is a phrase used to distinguish the one who resembles humanity (Israel) from the world-destroying beasts (the pagan nations).

The fact that "son of man" means "human being" is particularly important when we come to 1 Enoch. The English translations of this text are made from its earliest extant version, Ethiopic. The English translations employ the same phrase, "son of man," to render several different underlying phrases.

In addition to a phrase that literally means "this Son of Man," there is a more common phrase, "son of the offspring of the mother of the living." In this description, the human character of the being is underscored by saying that his descent is from other humans who descended from the first human woman. There are also one or two instances in which he is called, "son of woman."[5] What we learn from this is the following: (1) "son of man" was not a fixed title; (2) the various names rendered "son of man" in 1 Enoch underscore this exalted figure's human origin; so that (3) no early Jewish reader would have any reason to overinterpret this figure as divine in any sense other than Israel's God claiming a human being to stand in for God before humanity. For contemporary human readers, the best translation of the Gospels' "Son of Man" phrase is probably "the Human One." It is a title that captures both the humanity of Jesus and the special narrative he is claiming for himself as God's authoritative agent who must suffer and rise in order to take his heavenly throne.

Fourth, the discussion has brought us to probing 1 Enoch a bit further. As indicated immediately above, there are serious interpretive weaknesses in reading 1 Enoch's "son of human beings" as a second hypostasis of Israel's one God, beginning with the fact that the title clearly distinguishes the figure from God as a human being descended from humanity's primal parents.

A second significant problem is that 1 Enoch as we have it discloses the identity of this second, exalted, heavenly figure: it is the human seer Enoch himself (1 En. 71.14). This identification is perfectly sensible given the biblical story of Enoch. The mysterious saying of Genesis 5:24 that "Enoch walked with God and then was no more because God took him" led to considerable speculation that Enoch was taken to heaven to be with God. Given this background, Enoch as "son of humans" in 1 Enoch and Jesus as "the son of the human" in Mark's Gospel bear striking resemblance. Both live on earth, faithfully walking with God, prior to the heavenly glory and enthronement they receive.

In light of the rich history of idealized human figures enacting divine prerogatives that we see throughout the Hebrew Scriptures and Second Temple Judaism, there is little reason to think that the exalted God and

5. See Matthew Black, *The Book of Enoch, or I Enoch: A New English Edition with Commentary and Textual Notes*, SVTP 7 (Leiden: Brill, 1985), 206.

exalted messiah in 1 Enoch are, in fact, two aspects of the one God.[6] This is not the *prima facie* reading but a reading that must contend against the fact that the two figures are separate characters in the story, with the lesser being a stand-in for the former in a way that finds clear echoes in depictions of Adam, Moses, David, Solomon, and others in both biblical and postbiblical Judaism. The "son of man" is an exalted, heavenly figure. And the reason for this is God's exaltation of the human, Enoch, who faithfully walked with God.

Jesus in Mark is not so much God showing up to do strong, but ultimately meaningless tricks while in a human body on earth; instead, he is the consummate human, enacting what God intended humanity to be from the beginning and enabling his followers to participate in this same, renewed humanity, as Jesus reclaims the fullness of human potential on their behalf. This is what it means for Mark's Jesus to be the Human One.

The Arrival of the Lord

Psalm 110 is one of the most significant, and perhaps earliest, biblical texts to be employed by the early church to describe the person and work of Jesus.[7] In the Greek translation that most New Testament writers cite ("the Septuagint"), the name of Israel's God has been replaced by the word κύριος, which means "Lord." Thus Psalm 110:1 (109:1 LXX) states, "The Lord [i.e., YHWH] said to my lord [i.e., the king of Israel], 'Sit at my right hand until I make your enemies a footstool for your feet.'" Because the same word, "Lord" (κύριος), is used to refer to both Israel's God and God's human agent, this psalm simultaneously allows for the closest possible connection between the two figures and demands that we recognize them as separate entities. Thus, for Jesus to be addressed as "lord" in a formal sense means both that he speaks as the very voice of God and that he is the royal king who is not to be confused with YHWH himself. We can see this clearly in the allusion to Psalm 110:1 in 1 Corinthians 15:25–28, where Paul says that since God is subjecting everything to Jesus it is clear that God himself will *not* be subject.

---

6. For a full elaboration of idealized human figures in Second Temple Judaism, see Kirk, *Man Attested by God*, 44–176.

7. See C. H. Dodd, *The Apostolic Preaching and Its Developments* (London: Hodder & Stoughton, 1936), 14–16, 26–28.

The use of Psalm 110:1 in the early church provides a bridge for understanding how it is that YHWH texts from Israel's Scriptures can come to be applied to Jesus without there being an implicit claim that Jesus is YHWH. At the same time, however, to claim that Jesus is the Lord who comes with the dawning of the kingdom of God is to name him as the one in whom God's arrival to save God's people is made known. As "the Lord," Jesus is identified *with* God, but he is not identified *as* God.

This both/and of proximity and differentiation is consistent throughout the New Testament, and it should guide our interpretation of Mark's opening Scripture citation. There, as Winn notes, Mark consistently changes the speech of the divine voice. Whereas Malachi reads, "I will send a messenger before my face," Mark has, instead, "I will send a messenger before your face." The divine voice is both speaking of another who is not God and is bestowing on this nondivine figure the role of embodying the eschatological visitation of God promised in the prophets.

Such an interpretation coheres better with the prophecies of Isaiah and Malachi themselves than do attempts at making them speak of Jesus as an incarnation of YHWH. Throughout Israel's Scriptures, promises of divine presence and absence are realized not through incarnation but through signs on earth, often with human embodiment. Thus, the early chapters of Ezekiel tell a story of YHWH departing from Israel: he sees a vision of God riding on a chariot, departing from Jerusalem. But what everyone else in Israel saw was the armies of Babylon carrying them away. War, destruction, devastation, and exile are the tangible experience that "God has left us." Conversely, restoration to the land, abundance, healing, a rebuilt temple, the arrival of God's Spirit, and political glory were to be the signs that God had returned.

In Mark, Jesus is "the Lord" because he is God's appointed eschatological agent, the Christ ("anointed" king) whose authority is a harbinger of the arrival of God's reign. God's reign, in turn, is exercised through Jesus as the ideal human agent, fulfilling the roles anticipated by Adam and Eve in Genesis 1 or King David and his line.

This brings us to the similarities and distinctions between Jesus and YHWH at the transfiguration. Winn interprets this as a divine epiphany, given Jesus's lustrous appearance and the mountain scene. However, there are clear indicators that this is not a disclosure of Jesus's preexistent divinity but is instead a royal glory that awaits him. First, the divine voice tells the disciples, "This is my Son, listen to him" (Mark 9:7). To be "son of God" in the tradition of Israel's Scriptures and religion is not to be the eternal, second person of the Trinity; it is, more often, a way to depict humans who represent God's authority to the world. When Adam and Eve are created "in the image of God," this indicates that they are God's offspring, bearing the image of the Father, and that this is the reason they are entrusted with the role of ruling what is God's (Gen 1:26; 5:1–3). When an Israelite king is enthroned, Psalm 2 is read in which God says to the king, "You are my son, today I have begotten you" (Ps 2:7). In his baptism, Jesus receives the Spirit when God says, "You are my beloved Son" (Mark 1:11), an anointing that corresponds with David's reception of the Spirit upon his anointing (1 Sam 16:13). "Son of God" in Mark is a title for God's empowered king who must suffer and die.

Immediately prior to the transfiguration, Peter confessed that Jesus was the Messiah, Jesus predicted his death and resurrection, and Peter rejected the notion of Jesus as suffering Messiah (Mark 8:27–33). The transfiguration, then, is a divine approbation of Jesus's interpretation of his life: Jesus shines in glory, as he will after his resurrection; the divine voice confirms that Jesus is the Messiah by calling Jesus "Son," and the divine voice sides with Jesus against Peter about the nature of Jesus's messianic calling as it tells the disciples, "Listen to him." This is why, on the way down the mountain, Jesus can tell the disciples not to tell what they have seen until after he has been raised from the dead (9:9). What they have seen is an anticipation of the heavenly glory that awaits, not a disclosure of who he was before he came to earth. As "Son of God," Jesus is the suffering Messiah who will be glorified.

Ego Eimi

I wish to address the claim that saying ἐγώ εἰμι ("I am") is an allusion to the divine name in Exodus 3 because it is a common mistake that should not be perpetuated. Indeed, if one reads Winn's argument carefully, it becomes clear from his choice of words that he recognizes the weakness of the claim. Winn states that "I am" is "part of the response" or a "partial citation" of God's words to Moses when he sends him to Pharaoh at the burning bush. Emphasis should be placed on the word "partial"! In the Septuagint, after Moses asks for his name God says, "I am [ἐγώ εἰμι] the one who is; tell them 'the One Who Is' has sent you" (Exod 3:13–14). God does *not* say to Moses, "I am [ἐγώ εἰμι] has sent you." He says, "ὁ ὤν [the One who Is] has sent you." The phrase "I am" is simply the introduction to the substantive name, "The One Who Is," and bears no weight whatsoever as a stand-alone phrase. There is no reason to think that this commonplace phrase, on its own, alludes to Exodus 3.

In Mark, the phrase is used to affirm Jesus's messianic status, not his divinity. At his trial, Jesus is asked, "Are you the Christ, the Son of the Blessed?" Jesus replies, "I am [ἐγώ εἰμι], and you will see the Human One seated at the right hand of power." This is an affirmation that he is Messiah, God's appointed king, a claim he elaborates through a combined allusion to Daniel 7 and Psalm 110, both of which we have already discussed. The narrative in which the phrase is found is where we should first look for a sound interpretation of the phrase. This is a more reliable guide than allusions more likely to be heard by an English speaker than someone versed in the Greek translation of Exodus.

Making Sense of the Story

Winn has offered a powerful paradigm for reading Mark's Gospel. But it remains doubtful that a two-powers theology forms the backdrop for interpreting Jesus's identity in Mark (or other early Christian texts). Firmer, broader ground is found in the widespread Jewish tradition of identifying various human figures *with* God without thereby identifying them *as* God.

This latter alternative has the advantage of being able to navigate the Gospel of Mark as a coherent, unfolding story in a way that the two-powers Christology does not. Perhaps the greatest weakness of the arguments for a divine Jesus in Mark is that such divinity does not factor into the narrative of the Gospel. It does not coincide with what Jesus says about himself, what the narrator says about Jesus, or what the disciples say about him. It does not coincide with the consistent distinction that is always made between Jesus and God as separate characters in the story. And it does not contribute to the reader's understanding of how Jesus enacts the kingdom of God, gathers the people of God, or performs his great saving act on the cross. For all of this, Jesus as the Human One, the Son of God who is Israel's anointed king, Jesus the crucified who is now the risen and enthroned lord, makes for better interpretation.

Rejoinder

ADAM WINN

First, let me thank my fellow contributors for their engagement with my essay and their thoughtful responses. Such interaction certainly sharpens arguments, increases clarity in communication, identifies differences in presuppositions and methods, and illustrates the different ways in which one can read Mark's Gospel. Below, I respond to a variety of criticisms raised by the respondents.

"Two-Powers" Theology

It is not surprising that my presupposition regarding the prevalence of a "two-power" theology in Second Temple Judaism received criticism. As I noted at the outset of my essay, at least some of my fellow contributors would oppose this presupposition. I fully acknowledge that in my proposal of a normative "two-power" theology in Second Temple Judaism I am swimming against the stream of New Testament scholarship, and most New Testament scholars would put forward arguments much like those that Hurtado has issued in his response. Clearly this issue is a catalyst for significant debate and has tremendous implications for the guild of New Testament studies. But contrary to what Hurtado seems to communicate in his response (i.e., the *dubious* nature of such a position), a legitimate debate exists, and it is one in which the guild must engage. A full argument for this position cannot be made here, though I will respond to a couple of issues raised by Hurtado.[1]

1. For a more thorough argument, see Winn, "Identifying the Enochic Son of Man," as well as Boyarin, *Border Lines*.

Hurtado dismissed Philo's depiction of the Logos and the Targum's Memra theology as evidence for a "two-power" theology in Second Temple Judaism. For both, he follows a common line of argumentation, namely, that the Logos of Philo and the targumic Memra/Word of the Lord are simply metaphorical ways to speak of the way in which an utterly transcendent God could also be immanent.[2] However, Daniel Boyarin has rightly pressed this argument and demonstrated its weakness. Boyarin asks if Logos and Memra are merely theologically constructed metaphors that function as circumlocutions for God, created to maintain a theology of transcendence, then who actually was immanent in/with creation?[3] If the answer to this question is God and not some distinct expression of God, such as the Logos or Memra of God, then the very theology that Philo worked so hard to communicate through his complex thought and writing about the Logos is completely undone! Regarding the position espoused here by Hurtado, Boyarin claims that it "ascribes to the use of *Memra* [and I would include Logos] only the counterfeit coinage of a linguistic simulation of a theology of the transcendence of God without the theology itself."[4] In short, it seems that Hurtado and others who share his position are saying, "It walks like a duck, it talks like a duck, and its being a duck is central to the ontology of a duck, but it is not a duck!"

Interestingly, Hurtado calls on the landmark work of Alan Segal to support his position that Second Temple Judaism did not affirm two distinguishable deities. But Segal himself, in the very work Hurtado cites, claims that Philo's Logos would have been regarded as a heretical "two-power" theology by the later rabbis![5] On his assessment of Memra in the Targums, Hurtado calls on renowned targumic scholar Martin McNamara, yet in his

2. The earliest known espousal of such a position is from Rabbi Maimonides (twelfth century), but it has been adopted by many twentieth-century interpreters; see G. F. Moore, "Intermediaries in Jewish Theology: Memra, Shekinah, Metatron," *HTR* 15 (1922): 45–81. Moore is followed by many, including Hermann L. Strack and P. Billerbeck, *Das Evangelium nach Matthäus: erläutert aus Talmud und Midrasch*, Kommentar zum Neuen Testament aus Talmud und Midrasch 1 (München: Beck, 1922), 333; F. C. Burkitt, "Memra, Shekinah, Metatron," *JTS* 24 (1923): 158–59; C. K. Barrett, *The Gospel according to John: An Introduction with Commentary and Notes on the Greek Text*, 2nd ed. (Philadelphia: Westminster, 1978), 128; Craig S. Keener, *The Gospel of John: A Commentary*, 2 vols. (Peabody, MA: Hendrickson, 2003), 1:349–50; W. E. Aufrecht, *Surrogates for the Divine Name in the Palestinian Targums to Exodus* (PhD diss., University of Toronto, 1979).

3. Boyarin, *Border Lines*, 117.

4. Boyarin, *Border Lines*, 117.

5. See Segal, *Two Powers*, 173.

more recent work, McNamara notes the persuasive arguments of Boyarin and appears open to the Memra as a distinct divine entity.[6]

Perhaps Hurtado's most significant objection to the existence of a "two-powers" theology in Second Temple Judaism is the absence of any cultic worship offered to a second divine figure, such as God's Logos, Memra, or the Son of Man. Such an objection is unsurprising given the enormous weight Hurtado's body of scholarly work has placed on cultic practice for assessing divinity. I offer two responses to this objection. First, there are indeed places in Second Temple literature where such distinct divine figures receive cultic worship. In the Targums, the Memra is a recipient of such worship, as altars, burnt offerings, and prayers are offered to it (e.g., Gen 4:3–4; 8:20; 12:8; 13:4; 8; 22:8–13; Exod 33:9). And, against Hurtado, the Enochic Son of Man also receives such worship (though Hurtado contests such an assessment). Hurtado's common response to such arguments is that even if one sees such worship in Second Temple literature, one does not see it in the cultic practice of Second Temple Jews. To this claim, I offer my second objection, namely, if Memra, Logos, or Son of Man were understood in terms of immanent expressions of YHWH, that is, a true binitarianism, we should not expect to see in the cultic worship practices of Jews anything other than devotion to YHWH. In other words, the worship of YHWH would include the worship of any and all distinct expressions of YHWH, immanent or transcendent. Rather than regard the absence of cultic worship of God's Logos as evidence that it was not regarded as a distinct expression of YHWH, one could take it as the evidence that God's Logos (or Memra) was so intrinsically identified as YHWH that it would not be parsed out in cultic worship. In other words, to worship the Logos or Memra of YHWH was to worship YHWH. The Targums are telling here, as they depict Cain, Abel, Noah, and Abraham building altars and/or giving burnt offerings to the Memra. No doubt those who produced such a targumic tradition understood that when they were worshiping at the Jerusalem Temple, they were worshiping the same entity as these patriarchs, namely, the YHWH of Israel.

6. See Martin McNamara, *Targum and Testament Revisited: Aramaic Paraphrases of the Hebrew Bible: A Light on the New Testament*, 2nd ed. (Grand Rapids: Eerdmans, 2010), 161.

The Enochic Son of Man

Both Hurtado and Kirk levied criticisms of my assessment of the Son of Man figure that features prominently in the Parables of Enoch. Again, such criticisms are unsurprising, as I have engaged both Hurtado's and Kirk's treatments of the Enochic Son of Man in formal publication elsewhere. Because I can only address their criticisms here in a cursory manner, I direct the interested read to that publication.[7]

I should first address Hurtado's reference to Loren Stuckenbruck's recent work on the textual tradition of 1 Enoch. I do not have access to the yet unpublished paper that Hurtado cites, and thus my response is, unfortunately, constrained, and relies on Hurtado's summary of and citations from the paper.[8] Stuckenbruck no doubt offers a necessary and helpful word of caution to all who work on 1 Enoch and its relationship to the late Second Temple period. Stuckenbruck notes that, for the most part, we do not see major interpolations or omissions, but generally only the smaller types of textual variants typical for the transition of ancient manuscripts. Citing Stuckenbruck (via Hurtado), "The extant Ethiopic version . . . at best approximates what existed during the Second Temple Period, probably being nearly identical in some places, subtly changed in others, and wildly divergent elsewhere." Interpreters of 1 Enoch must then consider the evidence that would suggest relative stability of a text or significant instability. Evidence would no doubt include manuscripts that contain divergent readings and signs of clear and obvious interpolations or manipulation (e.g., clear Christian influence or content that betrays a post Second Temple date). What evidence exists regarding 1 Enoch's depiction of the Son of Man? With regard to manuscript evidence, without Stuckenbruck's paper there is little I can say. Yet I would contend that there is nothing in 1 Enoch's depiction of the Son of Man that suggests significant interpolation or manipulation. The Parables of Enoch and the Son of Man therein strongly resemble the Jewish apocalyptic literature of the late Second Temple period and seemingly are in continuity with the interpretive curiosity regarding Daniel 7 that existed

7. Winn, "Identifying the Enochic Son of Man."

8. Hurtado has given a more thorough summary of Stuckenbruck's paper in a blog post titled, "1 Enoch: An Update on Manuscripts and Cautionary Notes on Usage," *Larry Hurtado's Blog*, October 6, 2019, https://larryhurtado.wordpress.com/2019/10/06/1-enoch-an-update-on-manuscripts-and-cautionary-notes-on-usage.

during this time. There is also no indication of Christian influence on the Parables and their depiction of the Son of Man, a significant point given that the transmission history of 1 Enoch after the Second Temple period was largely the work of Christians. Perhaps the best evidence that the Enochic Son of Man has avoided such Christian manipulation is the identification of the Son of Man with the figure of Enoch (not Jesus!) in the extant manuscripts (whether this identification was original will be addressed below). In light of such evidence, it seems reasonable to conclude that with regard to the Son of Man figure, 1 Enoch has preserved for us a tradition that finds its origin in the Second Temple period. As such, one can, with appropriate caution, use that figure in assessing both Jewish conceptions of the one God of Israel and the Son of Man tradition in the Gospels.

I now turn to the assessment of the content of the Parables of Enoch and begin with Hurtado's claim that the Enochic Son of Man (ESM from here on) does not receive true worship in the Parables. According to Hurtado, this figure, who is God's eschatological and messianic victor, only receives honor through mere obeisance. But two significant factors work against such a conclusion. First, the ESM receives "obeisance" while sitting on the very throne of God, a detail that strongly evokes the setting of cultic worship and thus significantly undermines the conclusion that he is merely receiving the honor due a human king (1 En. 45.3; 51.3; 55.4; 61.8; 62.5–7; 69.29). Second, in addition to obeisance, the ESM is frequently described as being praised, blessed, exalted, and glorified (46.5; 62.6; and possibly 63.4). Strikingly, this same language is used in the Parables to describe the worship of the God of Israel (39.7, 12; 46.6; 61.9, 12). It would seem special pleading to conclude that such language communicates worship of the God of Israel but does not convey worship of the Son of Man. Such evidence has led many interpreters of the Parables to conclude that the ESM receives cultic worship and not mere obeisance—interestingly, Daniel Kirk is one such interpreter.[9]

While Kirk agrees that the ESM receives cultic worship, he disagrees that this figure should be identified as divine. Instead, Kirk identifies this figure as an idealized human and argues that such figures could receive

9. Kirk, *Attested by God*, 151–55; for additional examples, see J. A. Waddell, *The Messiah: A Comparative Study of the Enochic Son of Man and the Pauline Kyriọs*, JCTCRS 10 (London: Bloomsbury T&T Clark, 2011), 96–100; C. Fletcher-Louis, *Jesus Monotheism: Christological Origins: The Emerging Consensus and Beyond* (Eugene, OR: Cascade, 2015), 171–205.

cultic worship in the Second Temple period. But a human identity of the ESM is questionable. Many have argued that the ESM's identification with Enoch is a later addition to the Parables and is thus not a reliable marker of identity.[10] I have argued elsewhere that the various Ethiopic phrases for the ESM figure ("this son of man," "this son of the mother of the offspring of the living," and "son of woman") indeed convey a human appearance, but, contra Kirk, they do not necessarily convey a human identity.[11] In Jewish and Christian literature, angels often appear as human figures, as does even the God of Israel on occasion (see, e.g., Ezek 1:26–28). Finally, Kirk's claim that idealized human figures could be the recipients of cultic worship is highly questionable, and his evidence becomes extremely thin if one removes from it the ESM.[12] If Kirk is wrong, and Jews did not offer cultic worship to idealized humans, then the worship of the ESM is strong evidence for his divinity.

What of the appropriateness of bringing the ESM figure to bear on Mark's Gospel? Kirk argues that the background for Mark's Son of Man figure is Daniel 7 rather than the Parables of Enoch, and that in Daniel 7 the Son of Man is clearly a representative for the human people of Israel. I certainly agree with Kirk that Daniel 7 lies behind Mark's understanding of the Son of Man. Additionally, I have no disagreement with his interpretation of Daniel 7 in its original context. Yet, I raise two issues in response. First, I question why Kirk forces an either/or decision regarding Mark's use of Daniel 7 and the Parables of Enoch instead of allowing for mutual influence. As I argued in my essay, there is significant evidence that Mark was influenced by the Parables (or that they share a common tradition), a conclusion supported by many Markan interpreters.[13] Second, I would note that the Danielic Son of Man was clearly a source of interpretive curiosity in the Second Temple period and that it apparently went through significant

---

10. For discussion of such a position, see John J. Collins, *The Scepter and the Star: The Messiahs of the Dead Sea Scrolls and Other Ancient Literature*, ABRL (New York: Doubleday, 1995), 178–81; Michael A. Knibb, *The Ethiopic Book of Enoch: A New Edition in Light of the Aramaic Dead Sea Fragments*, 2 vols. (Oxford: Clarendon, 1978), 62–63; George W. E. Nickelsburg, "Discerning the Structure(s) of the Enochic Book of Parables," in *Enoch and the Messiah Son of Man: Revisiting the Book of Parables*, ed. Gabriel Boccaccini (Grand Rapids: Eerdmans, 2007), 42–43.

11. Winn, "Identifying the Enochic Son of Man," 299–300.

12. For a thorough critique of Kirk's claim that Jews worshiped idealized human figures, see Richard Bauckham, "Is 'High Human Christology' Sufficient? A Critical Response to J. R. Daniel Kirk's *A Man Attested by God*," *BBR* 27.4 (2017): 503–25.

13. For such interpreters see p. 222 above.

interpretive development, development for which the Parables are strong evidence. Such development is also seen in the Old Greek recension of Daniel 7:13, which reads, "I saw one like a son of man coming in the clouds of heaven *as* the Ancient of Days." Thus, instead of limiting the background to the Markan Son of Man to Daniel 7 within its original meaning and context, I contend that the Markan Son of Man was influenced both by Daniel 7 and the interpretive traditions that developed from it, such as the Parables of Enoch.

A "Reception" and Theological Reading?

The most surprising criticism of my essay came from Sandra Huebenthal, who characterized the essay as both a "reception" and a theological reading of Mark's Gospel. I believe such an assessment reflects a misunderstanding and mischaracterization of my essay and its aims. In response, I will address the charge of presenting a theological reading first. Huebenthal contends that my starting point is not the text itself, such as it is for both herself and Kirk, nor the historical setting of the composition, such as it is for Hurtado, but rather a reading grounded in theological assumptions. I strenuously object to such a characterization and contend that I am offering an alternative *historical* reconstruction of Jewish monotheism. It is one that challenges a significant consensus in the academy, to be sure, but one that is indeed *historically* rather than theologically grounded. Thus, I am doing nothing different than Hurtado himself, except that I am putting forward a competing understanding of Jewish monotheism. In fact, I would contend that both Huebenthal and Kirk are, to one degree or another, doing the same thing. All responsible readers of Mark must contend with the world in which the text was written, and that world can only be comprehended through historical reconstruction. Kirk's reading is heavily influenced by his reconstruction of the concept of the idealized human figure. Hurtado's reading is influenced by his reconstruction of cultic worship practices, both Jewish and Christian. Though less overt, Huebenthal's reading is influenced by, among other things, a reconstruction of Jewish monotheism that assumes a strict singularity of Israel's God.

The charge that I offer a "reception" reading is closely connected to this line of argument. To be clear, "reception" readings of Mark seek to reconstruct a *specific* setting of Mark's Gospel and then require reading the Gospel from the confines of that particular setting. I have indeed taken just such an approach in many of my formal publications on Mark, and in doing so I fully have recognized its limitations.[14] But such is not the approach I take in this essay. Instead, as I argued above, I offer a reconstruction of the *general historical* setting of Mark, that of Second Temple Judaism, a move made either explicitly or implicitly in virtually every scholarly reading of Mark, including those in this volume. Thus, in summation, the reading I offer in this volume is historical in nature, not theological, and it can be no more characterized as a "reception" reading than any of the other essays in this volume.

Neglecting Narrative?

To varying degrees, both Huebenthal and Kirk criticize my essay for its failure to allow the Markan narrative to shape my assessment of Mark's presentation of Jesus. In response to this critique, I first note that my essay focused on only one aspect of Mark's presentation of Jesus, namely, the question of Jesus's identity vis-à-vis the God of Israel. Additionally, from the outset of my essay, I specifically claimed that this aspect of Mark's presentation of Jesus was not a primary objective for the Markan evangelist or narrative. This claim reflects a key difference between the way Huebenthal and Kirk assess the role of narrative in interpreting a Gospel text and the way I assess such a role. Both Huebenthal and Kirk seem to give the totality of the text's meaning to its narrative aims, whereas I would contend that one can bifurcate primary narrative aims from authorial convictions that are secondary to narrative aims. As I argue in my previous responses to both Kirk and Huebenthal, within narratives, particularly ancient ones, authorial convictions that are unrelated to primary narrative aims can manifest themselves in the text. Ultimately, this criticism of Huebenthal and Kirk finds its origins in presuppositions about assessing the meaning of a Gospel text, presuppositions that I find misguided and the merit of which I question. Yet, where the criticism might have merit is if clear conflict existed between the demonstrable narrative aims of Mark and my proposed assessment of

---

14. See, e.g., Winn, *Reading Mark's Christology*, 1–28.

"nonnarratival" convictions. In other words, if it could be demonstrated that Mark's narrative clearly and without question precluded the possibility of Jesus being identified as YHWH, then my proposal would indeed be problematic. At a handful of points, Kirk has argued that just such a conflict exists. But as I have argued in my response to Kirk, the details of the Markan narrative that he sees in conflict with a divine identity of Jesus can be read in alternative ways, ways that not only allow for but also recommend a divine identity. I strongly contend that nothing in the Markan narrative demands a solely human identity for Jesus, and that some details of the Markan text work against such a conclusion.

The Question of Audience

In conclusion, I will address Huebenthal's question regarding the audience of Mark. She rightly notes that in my other publications on Mark that I argue for a gentile audience. She questions how my current reading of Mark, one that seems to require sophisticated understanding of Jewish Scripture, squares with the conclusions of my previous work. I offer a few considerations in response. First, while I do indeed believe that the audience for Mark's Gospel was gentile, I would contend that the author of Mark's Gospel was Jewish and very at home in the world of Jewish Scripture (particularly the LXX). Second, ancient authors often wrote on multiple levels, expecting the majority of their readers to perceive the most basic levels, but expecting a minority to perceive the more sophisticated levels. It is also quite probable that the more sophisticated levels of the text were explained to the audience either during a public reading or in later discussion or teaching of it. Third, it is possible that certain elements and/or pericopes of Mark's Gospel that were brought into the Gospel from oral tradition experienced little redaction from the Markan evangelist and simply reflect accepted understanding of Jesus's identity within the church, even a predominantly gentile one. In light of these considerations, I contend it is perfectly possible that the Gospel of Mark could be written for a predominantly gentile audience, but also incorporate and reflect sophisticated uses of Jewish Scripture and tradition that identify Jesus as the YHWH of Israel.

Concluding Remarks

What Is Said and Unsaid in Mark's Gospel

ANTHONY LE DONNE

This project has hinged on two questions. The primary question is seemingly simple. *Who is Jesus in Mark's Gospel?*

The answer to this first question is easy enough: Jesus is "Christ, the Son of God." This much is clearly stated in Mark's titular verse (1:1). Or, at the very least, the two titles "Christ" and "Son of God" provide the framework for an answer.[1] One of these titles is echoed by Peter's confession. The other is echoed by the centurion's admission.

> Peter: "You are the Christ." (8:29)
> Centurion: "Truly this man was God's Son." (15:29)

These short claims function almost as creedal statements. They are pithy, direct, and communicate a shared belief. In these cases, the reader shares the sentiment with the characters in the story.

The secondary question isn't so easy. *What does it mean that Jesus is Christ, the Son of God?*

While the initial question can be answered with a slogan, this question requires theological treatise. But Mark is not a treatise. It is a narrative. It is a story about Jesus, his disciples, his passion, and his vindication. In this story we learn that Jesus is *christos*, and because this title is placed at the very

1. We should keep in mind that Mark's first verse (or at least the title "Son of God") may be a later addition.

beginning and repeated at crucial moments, we might assume that a clear understanding of the story will reveal Mark's *Christology*. With this project, I've brought together a handful of scholars who specialize in Mark's story, with the hope that their conversation would illuminate Mark's Christology.

I have not been disappointed. Editing this project has been illuminating in ways that I couldn't have anticipated. But—I confess—I was hoping all along that the puzzle of Mark would remain a puzzle. I didn't want this book to provide a simple winning solution. Such an outcome would be suspicious to me because the question of *christos* in Mark is so very complex.

Looking back on this project, I have a better sense of why this is so. It is because Mark leaves so much unsaid. Take, for example, Peter's confession.

As the reader navigates through Mark 8, the story is about to plod toward the passion. This chapter features a dramatic turn in terrain from Jesus's career to Jesus's cross. If the transfiguration is the pinnacle of Jesus's revealed identity (Mark 9), and if the empty tomb is the proof (16:4–7), Peter's confession might be thought of as the preceding signpost (8:27–30).

Given the story as a whole, Peter's confession stands out as a singular moment. According to Huebenthal, it confirms Jesus as Isaiah's eschatological messenger. According to Hurtado, Peter makes a royal and messianic claim, which is later clarified in terms of divine sonship. For Kirk, the confession confirms Jesus's messianic authority but swings the story toward Jesus's suffering and death. Kirk and Winn agree that Peter lacks crucial awareness of the suffering that must follow. But Winn also suggests that Peter's confession (albeit incomplete) confirms what the narrator claims in Mark 1:1, that Jesus is "Christ, the Son of God."[2]

In sum, Peter may voice the right title, but he doesn't see the whole picture. This is made clear in Jesus's devastating rebuke (8:33). Huebenthal suggests that Peter and the narrator are voicing the same claim. She argues that—at this point in the story—Peter is confessing more than he can know. Hurtado strongly maintains that the titles "Christ and "Son of God" are distinguishable but complementary in Mark's story. As such, Peter is voicing a crucial (albeit limited) aspect of Jesus's identity. Both Kirk and Winn read Peter's confession as half correct, but woefully incomplete. Mark's

2. While Winn does not deal with Peter's confession in the present book, see his *Reading Mark's Christology under Caesar: Jesus the Messiah and Roman Imperial Ideology* (Downers Grove, IL: IVP Academic, 2018), 89–92.

story—and therefore Jesus's characterization—hasn't been revealed fully. So even if Peter has voiced the necessary creed, the full significance of that creed is not yet known. What is left unsaid in Peter's confession may well be as important as what is said.

To return to the signpost metaphor, we might think of the title *christos* like a green sign that declares: "San Francisco, ½ mile." The signage points the way and provides essential information. It might even be posted near the city. But the sign cannot tell you what the city is like. We could say the same about the title "Son of God." Just because we have the title right doesn't ensure that we understand what Mark means by it. Thus even an overt statement like that of the centurion requires some explanation. After witnessing Jesus's death, he says, "Truly this man was God's Son" (Mark 15:39 NRSV).[3] Does this man, like Peter, confess more than he knows? If so, Mark simply nods the reader in the right direction.

This is part of what makes the Gospel of Mark wonderful. Indeed, we might say that the entire Gospel is something of a signpost. The story repeatedly points beyond itself, remaining understated, while keying the reader's imagination. I've already mentioned Peter's confession, but consider two other crucial elements of this narrative.

First, consider what is (perhaps) Jesus's most direct claim to transcendence in Mark. The high priest asks Jesus, "Are you the Messiah [*christos*], the Son of the Blessed?" In reply to the high priest, Jesus says, "I am. And you will see the Son of Man seated at the right hand of the power, and coming with the clouds of heaven" (14:61–62). Let's assume for a moment that Jesus is referring to himself and that he is claiming divine authority to judge the nations (cf. Dan 7). Furthermore, let's set aside questions of whether this figure represents Israel, God's agent, or something more. Whatever this statement means, it's altogether grandiose! This statement stirs the imagination of the reader. We are pointed to an apocalyptic vision wherein Jesus wields divine power! *Yet it is a vision that we never see realized in Mark's story.* The high priest never gets to witness Jesus seated at the right hand of power or coming with the clouds of heaven. Within the confines of Mark, these words

3. We could translate this as "God's son," "a son of God," "a son of a god," or "the Son of God." Greek grammar does not solve the problem of when to supply the word "the." Moreover, Greek does not have any indefinite equivalents to the English articles "a" or "an." Predicate nominatives do not require the article.

only lead to disappointment. Jesus's claim only makes sense if it creates an expectation for what happens after Mark's story ends.

Second, consider the empty tomb. When the two Marys and Salome approach the tomb to anoint Jesus's corpse, they are met by a young man. He tells them,

> Do not be alarmed; you are looking for Jesus of Nazareth, who was crucified. He has been raised; he is not here. Look, there is the place they laid him. But go, tell his disciples and Peter that he is going ahead of you to Galilee; there you will see him, just as he told you. (Mark 16:6–7 NRSV)

The implication here is that Jesus has risen. The women and the other disciples will see Jesus again, presumably very soon in Galilee. *But without the help of an editorial addendum, this promise isn't realized in Mark's story.* According to Mark—even if we accept the longer ending and assume that the mother of James is also Jesus's mother—Jesus never sees his mother again. The story simply doesn't include this reunion. The young man's promise only leads to disappointment unless we imagine that the story continues after Mark's Gospel has concluded.

With these examples in mind, I appreciate Huebenthal's notion of a "suspended Christology." Rather than providing a definitive Christology, Mark open doors to possibility. In her view, the narrative refuses to assign Jesus divinity "explicitly." The story's ending (or lack thereof) prompts more questions than it answers. She explains that the story of the Gospel "extends far beyond the life of the character Jesus." If this is true, the story also invites imagination, speculation, and theological interpolation.[4] I want to heed her advice. I want to heed it, because reading Mark the way she does may help me to preserve Mark's irresistible mysteries. But I doubt I'll have the willpower to suspend my christological questions indefinitely.

Because at times the story seems to relish in implicit theology, Winn's two-powers paradigm is delightfully tempting. At times, Huebenthal casts her glance sideways to compare Mark with Isaiah, Paul, Josephus, etc. Such glances, of course, are inevitable. Winn's use of the Parables of Enoch has me

4. Mark 16:9–20 is proof that the Gospel invited theological interpolation. One might say that the Gospels of Matthew, Luke, and John also accept this invitation.

glancing at a few apocalyptic texts as well. Indeed, Mark's frequent appeal to apocalyptic language almost makes it necessary to read the Gospel alongside texts like Daniel, 1 Enoch, Jubilees, etc. When Jesus says, "You will see the Son of Man seated at the right hand of the power," I imagine that the storyteller expects that the audience will already know a few things about powers and principalities. Moreover, if Mark invites the reader to supply to the story what is left unsaid, there is perhaps no better place to start than Jewish apocalyptic literature.

Hurtado's reading also leaves room for Mark's implicit theology. Jesus's apocalyptic saying before the high priest leads Hurtado to assert that Jesus has a *unique* relationship to the Father. "Are you the Messiah, the Son of the Blessed?" asks the high priest. This provides Jesus with an opportunity to affirm both royal-messianic status and divine sonship. Hurtado writes, "Jesus's divine sonship carries its own, somewhat distinguishable, force connoting a unique relationship with God." In this case, Hurtado places a great deal of weight on the *connotation* of uniqueness. Because the story does not make Jesus's uniqueness an explicit claim, we are left to our best attempts to draw out what is implicit in Mark's connotation. Hurtado is a careful scholar who knows not to overreach with such claims; his nuance in this case is admirable. I would only add that Mark's story often resists definitive theological claims. So the question of Jesus's "unique and transcendent status" remains partially unanswered in Mark's story. At best the answer is implied. But Hurtado is certainly correct that others have run wild with the implication and that Mark must be situated within the wider world of these devotional activities.

Indeed, the nearest example of someone running with the implicit theology of Jesus's "right hand of power" claim is in Mark's longer ending (16:9–20). Mark's addendum provides a resolution to what Mark has left unresolved with Jesus's apocalyptic saying (14:62). The secondary interpolation explicitly claims that "the Lord Jesus, after he had spoken to them, was taken up into heaven and sat down at the right hand of God" (16:19).

This addendum resolves another unanswered problem in Mark's story, one that is underscored by Kirk. In Kirk's reading, God and Jesus are consistently presented as different characters. Kirk argues, "So distinct are the two characters that in the end the crucified Jesus can be abandoned by the God whom he has served and proclaimed throughout." Famously, Jesus cries out, "My God, my God, why have you forsaken me?" (15:34).[5] For Kirk, this is further evidence of the necessary distinction between Israel's God and Israel's royal Messiah.

I find his argument to be simultaneously compelling and vexing. Abandonment is an important theme in Mark's passion narrative. Judas betrays Jesus (14:10). The rest of his followers desert him and run away (v. 50). Driving the point home, Peter denies Jesus (vv. 66–72). The crowd that once praised Jesus calls for his execution (15:11–15). Finally, once completely isolated, Jesus cries out that his God has forsaken him (v. 34). Worse still, consider this: Jesus's words of forsakenness are the last words we hear from Jesus's lips in Mark's Gospel.[6]

I'll add another wrinkle: the abandonment of Jesus by his Father is never resolved in Mark! The reader is never given a cathartic moment whereby Jesus and God are reunited. If we stop reading at the empty tomb (16:8), we get no update on the relationship between Father and Son. Jesus's cry of abandonment in the previous chapter continues to echo without an answer. Ending without Mark's longer addendum leaves Jesus estranged. Or, at least, this could be implied by what is left unsaid.

The question, then, is this: *What sort of resolution are we to imagine if we look beyond Mark's abrupt ending?* The reader must speculate that Father and Son bridge the chasm between them. The reader is tempted to do this because the thought of a "beloved Son" who is ultimately estranged from both his mother and Father is too much to take! Mark's longer ending, therefore, offers relief to those who require it. Jesus is no longer forsaken in Mark's addendum; indeed, he is sitting at the right hand of God.

Here's my point: leaning too heavily on what is left unsaid in Mark has consequences. Perhaps we will construe too much and end up with

---

5. Some have argued that Jesus's quotation of Ps 22 is not a cry of ultimate abandonment. Rather, the outcome of Ps 22 provides an avenue of lament that leads to ultimate praise and the belief that God will rescue God's people. Following this line requires Mark's reader to supply the rest of the psalm, that which is left unsaid by Jesus but is echoed throughout Mark's passion narrative. Cf. Holly J. Carey, *Jesus's Cry from the Cross: Towards a First-Century Understanding of the Intertextual Relationship between Psalm 22 and the Narrative of Mark's Gospel*, LNTS 398 (London: T&T Clark, 2009). My own view is that Jesus's cry from the cross expresses just what it sounds like: a sense of being forsaken. Even if Mark has the larger context of the psalm in mind (implying eventual hope), the cry from the cross underscores a singular moment of lament.

6. This fits with the theme of God's "hiddenness" in Mark's Gospel; cf. Stephen C. Barton, *The Spirituality of the Gospels* (Eugene, OR: Wipf & Stock, 2006), 39–69. Barton explains that "in Mark we are struck most by the hiddenness of God and, at the end, Jesus's mysterious absence" (39).

a story that does violence to Mark's distinctive voice. At the same time, Mark repeatedly requires us to supply untold parts of the story. This, I am convinced, is why the Gospel of Mark continues to generate so much fruitful discussion. It is also why I am drawn to this story.

Returning to Peter's confession, all the scholars represented in these pages agree: Mark presents Jesus as the Lord's anointed one. Whether Peter represents the bigger picture, he gets this much right: "You are the *christos*" (8:29). So then, does *christos* mean kingship, spiritual authority, and/or suffering? Does the title confirm that Jesus is unique, transcendent, and/or divine? The answer depends on how you interpret what is both said and unsaid.

I'll finish by reiterating a point that the late Larry Hurtado often repeated. Hurtado was fascinated with how Mark presented Jesus's identity. He invested a large portion of his career to this question. But his view was that, while the Gospel of Mark speaks to questions of Christology, this is not its *raison d'être*. Rather, Mark is centrally concerned with Christian discipleship. The Markan Jesus is a pattern for the Christian life.[7] Mark is first and foremost a guide: baptism, ministry, and suffering. Then more suffering, and yet more, until Christians learn to die to themselves.

However we define *christos* theologically, the story of Mark intends to teach us the shape of a life in Christ. As such, it is a story that informs the many, many stories of would-be followers. Mark is a story that leaves a great deal unsaid so that readers are invited to supply what is only implied. In doing so, the reader (indeed, the implied disciple) is asked to inhabit the story, to learn to follow Mark's Jesus to the cross and beyond, and to continue to do so even after the story ends.

7. Larry W. Hurtado, "Following Jesus in the Gospel of Mark—and Beyond," in *Patterns of Discipleship in the New Testament*, ed. Richard N. Longenecker (Grand Rapids: Eerdmans, 1996), 9–29.

Contributors

Sandra Huebenthal (Dr. theol., Philosophisch-Theologische Hochschule Sankt Georgen, Frankfurt) is professor of exegesis and biblical theology at the University of Passau. She completed her habilitation in New Testament at Eberhard Karls University of Tübingen. She is the author of *Reading Mark's Gospel as a Text from Collective Memory.*

Larry Hurtado (PhD, Case Western Reserve University) is emeritus professor of New Testament language, literature and theology at the University of Edinburgh. He is the author of *Mark* in the New International Biblical Commentary series and *Lord Jesus Christ: Devotion to Jesus in Earliest Christianity.*

Chris Keith (PhD, University of Edinburgh) is research professor of New Testament and early Christianity and director of the Centre for the Social-Scientific Study of the Bible at St Mary's University, Twickenham. He is the author of *The Gospel as Manuscript: An Early History of the Jesus Tradition as Material Artifact* and *Jesus against the Scribal Elite: The Origins of the Conflict.*

J. R. Daniel Kirk (PhD, Duke University) is the author of *A Man Attested by God: The Human Jesus of the Synoptic Gospels* and *Jesus Have I Loved, But Paul? A Narrative Approach to the Problem of Pauline Christianity.*

Anthony Le Donne (PhD, Durham University) is professor of New Testament at United Theological Seminary. He is the author/editor of several books and articles. He serves as executive editor of the *Journal for the Study of the Historical Jesus.*

Adam Winn (PhD, Fuller Theological Seminary) is associate professor of New Testament at University of Mary Hardin Baylor. He is the author of *Reading Mark's Christology under Caesar: Jesus the Messiah and Roman Imperial Ideology.*

Scripture Index

Luke

John

Acts

Romans

1 Corinthians

Galatians

Philippians

Colossians

Hebrews

Revelation

Subject Index

Author Index